TWO
WHEELS
GOOD

TWO WHEELS GOOD

The History and Mystery of the Bicycle

JODY ROSEN

CROWN
NEW YORK

Published in the United States by Crown, an imprint of Random House,
a division of Penguin Random House LLC, New York.

CROWN and the CROWN colophon are registered trademarks of
Penguin Random House LLC.

Portions of this work were previously published in slightly different form.
Portions of the chapter "Uphill" originally appeared in *T: The New York Times
Style Magazine* in 2014. Portions of the chapter "Beast of Burden" originally
appeared in *T: The New York Times Style Magazine* in 2016. Portions of the
chapter "Mass Movement" originally appeared in *The New York Times
Magazine* and *The New Yorker* in 2020.

Library of Congress Cataloging-in-Publication Data

Names: Rosen, Jody, author.
Title: Two wheels good: the history and mystery of the bicycle / Jody Rosen.
Description: First edition. | New York: Crown, [2022] |
Includes bibliographical references and index.
Identifiers: LCCN 2021054101 (print) | LCCN 2021054102 (ebook) |
ISBN 9780804141499 (hardcover) | ISBN 9780804141505 (ebook)
Subjects: LCSH: Bicycles—History. | Cycling—History.
Classification: LCC TL400 .R67 2022 (print) | LCC TL400 (ebook) |
DDC 629.227/2—dc23/eng/20211116
LC record available at lccn.loc.gov/2021054101
LC ebook record available at lccn.loc.gov/2021054102

Printed in the United States of America on acid-free paper

crownpublishing.com

2 4 6 8 9 7 5 3 1

First Edition

Book design by Susan Turner

For Lauren, Sasha, and Theo

CONTENTS

VOYAGE TO THE MOON

Cycles "Brillant." Advertising poster by artist
Henri Boulanger (alias Henri Gray), 1900.

I n the 1890s, advertising posters depicted bicycles in outer space.
These are some of the most famous images of the bicycle ever
created: they show bikes pressed against the firmament, bikes
streaking past comets and planets, bikes coasting down the slopes of
sickle moons. The riders of these bicycles are often women—or,

rather, goddesses. They have bare breasts and rippling Grecian garments and long hair that trails behind them like a jet stream. In one
advertisement, for the French bicycle company Cycles Sirius, a
nearly nude cyclist rides sidesaddle across a starry sky, her eyes
closed, her smiling face thrust upward in ecstasy. The image says
that a bicycle is a conduit of otherworldly pleasure. A bike ride can
shoot you to the stars; a bike ride could give Aphrodite an orgasm.
A poster designed in 1900 for another French firm, Cycles Brillant,
pictures two barely clad female figures adrift in the Milky Way. One
of them, with fairy wings on her back and an olive bough in her left
hand, is reaching up toward the front wheel of a bicycle that hovers
overhead like an orbiting sun. The bike is spotlit and radiant, re-
flecting the glow cast by a diamond that floats nearby. In this surreal
vision, the bicycle itself is a deity, a heavenly body beaming light
down to Earth.

These posters date from the turn-of-the-century cycling boom,
the brief period prior to the rise of the automobile when the bicycle's dominion was uncontestable, and when bike manufacturers,
facing a glutted marketplace, sought to distinguish their products
with eye-popping art nouveau ads. But the celestial bicycle wasn't
just a huckster's hard sell. The first proto-bicycle, a curious two-
wheeled contraption that had neither pedals nor cranks nor a chain,
was likened by its admirers in the late 1810s and early 1820s to
Pegasus, the winged stallion of Greek mythology. Nearly five decades later, a chronicler of the velocipede craze in Paris marveled
that the vehicles had "been brought to such perfection, both for
velocity and lightness" that they gave the appearance of "flying
through the air." A cartoon from the same period made the connection explicit. It showed a man in top hat and tails straddling a velocipede suspended on either end by hot air balloons, with rotor blades
for wheels and a brass spyglass mounted on the handlebars. The
bike is seen soaring above Paris, on its way out of town. A caption
reads: VOYAGE A LA LUNE.

A flying bicycle. A bicycle that slaloms between the stars. A bicycle you can pedal to the moon. Popular culture has never let go of these ideas. In the mid-twentieth-century, manufacturers marketed bikes with sleek contours suggestive of jumbo jets and brand names that evoked air and space travel: the Skylark, the Skyliner, the Starliner, the Spaceliner, the Spacelander, the Jet Fire, the Rocket, the Airflyte, the Astro Flite. Flying bicycles appear in children's literature and pulp novels and science fiction. In *Bikey the Skicycle and Other Tales of Jimmieboy* (1902), by the American author John Kendrick Bangs, a young boy has a magical bike that is capable of speech and flight. Boy and bicycle go wheeling above church steeples, across the Atlantic, over the Alps, and up into space, where they cycle on the outer ring of Saturn—"a beautiful golden road" thronged with "bicyclists from . . . all parts of the universe." A Robert Heinlein novel from 1952, *The Rolling Stones,* tells the story of teenage siblings, residents of a colony on the moon, who take their bicycles to Mars to go prospecting for radioactive ore. ("A miner's bike would have looked odd in the streets of Stockholm . . . but on Mars or on the Moon it fitted its purpose the way a canoe fits a Canadian stream.") Today, tales of space travel by bicycle give voice to distinctively twenty-first-century questions of politics and identity. *Trans-Galactic Bike Ride,* published in 2020, is an anthology of "feminist bicycle science fiction stories of transgender and nonbinary adventurers."

And of course, there is the famous scene in *E.T. the Extra-Terrestrial* when a bicycle rises out of a pine forest on the edge of suburban tract land and climbs into the sky. It's one of the most indelible tableaux in cinema: a BMX bike, piloted by a ten-year-old earthling, with an alien in the handlebar basket, silhouetted against Steven Spielberg's preposterously big and bright full moon.

These are potent fantasies. They bespeak a primal desire to cast off the bonds of gravity, to speed away from Earth itself. But are they just fantasies? In 1883, the British physician and writer Benjamin Ward Richardson predicted that the "new and independent gift of progression" with which bicycles had endowed human beings would soon be dramatically extended: "The art of flight will be the practical outcome of the grand experiment which is now going on." During the last years of the century there were countless efforts to merge the bicycle and the airship. Newspapers and scientific quarterlies announced the inventions of "the Aerial-Cycle," "the Luftvelociped," "the Pegasipede." There were designs for bikes with whirling rotors, with whipping fan blades, with kite-shaped sails; there were proposals for dirigibles powered by squadrons of cyclists. These machines never reached the sky, but on December 17, 1903, twenty years after Richardson published his prognostication, the *Wright Flyer* took off over Kill Devil Hills in Kitty Hawk, North Carolina. Orville and Wilbur Wright were bicycle mechanics and manufacturers whose crucial breakthroughs in understanding the phenomena of lift and drag came when they attached a strange apparatus to the handlebars of a bike—a bicycle wheel, mounted so it spun horizontally, festooned with drag plates and model "wings"—and went pedaling through the streets of Dayton, Ohio. The brothers applied further lessons on balance, stability, and flexibility that they had learned from bicycles to design their plane, and they built it using tools and components straight out of their bike shop. The aviation age was, as Richardson forecast, an extension, a result, of the cycling boom.

Today there are machines that resemble the bicycle-airship hybrids imagined in the nineteenth century: pedal-driven helicopters and ornithopters and other light aircraft, designed by engineers in the aerospace laboratories of leading universities. Other visions remain unfulfilled. In the run-up to the 1971 Apollo 15 mission, NASA briefly entertained the idea of equipping astronauts with electric bicycles. A NASA photograph documents a test run: a rider in a full space suit is shown astride a prototype "lunar mini-bike," navigating the low-gravity training environment that astronauts nicknamed "the vomit comet." The mini-bike was eventually shelved in favor of the four-wheeled lunar roving vehicle, or "moon buggy." In space, as on Earth, car culture trumped the bicycle.

But the dream of a bike on the moon did not die. The leading advocate was David Gordon Wilson, an MIT professor and the author of *Bicycle Science,* the "bible" of bicycle engineering and physics. Years after NASA abandoned the project, Wilson continued to champion the use of pedal-powered vehicles by astronauts. The bicycles Wilson proposed accommodated two cyclists and were semi-recumbent; the design called for metallic mesh wheels engineered to ply the dusty lunar surface and parallel loops of high-tensile steel wire in place of a traditional chain drive. Wilson claimed that these bicycles would provide necessary exercise while serving as transport for astronauts on research expeditions. The lunar cyclist would experience novel climatic conditions, enjoying "the freedom conferred with having no wind resistance with which to contend." Wilson supported his proposals with precise calculations: "The 'cruising' speed for an astronaut, fully equipped, pedaling a two-man vehicle alone across uncompacted lunar soil would be 27.5 feet per second, or 18.75 mph."

Wilson's ideas about travel in outer space were not limited to bicycles on the moon. In a 1979 article he described life in "a space colony established on an artificial satellite." He pictured "planes with supine pedaling pilots" cruising over the colony's skyline. These aircraft would be available for free to all residents of the colony in a system Wilson likened to the White Bicycle Plan, the bike-sharing program formulated by anarchists in mid-1960s Amsterdam. But he imagined a bicycle culture unlike any on Earth. "The picture I have tried to portray of human-powered transportation in future lunar exploration and in space colonies is far from the slow, tiring, second-class systems to which bicycle transportation seems to have been relegated here on earth," Wilson wrote. "Planes would be capable of acrobatics. A popular sport would be reenactments of famous battles from the First World War. Parachutes would probably be unnecessary. An aerial collision would result in both planes and pilots floating gently to the ground."

———

Nine decades before David Wilson wrote those sentences, a momentous event in the history of transportation took place in Ireland. John Boyd Dunlop was a forty-seven-year-old Belfast-based veterinarian of Scottish birth. Dunlop had never ridden a bike, but his nine-year-old son, Johnnie, spent hours at a time racing his tricycle with friends on the paved track in a local park. Johnnie often complained to his father about the trip between the park and the Dunlop home. The ride was fine so long as Johnnie stuck to level macadam paths, but when the route veered onto the rougher terrain that prevailed in much of the city—streets laid with granite paving stones and threaded by tram tracks—pedaling became laborious, and the journey uncomfortable. Dunlop was familiar with the issue. Crisscrossing Belfast on his veterinary rounds, Dunlop had often noted the unpleasant vibrations that shook the horse-drawn carriages and dogcarts in which he traveled. Those vehicles, like Johnnie's tricycle, had solid tires that juddered and dragged on all but the smoothest roadways.

Dunlop was a thinker and a tinkerer. He looked the part. He had sharp, skeptical eyes and a long professorial beard, as thick and geometric as a topiary hedge. He liked to apply his intelligence to practical problems and to devise solutions, to use his head and hands to bring new things into the world. He designed and built a number of instruments for use in his veterinary surgery. He sold medicines for dogs and horses that he had developed and patented himself. He had "an abiding interest in the problems of road, rail and sea transport" and was intrigued in particular by the mechanisms of wheels, a fascination, he said, that began in childhood, when he observed the way wooden agricultural rollers moved over the furrows on his family's farm in Ayrshire, in southwest Scotland. Now, in the autumn of 1887, he turned his attention to the question of his son's cycle rides. Could Dunlop contrive improvements to Johnnie's tricycle that would make the boy's commute more tolerable and, perhaps, give him an advantage in those races in the park with friends?

Dunlop focused his attention on the tricycle's solid rubber tires. A better-designed tire would be durable enough to withstand the punishments of the road but sufficiently flexible to offer a less jarring ride as it passed over uneven ground. Smoother cycling, Dunlop suspected, would also mean speedier cycling. In physics terms, he was grappling with questions of rolling resistance and shock absorption. "It occurred to me," he wrote years later, "that the problem of obtaining speed or ease of propulsion . . . might be solved by a peculiar mechanical arrangement of cloth, rubber and wood."

Rubber, in particular, held the key. Dunlop's idea was to take a length of rubber tubing, fill it with some substance, and attach the tube to the cycle wheel, interposing a cushion between the wheel and the surfaces over which it rolled. He first tried using a water-filled hose pipe. When that yielded poor results, he began to experiment with another substance: compressed air. Dunlop pumped air into a tube of sheet rubber, as you would to inflate a soccer ball; he covered that air-filled tube with an outer layer of linen and affixed it to the circumference of a large wooden disk. A series of trials in the yard of Dunlop's veterinary establishment proved that this apparatus rolled farther, and with greater ease, than a conventional cycle wheel. Dunlop then built proper prototypes: a pair of wooden cycle-wheel rims, three inches wide and thirty-six inches in diameter, to which he fastened the inflated rubber tubes, sheathed in canvas and an additional outer layer of sheet rubber.

Dunlop secured these tires to the rear of his son's tricycle on the night of February 28, 1888. Immediately, Johnnie set out for a ride, "eager to have a speed trial of his new machine." It was just before ten P.M., an hour when Belfast's streets were generally free of traffic. "The moon was full and the sky clear," Dunlop wrote. "As it happened there was an eclipse of the moon so [Johnnie] came home. After the shadow of the moon had passed he went out again and had a long run. The next morning, the tyres were carefully examined and no scratch could be found on the rubber."

We cannot know what went through the boy's mind as he pedaled his newly swift and smooth-running tricycle over the moonlit cobbles. Although his father recounted his memories of the event many times and wrote about it in a book, Johnnie's thoughts were never documented. But the significance of that February 1888 tricycle ride is a matter of record: it was the world's first cycle journey on pneumatic tires. Five months later, John Boyd Dunlop was granted a patent for "An Improvement in Tyres of Wheels for Bicycles, Tricycles, or Other Road Cars," a breakthrough that sent millions racing into the last decade of the nineteenth century on two wheels.

Today the Dunlop name is known worldwide, thanks to the eponymous tire company. During Dunlop's lifetime, a footnote complicated his claim on history. In 1890, Dunlop's patent was rescinded after the discovery of an earlier invention that had been unknown to him. Nearly a half century before, another Scotsman, Robert William Thomson, had made the same imaginative leap, receiving a patent for a new kind of carriage wheel containing an air-filled sleeve, a device that "intercepted vibration from the road" before it reached the wheel's rim. The name Thomson gave to his creation had a poetic ring: "Aerial Wheels."

———

The connection we make between cycling and flying is metaphorical. You might even call it spiritual: an expression of the powerful feelings of freedom and exhilaration we experience when we ride bikes. But it is also a response to a physical fact. If cyclists imagine themselves to be flying, it is because, in a sense, they are.

When you ride a bicycle, you're airborne. The wheels that spin beneath you slip a continuous band of compressed air between the bike and the road, holding you aloft. That floating feeling, that sensation of airy buoyancy, is heightened by the way the bike bears your body: your legs do the work of propelling the vehicle, but the job of supporting your body weight is outsourced to the bicycle itself. Today you can attach an inflatable saddle to your seat post and sit back on a pillow of air even as your bike's wheels turn on air. Perhaps you are riding down an empty road on a quiet night; maybe, like Johnnie Dunlop, like Elliott and E.T., you are riding on a night lit by a full moon. Your bicycle will not take you on a voyage to the moon, but it is not quite earthbound, either. You're in another world, an intermediary zone, gliding somewhere between terra firma and the huge horizonless sky.

TWO
WHEELS
GOOD

BICYCLE PLANET

A woman and child on a bicycle, Mzimba District, northwestern Malawi, 2012.

Cycle tracks will abound in Utopia.
                    —H. G. WELLS, *A Modern Utopia* (1905)

Mankind has invested more than four million years of evolution in the attempt to avoid physical exertion. Now a group of backward-thinking atavists mounted on foot-powered pairs of Hula-Hoops would have us pumping our legs, gritting our teeth, and searing our lungs as though we were being chased

*across the Pleistocene savanna by saber-toothed tigers. Think
of the hopes, the dreams, the effort, the brilliance, the pure
force of will that, over the eons, has gone into the creation of
the Cadillac Coupe de Ville. Bicycle riders would have us
throw all this on the ash heap of history.*

—P. J. O'ROURKE, "A Cool and Logical Analysis of
the Bicycle Menace" (1984)

For two centuries, people have looked at the bicycle and dreamed out-of-this-world dreams. Those whose bicycle reveries do not extend to the realm of the moon and stars have nonetheless made huge claims for the humble two-wheeler. Bicycles have stirred utopian visions and aroused violent emotions, given rise to crackpot theories and inspired reams of purple prose. The bicycle took decades to evolve, passing through fitful stages of technical development, from the primeval "running machine" of 1817 to the boneshakers and high-wheelers of the 1860s and '70s to the so-called safety bicycle of the 1880s, whose invention gave the bike the classic form we recognize today and launched the fin de siècle cycling boom. But in each of these eras, the bicycle was hailed as revolutionary, a paradigm shifter, a world shaker.

The bicycle was the realization of a wish as ancient as the dream of flight. It was the elusive personal transport machine, a device that liberated humans from their dependence on draft animals, allowing individuals to move swiftly across land under their own power. Like another nineteenth-century creation, the railway locomotive, the bicycle was "an annihilator of space," collapsing distances and shrinking the world. But a train traveler was a passive rider, sitting back while coal and steam and steel did the work. A cyclist was her own locomotive. "You are traveling," wrote a bicycling enthusiast in 1878. "Not being traveled."

As decades passed and successive bicycle crazes gripped Europe and the United States, momentous transformations were ascribed to bikes. The bicycle was praised as a class leveler, a cleanser of bodies, a liberator of spirits, a freer of minds. "Bicycling . . . has done more to emancipate women than anything else in the world," said Susan B. Anthony in 1896. "It would not be at all strange," wrote a *Detroit Tribune* editorialist that same year, "if history came to the conclusion that the perfection of the bicycle was the greatest incident in the nineteenth century."

We may be inclined to dismiss these claims as period pieces, hyperbole typical of a bygone age. But the case that has been made for bicycles in the late twentieth and early twenty-first centuries is no less bombastic. In the 1970s, activists on both sides of the Atlantic championed the bike on ecological and spiritual grounds. The bicycle was a remedy for the car culture that was choking cities and polluting skies; bikes also embodied progressive values, the lofty ideals of peace, love, and unity. In the words of a '70s "pedal power" manifesto: "Perhaps an interface between East and West is the bicycle, the machine which makes us all brothers and sisters." Now, with climate change threatening life as we know it, the rhetoric has grown more messianic. The bike advocates of our time speak of "the noblest invention," "the most benevolent machine," "rideable art that can just about save the world." The bicycle of the nineteenth century was a marvel; in today's formulations, it is moral. It was enchanted; now it's enlightened. Bicycles are great—but, more to the point, bicycles are good.

———

Are the bicycle's venerators wrong? You could say that the bike's preeminence is irrefutable. There are approximately one billion cars in the world today. There are twice as many bikes. The number of bicycles manufactured this year in China alone will exceed the total worldwide production of automobiles. The cities and towns we inhabit, our economies, our laws are designed for cars; we hop between continents on airplanes. Yet we live on a bicycle planet.

Around the world, more people travel by bicycle than by any other form of transportation. The bicycle is the primary means of transport in the rural hinterlands of the Southern Hemisphere and in city centers of northern European capitals. There are twenty-three million bicycles in the Netherlands—five million more bikes than there are Dutch citizens. Almost anyone can learn to ride a bicycle. Nearly everyone does.

The bicycle's ubiquity is a testament to its versatility. A bicycle is a vehicle for transport and for sport, for leisure and for labor. We ride bicycles to deliver the mail, to tour the countryside, to burn calories and tone muscles. A bike can be a child's toy and a commuter vehicle that brings that child's mother to work.

Bikes are people movers and load bearers, carriers of bodies and carters of stuff. Thousands of pedal-driven taxis jam the streets of Singapore and Manila. Subsistence farmers in Vietnam, India, and other countries use modified bikes to plow and till and harrow. In Peru, bicycles function as mobile fruit and vegetable stalls; in Zambia, cycles bring goods to marketplaces and the sick to hospitals. In much of the world, it is pedal power that keeps cities running, that keeps commerce flowing, that stands between life and death.

The bicycle's continuing relevance upends myths of progress, challenging our convictions about history's steady forward march and the linear course of technological advancement. It also defies simple logic. In many ways, bikes are impractical. A bicycle can't zip down turnpikes or cross oceans. It won't keep you dry in a rainstorm; riding in the snow is treacherous. "Get a bicycle," wrote Mark Twain in 1886. "You will not regret it, if you live."

These cautionary words still apply. If you ride your bike every day in New York City, as I do, you are tempting fate, throwing yourself in the path of steamrolling motorists and the swinging doors of parked cars. One cyclist memorably likened the sound of an opening car door to that of a gun being cocked. "The cyclist is a suicide apprentice," wrote the Mexican essayist Julio Torri. "Since cars have multiplied in our streets, I have lost the admiration with which I formerly regarded bullfighters and I have reserved it for bicyclists."

Other nineteenth-century inventions—the steam engine, the

typewriter, the telegraph, the Daguerreotype—have been rendered obsolete or modernized beyond recognition. The bicycle, though, is essentially unchanged, a machine of improbable simplicity, elegance, and ingenuity: two wheels of equal size, two tires, a diamond-shaped frame, a rear chain drive, a pair of pedals, handlebars, a seat—and on that seat, a human being who is both the vehicle's passenger and its engine. This was the design of English inventor John Kemp Starley's breakthrough Rover bicycle of 1885. The bicycle Maurice Garin pedaled to victory in the inaugural Tour de France in 1903, the bike Albert Einstein rode around the Princeton University campus, the Flying Pigeon roadster enshrined by Deng Xiaoping as a glory of China's social compact; the bikes ridden by X Games competitors, by food deliverymen, by migrants navigating the no-man's-land on the San Diego County side of the U.S.-Mexico border, by agents of the U.S. Border Patrol's bicycle unit who police that no-man's-land, by weekend warriors wrapped in spandex, by "anarcha-feminist" cycling collectives; my bicycle, your bicycle— they're all more or less the same machine, barely modified versions of that pioneering Rover. Even e-bikes, which augment the old-fashioned pedal-and-crank with battery-powered electric motors, do not alter the underlying design. Decades and centuries pass; revolutions, technological and otherwise, remake the world. The bicycle keeps rolling along.

———

Where the bicycle goes, controversy flares and culture wars erupt. People often express surprise to find bikes at the center of fierce debates about some of the most central issues of our time—not just predictable squabbles about transit policy but broader questions of class, race, morality, sustainability, the very future of life on Earth. The furor that surrounds the bicycle seems antithetical to the thing itself, a quaint, even cute, vestige of the Victorian world. But the bicycle has always been a lightning rod. The purple ink has flowed in both directions: for every paean to the bicycle there has been an answering screed, proclaimed in words of high dudgeon.

The outcry began at the beginning, circa 1819, when the first primitive two-wheelers were met by criticism and legal suppression on three continents. The machines gained favor among the wealthy and fashion-conscious, and promptly became targets of populist ridicule. ("A curious two-wheeled vehicle called the Velocipede has been invented which is propelled by jackasses instead of horses.") Carriage drivers and pedestrians objected to the presence of velocipedes on roads and footpaths; crackdowns followed. Velocipede riding was banned in London in March 1819; similar restrictions were soon imposed elsewhere. An American newspaper editorial urged citizens to "destroy" velocipedes, and mob violence was visited on both the vehicles and their riders.

This earliest bicycle backlash bears a striking resemblance to those that have followed. Class-based antagonisms; contestation over the right to roadways; a sense that the bicycle is by definition absurd and illegitimate, a thing to be mocked and dismissed and, if possible, obliterated altogether—these are features of anti-bike agitation to this day. At the height of the 1890s bike boom, the criticism took on a more hysterical tone. In the United States, Britain, and elsewhere, cycling fever provoked outrage and moral panic. Bicycles were denounced as a threat to traditional values, public order, economic stability, women's sexual purity. Bike-riding villains blazed across the pages of the yellow press; in medical journals, cycling maladies were diagnosed: bicycle face, bicycle neck, bicycle foot, bicycle hump, cyclomania, "kyphosis bicyclistarum." Anti-bicycle invective thundered from church pulpits and filled the manifestos of moralists. "[The] bicycle runs for Satan," pronounced the Women's Rescue League of the United States in 1896. "The bicycle is the devil's advance agent, morally and physically."

Again, our inclination to roll our eyes at yesteryear's excesses must be checked against the rhetoric of our own time. The terms of the disparagement have shifted, but the fervor remains. Where turn-of-the-century critics decried the bicycle as a malignant force of modernity, P. J. O'Rourke sees an affront to progress, a machine for "backward-thinking atavists." O'Rourke may be exaggerating his indignation for satirical effect—but perhaps he isn't? Consider the social science. A 2019 Australian study explored the negative view of cyclists that prevails "in many countries," prejudice that is expressed in "public and humorous references to violence against cyclists" and in actual physical assaults on cyclists. The researchers posited that in societies organized around motor vehicles, cyclists are subject to processes of dehumanization: "On-road cyclists . . . look and act differently to typical 'humans.' They move in a mechanical way, and their faces are often not seen by motorists, blocking empathetic responses that might humanize them." To automobile drivers who regard the roads as their domain, bicycle riders appear to be alien others, pests that must be shooed away or stomped out. ("Many informal slurs against cyclists refer to them as 'cockroaches' and 'mosquitos.'") The study concluded that 49 percent of non-cyclists regard cyclists as "less than fully human."

———

This book tells a story about bicycle love and bicycle loathing. It explores the powerful affection and antipathy that bicycles inspire, and the way those attitudes have reverberated through history and culture and the minds and lives of individuals. It's a drama that is unfolding at this moment on a vast scale. Today, we are seeing a huge surge in cycling, propelled by an explosion of bicycle commuting in cities around the world. The global bicycle market has grown by billions of dollars over the past decade; analysts predict that the market will hit $80 billion by 2027. These numbers reflect the scope of a cycling craze that has reached a wider and more socially diverse swath of humanity than those of the past. Two hundred years after the bicycle's invention, we are experiencing the biggest bike boom of them all.

Bike booms bring bike battles. New cycling infrastructure is rising on city streets, bicycle-sharing programs are proliferating, pedal-assist e-bikes are buzzing along in a thickened stream of two-wheeled traffic—and once again, disputation between bike lovers and loathers has risen to a shrill pitch. The vehemence of that conversation says something about the bicycle's stature, the awareness, among advocates and critics alike, that bikes are once again transforming the places we live and the way we live in them. Past cycling booms can in many cases be traced to changes in technology and the development of new kinds of bikes. But the current wave seems to have been brought on by larger forces, by the crises and dilemmas gripping the globe in the third decade of the third millennium. In the ecologically imperiled, rapidly urbanizing, traffic-clogged, socially turbulent, pandemic-plagued twenty-first century, the nineteenth-century two-wheeler is a relic whose time, it seems, has come.

The quarrels that have shaped the bicycle's past and are roiling its present are the focus of many of the chapters that follow. The politics of the bicycle may seem to be self-evident. In the United States, we associate bikes with progressive views and values: with blue states and green policies; with hipsters and bourgeois bohemians; with the renegade protesters of Critical Mass, whose guerrilla group-rides aim to promote cyclists' rights; and with others who lean left. These are clichés, of course; there are countless bike riders to whom these stereotypes don't apply. But the bicycle's relationship to progressivism and radicalism is grounded in history.

Among the first major cycling organizations were socialist bicycle clubs in 1890s Britain, which hailed the bicycle as an egalitarian "people's nag." Through the decades, the bicycle has retained its countercultural potency. A manifesto issued by the Provo, the 1960s Dutch anarchist group behind the world's first bike-sharing plan, envisioned a revolutionary affiliation of "mods, students, artists, rockers, delinquents, ban-the-bombers, misfits . . . those who don't want a career, who lead irregular lives, who feel like cyclists on a motorway."

Governments have long recognized the bicycle as a means of resistance. One of Adolf Hitler's first acts upon assuming power, in 1933, was to smash Germany's cycling union, the Bund Deutscher Radfahrer, which was associated with anti-Nazi political parties and was capable of assembling tens of thousands of cyclists in the streets. Later, German soldiers in Denmark, the Netherlands, France, and other countries confiscated bicycles from the local populations. To a repressive regime or an occupying army, the bicycle was a menace, a device that could be used by dissenters to sneak up and speed off, to organize and mobilize and elude.

The bicycle's reputation as a catalyst of social change is based above all on its role in the women's movement. At the turn of the century, feminist reformers in the United States, Britain, and continental Europe adopted bicycles as totems of changing values and tools of protest. (In Elizabeth Cady Stanton's words: "Women are riding to suffrage on a bicycle.") Cycling offered women a new kind of autonomy, while dispelling myths about their physical frailty. And bike riding provided the impetus for another kind of liberation, freeing women from the constrictions of Victorian clothing, the architectural bustles and whalebone crinolines that made it impossible to mount, let alone ride, a bicycle. Female cyclists embraced "rational dress"—most famously, bloomer pantaloons, which became, along with the bicycle itself, a symbol of emancipated New Womanhood.

Today, the bicycle remains a flashpoint in the struggle for women's rights. Authoritarian governments in Asia and the Middle East have periodically imposed bans on cycling by women. In 2016, Iran's supreme leader, Ali Khamenei, proclaimed a fatwa prohibiting women from biking in public on the grounds that it "attracts the attention of male strangers and exposes society to corruption." Iranian women responded by posting photos on social media of themselves on their bikes, and by writing slogans on their clothing such as "Do not be sexually tempted; I am merely riding a bicycle." The ban was widely defied and not strictly enforced, but hardline clerics in several Iranian provinces have continued issuing edicts against women cyclists. In recent years, women in Iran have had their bikes confiscated, have faced arrest and other forms of "Islamic punishment," and have reported physical attacks and sexual assaults. For millions of women across the world, bike riding remains inherently political, an act of defiance and a claim of freedom undertaken at personal risk.

These stories loom large in bicycle lore. Many accounts of the bicycle's history emphasize its role as a liberating force and portray cyclists as heroic underdogs. This framing resonates with a romantic conception of the bicycle as insurgent and "punk," a scourge of conservatism, corporatism, and car culture.

But the politics of the bicycle are complex; the facts do not always align with the pieties. Recently, scholars have begun unearthing a less hagiographic history. In many places, the bicycle first appeared carrying soldiers, settlers, prospectors, proselytizers, and other seekers of territory, treasure, and souls. The raw materials used to build bikes—the steel for the diamond frames, the rubber in Dunlop's magical tires and inner tubes—have been acquired at a cost to the environment and to human beings, in some cases, through systematic violence against indigenous populations in colonial states.

The high-minded story passed down in standard bike histories— humanity finding freedom and fulfillment pedaling a peaceable "green machine"—can therefore be counterposed with different scenes. Infantrymen, *gendarmes,* tax collectors, and other colonial officers riding bikes in British Malaya, in German Togoland, in French Algeria. Black servants in the West Indies chauffeuring plantation owners on cycle rickshaws. Bicycle-riding European missionaries in Malawi and India and the Philippines. White fortune hunters biking to oil fields in Nigeria and gold fields in the Australian outback. Bicycle battalions of both the British and Orange Free State armies, facing off on the fighting grounds of that paradigmatic Scramble for Africa conflict, the Second Boer War. Millions of Congolese people harvesting rubber in the jungles of the Belgian king Leopold II's Congo Free State—a genocidal system of forced labor instituted when the rubber market boomed during the bicycle craze.

The point, of course, isn't that bicycles are nefarious. The point is that bicycles have a complicated history, as real things in the real world often do—including, or perhaps especially, products of industrial capitalism. Consider the relationship of bikes and cars, whose genetic links are closer than most people know. Two decades before the Model T rolled out of Detroit, Henry Ford produced his first automobile, the Quadricycle. As the name suggests, it was a four-wheeled cousin of the bike, with a small frame, a seat for two passengers, and an ethanol-powered two-cylinder engine that drove the rear wheels, bicycle-style. Parts essential to the development of cars, from ball bearings to brake pads, were first developed for bicycles. Cornerstones of the automotive industry—the assembly line, dealer networks, planned obsolescence—were likewise pioneered by bicycle magnates, many of whom transitioned from bikes to the car trade.

Then there are the roadways themselves, which, in the United States, are a legacy of the Good Roads Movement, a turn-of-the-century political crusade led by cyclists. The Interstate Highway System, suburban sprawl, strip malls: the credit, and the blame, for these features of the American landscape is usually ascribed to car culture, but their origins can be traced to the vision of coast-to-coast "macadamization" first advocated in the 1890s by the then-powerful "bicycle bloc." Bike activism, more or less literally, paved the path for the car. "It is the task of critical historians of the bicycle to help recover the real history of the complex material relations between ₋he bicycle, the automobile and the roads they share," the social historian Iain Boal has written. "Bicycle purists, who imagine that they are somehow unambiguously an antithesis to motorists, need to rethink this fantasy."

These complexities are not just artifacts of ages past. The

present-day cycling boom has surfaced racial and social class tensions. In many American and European cities, bike-sharing schemes and other pro-cycling measures are tied to efforts to attract global capital and to policies that exacerbate economic inequality. Researchers have correlated the building of new cycling infrastructure and the predations of real estate developers, showing that bicycle lanes often serve as "maps of gentrification." Gentrification is also an issue in the world of cycling advocacy, whose ranks are dominated by white men. The term "invisible riders" has gained currency among critics who decry the marginalization of Black, Latino, female, and working-class cyclists by establishment activists. The political rage expressed by certain cycling activists is arguably a reflection of entitlement: riding a bike in traffic, a white guy may experience structural inequities he encounters nowhere else in life.

The truth is, the politics of the bike are always up for grabs. In the pandemic summer of 2020, Black Lives Matter demonstrators poured into the streets of American cities, many of them on bikes. They were met there by another group of cyclists: heavily armored bicycle cops, who deployed violent crowd-control tactics and weaponized the bicycle itself, using bikes to bludgeon protesters. Perhaps the bicycle is the noblest invention, the most benevolent machine; but the nobility and benevolence aren't inherent. The ideal of the bicycle, like the ideals of justice and equity, is subject to an ongoing struggle—a fight that sometimes unfolds block by block.

———

I've tried to keep these complications in mind while writing this book. There is a lot of history in the chapters that follow, but this isn't a history of the bicycle per se. Major themes have been left to other chroniclers. I pay little attention, for example, to the sport of cycling, a subject that occupies kilometers of shelf space in the bicycle library.

My aim is to highlight some different stories. Traditionally, bicycle historians have told a transatlantic tale, concentrating almost exclusively on Europe and the United States. A similar provincialism is displayed by activists. The influential urban designer and cycling advocate Mikael Colville-Andersen has popularized "Copenhagenize" as a watchword of today's pro-cycling movement, anointing the bicycle-friendly Danish capital as the spiritual center of the bicycle universe.

But the vast majority of bikes and cyclists are nowhere near Denmark. Statistically speaking, a twenty-first-century cyclist is far likelier to be a migrant worker in an Asian, African, or Latin American megacity than a white European exemplar of "cycle chic" (another Colville-Andersen coinage). The issues that preoccupy bicycle advocates in the West—bike commuting as a planning priority and "lifestyle choice"—have little connection to the reality of the hundreds of millions for whom cycling is simply a necessity, the only viable and affordable means of travel.

In the developed and the developing world alike, the bicycle is an urban machine, and much of this book is devoted to tales of the city. Of course, there are millions of rural cyclists. Practically from the moment of its invention, the bicycle was extolled as a means of escape from the metropolis, a vehicle that could whisk frazzled urbanites to greener pastures and cleaner air. But bikes were created in and by and for cities. Whatever the future holds for bicycles, that destiny will surely play out on city streets.

In fact, the fate of cities may be predicated on bikes. Demographers estimate that by 2030, 60 percent of the world's population will be living in cities. On a planet of sprawling megalopolises, in an age of climate crisis, the problem of urban transit is no longer a mere quality-of-life question, a matter of aggravating traffic jams and unpleasant commutes. The way we travel may determine not just how we live, but if we do.

Increasingly, public opinion is tilting toward a belief long held by cycling advocates: cars are killing us. Researchers say that motor vehicles are the largest net contributor to climate change. The problem will not be solved by electric or hybrid automobiles, since tire wear and other non-tailpipe pollutants account for a large percentage of vehicle emissions.

The climatic effects only scratch the surface of car culture's toll. The automotive age is an age of carnage. Globally, some 1.25 million people die in car crashes each year, an average of more than 3,400 deaths per day. Automobile accidents are the leading cause of death among young adults ages fifteen to twenty-nine worldwide. An additional twenty to thirty million people are injured or disabled each year on the world's roads.

Then there are the larger geopolitical consequences of car culture: the dubious alliances formed and principles forsaken, the wars fought and lives lost, in order to keep the petroleum flowing.

Against this ghastly backdrop, the bicycle takes on a virtuous glow. "The bicycle is the most civilized transport known to man. Other forms of transport grow daily more nightmarish. Only the bicycle remains pure in heart." When Iris Murdoch wrote those words, in 1965, she could hardly have imagined our world, where plutocrats in global capitals rent helicopters to swoop over streets paralyzed by traffic.

There are signs that history may be reversing course. With the outbreak of the Covid-19 pandemic in early 2020, millions turned to bike riding as a way to get around while maintaining social distance. Cyclists found themselves pedaling through a locked-down world, on eerily empty streets cleared of most pedestrians and motor vehicle traffic. Suddenly, the great cities of the world were cycling cities. It was a strange blend of dystopia and utopia. The vacant cityscapes were like disaster-movie scenes of apocalypse—but they offered a hopeful glimpse of the future, a time when bikes might navigate serene streets beneath skies undarkened by exhaust fumes. Whether or not bicycles can "save the world," there is little doubt that a city with lots of bikes and few cars will be a safer, saner, healthier, more habitable, more humane place.

A favorite slogan of bicycle activists goes: "Two wheels good, four wheels bad." It's a cheeky paraphrase of Orwell, but the motto smacks of sanctimony: the certainty that bikes are morally superior to cars, and that cyclists are nobler than motorists.

Yet "Two wheels good" is also a plain statement of fact. In a world of bum deals, a bicycle offers an excellent return on investment. Bikes are cheap and durable and portable and take up little space. A bike can carry you down the road five or ten or two hundred miles; when you get home, you can carry the bike upstairs into your apartment. Try doing that with a sports car or a pickup truck.

Cyclists get back more from their bikes than they put in. A bicycle is a remarkably effective device for converting human exertion into locomotion: on a bike, a person moves four times faster than on foot while expending five times less energy. "The bicycle is the perfect transducer to match man's metabolic energy to the impedance of locomotion," wrote the philosopher and social critic Ivan Illich two generations ago. "Equipped with this tool, man outstrips the efficiency of not only all machines but all other animals as well." Even digital age utopians, with their blazing faith that everything on Earth can be optimized by "tech," must bow before the unbetterable efficiency of the steampunk two-wheeler. None other than Steve Jobs called the personal computer "a bicycle for our minds."

Or maybe the machine for our minds is the bicycle itself. Many of us know that our brains feel invigorated, our vision sharper, our senses keener, when pedaling a bike. Bike riding is the best way I know to reach an altered consciousness—not an ennobled or enlightened state, exactly, but definitely an enlivened one. A bike ride is better than yoga, or wine, or weed. It runs neck and neck with sex and coffee. It's also, in my experience, an antidote for writer's block. If you're stuck, if you need to ungum the synapses and lift dust off the cerebral lobes, take a trip on two wheels and the words will begin tumbling out. Eventually, for better or worse, you may find you have a book's worth.

THE BICYCLE WINDOW

The so-called bicycle window, St. Giles' Church, Stoke Poges, Buckinghamshire, England.

S t. Giles' is a small parish church that sits on a patch of pleasantly shaded land in the village of Stoke Poges, Buckinghamshire, twenty-five miles west of London. There has been a house of worship on this site since Saxon times. The oldest part of the church building, its rough-hewn stone tower, dates from the period of the Norman Conquest.

The place is also holy ground for literati of a certain age and inclination. It was at St. Giles', in 1742, that Thomas Gray conceived "Elegy Written in a Country Churchyard," a meditation on death and bereavement that was once among the most celebrated poems in the English language, a fixture of syllabi until tastes swung to less orotund verse. Today, Gray himself is in the churchyard, in a grave marked by an altar-shaped tombstone that sits just outside a chapel window on the building's east façade. St. Giles' is a lovely place, tranquil and picturesque, an ideal spot for a rest—eternal or merely momentary. If you find yourself there on a mild evening, you will take in a setting little different from the one immortalized by Gray:

> *Now fades the glimmering landscape on the sight,*
> *And all the air a solemn stillness holds,*
> *Save where the beetle wheels his droning flight,*
> *And drowsy tinklings lull the distant folds.*

My visit to St. Giles' came in the spring, on a day of warm breezes and pouring sunshine. The panorama—church, churchyard greenery, surrounding countryside—was unreasonably pretty, and as I strolled the long path that snakes through St. Giles' grounds, the birds were singing so wildly that I punched up the Voice Memos app on my iPhone and made a recording. Looming about one hundred yards to the south of the church was the Manor House, a sixteenth-century estate once owned by Queen Elizabeth I, and later by Sir Thomas Penn, the son of William Penn, Pennsylvania's founder. For an American who had spent little time in the leafy home counties but many hours reading nineteenth-century novels and watching costume-drama adaptations of those novels, the scenery was exotic but familiar. I half-expected to see Dame Maggie Smith bustling out of the church in period dress.

The person who materialized instead was St. Giles' minister,

Reverend Harry Latham. With a couple of adjustments to his wardrobe, Latham himself might have stepped from the pages of Jane Austen. He was the picture of the handsome country vicar. He was perhaps forty-five years old, but he had the unlined face and full hairline of a younger man. He wore wire-rimmed glasses and a pinstriped shirt with a clerical collar. There was a faint musical lilt when he spoke, and his manner was soothing. Latham has a second pulpit about a mile up the road at St. Giles' sister church, St. Andrew's, where the congregation is younger and the services more informal, with sermons augmented by guitars and drums and sing-alongs. It is easy to picture Latham in either role: intoning the Beatitudes beneath St. Giles' medieval vaults or strumming an acoustic on the altar at St. Andrew's, his feet tapping along in open-toed sandals.

I had phoned a few months earlier to arrange a meeting, and followed up with emails, including one on the evening before my arrival. But as I faced Latham that afternoon in the churchyard, it was apparent that he had no idea who I was or what I could be doing there. I watched him take me in, cap to sneakers, registering the facts of the case: I was a stranger, my accent was American, I was clearly seeking neither pastoral care nor communion with the ghost of Thomas Gray. He came to the obvious conclusion. "You're looking for the bicycle window," Latham said.

———

The bicycle is a definitively nineteenth-century thing. It was the product of hard science and machine age engineering, of mass production and global trade. It was a creation of Victorian commercial culture, blown up big and spread wide by billboards and newspaper advertisements and popular songs. The bicycle stood for modernity and for modernism. "Lady Progress" was the mascot of the first periodical devoted to cycling, *Le vélocipède illustré*, published in Paris beginning in 1869. Drawings that appeared above the magazine's masthead depicted a female cyclist in a heroic pose, leaving dust in her wake as she streamed forward on two wheels, clutching a banner, with a headlamp lighting the way. The image winked at Delacroix's *Liberty Leading the People* while linking the bicycle to the hallmarks of changing times: women's liberation, new technology, speed, freedom. Decades later, Picasso, Duchamp, and other artists and writers still enshrined the bicycle as an emblem of the avant-garde.

Yet a crucial truth about the bicycle, as a historical and technological phenomenon, is that it arrived illogically late. It was an anachronism at birth. The first bike came into the world a decade and a half after the invention of the steam locomotive. By the time the bicycle achieved its ideal form, the automotive revolution was stirring. The groundbreaking Rover bicycle hit the market in 1885; that same year, Gottlieb Daimler introduced his proto-motorcycle, the *Einspur,* and Karl Benz built his first *Motorwagen.* The knowledge and materials required to create a bike have been around since the Middle Ages, but it took centuries for the forces of fate and fancy to align and give the world the thing itself.

Perhaps this is why the bicycle library is cluttered with apocrypha: fantasies and hoaxes and bogus origin stories, projected centuries and even millennia back into history. Victorians dreamed of bicycles in antiquity, envisioning Roman velocipede cavalries and gilded bicycles waiting to be excavated from pharaohs' tombs in the Valley of the Kings. The idea was echoed in the advertising art that pictured bicycles alongside figures from classical mythology. The surrealist jokester Alfred Jarry may have had such visions in mind when he wrote his satirical retelling of the crucifixion story, "The Passion Considered as an Uphill Bicycle Race" (1903), in which Jesus punctures a tire with his crown of thorns and lugs his bicycle up the hill to Golgotha:

> The bicycle frame in use today is of relatively recent invention.
> It appeared around 1890. Previous to that time the body of the
> machine was constructed of two tubes soldered together at right

angles. It was generally called the right-angle or cross bicycle. Jesus, after his puncture, climbed the slope on foot, carrying on his shoulder the bike frame, or, if you will, the cross.

No one could mistake Jarry's jape for fact. But myths have slipped into history books and popped up in respectable journalism. "Bicycles appear in the bas reliefs of ancient Babylon, Egypt, and Pompeii," asserted *The New York Times* in 1974, breezily revising the birth date of the bicycle by thousands of years. Among scholars, the search for a lost ur-bicycle continues. It is as if the reality of the machine's nineteenth-century origins remains at some basic level unbelievable, even to those most conversant with the history. Researchers grasp at scraps, identifying supposed bicycle progenitors: a fifteenth-century wood carving showing what may be a toy tricycle, a treadle-operated seventeenth-century "invalid carriage," a variety of other human-powered machines propelled by the turning of cranks and the pumping of handles.

This antecedent spotting can be enjoyable, even when it is far-fetched. At least two works by Hieronymus Bosch have been noted for their depictions of putative proto-bikes, and it is fun to imagine that the bicycle began as a figment of that great freakish mind. One Bosch drawing, *Witches* (c. 1500), features a kind of primitive unicycle: a woman is pictured astride a large wooden wheel, to which her feet are attached by pedal-like straps. This device is shown rolling through a typically grotesque Boschian landscape; it appears to be headed for a crash with a nude figure whose rear end is being probed by a long-beaked bird.

Another Renaissance master was at the center of a notorious bicycle hoax. In September 1974, newspaper readers around the world were startled by the announcement that a sketch of a bicycle had been discovered in Leonardo da Vinci's Codex Atlanticus, a previously unpublished compendium of the artist's drawings and writings. The drawing was said to be the work of Leonardo's student and servant Salai, based on a design by Leonardo himself. Scholars

greeted the claim with skepticism. The sketch was suspiciously detailed and modern-looking, showing a bike with a crank, pedals, a
rear-driven chain wheel, and a mudguard. A raft of evidence has
since confirmed that the image is counterfeit, likely scribbled into
the Codex between 1966 and 1969 by a person whose intent may
have been humorous rather than fraudulent. An art historian at
UCLA found that the page of the Codex where the bicycle now appears previously featured abstract geometric jottings, two circles
intersected by arcs. These may have suggested the shape of a bicycle to the prank's perpetrator, who completed the job with a few
quick pen strokes.

Some speculate that the drawing of "Leonardo's bicycle" was
the work of a mischievous monk at the Abbey of Santa Maria di
Grottaferrata, near Rome, where the Codex was housed for years
while undergoing restoration. But the culprit may never be identified. The question, in any case, is not whodunit but why an obvious
forgery was greeted with credulity and enthusiasm, by the public at
large and by officialdom. As the cycle historians Tony Hadland and
Hans Erhard-Lessing have noted: "The Italian cultural bureaucracy . . . still upholds 'Leonardo's bicycle.'" The stubbornness may
be explained by the wry words of the writer Curzio Malaparte: "In
Italy, the bicycle belongs to the national art heritage in the same way
as Mona Lisa by Leonardo, the dome of St. Peter or the *Divine
Comedy*. . . . When you say in Italy that the bicycle has not been
invented by an Italian . . . then a long shudder will run down the
peninsula's spine, from the Alps to the Etna."

Italy is hardly the only bastion of what we might call bicycle
nationalism. The historiography of the bicycle is clouded by competing priority claims, clashing accounts of the bike's creation and
evolution that reflect a struggle for patriotic bragging rights. Paul
Smethurst, the author of *The Bicycle: Towards a Global History*, has
described the politics behind these battles over the bicycle's lineage:
"As soon as individuals—and by extension nations—are credited
with great inventions, ideas or works of art, edifices of mythological

proportions can emerge. In the chauvinistic and sometimes jingoistic atmosphere of 19th-century Europe such edifices bolstered national prestige, and in the modern era technological advances have been especially valued."

At least one creation myth came from outside Europe. In 1897, the diplomat and politician Li Hongzhang declared that the bike was an ancient Chinese invention. Li told a group of American journalists that the bicycle was developed at the time of the Yao dynasty, around 2300 B.C. The vehicle was known as the "happy dragon," and it grew so popular that it disrupted China's social order: women neglected their household duties to spend their time riding, and the emperor was forced to impose a ban. This was a clever yarn, neatly accounting for the happy dragon's disappearance while evoking current events: the rise of bicycle-riding feminists, and the backlash against them.

Li, a famous raconteur, may well have spun his fairy tale spontaneously, from whole cloth. But certain priority claims appear to have been deliberately concocted as government propaganda. A 1949 article in the Soviet journal *Physical Culture and Sport* detailed the heroics of Efim Artamonov, a Russian serf who invented a high-wheeled bicycle in 1801, nearly seven decades before similar machines appeared in western Europe. According to the article, Artamonov hand-built the bike, which he then rode eleven hundred miles, from his home in Verkhoturye, in the Urals, to Moscow, where he presented it to Czar Alexander I as a wedding gift. (The czar rewarded the inventor by freeing him from serfdom.) A year after its publication in *Physical Culture and Sport*, the Artamonov story was codified with an entry in the *Great Soviet Encyclopedia*, and soon thereafter a replica of the landmark bicycle was installed in the Polytechnic Museum in Moscow. There's no mistaking the Cold War imperatives behind this legend, which established Soviet primacy in bicycle history while hitting familiar notes about the glory of Russian workers. ("Artamonov, who with his invention anticipated the modern bicycle by many years, serves as an example of native wit and ingenuity.") The claim was debunked as pure fiction by scholars who dug into the archives following the collapse of the USSR. Nevertheless, a bronze monument with an inscription proclaiming Artamonov the inventor of the bicycle still stands in the Ural city of Yekaterinburg.

The Artamonov hoax has the flavor of Jorge Luis Borges, sending the student of bicycle history into the bibliographical labyrinths, chasing footnotes that lead to blank walls. Another nineteenth-century literary fraud aimed to establish French patrimony for the bicycle. The perpetrator was a Parisian journalist who, in a move Borges would have savored, upgraded his pedigree by adding an aristocratic "de Saunier" to his given name, Louis Baudry. It was under that nom de plume, in 1891, that Baudry published *Histoire générale de la vélocipédie*, which dated the birth of the bicycle to exactly one hundred years earlier—smart marketing on the author's part, since it meant that the publication of his *Histoire* coincided with the bicycle's centennial. According to Baudry, the first bicycle was a "rigid" two-wheeler (it had no pedals or steering apparatus) crowned with a decorative head carved in the shape of a horse or lion. The vehicle was called the *célérifère* and was invented, Baudry wrote, by a nobleman, the Comte Dédé de Sivrac. Neither the *célérifère* nor the Comte de Sivrac ever existed, but the falsehoods have been repeated in books ever since, and bicycle museums in Europe and the United States have exhibited replica *célérifères*. Baudry did not disguise his jingoism, concocting an entirely French first quarter-century of cycling history, stretching from the Reign of Terror to the Bourbon Restoration, spiced with evocative scenes: a *célérifère* unveiling in the Palais-Royal, *célérifère*-mounted mailmen plying Paris streets. But Baudry was rhetorically shrewd, pooh-poohing the *célérifère* as homely while championing it as the First—an epic humblebrag. "M. de Sivrac's invention was but a poor little naked seed!" he wrote. "What sweat, what tears, what expense, what years it took to produce fine bicycles from the primitive *célérifère* of the eighteenth century!"

The most telling passages in Baudry's tract were those that lashed out at non-French claimants to the bicycle's invention. His animus was aimed especially at France's neighbor to the northeast. "Could a brain from the other side of the Rhine have conceived the [bicycle]?" he wrote. "Is that plausible after all?"

Baudry had in mind a particular Rhinelander: Baron Karl von Drais, a minor nobleman, originally from the city of Karlsruhe, on the western edge of the German Confederation, in the Grand Duchy of Baden. Baudry's loathing for Drais was intense; at times in his *Histoire*, it seems that Baudry can hardly bring himself to write Drais's name. ("The Badenian was merely a thief of ideas.") But the record is clear. The crucial breakthroughs that brought the bicycle into existence took place in the brain of Karl von Drais. It was Drais who devised the first bicycle, which rolled into the world in the city of Mannheim, on the eastern bank of the Rhine, in the late spring of 1817.

———

The basic facts of the story have been established. On June 12, 1817, Drais unveiled the invention he called the *Laufmaschine,* or "running machine." That day, Drais made a short demonstration ride on a road that ran south from central Mannheim, covering a distance of eight miles in just under an hour. It is unknown how many onlookers were present for the *Laufmaschine*'s debut, but those who were would have been impressed—and, perhaps, tickled—by its novelty. It had two wheels, each approximately twenty-seven inches in diameter, arranged in a line, one wheel in front of the other. The wheels were connected by a wooden slab, which was fitted with a cushioned saddle. The rider centered his weight on the vehicle, straddling the seat, and rolled the wheels forward by pushing off the ground, one foot at a time—the "running" motion that gave the *Laufmaschine* its name. The steering mechanism was a kind of tiller, a long pivoting pole hitched to the front axle. If the rider came to a hill or other terrain that was difficult to navigate by the usual means, he could dismount, rotate the steering rod forward, and use it to drag the *Laufmaschine* behind him. There was a brake, too, operated by a pull cord. To thwart copycats, Drais placed the brake on the front section of the frame, where it was hidden by the rider's legs.

The design was clever in several ways. Drais situated the saddle toward the rear of the frame, at a height low enough for the user's legs to reach the ground. On the other end of the *Laufmaschine*, Drais placed a padded rest for the forearms. This arrangement held the rider's body in an optimal position—back erect, torso slightly tilted forward—providing comfort and ensuring efficient movement. "The instrument and the traveller are kept in equilibrio," Drais noted in his first published description of the invention. He had hit upon the defining oddity of bicycle mechanics: the symbiosis between man and machine, between the bicycle and the rider who is also the power source. Drais's intuition about ergonomics was matched by an eye for aesthetics. The *Laufmaschine* was primitive by comparison with the bicycle as we have come to know it, lacking many key features, notably pedals. But its silhouette—the slender frame that loops on either end into wheels of equal size—is recognizably that of a bike. To behold the *Laufmaschine* in 1817 was to glimpse the future.

Nevertheless, those who witnessed Drais's first ride might have been more amused than amazed. To early-nineteenth-century eyes, the *Laufmaschine* told a visual joke: it was a parody of a chariot. Drais had commissioned a cartwright to construct the machine, and the building materials—the frame of seasoned ash, the spoked wooden wheels wrapped in iron hoops—were carriage materials. It was, in short, a horse-drawn cart that had somehow become separated from the horse and most of the cart, and fallen under the command of a toiling human being. The *Laufmaschine*, critics quipped, was a coach that forced its passenger to walk in the mud, while burdening him with the labor normally delegated to a four-legged beast. It was a contraption that "turned a man into a horse."

In fact, the first person to make the comparison to horses was Drais himself. He touted the *Laufmaschine* as a horse replacement, offering travelers a new kind of autonomy and, under the right conditions, greater speed. "When roads are dry and firm, [the *Laufmaschine*] runs on a plain at the rate of eight or nine miles an hour, which is equal to a horse's gallop," Drais wrote. "On a descent, it equals a horse at full speed." For Drais, the *Laufmaschine* was a "facilitator" and an "accelerator," a device that augmented a person's own natural powers of locomotion. The machine did not dehumanize its rider—if anything, it superhumanized him, allowing him to travel faster, more efficiently, more freely.

This was the message Drais carried across Europe in the half decade following the *Laufmaschine*'s introduction. He spent several years refining the design, creating new *Laufmaschine* models— tandems, three- and four-wheeled variations, a *Laufmaschine* with an extra passenger seat "for a lady"—while seeking to secure patents in different territories. Drais was an imperfect proselytizer, an oddball who alienated as many people as he charmed. He had been born Karl Friedrich Christian Ludwig Freiherr Drais von Sauerbronn in Karlsruhe in 1785. The Drais family was titled but not wealthy. His mother was born the Baroness von Kaltenthal; his father, Baron Wilhelm von Drais, was privy councillor to the grand duke of Baden, Karl Friedrich. Karl was named after the duke, who attended his christening.

As a child, Karl showed a keen interest in machines and devised new ones of his own. When he reached his teenage years, it was decided that he should pursue a career in civil service, and he enrolled in a school of forest administration run by his uncle. Drais later studied architecture, physics, and mathematics at the University of Heidelberg, but a career in forestry was deemed his best professional option.

In 1810, Drais secured an appointment as the grand duchy's chief forester. The title was impressive, but the job was hardly a job at all. It was a ceremonial post: Drais received a salary but did basically no work. He went officially "off duty" in 1811, continuing to collect his pay while living in Mannheim and pursuing private obsessions. Effectively, the government was providing him with a stipend to daydream and tinker. It was a good investment. Drais would go on to invent a periscope, a wood cooker, a meat grinder, a machine that recorded piano music on paper, the earliest keyboard typewriter, and the first shorthand transcription machine. In a portrait painted when Drais was in his early thirties, he has the eccentric look of a gentleman inventor: ill-fitting coat, tousled hair, glassy faraway gaze.

Drais was particularly interested in the problem of transport. Breakthroughs in science, medicine, and engineering had radically transformed everyday life in Europe, yet the horse-drawn vehicles used to move human beings over land had not been meaningfully upgraded for centuries. In 1813, Drais tried his hand at an improvement, designing a four-wheeled carriage, to be piloted by two or more people, with a foot-powered crank and a hand-operated "rudder" for steering. He called it the *Fahrmaschine*, the driving machine. The device had a variety of technical shortcomings, but it was the clear forerunner of the two-wheeler that Drais would soon conceive.

What prompted Drais to dream up the *Laufmaschine*? The question has vexed historians. Hans-Erhard Lessing, Drais's biographer, has argued that the invention of both the *Fahrmaschine* and the *Laufmaschine* are linked to crop shortages, which turned Drais's thoughts to the possibility of horseless travel, a means of personal transport not reliant on stores of oats or corn. In the case of the *Laufmaschine*, Lessing says, the precipitating event was a global cataclysm: the "super-colossal" eruption of Mount Tambora, on the Indonesian island of Sumbawa, which sent a towering column of ash skyward on April 10, 1815. The following year, the ash cloud reached the Northern Hemisphere. The result was the climatological and ecological disaster known as "the year without a summer." Winter temperatures and blizzards continued into the summer months of

1816, destroying harvests in Europe and North America. The Rhine River valley was one of the places hardest hit, and Lessing theorizes that the chaos there—devastating crop shortfalls and deaths of horses on a mass scale—compelled Drais to once again take up the horseless transport problem. It is a seductive origin story: the bicycle's creation was heralded by the largest volcanic explosion ever recorded, a literal big bang.

Still, it is just a theory, and the murk surrounding Karl von Drais's eureka moment may never lift. As for the *Laufmaschine's* decline: that story is well known. It enjoyed a brief vogue in several European and American cities, fell out of favor within a few years, and stands today as an oddity: a technological landmark that is also a curio, a historical flash in the pan.

Yet the *Laufmaschine* was revolutionary. Several decades elapsed between the introduction of Drais's machine and the invention of a pedal-driven two-wheeler, and another thirty-odd years passed before further refinements gave us the modern bicycle. But none of these bikes would have existed had Drais not established what scholars call the "two-wheeler principle," the single-file lineup of two wheels. For that leap of the imagination alone, Drais merits the heady title *Vater des Fahrrads,* Father of the Bicycle.

During his lifetime, acclaim eluded Drais. Infamy did not. His life was tumultuous, shaken by great events of the age and by the cutthroat politics of his caste. In 1822, he was targeted by student mobs in the aftermath of a controversial legal decision made by his father, then the highest-ranking judge in Baden. Drais fled to Brazil, where he hid out for years, working as a land surveyor on the plantation of a German-Russian nobleman. He returned to Baden in 1827, but he came under fire for his increasingly liberal-nationalist views and support for democratic reforms. He was harassed by the authorities, who slandered him as a madman and a drunk. The press played along, dubbing Drais "the foolish forester" and deriding him as an inventor of useless machines. There were efforts to commit him to sanatoriums, and he survived at least one assassination attempt. In 1848, following France's "February Revolution," he renounced his noble title, taking the name "Citizen Karl Drais." But in 1849, when an uprising in Baden failed, his assets were seized and his pension cut off—repayment, the government said, for "the cost of revolution." Drais retreated to his hometown of Karlsruhe, where he lived just a few streets away from the home of another pioneer of mechanized transport, Karl Benz, a child at the time. Drais died, destitute, on December 10, 1851. A *Laufmaschine* was among his scant possessions at the time of his death. He was buried in Karlsruhe, beneath a gravestone that made no mention of his inventions, summing up his life's work in bland bureaucratese: "Chamberlain, Forester, Professor of Mechanics."

———

Researchers do not agree on all aspects of the *Laufmaschine* story. Hans-Erhard Lessing's "year without a summer" hypothesis has become a part of the official narrative, asserted as a fact in books and other commemorations. In 2017, on the bicentennial of Drais's first ride, Germany issued a silver twenty-euro coin featuring depictions of the *Laufmaschine* and the Tambora eruption. Yet Lessing has stated plainly that the theory is based on circumstantial evidence, with no testimony from Drais himself connecting the *Laufmaschine*'s invention to the climatic catastrophe of 1816. (In fact, the only inspiration cited by Drais himself was ice-skating—a clear precedent for the push-and-glide motion used to propel the *Laufmaschine*.) Paul Smethurst has suggested that "environmentalist revisionism" may be behind the acceptance of the "year without a summer" narrative. "The bicycle has gained a symbolic role as a 'green machine' in the 21st-century, so it might seem 'natural' to associate its invention with an environmental crisis of 200 years ago," Smethurst writes.

Other scholarly quibbles are more pedantic, such as the argument that the *Laufmaschine* should not be classified as a bicycle, since it lacked pedals. Bicycle history holds many milestones, a long sequence of design breakthroughs and mechanical enhancements that came after Drais. There are plenty of firsts to go around, and various nations—France, England, Scotland, the United States, Italy, Japan—can claim pivotal roles in the bike's technical development. But the primacy of the *Laufmaschine*, its status as the ur-bike, is unchallenged today by all but cranks and fantasists.

Of course, dreams do persist. There are bicycle obsessives who care little for the fine points of scholarly disputes or nationalist priority claims. Their love strikes a more mystical chord. For romantics like these, the search for the bike's origins leads to Stoke Poges, to St. Giles' Church, and to the bicycle window.

Inside the church, on the building's west-facing wall, there is a stained-glass window framed by an ogive arch. The window's centerpiece is a World War II memorial listing the names of eight St. Giles' congregants who died in the war. Just above and to the right of the memorial is an additional piece of glass, measuring eighteen inches by eighteen inches, which was not part of the original design and sits rather awkwardly, like a crude patch, atop the window's harlequin pattern of colored panes. The panel holds an enigmatic image: a small muscle-bound male nude, a cherub perhaps, is blowing a horn while straddling a strange device with a single spoked wheel.

This is the so-called bicycle window. No one is certain where or when it was created, or what exactly it portrays. Its provenance has been traced by different investigators to fifteenth-century Flanders and sixteenth-century Italy. Some have suggested that the contraption it depicts is a medieval land-surveying tool known as a waywiser. (The knotted string that appears in the upper left portion of the panel is similar to those found on waywisers.) Others point to passages in the Book of Ezekiel that describe cherubs riding wheels, and to religious paintings and mosaics depicting such scenes.

What is clear, in any event, is that the bicycle window has nothing to do with bicycles. It is evidently a section of a larger stained-glass composition; details that could clarify what kind of apparatus the horn player is riding have been cut off, leaving fragmentary images within the panel's borders. The rear of the machine arcs into what appears to be a circular shape. But it is a wild leap to conclude that this truncated form is the rear wheel of some kind of bike or bike-like vehicle.

Nevertheless, many have drawn that conclusion. Word of the window's existence first began to circulate when the members of a cycling club visited Stoke Poges in 1884. Reports surfaced in cycling magazines, and a sketch of the window appeared in one of the earliest bicycle histories, Harry Hewitt Griffin's *Cycles and Cycling* (1890), above a caption that dated it to the seventeenth century and offered no hedging language: "The church window cyclist of 1642." In his text, Griffin went further, construing the St. Giles' window as a historical missing link, a "clue to the student who is desirous of tracing manual locomotion to its birth."

By the turn of the century, the lore of the St. Giles' window had spread sufficiently that guidebooks touted it as a tourist draw on par with Thomas Gray: "Every visitor to Stoke Poges visits Gray's tomb, and no less a matter for pilgrimage has the so-called 'Bicycle Window' become of late years." "Pilgrimage" was the right word. Even those not prone to fantastical thinking may have found their imaginations inflamed by the atmosphere of St. Giles'—by the sight of a "sacred bicycle," consecrated in stained glass among the arches and archangels.

Today bicycle pilgrims still come to St. Giles', though not, according to Reverend Harry Latham, in the numbers they once did. Still, when Latham brought me into the church that afternoon, it was clear that this was a tour he had given before. Architecturally, St. Giles' is a hodgepodge, telling a centuries-long story of building and rebuilding. There are Saxon windows, Norman walls, a Gothic nave, a Tudor chapel, late-seventeenth-century hatchments, Victorian arches. Latham and I were alone, and the place was very quiet, still, and dark. It was dank, too. The weather outside was warm, but

inside the church, it was chilly: the cold and wet of a thousand English winters had blown into the building and never left. Latham led
me past the Easter Sepulchre, a tomb containing the mortal remains
of Sir John de Molyns, a fourteenth-century knight. Latham said:
"Before I show you the bicycle, I need to show you the place that it
came from."

On the south side of St. Giles', just opposite the wooden porch
entrance to the building, there is a separate entryway that leads into
a little vestibule. This place is known as the Manor House Entrance.
As the name suggests, it once served as a private way in and out
of the church for the residents of the neighboring stately home,
a place for St. Giles' fanciest congregants to gather themselves,
and to discard wet clothes on a rainy day, before stepping into the
sanctuary. Eventually the occupants of the Manor House stopped
using the entrance, and the vestibule became a kind of storeroom
where St. Giles' clergy kept bulky items: cleaning supplies, gardening equipment, a bicycle or two. "Today we use it as a kitchen-
ette," Latham said. There was a small table in one corner, next to a
mini-refrigerator.

The oddest features of the room are two small south-facing windows that are hung with what is best described as stained-glass col-
lages. These windows hold a weird array of ornaments and images:
floral motifs, swags, scrollwork, dogs, birds, fierce-looking griffins
holding coats of arms in their beaks. For years, the bicycle panel sat
in these windows too, another element in a surreal jumble. Some
decades ago, the clergy at St. Giles' got tired of bringing visitors into
the vestibule to view the bicycle window. So they cut the panel out
of the window and installed it in the church proper.

In fact, the bicycle panel was twice decontextualized. Its first
home was neither the sacred confines of the sanctuary nor the adjacent vestibule but an entirely different building: the Manor House.
"The vestibule was built when they were downsizing the Manor
House," Latham said. "This was in the mid–seventeenth century,
we think. They obviously had some scraps of glass from the house

they wanted to recycle." In other words, the bicycle window was originally a domestic oddity, an adornment of a noble family's posh digs. Perhaps Queen Elizabeth herself laid eyes on it when she visited the Manor House in 1601. Latham said: "They brought the stained glass from the Manor House and threw it in here. I don't think much care was taken with it, frankly. I mean, it's a mishmash."

Latham led me through a little corridor, back into the sanctuary. He said: "I think it was a good idea to pop the bicycle window into the church. I'm sure it was irritating having to bring people through. So, you know, 'Let's put it where everyone can see it.' Then there's no more problem. And now it's become part of the furniture. Anyway, there it is."

There it was. The sunlight was glancing down on St. Giles' west façade, and on the other side of those walls, where Latham and I now stood, the backlit bicycle window had a somber glow. There is a feeling that sometimes steals up on me when I'm someplace beautiful and ancient, like St. Giles'. The stones and the bones; the dusty light and the musty air; the history, the mystery. The solemn majesty of such an atmosphere doesn't so much inspire faith as ignite self-doubt, overwhelming whatever confidence I have in the power of my own mind and the worth of my worldly knowledge—throwing into question any inklings I might hold about the riddles of the universe, bicycle genealogy included. Latham stood patiently alongside me for several minutes while I studied the window, stepping forward, stepping back, snapping photos, and gazing at the thing again. There was no denying: it was a strange and alluring artifact. The toes of the rider's right foot appeared to be reaching down to touch the ground, and his left foot was raised in the air. It was not crazy, I had to concede, for a viewer to suppose that this personage was moving his thingamajig forward by the same push-and-glide motion with which Karl von Drais had impelled the *Laufmaschine*. I asked Latham if he thought the contraption looked like a bicycle. "Not really," he said. "But I suppose it looks enough like one."

We exited St. Giles', stepping back into the bright blusteriness of a spring day in Buckinghamshire. Latham led me around the church's exterior, pointing out some more features of the architecture. Eventually we arrived at the spot where a granite slab commemorated the churchyard's famous occupant: *Opposite to this stone in the same tomb upon which he has so feelingly recorded his grief at the loss of a beloved parent are deposited the remains of Thomas Gray.* Latham said: "A thing that you learn doing this job is that people like mysteries. They like mysteries, I think, as much as they like certainties."

DANDY CHARGERS

Hobbies; or, Attitude Is Everything, Dedicated with Permission to All Dandy Horsemen. Hand-colored etching, published in London, 1819.

ondon, 1819. A crowd has gathered in Paddington to witness a sporting event, of a sort. It is a race that will follow a semicircular course, bending through the genteel streets and squares on the eastern side of the Edgeware Road, moving west out to the Grand Junction Water-Works, before turning south and then east to finish at Tyburn Turnpike, at the northeast corner of Hyde Park.

As battles staged in London streets go, it is a high-toned affair. The contest pits a lord against an earl, and a collection of the well-born and well-dressed have gathered to look on, wearing fine muslin and crisp breeches worthy of an afternoon at Ascot. This is a stakes race, after all, with a prize of one hundred guineas promised to the victor. Yet no horses will be run today. Instead, this contest will showcase that latest sensation, that celebrated and maligned novelty that goes by various names—the velocipede, the hobby-horse, the pedestrian curricle, the swiftwalker, the accelerator, the perambulator, the draisine—but is most colorfully known by moni-kers that testify to its popularity in the beau monde to which the lord and earl belong: the dandy horse, the dandy hobby, the dandy charger.

Someone has fired a pistol. The racers are off, swinging their legs and pushing off on paving stones to drive their vehicles forward. The sight of these two-wheelers in motion is by turns impressive and absurd. On straightaways and on level ground, the machines do well, traveling with an easy gliding motion that might even be called elegant. But when the road slopes upward, the racers grunt and strain, and on the downhill stretches and sharp turns, toil often turns to panic, a flurry of furious tugging at hand brakes and clumsy manipulating of steering bars to keep the contraptions vertical and above the London dust.

For the first half mile or so, the lord and the earl run virtually neck and neck. Then, as they near the waterworks, the racers' eyes bulge at an unwelcome sight. A cow has dashed onto the path. The earl swerves clear but the lord maneuvers too slowly, plowing straight into the beast and crashing hard amid a tumult of cursing and bovine lowing. The fallen rider is helped to his feet by a chimney sweep. He brushes himself off and starts up again, trailing by some distance now but riding hard. A short while later, as the riders approach the corner of Connaught Mews, just north of Hyde Park, it is the earl who veers off course—slipping, tipping, nearly hurtling to the pavement. This lapse allows the lord to close the gap, and moments later, when the pair arrive at Tyburn, they are in a dead heat. As they cross the line it is impossible for anyone in the cheering throng to discern which dandy has charged to the finish first.

This was likely one of the first bicycle races held in England, one of the first anywhere, for that matter—assuming that it actually took place. The story is recorded in a pamphlet, *An Accurate, Whimsical, and Satirical, Description of the New Pedestrian Carriage, or Walking Accelerator!!*, written by a certain John Fairburn. It is a contemporary source, published in 1819, the year the race is reported to have been run. But there are reasons to believe that the account is more whimsical and satirical than accurate, another vivid piece of bicycle apocrypha. The racers are identified only as "Lord Y____" and "the Earl of B____." That wager of one hundred guineas, nearly $10,000 in today's money, seems steep, even for profligate peers. The slapstick elements of the account—the sudden appearance of cows and chimney sweeps, darting onstage from the wings—suggest an effort to juice the plot. Then there is the kicker to the story, in which Fairburn reports that the race transfixed *le tout London* and that news of the results was sent by carrier pigeon to George, the Prince Regent, at his seaside retreat, the Royal Pavilion in Brighton.

But if the story is not, strictly speaking, factual, there is truth in it. As Fairburn's lively narrative suggests, history's first cycling craze played out as a Regency farce, with dramatis personae drawn from England's upper crust. The *Laufmaschine* made its way first to France, where Karl von Drais secured a patent in early 1818. News that Parisian swells had taken to riding a machine called the *draisienne* or *vélocipède* filtered across the channel; later in 1818, the two-wheeler materialized in Bath, where a German acquaintance of Drais's had a model built by a local artisan. Soon after, a London coachmaker, Denis Johnson, was granted a patent for "a Pedestrian Curricle or Velocipede." Johnson's machine incorporated modifications to Drais's blueprint and added some tweaks of his own devising. Johnson refined the steering apparatus and substituted metal for wood in certain areas to create a sturdier machine. He also designed an adjustable seat, which could be raised or lowered to accommodate riders of differing heights. Other manufacturers soon popped up, selling their own variations or—more often, perhaps—pirated copies of Johnson's velocipede in violation of his patent.

By the turn of 1819, several hundred of the new vehicles were in use across England. Their presence was felt on city streets and country lanes, from Winchester to Canterbury to Hull to rural Hampshire, where a woman was killed when her horse, startled by a passing velocipede, threw her from her cart. In Manchester, Sheffield, and Leeds, crowds gathered for demonstrations of velocipede riding. Denis Johnson, hoping to drum up sales, went on tour, traveling to Birmingham, Liverpool, and other cities to exhibit his machine in hotels and music halls. There were velocipede races. Many were informal competitions, like the race depicted in Fairburn's pamphlet. On one occasion, hundreds assembled on a road outside Glasgow where, word had it, a velocipedist would be showcasing his machine. "Thus they were hoaxed," a newspaper reported, "for no dandy horse appeared."

The fad was centered in London. "In the New Road [velocipedes] might be seen in great numbers running every fine evening especially near Finsbury Square, and the top of Portland Road, where they were let out for hire by the hour," recalled one Londoner. "Rooms for practice were opened in several parts of town." A newspaper likened the obsession with velocipedes to the interest generated by the visit to England of a Persian emissary seeking assistance in his nation's conflict with the Russian Empire: "To-day, nothing is spoken of but the Persian Ambassador, or the Velocipede." On the variety stage, skits and songs sent up the velocipedes as a trendy folly. "The nothing of the day is a machine called the velocipede," wrote John Keats, the poet, in March 1819, in a letter from London to his brother and sister-in-law. Keats professed bafflement at the popularity of the strange "wheel carriage to ride cock-horse upon."

The meanings ascribed to the new invention in the French and

English capitals conformed neatly to national stereotypes. The Parisian *vélocipède* signified sex: it was said that couples rented his-and-hers two-wheelers in parks and *bois* and rode to secluded spots to tryst. In London, the vehicles were emblems of social class. The price of a velocipede was dear. (Eight guineas, Keats noted in his letter.) The velocipede craze was not restricted to the elite; the proliferation of instructional schools and the by-the-hour rental market bespeaks more widespread popularity, and there are contemporary accounts of country clergymen using velocipedes to make their rounds visiting parishioners. But they held special allure for the subset of rich Englishmen who were infatuated with novelties and dedicated to amusement.

This social type—young, carefree, flamboyantly dressed, with ample funds and free time to commit to the pursuit of what most would call frivolous pleasures—had been an object of fascination in England since the 1770s. But the figure of the dandy gained new prominence in the second decade of the nineteenth century, when King George III, beset by mental illness, was judged unfit to rule, and his eldest son, Prince George, was installed as his proxy. The prince had long been notorious for his dissolute habits: his ravenous appetite for food and sex and art, his wild parties, lavish spending, huge debts, and general disdain for duty and propriety. Some held out hope that the responsibility with which the prince was now entrusted would bring a change in demeanor. But with greater power came more opportunities for George to indulge his vices, and he took them.

During his reign as regent, from 1811 to 1820, George turned over the business of governing to his ministers, chiefly the prime minister, Lord Liverpool, absolving himself of responsibility for nearly all affairs of state, including the ongoing war with Napoleon's France. While Britain endured the costly final years of that conflict, and faced an onslaught of domestic crises, the prince devoted himself to high living. The excess of the period was exemplified by the Royal Pavilion, the opium-dream Orientalist palace designed for the prince by architect John Nash, and by the parade of aristocrats and hangers-on who flocked there to eat, drink, and debauch beneath its psychedelic domes and minarets. This circle included George's various mistresses and many prominent men of fashion, among them the ne plus ultra of dandies, the prince's old Eton chum Beau Brummell.

The exploits of the prince and his set transfixed and scandalized the public. Everyone and everything connected with the milieu was imbued with glamour and subject to populist resentment. Thus the velocipede, which gained fame and, in short order, infamy. Newspaper readers learned that velocipedes were fixtures on the grounds of the prince's estates and adornments of his parties. In August 1819, the London-based *Morning Post* described the regent's birthday celebration at Windsor Castle, an extravagant affair featuring "a variety of juvenile amusements," including "eating of buns while hopping," "wrestling for a jacket," and "dandy horse racing." Newspapers reported that the Prince Regent's guests were in the habit of commuting to the Royal Pavilion on two wheels. ("It is now become quite common for persons to come down to Brighton from London on Velocipedes.") George himself took an interest in the machines: he was said to have purchased four of them, which were conveyed from London to the Royal Pavilion by army officers with "all the wagon-train pomp of a peaceful military parade." It is unclear if the prince himself was a velocipede rider, but the idea provoked much amused commentary, due to his considerable girth.

You did not need to be among the elect on the royal guest list to catch a glimpse of the velocipede. "In Hyde Park, all fashionable men cross its saddle," went the lyrics of "The Perambulator; or, Pedestrian Dandy Hobby Horse," a song published in 1819. Hyde Park was London's velocipede mecca, and dandies predominated. ("If we are *literally* to shoot the folly as it flies," wrote one observer of the velocipede scene, "Hyde-park, on a Sunday would be strewed with dead, and not a Dandy left to tell the tale.") The understanding that velocipedes were, first and foremost, the playthings of "idle and titled" men-about-town was amplified in the quips of commentators and the sardonic rhymes of poets:

> *Pray have you not seen*
> *That most clever machine,*
> *That's to drive out of England each prime bit of blood;*
> *And the dandy who rides,*
> *Has the pleasure besides,*
> *Of carrying his steed, and of walking in mud.*

There were fiercer denunciations. In May 1819, a newspaper editorialist lamented the "disgrace and odium of Dandyism" that had tainted the velocipede, distracting attention from its innovative design and its usefulness as a means of "muscular exertion." For a writer in the political weekly *The Gorgon*, the velocipede was a symptom, and a symbol, of the depravity of England's elites: "What are these lay-lords, as they are called, with which the country is burdened? Idle young fellows . . . who spend their time in galloping about the Park, and riding the Dandy horse—while the labourer is perishing with hunger, the merchant cannot sell his goods, nor the farmer cultivate his land, because of the taxes they pay to support the spendthrifts."

The virulence of this criticism reflects the wider politics of the day. Britain in the early nineteenth century was convulsed by change and social unrest. The rise of industrialized production, the enactment of free trade policies, the deprivation and loss engendered by the war with France—these transformations and traumas roiled the British public and poured fuel on smoldering class tensions. Throughout the Regency period, as much as a third of England's population faced starvation. Food riots and other rebellions erupted and were met by military crackdowns. More British troops were called up to combat machine breakers during the Luddite uprisings of 1811–13 than had been deployed by Wellington against Napoleon's forces in the Iberian Peninsula a few years prior. In August

1819, the British calvary stormed into a crowd of sixty thousand protesters who had assembled in Manchester's St. Peter's Field to demand parliamentary reform. Eighteen people died and hundreds were injured in the so-called Peterloo Massacre, "the bloodiest political event of the nineteenth century on English soil."

This was the backdrop to England's velocipede craze. Whatever inherent appeal the machine may have held—as a technological wonder, as a symbol of progress, as an amusing curio—was overwhelmed by its association with the callous ruling class. The knowledge that the velocipede had reached English shores via France added to the umbrage. In Regency England, Francophilia was rampant among "all those with the slightest pretension to fashion or taste." Throughout the Napoleonic Wars, English elites maintained their French allegiances and affectations—peppering their speech with French phrases, stocking their cabinets with Sèvres porcelain, filling their glasses with Bordeaux, and "hanker[ing] after Paris as their spiritual home." The vast majority of the English held virulent anti-French views, and the sense of betrayal—the conviction that the indulgences of the upper classes were not only decadent but treasonous—lingered when the war was over. In June 1819, almost exactly four years to the day after Napoleon's defeat at Waterloo, a comedian appeared onstage at London's Covent Garden Theatre. Riding a velocipede and clad in the costume of the dandy, he recited flowery verses praising his Parisian *"cheval de bois."* The joke would have been lost on no one.

The most vivid satire was the work of caricaturists, who churned out etchings and engravings lampooning the velocipede fad. (In 1819, a London journalist noted that the velocipede "contributes to the amusement of passengers in the streets in the form of caricatures in the print shops.") Rendered in the bold colors and cartoonish style of the period, the prints reflected the understanding that velocipedes were a public safety hazard, a threat to life or, at least, limb. They showed madcap scenes, images of an out-of-control machine barreling at top speed toward an inevitable crash.

But it was the riders who were the prime subjects of ridicule. Caricaturists depicted dandies in their finery, stuffed into top hats and half-swallowed by cravats, struggling to maintain a grip on careering velocipedes. Many cartoons conflated velocipede riding with sexual perversion. A frequent target of the caricatures was the Prince Regent, who was portrayed in preposterous erotic situations, straddling both a two-wheeler and a mistress. One print, thought to be the work of the famous illustrator George Cruikshank, shows the prince splayed facedown across a velocipede beneath its rider, the prince's mistress, Lady Hertford. The prince has a bit in his mouth, and Lady Hertford tugs at the reins with her left hand; her right hand, raised high over her head, grips a horse whip. In the background we glimpse a second velocipedist, the prince's brother Frederick, the Duke of York, who appears to be savoring the sadomasochistic scene.

Historical patterns are assembling here. We can see similarities between the anti-velocipede uproar of the Regency period and the scorn directed at today's cycling dandies, "hipsters," with their fixed-gear bikes and fashion-forward looks. There are other echoes of today's bicycle controversies. Populist contempt for velocipedes may have been based largely on their reputation as toys of the rich. But what doomed the first bicycle, in England and elsewhere, was NIMBYism: the belief that velocipedes were unrightful intruders, welcome neither on the roadways, where horses and carriages traveled, nor in the parks or on the sidewalks, which were the domain of pedestrians. "The crowded state of the metropolis does not admit this novel mode of exercise," pronounced a London newspaper in March 1819. Velocipedes were dangerous, critics said, ungovernable things that posed a menace to men and beasts, to say nothing of the fools who chose to ride them.

The problem was fundamental, built into a machine whose steering mechanism was poorly engineered and whose brakes were inadequate. Riders caught their wheels on ruts and went flying; they struck other velocipedes and swerved into the paths of pedestrians and horse-drawn cabs. Newspapers recounted stories of collisions and smashups: velocipedists who skidded into fence posts, who were thrown to the floor in practice rooms, who slammed into walls and gates and docks. There were reports of broken bones, cracked teeth, and crashes in marketplaces that upended vendors and scattered wares. An epidemic of "ruptures," or hernias, was said to have afflicted those who "indulged themselves in the Sunday use of this vehicle." Looking back on the phenomenon years later, a Londoner recalled the hysteria velocipede accidents provoked among certain citizens:

> When quietly disposed people saw a velocipede come rattling towards them down a steep hill, rush by like a thunderbolt, going every moment faster and faster, and finally behold the rider terminate his furious career by plunging with frantic desperation, headlong into a deep ditch up to his eyes in mud, respectable people were at a loss to account for his violent conduct, and in their own minds ascribed it to mental alienation— a sort of temporary insanity brought on by velocipedes; while others could not help thinking of a certain herd of swine, that under satanic influence ran violently down a steep place into the sea, and perished among the waters.

The backlash against velocipedes had a violent edge. In Hyde Park, gangs of youths swarmed riders and chased them away. Sometimes the vehicles were seized by mobs and vandalized. Once, when a few velocipedists joined hundreds of horsemen on a stag hunt in Epping Forest, northeast of London, "the hobbies ultimately became objects of attack and were demolished." The actions of these vigilantes were soon given an official imprimatur. In 1819, a ban on velocipede riding was decreed in London. Injunctions were enacted elsewhere in England, and in other far-flung locations that Karl von Drais's invention had reached. Bans were imposed in Milan, New York, and Philadelphia. In New Haven, Connecticut, a newspaper editorial advised citizens to "seize, break, destroy, or convert to their own use as good prize, all such [velocipedes] found running on the side-walks." The vehicles materialized in distant corners of the British Empire, and a familiar series of events unfolded. "It would seem that the Dandies of Calcutta, mounted on their Velocipedes, have become rather troublesome to the worthy citizens of that metropolis," quipped the London *Sun* in May 1820, reporting that the city's governor-general had instituted a velocipede prohibition.

For a time, zealous riders flouted these laws. But the blow was struck. The two-wheeler had been deemed illicit, and that judgment would hold. The London press, which just months earlier had portrayed velocipedes as the height of fashion, now called them passé. "Great expectations were at one time formed of those things called Velocipedes," a newspaper declared in the summer of 1820, "but they have been found so crazy and laboriously manageable that they are altogether abandoned." The fashion-conscious moved on to new sensations, and there were fresh inventions to excite the imagination of technophiles: "All the catalogue of dandy chargers hitherto invented are not to be compared with the new mode of traveling by steam-boats."

Other changes were afoot. With the death of George III in 1820, the prince ascended to the throne. King George IV was unreconstructed, still lazy and dissipated. ("A more contemptible, cowardly, selfish, unfeeling dog does not exist than this king, with vices and weaknesses of the lowest and most contemptible order," wrote the privy councillor and diarist Charles Greville.) But King George was a depleted force who spent his final decade in steep decline: blind in one eye, morbidly obese, racked with gout and dropsy, doped up on laudanum. The Regency receded into history, and to the extent that the velocipede was recalled at all, it was as a footnote from that era of excess and frivolity. In 1822, a literary critic, writing dismissively of Lord Byron, judged the poet "as ephemeral as a Brummel or a Velocipede."

But there were voices in the wilderness—those who remembered the velocipede fondly, and who glimpsed its future. The historical record has preserved a couple of these visionaries. The anonymous author of an 1829 letter to the London-based science journal *The Mechanics' Magazine* hailed the velocipede's "celerity, lightness, elegance, compactness, durability, and ease of propulsion," proclaiming it "one of the most promising inventions of this inventive age . . . far less worthy than most, of that oblivion into which it appears to have sunk." With impressive prescience, the letter writer suggested that the machine might be improved with the addition of "treadles and cranks."

Some eight years later, a more forceful case was mounted. In May 1837, just a month before the teenage Princess Victoria began her reign as queen, a man named Thomas Stephens Davies delivered a speech to a distinguished body in London. Davies was a mathematician and a member of the Royal Academy, a "gentleman of science" whose disquisitions typically had titles like "On the Equations of Loci Traced upon the Surface of the Sphere, as Expressed by Spherical Co-ordinates."

His address on this occasion, "On the Velocipede," fell outside his usual purview, and it stands as a remarkable piece of bicycle literature: both a requiem and a prophecy, and one of the most far-seeing defenses of the two-wheeler ever recorded. The lecture was given in Woolwich, in southeast London, at the Royal Military Academy, an august institution for which Davies had recently authored a multivolume mathematics textbook. The audience that day was full of stolid, serious types, scholars and career soldiers. Davies knew they would be puzzled by his praise song to a machine, which, at that late date, was obscure to most ("[Today] a velocipede is as rare as a black swan, and the young people now rising up scarcely know what it is") and regarded by those who did remember it as obsolete. "It has been suggested to me," he said, "that I ought to apologize to you for bringing before you a subject that may appear to some persons too trifling to merit the attention of the members of this institution."

But Davies insisted that the velocipede was worthy of reconsideration. It was, he said, a "remarkable invention," which had been "persecuted" and "put down" before its time. He conceded that the velocipedes had design deficiencies, and that riders had difficulty controlling the machines when they reached high speeds. But Davies argued that neither design flaws nor dandies were behind the velocipede's demise. The cause was narrow-mindedness and philistinism, the outcry of the "braying" hordes who oppose anything new and unfamiliar on principle: "When umbrellas were first brought out, they brayed at them, and when the steam engine got coming they raised with one content a bray so loud that it was heard across the Atlantic and re-echoed back from North America."

In the case of the velocipede, Davies said, the braying had proved decisive. But was it fatal? Davies thought perhaps not. Squinting into the distance, he caught sight of a day when Karl von Drais would be vindicated—when the velocipede, or a descendant of it, would once again flash into view. "I am persuaded that many of you will think with me, that a new machine ought not to be laid aside and forgotten, until its principle or theory has been fairly enquired into," Davies said. "An original idea should not be lost sight of, for, if the inventor himself does not see the full extent and application of it, those who come after him may."

3

ART VÉLO

A man working on a bicycle wheel, circa 1890s.

Before bicycles worked well, they looked good. As a means of safe and reliable locomotion, Karl von Drais's proto-bike left much to be desired. But as an objet d'art, it could not be gainsaid: with its curvaceous silhouette, its graciously hooped and spoked wheels, the machine cut a lovely figure.

The same was true of the inventions that followed Drais's in the decades-long saga of refashioning and refining that brought us the modern bicycle. The bike that touched off a cycling craze in 1860s France was nicknamed "the boneshaker" because of the punishment its wrought-iron frame and ironshod wooden wheels inflicted on riders. The high-wheeler or "ordinary" or penny-farthing, the famous bike of the 1870s and early 1880s with a small wheel in the back and a huge one in front, was difficult to mount and dangerous to operate. Penny-farthing riders were prone to "taking a header," flying headfirst over the handlebars. The name given to the breakthrough bike that ushered in the great cycling boom of the 1890s— the safety bicycle—testifies to the hazards of the models that preceded it. Yet like the *Laufmaschine,* the boneshaker had elegant looping lines, and the penny-farthing ranks among the most visually striking transport machines ever devised.

Today it may seem surprising that the bicycle was *invented* at all. Two inline wheels of equal size, with a chain drive on the rear wheel and a diamond-shaped frame—the classic safety bicycle form feels preordained, as natural as a human being with two arms and two legs. The bicycle's geometry pleases the eye: the sweep of the handlebars, the flow of the tubing, the spindly lacing of the spokes. Your bike might be standing still, resting jauntily on its kickstand, but its streamlined contours give it the look of a thing in motion. Simone de Beauvoir described a bicycle whose appearance was "so lissome, so slender, that even when not in use it seemed to cut through the air."

There is a kind of person who likes to look at bikes as much as he likes to ride them. I remember the first time I screwed a hook into the ceiling of a studio apartment and hung a bike lengthwise from its rear wheel. My ride to work was now also my décor, an artwork that dominated the small living space. At night, with the lights off, the rims and spokes would catch the glint of streetlamps from the sidewalk outside. When I spun the front wheel, reflections reeled across the wall like a disco ball light show.

I was not the first to take pleasure in this spectacle. Marcel Duchamp recalled the mesmeric effect of his famous readymade sculpture *Bicycle Wheel* (1913), a twenty-six-inch wheel mounted upright
on a stool. "To see that wheel turning was very soothing, very comforting," Duchamp said. "I enjoyed looking at it, just as I enjoy looking at the flames dancing in a fireplace." For Adolf Loos, the
architect and design theorist, the bicycle was a near-perfect piece of
art, comparable in purity to the great creations of the ancient world.
A Greek vase, Loos said, is "as beautiful as a bicycle."

Bicycle design tells important stories. History speaks in the language of lugs and cranksets, in the height of bottom brackets, the
shape of saddles, the slope of top tubes. The whimsical penny-
farthing carries a lost Victorian world on its enormous front wheel.
The Schwinn Sting-Ray, with its low-slung "wheelie" frame and
elongated banana seat, is a piece of Americana as evocative of the
funky late 1960s and early '70s as bell-bottom jeans or Sly and the
Family Stone's *Greatest Hits*. Compare the slender, austere cruisers
and roadsters that predominated in midcentury Europe to the
American bikes of the period, with their bulging balloon tires and
hefty frames with stylized motorcycle-style "gas tanks." Clashing
worldviews come into focus: on the one hand, an urban society in
which bikes were utilitarian machines, integral to everyday life; on
the other, a car culture that had relegated bicycles to the status of
children's playthings and surrogate motor vehicles, with "petro-
fetishism" built into the bike frames themselves.

The main story the bicycle tells is one in which utility, simplicity,
and beauty are indistinguishable. This is why Loos and other Bau-
haus theorists, those wagers of war on ornament, hailed the bicycle
as an embodiment of modernist ideals. The bicycle expresses the
principle of "form follows function" with a transparency that is
matched by few other human creations. To understand the workings of most machines, you must bury your nose in a user's manual,
then bury your head in the machine's innards. A car conceals its
mechanisms beneath covers and hoods and glossy paint and with

the underside of its chassis. But the bicycle, wrote Roderick Watson and Martin Gray, "comes to us . . . naked": "wheels, pedals, chain, crank and forks demonstrate their purpose and only their purpose, with scarcely an ounce of surplus matter." The modern bicycle has just a few dozen functioning components, and they are in general durable and easy to maintain. The most vulnerable part of a bicycle, the tires' inner tubes, can be repaired or replaced quickly and cheaply.

There have been many innovations in bicycle design and construction since the arrival of the safety bike. Derailleurs, disc brakes, titanium and carbon-fiber frames—innumerable new components and building materials have appeared on the scene. Whole new genres of bikes have come into the world. There are collapsible bikes that fold on hinges so you can carry them around like a backpack or briefcase; there are bicycle designs that you can download on open-source websites and print out on a 3D printer. But the basic shape, the classic safety bicycle silhouette, remains and reigns. Lewis Mumford wrote: "In every art there are forms so implicit in the process, so harmonious with the function, that they are, for practical purposes, 'eternal.'" Mumford had in mind such things as the safety pin and the drinking bowl, whose antiquity would seem to justify the heady designation "eternal." In historical terms, the bicycle is a new thing, but its form feels as fundamental and inviolable as any pin or bowl or Grecian urn.

———

It begins with, what else, two wheels. In English, we call the machine a bicycle because of that pair of wheels—those twin "cycles," a word derived from the Greek for "circle." The writer Robert Penn has made the amusing observation that you could subtract nearly every component essential to the modern bike besides wheels—sprockets, chain, brakes, pedals—and you would still have a bicycle. (In fact, you would have stripped the thing back to Drais's elemental

Laufmaschine.) But the wheels are nonnegotiable: take those away and you won't travel far.

The bike wheel has a combination of strength and lightness, stability and flexibility—qualities that distinguish the bicycle's mechanism in general. Similar characteristics are exhibited by suspension bridges, to which spoked bicycle wheels have often been compared. Both bike wheels and bridges rely on the tensile strength of a network of wires; both have a weight-bearing capacity that seems improbable given their elegant, even delicate, appearance. The bicycle wheel is one of the strongest of all human contrivances, capable of supporting approximately four hundred times its own weight. In theory, a buffalo could pedal a bike without the wheels buckling under the load.

The first generations of bicycles had what were more or less carriage wheels, made of iron and wood, with fixed spokes built from those same materials. The wheels were heavy and rigid and not ideally engineered to withstand the burdens the bicycle and rider placed on them. As the wheel rotated, the weight was transferred to, and considerable stress placed upon, the spoke nearest the ground at the bottom of the wheel.

A breakthrough in wheel design came in the late 1860s and early 1870s, with the introduction of wire spokes. The conventional bicycle wheel of today has twenty-eight, thirty-two, or thirty-six spokes, which yank the hub and rim toward each other, keeping the wheel in a state of tension. These wheels can bear the load of cyclist and frame at any point on their circumference and tolerate pressure from different areas and angles: the stress that is exerted from underneath as the wheel moves over the road, torsional stress from the chain as it drives the rear wheel forward. In earlier stages of wheel development, spokes were threaded from hub to rim radially, but designers figured out that a tangential pattern—in which the spokes stretch out from the hub at angles in an overlapping configuration—made the wheel more resistant to warping. Also, tangential spoking is an eye-catcher. Lowrider bicycles, the extravagantly blinged and bedazzled customized bikes made famous by Latino cyclists in Los Angeles, feature as many as 144 spokes, often chrome- or gold-plated. Lowriders are perhaps the purest expression of bike-as-art-object, since in many cases they are bikes that cannot be ridden: the bottom brackets sit too close to the ground for the pedals to be turned. Like Duchamp, lowrider devotees look at the bicycle wheel and see fire, a metallic flicker and flare that they cannot resist stoking to maximum brightness.

You can gaze at the bicycle wheel; you can also listen to it. The faint click and purr of the rotating bike wheel is a sound as soothing as any in nature—as lulling as the trickle of water over stones in a riverbed. The bike wheel can make all kinds of music. A young Frank Zappa appeared on *The Steve Allen Show* in 1963, producing eerie tones by scraping at the spokes of a cruiser bike with a bass bow. (Zappa told an amused Allen that he'd been playing the bicycle for "about two weeks.") Bike builders sometimes test wheels using tuning forks, plucking the spokes like guitar strings to determine if they sound the same pitches and are, therefore, correctly tensioned.

The process of adjusting spoke tension such that the rim will spin freely between the brake pads is known as "trueing" the wheel. For the philosophically disposed, the trued bicycle wheel embodies grander truths. The trued wheel plays notes in tune; the trued wheel obtains a Euclidean ideal. The spokes that stretch between the hub and the rim are engaged in a tug-of-war, each end straining against the other to hold the wheel in a perfect circle.

————

Examine the bicycle and you will find more circles, and circles within circles. There are those Dunlopian circles, the tire and the inner tube, a circular sleeve cradling an air-filled ring. There are the various circular parts and pieces—clamps and washers, bolts and bushings—that make up the bicycle's components and fix them in place. There is the chainring and the rear wheel sprocket, toothy disks along whose circumference the chain is impelled.

The development of the chain drive may rank as the most significant milestone in bicycle design, after Drais's choice to arrange two wheels in a line. The first phase in the evolution came in the 1860s, with the invention of the boneshaker velocipede, which reconfigured Drais's running machine as a pedal-powered device. This velocipede was a "direct-drive" vehicle: a rotary crank and pedals were affixed to the hub of the front wheel, and each rotation of the crank spun the front wheel around exactly once. To reach a higher "gear"—to make the bike travel faster with each revolution of the crank—the circumference of the wheel had to be increased. Thus the penny-farthing, whose gargantuan front wheel offered higher gear ratios but made cycling challenging and risky. A poorly taken bump in the road could result in the dreaded header— a plunge over the handlebars, a bruise, or a broken bone, or a broken neck, or a skull cracked like an eggshell.

These problems consumed the attention of mechanics and tinkerers for more than a decade. The solution came, at the end of the 1870s, with a new bicycle design that replaced the direct drive with a drivetrain transmission: a contraption that transferred the energy produced by the pedaling cyclist to the bicycle's wheels via a chain. Earlier experimenters had tried connecting chain drives to the front wheel. But now the crank and pedal were shifted to the center of the bicycle, and the chain was looped from the crankset back to the rear wheel. When the pedals were pressed, the crank turned, the chain was activated, and the rear wheel was dragged forward, setting the bike in motion.

It was a simple and ingenious improvement. By running the chain between different-sized cogs—the larger chainring on the crankset and the smaller rear-wheel sprocket—the bicycle achieved a gearing effect: for every rotation of the pedals, the rear wheel revolved multiple times. This allowed the penny-farthing's jumbo

front wheel and miniature rear wheel to be discarded in favor of—
at first, on the earliest model safety bikes—wheels of similar size,
and, soon enough, equal-sized wheels, which made the bicycle easier to mount and operate. The front wheel could now be used simply to steer, a far less complicated arrangement than a steering
apparatus that doubled as a pedal drive. In short, the chain drive
was a great democratizer. It made the bicycle safer and simpler,
transforming cycling from an activity dominated by sportsmen and
daredevils into a mode of transportation open to more or less
anyone—children, the elderly, the unathletic. Crucially, the invention of the safety bicycle refuted the theory—espoused by men,
mostly—that cycling was beyond the ability of women, who were
considered too delicate to brave the rigors of the boneshaker and
the penny-farthing.

In technological terms, the bicycle's chain drive was historic, a
solution to conundrums pondered for ages by humankind in its
quest for better tools. Hand-cranked devices had been in use since
antiquity, but the safety bicycle's drivetrain exploited the leg muscles, the largest in the human body, to create a motor of extraordinary efficiency. Once again that talismanic form, the circle, comes
into play. The efficiency of the bicycle is based on the conversion of
reciprocating motion—the up-and-down action of feet pressing
pedals—into rotary motion, the dreamy circular revolutions of the
pedals and crank. (In cycling slang, a rider with poor pedaling technique, or a rider whose technique slips as fatigue sets in, is said to
be "pedaling squares.") The result is energy-optimizing. As Robert
Penn has written: "Cycling with regular pedals and cranks, our legs
only push on the pedal for a small part of each pedal rotation: about
60 degrees. For the other 300 degrees of that revolution, the main
muscles in that leg—hamstrings and quadriceps—are at rest, and
able to absorb blood, carrying replacement energy."

The other essential bicycle shape is the triangle. The classic diamond bicycle frame, codified in the 1880s with the invention of the
safety bike, is in fact made up of two linked triangles. One of the

triangles comprises the top tube, down tube, and seat tube; the second also incorporates the seat tube, from which the seat stays and chain stays angle back to the rear wheel axle. There are other, subtler triangles on the bike frame, formed by the front fork and chain stays, which connect, respectively, to the axles of the front and rear wheels. Structural engineers have long recognized that the triangle is the strongest geometric shape, resistant to deformation even when placed under great stress. A bicycle that has suffered a big crash may have a bent fork, wheels folded over like tacos, and various other ravaged bits and pieces. But the frame is likely to be intact. The underlying integrity of that frame configuration has allowed designers to incorporate progressively lighter materials—tubes made of aluminum or titanium or carbon fiber—without sacrificing stability. The triangles hold their shape.

Many other variables go into the making of frame geometry and the function of any given bicycle. The lengths and widths of the tubes, the angle of the steering axis, the positioning of the bottom bracket, the length of the wheelbase—these and other factors affect how the frame fits the rider, the speed at which the bike will travel, and how well it will handle. There have always been deviations in frame layout; the twenty-first century has brought radical new bicycle designs and novel frame shapes. But the diamond is the standard—most newfangled frames are, in truth, just variations on the theme. "It is unlikely that the diamond frame will ever be surpassed as a way to build a rigid-frame bicycle using joined tubes as a construction medium," wrote the bicycle builder Sheldon Brown. "It is one of the most nearly perfect pieces of design known."

———

Machines with perfect designs, like those with imperfect ones, do not appear by magic. To build a bike, raw materials must be gathered and transported. The raw materials in, for instance, a road bike with an aluminum alloy frame may include aluminum, steel, iron, copper, manganese, magnesium, zinc, chromium, titanium, mineral oil, sulfur, carbon black, synthetic rubber, and natural rubber. These materials are mined from the earth or extracted from plants or cooked up in factories. During the manufacturing of the bike and its varied parts, further processes of refinement and treatment take place: grinding, smelting, hydroforming, extrusion, and vulcanization, among others. At each stage, waste and emissions are produced. Many of us take comfort in the knowledge that, by riding bikes, we are making an ethical and environmental choice. But bicycles do not float free from the realities of their creation: the resource extraction, energy consumption, and human labor involved in the manufacturing of a bike exacts a cost. The two-wheeler leaves a footprint.

Just how big a footprint is hard to say. The bicycle industry is global and byzantine. Most of today's bicycles include parts manufactured in several different countries. Researchers who have attempted to write about the life cycle of bicycles have found it difficult to follow the supply chains to their origins—to pinpoint the open pit mine in Guinea or Ghana or China where the bauxite ore, the primary source of an aluminum bicycle frame, was originally dug up, or to identify where in the world the natural rubber in a bike tire was harvested. Suffice it to say, the extractive industries involved in the earliest stages of a bicycle's life cycle have—to be generous—spotty environmental and human rights records, and it is sentimental to suppose that bikes, by virtue of being bikes, arrive in this world clean and green. Nor should we be naïve about the conditions under which bicycles are assembled in factories. Journalists have uncovered labor abuses in the bicycle industry, including the exploitation of child bike factory workers in such places as Cambodia and Bangladesh.

The historical record is darker still. We need look no further than John Boyd Dunlop and the pneumatic rubber tire. In the standard version of bicycle history, the tale of Dunlop's invention is narrated—as in the Prologue to this book—as a technical and mercantile triumph, the final breakthrough that set the late-nineteenth-century bike boom in motion. But that story fails to trace the rubber in the countless tires and inner tubes back to the source: to rubber plantations in the Amazon basin and to the "red rubber" terror in the Belgian Congo, where millions died harvesting latex from *Landolphia owariensis* vines. In Brazil, one person perished for every 150 kilograms of rubber reaped; in Congo, the figure was one death for every ten kilograms of rubber. "If you were one of the millions all over the world who started riding a bicycle in the 1890s 'bicycle craze,' you may have coasted on a cushion of Congo rubber," writes the historian Maya Jasanoff. The connection between the turn-of-the-century boom and the humanitarian and ecological infamies perpetrated by European powers extends to at least one more natural resource: asphalt, mined by exploited laborers in the English colonial territory of Trinidad, and used to lay the smooth surfaces over which so many European and American cyclists rolled their wheels.

This grim record may temper our enthusiasm for the Great Man version of bicycle history, with its pantheon of illustrious European inventors and innovators. Their achievements are impressive nonetheless. Alongside Drais and Dunlop and the safety bicycle pioneer John Kemp Starley, cycling historians enshrine such names as Pierre Michaux, a Parisian blacksmith believed by some to have produced the first boneshaker velocipedes, and Eugène Meyer, whose work was crucial to the development of the high-wheeler. There are contributors to bicycle anatomy at the molecular level. A key figure is Jules-Pierre Suriray, the Parisian bicycle builder who patented the ball bearing, that "atom of the Machine Age," essential to the operation of not just bikes and cars but everything from fishing reels to air conditioners to computer hard drives to the Hubble telescope and the Mars rover.

The record is muddled by the usual disputes about provenance. Historians debate whether credit for the invention of the pedal bike should go to Michaux or to various fellow travelers in the mid-

nineteenth-century French bicycle trade. (In recent years, a new
scholarly consensus has formed around Pierre Lallement, a French
mechanic who moved to Connecticut and was granted the first U.S.
patent for a pedal-driven velocipede in 1866.) There is also the controversial case of Kirkpatrick Macmillan, a blacksmith from Dum-
fries, Scotland, who, according to some sources, invented a pedal
bicycle, with a rear wheel drive powered by treadles and rods, in the
1830s.

The story of the bicycle's evolution is also industrial history, a
tale of innovative products and the companies that brought them to
market. Bike booms and boomlets have been spurred by the introduction of new kinds of cycles: tricycles in the 1880s, racing bicycles
in the 1930s, derailleur and BMX bikes in the '60s and '70s, mountain bikes in the '80s, the e-bikes of the present day. Connoisseurs
of bicycle components and equipment have their own canons of beloved parts and hallowed parts makers. The mystique surrounding
such producers of bike components as Campagnolo, Shimano, and
SRAM, and the zealousness with which bicycle "gearheads" choose
sides among and pledge allegiance to these brands, is a subject worthy of its own tome.

But it is wrong to view the bicycle as a thing that has been
handed down from on high, bestowed on the world by heroic individuals and visionary manufacturers. The bicycle is a populist project, the result of grassroots innovation and an exchange of knowledge
that runs in all directions. A defining quality of the bicycle's form is
its openness to hacks and interventions, to rejiggering and retrofitting. The simplicity and legibility of the bicycle's mechanism has
brought out the mad scientist in millions. A curious child with a
decent set of wrenches can strip a bike down to the bearings and
build it back up again, adding bells and whistles if so inclined.

The culture of popular mechanics that began in the late nineteenth century was initially dominated by cyclists who discovered
how simple and enjoyable it was to jury-rig their safety bikes. "There
are two ways you can get exercise out of a bicycle," wrote the English

humorist Jerome K. Jerome in 1900. "You can 'overhaul' it, or you can ride it." The vast numbers of hybridized bikes and bike-like machines—bikes you can pedal through the air, bikes you can ride across the water, bikes you can lie down in as if on a daybed—reflect the ease with which the bicycle can be modified and the conviction that bikes are, that bikes *should be,* infinitely accommodating of new forms and alternative functions. In 1886, an American journalist mocked the compulsion to create bicycle crossbreeds: "When we finally get a full-rigged bicycle, with its steam engine, mainsail, spinnaker, and all the other appliances suggested or invented, we shall have a new means of suicide which cannot fail to become popular."

Altered bikes have altered the course of historical events. The bicycle first arrived in Vietnam as a tool of empire: a favored form of transport and recreation for colonial officials in French Indochina and a cash cow for French manufacturers, who for years operated with something close to a monopoly in Vietnam. But the locals soon adopted the bicycle to their own ends, including anti-colonial resistance and guerrilla military actions against French and, later, American occupiers. The Vietnamese used bikes both to transport explosives and *as* explosives, concealing bombs in the hollows of seat tubes or top tubes. A secret American military report issued in May 1966 noted the practice with alarm: "Sometimes the bicycle itself is the instrument of death, its hollow tubular frame packed with plastic explosive and the timing devices located under the saddle. Terrorists ride the bicycle into the area, lean it up against the building to be destroyed, set the fuse, and walk off." In subsequent decades, "bike bombs" have become familiar features of asymmetrical warfare and struggles against occupying powers. In the so-called war on terror, American forces in Iraq and Afghanistan were frequently targeted with explosives hidden in and attached to bicycles.

The impulse to strip down and soup up has given the world new kinds of bikes and new ways of biking. The origins of the modern mountain bicycle can be traced to a group of cyclists in Northern California in the 1970s who altered vintage bikes so they could go riding up and down Mount Tamalpais, a famous peak in Marin County. The cyclists renovated prewar Schwinns—reinforcing the frames, replacing the handlebars, adding new tires, gearing, cranks, and brakes—to create "klunkers" capable of navigating footpaths that sloped nearly thirteen hundred feet through rugged terrain on the face of Pine Mountain, one of Mount Tamalpais's foothills. The nickname the riders gave to this trail, Repack, paid tribute to their down-and-dirty handiwork: the cyclists' screaming descents left their coaster brakes squeaking and smoldering, necessitating the frequent repacking of brake hubs with grease.

Eventually one of the top Repack racers, Joe Breeze, began to design, build, and sell his own line of purpose-built mountain bikes. The bicycle industry soon followed suit. By some measures, the mountain bike is the most popular model of bicycle to reach the public since the safety. Its sturdy construction, low gear ratios, shock-absorbing suspension systems, and easy handling have made it a favorite of millions of riders who will never get anywhere near an off-road trail.

Today, DIY experimentation remains a fundamental aspect of bicycle culture, and a foundation of bicycle subcultures. The developing nations of Asia, Africa, and Latin America, where cycles serve a wide variety of utilitarian functions, are hotbeds of customization: overhauls that turn two-wheelers into three- and four-wheeled cargo vehicles, novel designs that deploy pedals and drivetrains as power generators to run tools and electrical systems. In certain bohemian enclaves, bicycle building is a political act and an expression of dissident identity. The "freak bike" or "mutant bike" movement, a punk- and anarchist-affiliated scene concentrated in American cities, is dedicated to the construction of bicycles of odd shapes and sizes, scrapped together from scavenged parts. Freak bikes give physical form to the ideals of recycling and reuse. The freak bike's battered, proudly low-tech look makes an anti-consumerist statement—spurning the gleaming machines that roll off the factory floors of mass manufacturers and the upmarket artisanship of bespoke bike builders—while treating the bicycle as a punk art object, a medium of absurdist play and display. No one who has shared a city street with an armada of mutant "tall bikes"—seven-foot-high contraptions with "ape hanger" handlebars and three diamond frames welded together in a vertical stack—will think the same way about the art of the *vélo*.

Those who have no interest in or aptitude for grimy bicycle bricolage can nonetheless derive a unique kind of hands-on pleasure from a bike. The click of the grip shifter as you change gears. The action of the calipers as your brake pads clench the rims. In an age dominated by alienating frictionless interactions with digital devices, the bicycle offers a throwback, a reminder of the tactile satisfactions of machine age technology. There is poetry in the workings of the bicycle's components. "To consider the endless perfection of the chain, the links forever settling about the cogs, is a perpetual pleasure," wrote the literary scholar Hugh Kenner. "To reflect that a specified link is alternately stationary with respect to the sprocket, then in motion with respect to the same sprocket, without hiatus between these conditions, is to entertain the sort of soothing mystery which . . . you can study all your life and never understand."

The most important bike component is the engine, otherwise known as the rider. The essence of the bicycle's design lies in its uncanny fusion of machine and human being. Builders of high-end custom bicycles use computer programs and mathematical formulas to provide fine tailoring, precisely fitting the bike frame to a person's frame. But even the rider of a scrap-heap junker can experience the strange sensation of becoming one with the bike. In "Le Vélocipède" (1869), the poet Théodore Faullain de Banville pictured the cyclist as "a new animal / . . . Half wheel and half brain." Flann O'Brien, one of the great bicycle bards, described "people in these parts who nearly are half people and half bicycles . . . [who] get their personalities mixed up with the personalities of their bicycle as a result of the interchanging of atoms of each of them." These chimeric metaphors may be the closest we can get to capturing in words the feeling of a particularly free-flowing ride, when your body and being—shoulders, hands, hips, legs, bones, muscles, skin, brain—seem to be inseparable from the strong but supple bicycle frame. At such moments, to conceive of the bike as a vehicle is perhaps not quite right. It may be more accurate to think of it as a prosthesis. Ideally, it is hard to say exactly where the bicyclist ends and the bicycle begins.

4

SILENT STEED

"Horsey," an "attachable bicycle ornament." Created in 2010 by Korean designer Eungi Kim.

For millennia, civilization moved to a soundtrack of falling hooves. It was the rhythm of travel, the metronome marking the time of a journey: *clip-clop, clip-clop, clip-clop.* Horses' footfalls amplified the quiet of rural roads. In cities, horses moving across cobblestones made a bustling background din. The sound brought pleasure: "The hoofs of the horses!—Oh! Witching and sweet / The music earth steals from the iron-shod feet," wrote the poet Will H. Ogilvie. It was also a terrifying sound, a herald of death, as in the Book of Jeremiah: "All who dwell in the land will wail at the sound of the hooves of galloping steeds, at the noise of enemy chariots and the rumble of their wheels." In any case, the sound was ubiquitous and inescapable. To journey over land at speed was to move to the accompaniment of a familiar racket.

The bicycle offered an undreamed-of novelty: nearly silent high-speed travel, a vehicle that shot you across the land atop spinning wheels that made almost no sound at all. Bikes snuck up on the nineteenth century. "There is something weird, almost uncanny, in the noiseless rush of the cyclist as he comes into view, passes by, and disappears," a journalist declared in 1891. Today it is surprising to discover how many early observers expressed wonder, first and foremost, about the sound the bicycle made—or, rather, didn't make. This was thought to be socially transformative. In 1892, a writer predicted that bicycles would eliminate the "harsh rattle and clatter" of horse-drawn vehicles, eradicating "the main source of the nervousness that so universally afflicts city dwellers." Wags coined a nickname, drawing a distinction between the new machines and the old stomping, snorting pullers of carts and carriages. The bicycle was "the Silent Steed."

There were other nicknames. The iron horse, the mechanical mount, the nickel-plated stallion, the steel palfrey, the two-wheeled Bucephalus. In France they spoke of the *cheval mécanique;* in Flanders, the bicycle was a *vlosse-peerd,* a "floss-horse," a punning Flemish approximation of "velocipede." At one time, the Chinese referred to the bicycle as "the foreign horse." Epithets in this vein date to the dawn of the bicycle age. When the English gave equine nicknames to Karl von Drais's *Laufmaschine*—the hobbyhorse and dandy horse and dandy charger—they were underlining the obvious. Of course, Drais himself was explicit about the connection. It was no accident that the destination of Drais's first ride was the Schwetzinger Relaishaus, a coaching inn, where mail-delivery horses were stabled and weary horses could be swapped for those with fresh legs.

The ideological battle pitting the bicycle against the car has nothing on the nineteenth-century showdown between the bike and the horse. At stake was not just the question of noisy versus "silent" transport. The bicycle-horse clash set the modern world against the old days and old ways, urbanity against agrarianism, machines against nature. It was an argument about progress and obsolescence. It brought heady hopeful visions crashing into dire apocalyptic ones.

It was not the first such drama to hit the nineteenth century. Similar controversy had erupted decades earlier with the arrival of the steam locomotive, which was likewise branded "the iron horse." But in that case, the analogy was imprecise. A train traveled on tracks, shuttling between fixed points, carrying passengers en masse. The bike was personalized transport, "a single horse that obeyed only one master," as the historian David Herlihy has written. Like a horse, a bicycle could take you door to door or—in the conceits of poets, at least—over the hills and far away:

> The shadow of my silent steed
> Flies over hill and vale
> As swiftly as the clouds that speed
> On Notus' fav'ring gale.
> No whip, no spur, its sleek thigh wounds;
> Nor galls the chafing rein;
> But free as Helios' steed it bounds
> Across the shining plain.

The comparison made sense. A bicyclist straddled his machine like a horseman astride his mount; to this day, the cushion attached to a bicycle's seat post is called a saddle. In early cycling literature, writers ascribed horsey qualities to bikes: "[The velocipede] is light, and little, and leans lovingly against you for support. Its gait is uniform and easy"; "It quivers like an animal under its thick skin of nickel and enamel; it whinnies at times"; "It runs, it leaps, it rears and writhes, and shies and kicks; it is in infinite restless motion, like a bundle of sensitive nerves; it is beneath its rider like a thing of life."

The first generations of cyclists, who learned to ride as adults, construed the bike as horselike in its unruliness. Like a mustang, a bicycle needed to be "broken." Bicycles, wrote Jerome K. Jerome, "will try all the lowest dodges to get rid of their riders; they try to climb up the sides of houses and walls; lie down in ditches; stand on their heads for no apparent reason; buck-jump; wage war against cabs and omnibuses; and do everything they can think of to make it unpleasant for their rider until he shows them he means to be obeyed." In "Taming the Bicycle" (1886), Mark Twain recounted his struggle to master his high-wheeled ordinary. Twain wrote: "Mine was not a full-grown bicycle, but only a colt—a fifty-inch, with the pedals shortened up to forty-eight—and skittish, like any other colt." This horse was prone to throwing its driver:

> Suddenly the nickel-clad horse takes the bit in its mouth and goes slanting for the curbstone, defying all prayers and all your powers to change its mind—your heart stands still, your breath hangs fire, your legs forget to work, straight on you go, and there are but a couple of feet between you and the curb now. . . . You whirl your wheel *away* from the curb instead of *toward* it, and so you go sprawling on that granite-bound inhospitable shore.

The bicycle posed peril of a different sort to those whose livelihoods were dependent on horses. A satirical etching from 1819, at the height of England's velocipede craze, depicts a blacksmith and a veterinarian taking revenge on the newfangled "horse" that requires neither shoeing nor medicine. The blacksmith is shown smashing the vehicle with a hammer; the veterinarian glowers over the crashed rider—a dandy, of course—while administering a dose from a giant syringe.

The scene was imaginary, but it reflected real anxieties. From the start, the bicycle was touted as a cost-effective alternative to horses. "What an expense would be saved in feeding, littering, far-riering, and doctoring!" wrote a London velocipede enthusiast in 1819. "A glue-pot, hammer, bag of nails, and a little oil, would sup-ply every want; if the head of a dandy charger were shot off, the rider would only have to dismount and nail it on again." A half cen-tury later, J. T. Goddard, one of the bicycle's first self-styled histori-ans, expressed a similar sentiment: "We think the bicycle an animal, which will, in a great measure, supersede the horse. It does not cost as much; it will not eat, kick, bite, get sick, or die." Bike manufactur-ers seized on this sales point. A famous Columbia Bicycle advertise-ment hyped the company's high-wheeler as "An Ever-Saddled Horse Which Eats Nothing."

Not everyone was buying the comparison. In 1868, a New York journalist scoffed at the idea of a bicycle race, envisioning a horse race without horses: "We may imagine the race courses devoted to contests of this description, with hundreds of excited gentlemen beating each other over the head with their whip handles, instead of their horses." A French cartoonist went further, depicting cyclists churning around a track while racehorses take in the contest from the grandstand, lounging beneath parasols. Others spoofed the idea of bicycles engaged in equestrian activities associated with elites, like polo and hunting with hounds.

But reality outpaced parody. In 1869, a tournament hosted by the Liverpool Velocipede Club included cycle-mounted fencing, jousting, and javelin throwing. Bicycle polo clubs proliferated in the United States and Britain. Bikes infiltrated country gymkhanas, re-placing horses in such games as tent pegging and Maypole plaiting. On the estates of the gentry, bicycles were fashionable. An 1895 dispatch on cycling in Paris noted the trend: "A new race of servants has come into being—the bicycle groom. . . . In great country houses the post is no sinecure as guests come in droves, and all of them can ride."

A humorous trope of the period pictured the cyclist as a modern-day knight-errant, perched on "no steed but trusty Wheel." The most famous example is again found in the pages of Mark Twain: the scene in *A Connecticut Yankee in King Arthur's Court* (1889) where a detachment of cycling Lancelots—"five hundred mailed and belted knights on bicycles"—stream into view. But once more, truth surpassed fiction. The French army deployed bicycle soldiers for reconnaissance missions in the Franco-Prussian War of 1870–71. By the 1880s, the armed forces of every major European nation had bike battalions. The relative merits of bicycle cavalries and the traditional kind was a subject of much discussion among military strategists. An editorialist in the *Journal of the Military Service Institution of the United States*, writing in 1896, judged bicycles superior to horses in several crucial areas: "When the horse is badly injured he becomes an encumbrance. . . . [A bicycle] is, moreover, easier to conceal, and more apt to be found in its place of concealment on the return of its owner."

The greatest military benefit offered by bikes was in the area of stealth: "The bicycle is noiseless, thus possessing a manifest advantage over the horse, both as to foot beats and neighing." On the battlefield, riders of the silent steed could take their foes by surprise. A crucial testing ground for the military bicycle was the Second Boer War (1899–1902), that grubby competition between the British Empire and the two Boer Republics for dominion over Southern African land and the diamonds and gold beneath it. When British Army infantrymen outfitted with folding bicycles first appeared in the war theater, an Orange Free State soldier joked, "Trust the English to invent a way of traveling while sitting down." But both the British and the Boer sides learned that bikes were suited to the terrain and tactics of that conflict: troops moving more quickly than on foot and more quietly than on horseback could flourish, outflanking the enemy and staging sneak attacks.

It was the Boer army's bicycle reconnaissance outfit, the Wiel-rijders Rapportgangers Corps, that pressed the advantage. Their leader was Daniel Theron, a cunning and fearless commando who had earlier won renown as a "crack horseman." Theron's men tormented the British, pushing their bikes through dense brush and across open fields, staging ambushes on key positions, blowing up rail yards and bridges, capturing hundreds of enemy soldiers and officers, and freeing Boer prisoners of war. Lord Roberts, the British commander in chief, called Theron "the hardest thorn in the flesh of the British advance." Roberts deployed 4,000 troops to eliminate the Boer unit of just 108 cyclists and placed a bounty on their commander's head. Theron was finally killed in September 1900 when he encountered members of Marshall's Horse, an elite British cavalry unit, while scouting alone behind enemy lines. Theron did not go quietly. He shot seven British cavalrymen, killing four, before falling amid "an inferno of lyddite and shrapnel." The Brits had learned their lesson: shortly after Theron's death, they quadrupled the size of their bicycle force.

———

Among civilians, another battle raged. Equestrians had their maxims and gibes: *A horse doesn't fall over when it stands still. You cannot pet a bicycle. A horse always shies away from an oncoming object; a bicycle always shies into it.* Bike partisans retorted: *A bicycle never needs to be lassoed. Bicycles don't foul the roads with manure. Bicycles don't drop dead and leave behind a rotting carcass.* The quips resonated with more high-minded arguments. Progressive reformers, who pushed for sanitary conditions in cities, preferred bicycles to horses, which polluted streets and could spread disease. Reformers also embraced the bicycle on the grounds of animal welfare. Charles Sheldon, the American Congregationalist minister whose 1896 novel *In His Steps* popularized the phrase "What would Jesus do?," took the position that the bicycle was the ethical choice: "I think Jesus might ride a wheel if He were in our place, in order to save His own strength and the beast of burden."

The bicycle's association with feminism disposed traditionalists toward the horse: it was pointed out that a woman on horseback could sit sidesaddle, allowing her to wear a long dress, rather than the bloomers favored by the bicycle-riding New Woman. Cycling advocates, meanwhile, championed the two-wheeler as an alternative to emasculating travel by horse-drawn carriage, that "luxuriously effeminate style of locomotion."

Much of the talk about bikes and horses revolved around social class. It took decades for the dandy horse to become "the people's nag"—for the plaything of Regency elites to evolve into an affordable, democratic horse alternative. The boneshaker velocipedes and penny-farthings of the 1860s and '70s were *haute bourgeois* status symbols. The change came in the 1880s, with the arrival of the safety bicycle, which brought affordable two-wheelers to the masses. Of course, bikes remained popular among the well-to-do, as the bicycle grooms of Belgravia and Berkshire could attest. But as bicycles proliferated across the social spectrum, the horse was held up as a marker of class distinctions. An 1895 newspaper editorial typified the snobbery of certain bicycle critics: "One of the most interesting things in life . . . is the young man who never rode a horse more than two or three times in his lifetime expatiating to all his friends on the great saving that he makes in the hire of horses by owning a bicycle."

Behind such supercilious pronouncements, we sense alarm and, perhaps, dread. The frenetic action on fin de siècle roadways—bikes swarming and darting alongside horse carts on streets thick with traffic—foretold further upheavals, a more fluid and hectic social order. The horse-drawn carriage represented gentility, ancient hierarchies, time-honored entitlements; the bicycle was anarchic and insurgent, an agent of chaos and change. "What is the one symbol that used to mark the rich man from the poor man?" asked John D. Long, the U.S. secretary of the navy, in an 1899 speech. "The rich man could ride while the poor man goes afoot." Now, Long said, that divide had been eradicated: "The man who owns a bicycle rides his own steed. He throws dust in the face of the man in the carriage."

The bike-horse showdown was not just metaphorical and rhetorical. In Europe and the United States, a political and legal argument revolved around questions of taxonomy: What exactly was a bicycle? Was it a mere plaything? Or was it a lawful and legitimate vehicle, a "carriage" in its own right? In American cities, ordinances banning bicycles from streets and parks were challenged by activists in court and, often, on the roads themselves, through direct action and deliberate defiance of laws.

A complaint leveled at bicycles was that they frightened horses. The bicycle's silence was regarded as a menace: bikes were prone to stealing up on horses, causing accidents and sowing mayhem. It was said that bicycles spooked horses, drove horses "crazy," caused horses to throw riders and crash tow carts. The prerogatives of horsemen were aggressively enforced by teamsters, hackney cab drivers, and others who made their living in the horse-and-wagon trade. Coachmen placed their carriages at right angles to the road to prevent cyclists from passing, organized blockades, and turned their horses into the paths of cyclists to strike them down. A cyclist who left a bike unmanned at the curbside might return to discover that "a teamster's horse [had] knocked it over and trampled upon it until it almost lost all resemblance of a bicycle." In 1895, a New York City teamster, Emil Rothpetz, was arrested for spitting at cyclists from the rear of a fellow horseman's vehicle. The presiding judge remanded Rothpetz to prison for four days, expressing hope that the sentence would serve as an example to the many truckmen "who appear to take delight in annoying those who ride the wheel."

The road rage ran in both directions. In the cycling press, reports of accidents and infamies perpetrated by horsemen were standard fare. The American touring cyclist and writer Lyman Hotchkiss Bagg, a prolific chronicler of his bicycle travels under the pen name

Karl Kron, was an acidic disparager of horses and their drivers. In his 1887 tome *Ten Thousand Miles on a Bicycle,* Bagg wrote, "Delight in the dangerous pastime of driving skittish and unmanageable horses would be worth no more than a passing remark, except for the fact that the mere act of purchasing a horse creates the curious hallucination that he simultaneously purchases an exclusive right to the public highways." The epithet Bagg coined for entitled horsemen is with us still: "Road hog."

———

The bicycle-horse rivalry did not escape the notice of entrepreneurs and impresarios. There was money to be made. Beginning in the 1880s, Americans packed indoor arenas and outdoor fairgrounds to view races between bicycles and horses. These events were often promoted as symbolic showdowns: "A contest between the old and the new, a trial between the most primitive form of aided progression and the most modern of all mechanical motive powers." In one famous race, held at San Francisco's Mechanics' Pavilion in the spring of 1884, the horseman Charles Anderson faced the cycling team of Louise Armaindo and John Prince. The match was a test of strength and stamina that followed the model of a six-day bicycle race, unfolding in daily noon-to-midnight stages over nearly a week, with the winner determined by the total number of laps completed and miles covered. The horseman rode on an outside track that edged close to the grandstand; the cyclists raced on a separate inside track marked in chalk on the pavilion floor. The ultimate victory went to Anderson, who completed a total of 874 miles to his opponents' 872. But it was Armaindo, a Canadian racing cyclist known for flamboyant showmanship, who captivated the crowd and the press. "Her mighty limbs sent the bicycle spinning round the track," the *Daily Alta California* reported. "It was funny to see the horses stare with open eyes full of wonder at Armaindo, as her bright machine flashed past them."

Bicycle-horse races were also popular in Britain and Europe. Sometimes these competitions served as proxy geopolitical skirmishes. In 1893, Samuel Franklin Cody, a Buffalo Bill imitator from Iowa who called himself "the King of the Cowboys," barnstormed England and the continent, challenging leading cyclists in a series of races that attracted throngs and inspired blanket newspaper coverage.

Cody had a flair for self-promotion. He wore a broad-brimmed hat and a buckskin jacket and had a drooping mustache; he regaled interviewers with tall tales about rustling cattle and battling Sioux Indians. His most celebrated race took place in October 1893, when he faced off against the French racer Meyer de Dieppe, in a match that drew thousands to the Paris suburb of Levallois-Perret. The contest played to European prejudices, casting the New World as old-fashioned, a land where colorful yokels roamed the open plains on horseback. Europe, by contrast, was the home of the bicycle—the place of urbanity, technology, the future. Perhaps this took the sting out of Cody's defeat of Meyer in the Levallois match and his many subsequent triumphs on his European tour. These victories reportedly earned Cody a small fortune from both prize purses and his own side wagers. Cody also gained a new nickname: newspapers now hailed *Le roi des cow-boys* as *Le tombeur de vélocipédistes*.

But cyclists would inherit the earth. At least it seemed that way in the 1890s. In the United States, bicycle activism reached an apotheosis during the 1896 presidential campaign, when Republican William McKinley and Democrat William Jennings Bryan competed to win the endorsement of the League of American Wheelmen (LAW) and secure the votes of the "bicycle bloc." Founded in Newport, Rhode Island, in 1880 by the Columbia Bicycle mogul Albert A. Pope, the LAW consolidated the bicycle lobby by bringing thousands of local cycling clubs under the umbrella of a national organization. In its early years, its membership was composed largely of genteel gentleman cyclists. (Members included John D. Rockefeller, John Jacob Astor, and other Gilded Age titans.) By the

time of the McKinley-Bryan race, the LAW was powerful and populist, with a membership of more than one hundred thousand. It
was also racist. The group's constitution, ratified in 1894, prohibited
membership by non-whites; because the LAW was also the governing body of U.S. bicycle racing, non-white riders were banned
from most American cycling competitions. The 1897 edition of the
LAW's annual meeting, a four-day gathering in Philadelphia, concluded with a "great bicycle parade" in which twenty-five thousand
members rolled through the streets in costume; many riders wore
blackface or impersonated other ethnic and racial types, including "Japs, Indians, Esquimaux . . . and South Sea Islanders." (For
decades, minstrel-show performances were staples of LAW events
held by both local chapters and the national organization, and many
LAW-affiliated cycling parades and protests featured members riding in blackface.) The LAW dissolved and was revived two times
over the decades, but it wasn't until 1999 that the organization (now
the League of American Bicyclists) formally repealed the racial
prohibition.

If the LAW wasn't socially progressive, it was politically savvy,
and prescient. Its membership united behind the organization's defining mission, the Good Roads Movement, a push to clear the
"sand, gravel, mud, stones and muck holes" and thread the vast nation together, connecting American cities to the countryside with a
network of safe, smoothly paved streets and highways. A similar effort was under way in England; Europe was decades ahead in paving over existing road networks with macadam. But in the United
States, the condition of the roadways, particularly outside urban
areas, was dire. "No nation can advance in civilization which does
not make a corresponding advance in the betterment of its highways," wrote Pope in an 1893 open letter to Congress. The language
is noteworthy. The goal, the LAW emphasized, wasn't merely to
modernize the United States but to civilize it, to bring the young
country onto equal terms with Europe and to continue the expan-
sionist "advance" of the settler colonial state. The fact that many of

the existing roads on the North American continent were Indian trails was unstated but implicit. As was the fact that, for a bicycle mogul like Albert Pope, good roads meant great business.

Now largely forgotten, the Good Roads Movement was one of the most consequential activist crusades in American history. Certainly it had momentous consequences for bicycles, horses, and their respective places in American life. The bicycle's "natural home" was in the city; to build bike-friendly roadways that stretched into the hinterland was to extend the bicycle's dominion, an incursion of the two-wheeled horse into the domain of the four-legged one.

In the mid-1890s, the horse was in decline in the United States on several fronts. The market for horses was depressed; the cause was widely believed to be the bicycle boom. In 1897, the New York *Sun* reported on slumping sales of hay, ascribing the downturn to "the bicycle, which has to a great extent superseded the use of horses." Bicycles were said to be behind the faltering businesses of livery stable owners and carriage builders. It was reported that horse tradesmen were shifting to the bicycle business: "The saddle- and harness-makers are . . . turning their attention to the making of bicycle saddles. Riding-academies have been turned into bicycle schools."

Historians recognize that the bicycle's role in this shift may have been overstated, that other factors—the general deflation of the 1890s, and the rise of electric streetcars to replace horse-drawn trains—were perhaps greater contributors to the horse's decline. But at the turn of the century, the issue was viewed in stark terms: "The bicycle has come to stay and the reign of the horse is over." In this period, the horse assumed a new character in the popular imagination, alternately idealized as sweet nature incarnate, a gentle frolicker of the fields, and disdained as "an untamable beast," "a willful unreliable brute" that brought filth and disease to cities and "belongs in the country." Whether you hallowed or scorned the horse, there could be no question that the creature was out of step with the times, an impediment to the progress the bicycle represented.

Of course, the parade of twentieth-century progress was not to be led by bicycles. The first Ford Model T rolled off a Detroit assembly line in 1908. The following year, just 160,000 bikes were sold in the United States, down from sales of 1.2 million a decade earlier. In Europe, it took longer for the bike to be shunted to the margins, but the advance of motor vehicles proved inexorable. The future belonged not to the silent steed but to the four-wheeled "horseless carriage," with its roaring, revving internal combustion engine.

Today's debates about bicycles and cars reiterate many arguments made in the bike-horse battles. Car culture regards bicycles as relics and nuisances, slowpokes cluttering the roads. Bicycle partisans state their claims in familiar moral terms. Like the late-nineteenth-century cyclists who reviled horses as polluters, today's bike advocates cite the ruinous effects of cars on public health and the environment. Another frequent complaint: the "infernal noise" of car-clogged cities, said by cycling advocates to be the cause of "stress-related illnesses."

As for horses: they have receded from our transportation debates, but they linger in collective consciousness. Automobile manufacturers still measure the capacity of their engines in units of horsepower. The horse has continued to haunt the story of the bicycle, too. In the United States, in the 1950s and '60s, the horse reemerged as a marketing angle in a bicycle industry focused on children. Manufacturers sold "boys' bikes" under names like the Bronco, the Hopalong Cassidy, and the Juvenile Ranger, evoking a mythic West roamed by wild mustangs and the heroic men who could subdue them. The bicycles were available in colors such as "Stallion Black" and "Palomino Tan"; many bikes came equipped with "cowboy" accoutrements. The Monark Silver King Company's Gene Autry Western Bike featured a rhinestone-studded frame, horseshoe-shaped safety reflectors, a fringed saddle blanket, and a "genuine leather holster with Red-handled official Gene Autry pistol." Suburban kids, riding bikes they pretended were horses, dreamed of the untamed frontier that had vanished beneath tens of thousands of miles of asphalt and concrete—the Interstate Highway System, a network of good roads vaster, and more inhospitable to bicycles, than the visionaries of the League of American Wheelmen could ever have imagined.

Comedy is a form of historic preservation. The bike-horse discourse of decades past resurfaces these days in the form of a visual pun. Over the years in New York City, I have encountered several bikes fitted at the handlebars with plastic horse heads. The gag is not unusual. On the internet you can find photos of cheeky bike-as-horse makeovers, bikes rolling along the route of Critical Mass rallies with papier-mâché pony heads leading the charge, bikes with children's hobbyhorses strapped to the top tube, tricycles with stylized horses' tails trailing between the rear wheels. Bicycle-unicorn crossbreeds are also big.

A few years back, a London design firm began marketing a device billed as "the leading bike-horse hybridiser in the world." The Trotify is a small component that attaches to a bicycle's front brake mount, where it claps together two pieces of coconut shell as the bike rolls forward. The sound that is produced is eerily identical to the one made by a cantering horse. This effect may startle fellow cyclists, who hear the clatter of hooves bearing down fast from behind. The silent steed is silent no more. While the bicycle's wheels spin almost noiselessly, the Trotify beats out an ancient rhythm, a song from yesteryear: *clip-clop, clip-clop, clip-clop.*

5

BICYCLE MANIA: 1890s

The Biggest People on the Road! Cover illustration by
Louis Dalrymple, *Puck* magazine (New York), May 1896.

1899, *Akron Daily Democrat* (Akron, Ohio)[*]

Chris Heller has filed a petition in Common Pleas court asking for a divorce from Lena Heller. He alleges gross neglect. To substantiate this he says that she refused and neglected to keep house or prepare meals. He says his wife is a victim of the bicycle craze and that she spent nearly all her time riding her wheel in company with people who were strangers to propriety.

1896, *The Wichita Daily Eagle* (Wichita, Kansas)

The bicycle has appeared in a new role—that of destroyer of a once happy home. The woman in the case is Mrs. Elma J. Dennison, formerly of 513 Fifth Street, Brooklyn, 23 years old, a "bicycle girl," who rides a man's wheel and wears bloomers. She was married to Charles H. Dennison in 1892. At that time she devoted herself to household duties which were soon increased by the arrival of two pretty children.

Then, in an evil hour, Mr. Dennison presented his wife with a bicycle. Mr. Dennison says that his wife developed the bicycle fever to such a degree that she neglected everything—her home, her children, and her husband. She lived only for her wheel, and on it. Soon she changed her bicycle for a man's wheel, then she discarded her skirts and adopted bloomers. Since then, she says, her husband has treated her cruelly, so that she was finally compelled to leave him. Now she has commenced a suit for a separation on the grounds of cruelty. Mr. Dennison contends that his wife is a bicycle fiend, and offers, with proof, the following letter, which she recently sent to him: "My Dear Husband—Meet me on the corner of Third Street

[*] All of the items in this chapter are excerpts from articles published in the popular press, or more specialized academic and medical journals, between the years 1890 and 1899. In many cases, I've transcribed the excerpts verbatim. In some instances, I lightly edited the passages in the interest of pace and clarity—condensing the text, or excising confusing period language or references.

and Seventh Avenue and bring with you my black bloomers, my oil can, and my bicycle wrench."

1896, *The World* (New York, New York)

Henry Cleating and his wife once lived happily together at Butler, near Paterson, N.J., but now they have gone to the divorce court, both of them, and all on account of her bicycle and bright red bloomers. He stated publicly last Saturday that he would sue her for absolute divorce, because she persisted in wearing bloomers, taking long bicycle rides and neglecting her household duties. Mrs. Cleating alleges, after she returned from a ride last Wednesday, her husband ran out of the house and pulled her to the ground so hard that her bright red bloomers were torn to shreds. While she fled, blushing and shrieking, into the house, Cleating, she says, got an axe, and smashed the bicycle into a snarl of bent spokes, gashed tires and ruined tubing. The bloomers are of no further use as bloomers but will serve as exhibits in the divorce suit.

1891, *The Essex Standard* (Colchester, Essex, U.K.)

Philip Pearce, alias *Spurgeon*, of 9, Warwick Road, Stoke Newington, aged 15, who on July 24 was sentenced to a month's hard labour by the Chelmsford Magistrates for stealing a bicycle of Mr. Alfred Boon, of Tindal Street, was discharged from the gaol on Aug. 22, but was immediately arrested outside on a charge of stealing other bicycles. The father said that up to Easter the boy has been in the Co-Operative Stores in the City, and he was a very good boy until seized with the "bicycle mania." That had been his ruin.

1895, *The Journal and Tribune* (Knoxville, Tennessee)

They arrived at Glen Island [N.Y.] on Thursday, July 11. They had their bicycles with them, and described themselves as John and

Peter Carlston, college students from Pennsylvania. Both were given jobs, and John was put in the dining room as a waiter. They rode about on their wheels a great deal and attracted considerable attention. Yesterday John went to wait on a man, and when he got near his table dropped his [tray] and ran. The customer started out after John, and the head waiter chased the elderly customer and caught him.

"That waiter is my daughter Tillie," said the elderly man. "She is masquerading in men's clothes."

The two young "men" were found in their room in tears. They confessed. They are the daughters of Henry Carlston, who lives in Chicago, near Oak Park.

"I am employed in the auditor's department of the Chicago & Northwestern Railroad," he said. "These are my daughters. The one who assumed the name of John is Matilda, twenty years old, and the one you call Peter is Harriet, aged eighteen."

"I lay this to the bicycle craze," he continued. "Both girls insisted on having bicycles, and then got to bloomers. Finally they have adopted male attire entirely."

1896, *The Des Moines Register* (Des Moines, Iowa)

Sunday the police developed a case of extreme cruelty. It was found that ex-Alderman Frank Dietz had fastened to his daughter's foot a heavy log chain, in order to keep her at home. The girl wanted to go out on her wheel and the father refused, and fearing that she might go while he was away, he used the chain.

1895, *The Allentown Leader* (Allentown, Pennsylvania)

A dispatch from Unadilla, N.Y., says that the opposition of a prospective mother-in-law to bicycles and bloomer costume resulted in a novel bicycle wedding. Mrs. Frank Moses has persistently opposed her 17-year-old daughter Florence, ever since she purchased her wheel and bloomers.

On two occasions the mother strewed tacks on the walks, to puncture the tires of her daughter's wheel, and another time nearly ruined her bloomer costume by besmearing her wheel with paint. Mrs. Moses, however, regarded Jerome Snow, her daughter's escort, as instrumental in inducing the girl to adopt the bloomers. When Mr. Snow called last week to invite Miss Moses to join in a cycling party, Mrs. Moses ordered him to leave and never return.

The daughter just then appeared, dressed for a cycling trip, and hastening from the house the couple soon disappeared down the road. The two journeyed several miles, discussing the unpleasant incident, when the young man suddenly exclaimed:

"Let's have a bicycle wedding tonight and settle this question."

"All right," said Miss Moses, "Where is the minister?"

The young couple were soon joined by a cycling party, one of whom was the Rev. Mr. Mead. The necessary arrangements being completed, the clergyman repeated the marriage ceremony, received the responses and pronounced the couple husband and wife while the wheels were making ten miles an hour.

1895, *The Century Illustrated Monthly Magazine* (New York, New York)

As a revolutionary force in the social world, the bicycle has had no equal in modern times. What it is doing, in fact, is to put the human race on wheels for the first time in its history. When we consider the increase in rapidity of locomotion which is attained, and the fact that it is self-supplied with such ease, it is not surprising that the changes required to meet the demands of the new order of things are so many and so radical as to amount virtually to making the world over again.

1896, *Munsey's Magazine* (New York, New York)

In every civilized land, the bicycle has become a familiar object; and even into some of the wildest corners of the earth it has penetrated. European royalties have taken to the wheel no less kindly than America's social lights. The young aristocrat of all the Russias, the Czar Nicholas, has been photographed with his wheel. Grouped with him were his cousins, the two tallest princes in Europe— George of Greece and Charles of Denmark. The latter not long ago taught his betrothed, Princess "Harry" of Wales, to ride—an accomplishment shared by the Princess Louise and several other members of Queen Victoria's family. Both lines of French pretenders are represented in the cycling world, Prince Napoleon and Prince Henry of Orleans being wheelmen. The former's kinswoman, the Duchess of Aosta, has somewhat scandalized her sedate brother, King Humbert, by "scorching" through the streets of Turin in the most emancipated costumes.

In Turkey it is not long since the bicycle was officially designated as "the devil's chariot," and its use was proscribed through the Sultan's domains; yet today it is stated that in the three cities of Constantinople, Smyrna, and Salonica there are more than a thousand wheelmen. In Egypt, the Sphinx looks down upon the bicycle with unmoved eyes. At the other end of the Dark Continent, British settlers have introduced the wheel along with the tennis racket and the cricket bat. All over the world, the story is the same, from Rio de Janeiro, where there is a fine racing track, to Cabul, where the Ameer has recently ordered a consignment of wheels for the benefit of the ladies of his harem.

1897, *The Muncie Evening Press* (Muncie, Indiana)

American bicycles have made their appearance in Arabia. About the only regions of the earth where the American bicycle has not penetrated lie beyond the Arctic and Antarctic circles.

1896, *The Journal* (New York, New York)

In all the wonder story of commerce and money dealings from the days of the Phoenicians there is no chapter so astounding as that which tells of the bicycle.

A toy, it has overturned the trade of nations within the compass of five fleeting years. There have been South Sea bubbles and fevers of gold and coal and oil. But all this history of money manias shows no parallel to the bicycle fever. It has set civilization by the ears.

Five years ago, in this whole wide country, not 60,000 bicycles were made or sold, and the solid, stolid, business-men made mock of the "playthings."

Mark the change. In this year of grace and pneumatic tires, four-fifths of a million of wheels will be marketed in the United States alone.

The leaders of the bicycle trade say that the average price for these machines is $80. Multiply. There will have been $66,000,000 spent this year in the United States alone for bicycles. The world is bicycle mad.

Man, woman, and child—the population of Christendom—is awheel. "Business hours" are only the intervals, now, that must elapse between trips upon the wheel. The butcher, the baker, and the candlestick maker may whistle for their pay so long as the bicycle vendor is well reckoned with.

The church? It is forgotten. The Sabbath? A cycling day. The theatre? Old-fashioned fun. The horse? Token and companion of gentlemanhood, a hack, browsing on the highway. Jewels? Watches? Clothing? The men who carried on those industries have turned their machinery to the making of rubber tires and ball bearings.

Tobacco has been forsaken. Wine is a mocker mocked at. Wheels and ginger pop. That is the order of the day. Railroad dividends are decimated. Politics has become merely a catering to the wheelmen's wishes.

1896, *The Forum* (New York, New York)

The economic effects of this new force in human affairs affords much material for curious and even amusing study. The loudest outcries come from the makers of watches and jewelry. Many of them have abandoned the business altogether and substituted for it bicycle-making.

It is stated by the journals of the tobacco trade that the consumption of cigars has fallen off during the present year at a rate of a million a day, and that the grand total of decrease since the "craze" really got going is no less than 700,000,000. The tailors say their business has been damaged at least 25 percent, because their customers do not wear out clothes so rapidly as formerly, spending much of their time in cheap bicycle suits which they buy ready-made. Shoemakers say they suffer severely because nobody walks much any longer.

The hatters say they are injured because bicyclists wear cheap caps and thus either save their more expensive ones or else get on without them. One irate member of the trade proposes that Congress be asked to pass a law compelling each bicycle rider to purchase at least two felt hats a year.

Saloon-keepers say that they suffer with the others, that their saloons are deserted on pleasant evenings, and that riders who visit them take only beer and "soft drinks." There are many other complaints of injury to trade which might be enumerated but I must content myself with the mention of only one other which is, perhaps, the most moving of all. It was made by a barber in New York City. "There is nothing in my business any longer," he said, "the bicycle has ruined it. Before the bicycle craze struck us, the men used to come in on Saturday afternoons and get a shave, and a haircut, and maybe a shampoo, in order to take their lady friends to the theatre, or go out somewhere else in the evening. Now they go off on a bicycle and do not care whether they are shaved or not. You see where it hurts our business is that when a man skips a shave today, we can't sell him two shaves tomorrow; that shave is gone forever."

1897, *The Anaconda Standard* (Anaconda, Montana)

The Rev. Thomas B. Gregory of Chicago has made a violent attack upon the bicycle. The Rev. Mr. Gregory says the bicycle is a menace to the mind. It annihilates the reading habit. The reading rooms and libraries as compared to what they used to be, are deserted. It is a menace to the health. It provokes heart disease, kidney affections, consumption and all sorts of nervous disorders. It is a menace to the domestic virtues. It breaks up and destroys the home. The children are turned into the street or left at home to look out for themselves while father and mother go spinning. It is a menace to morality. It makes women immodest. And when a woman throws off the beautiful reserve which the Almighty has placed around her she stands on dangerous ground. There is no telling what a woman will do after she has lost her womanliness. The bicycle opens the way for everlasting ruin to a multitude of young men and women who might otherwise escape.

1895, *The Oshkosh Northwestern* (Oshkosh, Wisconsin)

Whenever a healthful amusement becomes a mania, it ceases to be healthful. The doctors have invented the word *bicychloris* to designate a condition in which the blood is impoverished and the vitality of the system lowered from excessive wheeling.

1893, *Buffalo Courier* (Buffalo, New York)

Doctors seem to agree that there is such a thing as a bicycle disease, and no one who sees a rider bent in two over his machine, going

along as if a prairie fire or a band of wild Indians were after him, will
wonder at it. The bent position which is assumed by bicyclists, in
order to secure the greater amount of power over their machines
and to attain the highest degree of speed while running them, is attended with an unnatural flexion of the spine, which appears in the
region of the back and causes not only unsightliness of form, but in
boys of 14 years and under is fraught with serious and possibly fatal
consequences.

1896, *The Medical Age* (Detroit, Michigan)

The wheel is often the primary or exciting cause of serious rectal
trouble, and there is no affection of the rectum which it will not ag-
gravate. Cases of fissure, piles, and pruritus ani have developed
from bicycle riding, which resisted all treatment until the machine
was discarded.

In attacks of acute diarrhea, where the anus is excoriated from
watery evacuations, and the rectal mucus membrane congested and
often inflamed, the bicycle adds more fuel to the flame, and is often
the direct cause of fissure, rectal ulcer, or internal hemorrhoids.

Dr. John T. Davidson believes excessive use of the bicycle will
lead to sterility in the male, especially where there is already hyper-
aesthetic deep urethra from an old gonorrhea.

1896, *The Daily Sentinel* (Grand Junction, Colorado)

Of all the deformities produced by biking the strained, nervous expression known as bicycle face is the most pronounced. It is so common nowadays that a description of it here would be a waste of
valuable space.

The bicycle neck is also becoming more prominent every day.
Bicycle arms may be seen on the boulevard any pleasant day. The
fiend spins along with his elbows projecting outward as far as possible. He is usually so accustomed to this unusual position that he

finds it next to impossible to straighten his arms and assume any another when not riding.

Bicycle legs are also characteristic of this peculiar specimen. They are usually knock-kneed, with an abnormal development of the calf. The peculiar position causes him to toe in, producing bicycle toes, similar to pigeon toes.

As a result of indiscriminate riding, scorching and racing, we see a long, strained and nervous-visaged, crooked-necked, round-shouldered, narrow-chested, hump-backed, knock-kneed and pigeon-toed specimen of humanity.

1898, *Chattanooga Daily Times* (Chattanooga, Tennessee)

The wry-faced, hunchbacked, human monkey, otherwise known as the scorcher, is again at liberty. The scorcher is a menace to every pedestrian and to every decent bicyclist. He should be suppressed. The police should begin a vigorous campaign against him and he should be nabbed wherever found. It is of little concern that the scorcher is unmindful of his own safety; the concern is that he has no regard for the safety of others. A few days of solitary confinement in the county jail would have a salutary effect upon the scorcher.

1896, *Toronto Saturday Night* (Toronto, Canada)

The bicycle maniac should be shot on sight. The term fiend is no longer appropriate, for the fiend has brains, but the maniac is a reckless, wicked and irresponsible terror for whom no consideration should be shown. The newest of his minor performances is to scorch along the devil-strip on College Street and when he sees a rider approaching to yell, "Right of way," and accelerate rather than diminish his speed, thereby frightening women unaccustomed to such hoodlum conduct and sometimes causing serious injury to himself and his scared *vis-a-vis*. Prithee give us one trolley to run over him!

1897, *Saint Paul Globe* (Saint Paul, Minnesota)

Doctors of France are puzzled by a new mania which is afflicting women who ride bicycles. The feminine cyclists are becoming extremely cruel.

The first case which came into general notice was that of Mme. Eugenie Chantilly. An enthusiastic wheelwoman for a very long time, she even takes her wheel with her when she goes upon visits to friends some distance away. It was on one of those visits to a friend of her girlhood in Paris, Mme. Henry Fournier, that a strange affliction came upon her. Her hostess is also a wheelwoman, and the two went riding one morning along the boulevards which have made Paris famous.

When in the vicinity of the Jardin des Plantes, Mme. Fournier scorched ahead of her friend, and as she drew away from her, looked back laughingly over her shoulder and called to her "Adieu, mon amie." Mme. Fournier, who tells the story, said she received no response and looking back a moment later, saw her friend darting down upon her at terrific speed. She rode to one side thinking Mme. Chantilly would be unable to check herself by the time she came up with her, but what was her horror when her friend deliberately steered the wheel straight at her. Before Mme. Fournier could evade her, Mme. Chantilly had collided with her wheel and knocked her down. Mme. Chantilly rode back a few paces and then, riding at a lightning rate, actually rode over the prostrate form of Mme. Fournier.

Screaming with terror, Mme. Fournier attempted to rise but was repeatedly knocked down by her infuriated friend, and it was not until others came to the rescue that she was able to gain security from the repeated assaults of Mme. Chantilly.

Mme. Fournier's injuries were such that the constant care of a physician was required for several days. The physician, deeply interested in so singular an assault, took pains to investigate it and communicated with the insanity expert who had been called to examine into the condition of Mme. Chantilly.

Considering the case on the whole these two medical savants determined that they had discovered a brand new disease which was due solely to the bicycle. They also caused a careful inquiry to be made throughout France. They found seventeen women who had been seized with the same irrepressible desire to injure all cyclists of their own sex whenever possible. The doctors also found additional evidence that the mania inspired a keen delight in all things savoring of cruelty. One woman who was found torturing her dog, when asked the reason, said that she was illustrating the methods of the Spanish Inquisition.

1894, *The Chicago Tribune* (Chicago, Illinois)

The question, it seems to me: Does the New Woman spring from the bicyclist, or does the bicyclist spring from the New Woman? They are certainly cousins.

Is bicycling beautiful? What a question! The woman, perched on a tiny saddle, balancing herself on the wheel, cannot be anything but ungraceful. When she's in motion she reminds me of an octopus, with her arms and legs going at once.

1896, *The Nebraska State Journal* (Lincoln, Nebraska)

Miss Charlotte Smith, the president of the Women's Rescue League, says that bicycle riding by women is "leading them headlong to the devil," and proposes to have it stopped by an act of Congress.

1895, *The American Journal of Obstetrics and Diseases of Women and Children* (New York, New York)

A very grave objection has been made to the use of the bicycle among women, which, if true, would induce us to be exceedingly cautious in ever suggesting this exercise. It has been said to beget or foster the habit of masturbation.

It is perfectly conceivable that under certain conditions the bicycle saddle could both engender and propagate this horrible habit. The saddle can be tilted in every bicycle as desired, and the springs of the saddle can be so adjusted as to stiffen or relax the leather triangle. In this way a girl could, by carrying the front peak or pommel high, or by relaxing the stretched leather in order to let it form a deep, hammock-like concavity which would fit itself snugly over the entire vulva and reach up in front, bring about constant friction over the clitoris and labia. This pressure would be much increased by stooping forward, and the warmth generated from constant exercise might further increase the feeling.

1895, *The Medical World* (Philadelphia, Pennsylvania)

To my brethren I feel I must speak plainly and unreservedly on this subject. Have we not sexual troubles enough on our hands without opening Pandora's Box and hauling out a bike? It is a dreadful thing to think that the first thing that should render a young and pure girl conscious of her sexual formation would be her first ride on a bicycle. God save our girls, and keep them pure and virtuous!

1897, *The Cincinnati Lancet-Clinic* (Cincinnati, Ohio)

A word in regard to the tandem where used by a male and female. The sight of it is immodest to say the least—a tandem bicycle with a girl at puberty bent forward in what may be called a scorch attitude, and right behind her a fellow in a jumping bullfrog position, together working their legs in unison. Every city, town, and State should enact misdemeanor laws that would stop such double riding as may be seen on our streets on tandem bicycles.

1896, *The Sun* (New York, New York)

Among the bicyclists of the Boulevard she is known as the Woman in Black. On the police court records she appears as Carrie Witten. One name is probably about as near correct as the other. She got into the police court records because the ordinary wheeling pace wasn't good enough for her, and she took along with her, both on the wheel and to the court, a companion of the opposite sex. They rode tandem; they were arrested tandem; they were arraigned tandem.

It is revealing no secret to announce that Miss Witten is not slow in any sense of the word. Her ordinary bicycling costumes consists of a jaunty black cap, a modish black jacket, well-fitting black knickerbockers—not bloomers by any stretch of the imagination or otherwise—and black silk stockings. Moreover Miss Witten is a very pretty girl in that or any other costume. Clad in this fetching costume she travels along the Boulevard, not only frequently defying the law herself by her pace, but also inciting others (principally of the male sex), to lawlessness in their endeavor to keep her within view.

1896, *Cheltenham Chronicle* (Cheltenham, Gloucestershire, U.K.)

An extraordinary incident has occurred in Battersea Park. Miss Barlow, of Wandsworth Common, a well-known lady cyclist, entered the park on her bicycle about 3 p.m. Attracted, doubtless, by the fact that the lady wore "bloomers," instead of the orthodox skirts, a number of boys gathered round and pursued her, and their shouts soon caused a group of roughs to join in the chase. The lady went into the lake house for shelter, which was surrounded by a very demonstrative crowd. Eventually police assistance was procured and Miss Barlow was enabled to leave the park.

1897, *Public Opinion* (New York, New York)

Press Dispatch, Cambridge, England, May 21: Cambridge University today, by a vote of 1,713 to 662, rejected the proposal to confer degrees upon women. When the voting began the Senate House was thronged, and there were large crowds outside the building. Everywhere were posters inscribed: "Varsity for Men; Men for Varsity." The excitement continually increased, especially in the streets. An effigy of a woman in bloomers on a bicycle was suspended above the Senate House.

1896, *The Glencoe Transcript* (Glencoe, Ontario, Canada)

The bicycle fever will not have spent its fury before another craze has developed and taken hold of the community. The horseless vehicle is the coming sensation. The French and German builders cannot keep up with the demand for them. It is predicted that the fever will be due in this country in two years and that before five years have elapsed every city will be turned into a veritable pandemonium of wheels and automobiles.

1896, *The Philadelphia Times* (Philadelphia, Pennsylvania)

Are the days of the bicycle numbered, and the poor horse threatened with extinction?

Many people have heard of the real horseless carriages, but few have seen them. They are in the same category of public estimation as the bicycle was in the early seventies. But once fin de siècle society takes it up, the bicycle will have to step out and the horseless carriage will be "king," and as popular as the bicycle is at present.

In the days to come, when automobiles shall outnumber all other styles of vehicles and means of passenger and freight transportation on the streets, the present laws of the road must be radically revised. All streets and boulevards will be divided into two sharply defined sections, which will be indicated by a line of posts or a narrow strip of parking.

Perhaps the greatest boon to suffering humanity that this popular horseless carriage will afford will be the subjugation, humiliation and relegation to the past of that end-of-the-century freak, the cadaverous scorcher.

1899, *Comfort* (Augusta, Maine)

There are some who claim the automobile will replace the bicycle, but this is rank nonsense. Those who have become attached to their bicycles—there are several millions of bicycle riders—will not easily give up the pleasure of skimming along the country like a bird—or a scorcher!—for the more doubtful delight of riding in the cumbersome, ill-smelling automobile.

1896, *Fort Scott Daily Monitor* (Fort Scott, Kansas)

Those people who affect to believe the bicycle craze is dying out should peruse the following advertisement from a Buffalo newspaper: "Will exchange folding bed, child's white crib, or writing desk for lady's bicycle."

6

BALANCING ACT

Danny MacAskill, perched on high. Glasgow, Scotland, 2012.

Angus MacAskill was one of the biggest men who ever lived. Some have claimed that he was history's largest "true giant"—a giant who was not afflicted with gigantism, exhibiting no growth abnormalities or hormonal irregularities. His body was huge but proportional. He stood seven foot nine and weighed upwards of four hundred pounds. The palms of his hands were said to have measured six inches by twelve; his shoulders stretched nearly four feet across. Herculean feats of strength were attributed to him: he hoisted a twenty-five-hundred-pound anchor to chest height and carried it the length of a wharf, he single-handedly set a schooner's mast, he tore a fishing boat in two from stem to stern by yanking hard on a rope, he lifted a full-grown horse over a fence, he raised a 140-gallon barrel of Scotch whiskey to his lips and drank from it as from a jar.

He was born in 1825 in Berneray, Scotland. When he was six, he moved with his family to Cape Breton, Nova Scotia. At age twenty-four, he joined P. T. Barnum's circus. Giants, Barnum wrote in his autobiography, "were always literally great features in my establishment, and they oftentimes afforded me, as well as my patrons, food for much amusement as well as wonder." Barnum paired MacAskill with one of his star attractions, the three-foot-four dwarf General Tom Thumb, in an act that consisted of sight gags. Tom Thumb would tap-dance on the palm of MacAskill's hand or roost in his jacket pocket; sometimes the dwarf and the giant would square off in simulated fisticuffs. As a sideshow performer, MacAskill toured the United States, Europe, and beyond. He performed for Queen Victoria at Windsor Castle. (The queen presented him with a traditional Scottish Highland costume—Tartan kilt, tweed jacket and waistcoat, *sporran* pouch—tailored to his massive frame.) Eventually, MacAskill retired from show business and returned to the village of St. Anns on Cape Breton, where he ran a gristmill and, later, a dry goods store. He died in August 1863, at age thirty-eight, of brain fever. His coffin, locals said, was big enough to have served as a boat that could float three men across St. Anns Bay.

There is a replica of that coffin on display at the Giant Angus MacAskill Museum, which sits near the main commercial strip in the small village of Dunvegan on Scotland's Isle of Skye. The exhibit holds other artifacts: a life-sized statue of MacAskill that towers above a life-sized Tom Thumb statue, one of MacAskill's sweaters, a pair of enormous socks, an extra-long bed, and a chair modeled on one that MacAskill himself used. The chair is so large that adult museumgoers look like children when they pose for photos seated in it, their feet dangling inches above the floor.

The museum devoted to the giant is in fact quite small. It occupies a one-room thatch-roofed cottage at the bottom of a garden, outside the family home of Peter MacAskill. MacAskill, who claims Angus as an ancestor, opened the museum in 1989. The following year, MacAskill's youngest child, four-year-old Danny, was given a bicycle as a gift. It was a black-and-white child's Raleigh that MacAskill had found in a dumpster. The boy learned to ride in just a few days, and right away he began trying to do unusual things on the bike, barreling up and down the garden path, yanking the front wheel upward pop-a-wheelie-style, weaving and skidding, jerking the bicycle on top of, and over, rocks, chairs, and other objects. Danny was a wild kid, energetic and fearless, and from the time he'd learned to walk, his parents, realizing they had little choice, had let him crash around the front yard undeterred. He spent his days climbing trees, clambering to the roof of his parents' car and leaping off, scaling the side of the family home. Now he wondered: What would it be like to ride a bicycle on a tree or up the wall of a building, to summit the Giant Angus MacAskill Museum on his bike and fly back to the ground below? If he could climb and jump using his two legs, why couldn't he do it on two wheels?

By the time Danny was five years old, he was a familiar figure in Dunvegan, a little boy on a bicycle that he manipulated with startling ease, as if it was an extension of his limbs. He pedaled a mile uphill to school in the morning, and in the afternoon, he raced back with a mob of kids, all older than he, on downhill runs through the village's bendy streets. The older boys taught him how to ride hands-free, and he made a habit of it, streaking along the roads with his arms overhead. He rode whenever possible, in fair and poor conditions, in the daylight and in the dark. Winter days on Skye are short, and the weather is raw and wet. At three-thirty or four in the afternoon, the sun would disappear into the sea of the Little Minch, off the island's west coast, and Danny would bike for hours in the dark, on roads slick with rain.

In any case, he preferred his wheels off the ground. He learned to jump from the curb to the street and back again, and worked to increase the length of his leaps, extending the time he floated above the pavement, spokes spinning in the open air. His mental map of Dunvegan was a chart of obstacles and jumps at the level of the centimeter. He memorized which spots on which slab of curb he needed to hit at speed in order to go airborne. He biked so much that he altered the terrain, molding ridges of turf into miniature ramps he could kick off to get air.

By age eight, he was making bigger jumps, descending to the grass or gravel from walls and benches as high as four feet. He got a new bike, the BMX-style Raleigh Burner, and took on tougher challenges. He impressed his peers by landing a six-foot jump onto the concrete from the top of Dunvegan's bottle bank, a big metal container for glass recyclables. He fell often, and his legs would wind up pretzeled around his bike frame. But he bounced up, bruised and scraped but unbroken.

Etymologists have suggested that the name Skye comes from a Norse word meaning "isle of cloud." An alternative name, in Gaelic—Eilean Sgiathanach—has been translated as "winged isle," a reference, it is thought, to the shape of the island's coastline, which "can be viewed as a mighty bird with outstretched pinions, coming in to land, or to seize upon prey." Skye's topography pulls your line of vision upward, into the realm of the mists, and you can imagine how it might tug a child's thoughts toward dreams of flight, or approximations of flight on a bicycle.

The island sits just off the northwestern edge of the Scottish mainland, in North Atlantic waters warmed by the Gulf Stream. (Giant Angus MacAskill's birthplace, the Isle of Berneray, lies twenty-five miles farther to the northwest, across the Little Minch.) Skye is the largest of the Inner Hebrides islands, and the most northerly. On winter nights, the aurora borealis can often be seen from points along the coast. Skye's scenery is spectacular: green meadows, plunging glens, waterfalls that empty into crystalline pools, deep lochs ringed by volcanic rocks. The most famous feature of the island's terrain is the mountain range known as the Cuillin, serrated peaks that jut into the air to stab at the clouds. They look fantastical and cinematic, the kind of mountains where you expect to find a wizard with a staff, scanning the horizon for dragons. Sure enough, many movies have been filmed on the island. A scene in the time-travel epic *Highlander* (1986) captures Sean Connery and Christopher Lambert crossing broadswords on the Cioch, a famous crag that cantilevers out from a cliff face above a glacier-carved dell. It may be the most dramatically situated and least exciting action sequence ever shot: the actors are visibly petrified, standing with unmoving feet and waving their weapons with comical caution, knowing that a stumble of a couple inches in the wrong direction could send them plummeting.

Skye is the setting for many legends, stories of magic and violence that speak of the island's wild landscape and reflect a history marked by bloodshed and clan warfare. Dunvegan Castle, which looms over an inlet on Skye's northwestern shore, holds several heirlooms of the chiefs of Clan MacLeod, including the Fairy Flag, whose mere unfurling is thought to have extinguished fires, turned battles in the favor of the MacLeods, and rid Skye of a plague that was devastating its cattle. There are various accounts of the flag's origins. In one story, fairies bestowed the flag on an infant MacLeod chieftain; in another, it was a farewell gift given to a chieftain by his fairy lover. Less beneficent creatures are said to have inhabited Skye: "water bulls" with fiery nostrils that stampeded out of the sea to wreak havoc onshore; demon greyhounds that haunted mountain passes; a headless monster, the *Coluinn gun Cheann,* that stalked the island's pathways at night and left behind mutilated corpses. Legend holds that the jagged Cuillin range was formed when a male and female giant faced off in a days-long sword fight, carving up the mountains with their errant swipes. The devil himself is supposed to have appeared one night on a ridge in the Trotternish, Skye's northernmost peninsula.

It is not a place for fainthearted people, or for coddled children.

When Danny MacAskill wasn't riding his bike, he roamed Skye, leaving wreckage in his wake. He took his grandfather's Second World War machete into the woods to hack at tree trunks and branches. He snuck saws into school and spent his lunch period carving up tree limbs. He liked to watch things crash and burn. He and his friends climbed up mountains and used iron bars to roll boulders off the edges of cliffs, into the sea. They gathered driftwood and lit bonfires with lawnmower petrol. Danny was asked by teachers at school what he wanted to be when he grew up. He said, "Demolition expert," imagining a daily routine of dynamiting buildings. When they were still preteens, Danny and his friends would get hold of old cars that were set to be scrapped and go careening around meadows at high speed. The game would end when the boys sent the empty car rolling downhill to smash into the woods. The kids would scramble to the roof of a nearby house to watch flames consume the wreck.

Always, there was the compulsion to get air. On beachcombing excursions, Danny found old fishing nets that had washed up on the coast. He dragged the nets back to Dunvegan, attached them to scraps of netting from soccer goals, and rigged them up in trees, so he could swoop out of the branches, Tarzan-style. With friends, he built a treehouse in an oak that sat atop a hill behind the MacAskill home. The boys found a huge length of six-millimeter rope in someone's father's shed and stretched it from the treehouse to a fence more than a hundred yards away. They used it to do "flying foxes," zip-lining to the ground from the fifty-foot-high treetop. "I had freedom, growing up in Skye," Danny MacAskill says. "I unleashed my energy on the wilderness."

Most of the time, he did so while hunched over handlebars. When Danny was eleven, he moved on from the Raleigh Burner to a mountain bike. He began to soak up the culture of mountain cycling, in particular the sport called mountain bike trials, in which riders compete to pedal, hop, and jump their two-wheelers over obstacles without letting their feet touch the ground. It's a cycling sport that upends various conventions of cycling, including the appearance of the bicycles themselves. (Many trials bikes have no seat.) Danny and his friends traded magazines that documented the trials scene and watched the videos that circulated, in those days before online streaming, on VHS cassettes obtained by mail order and via samizdat networks of enthusiasts.

He was mesmerized in particular by one famous video, a 1997 film called *Chainspotting*, which featured several cyclists performing stunts on the streets of Sheffield, England, and in various other locations. Unlike the riding in competitive mountain bike trials—contests staged within a taped-off course, with carefully arranged obstacles and judges determining winners and losers—the "street trials" cycling showcased in *Chainspotting* was informal and improvisational, heeding no rules or boundaries. The riders in the video hurdled park benches, rode across water tanks, balanced their bikes on bollards and hopped from bollard to bollard, turned 360s while dropping to the ground from ten-foot walls. Street trials has roots in other so-called extreme sports—skateboarding and snowboarding and "freestyle" BMX riding—but places even greater emphasis on tricks, wit, and vision. It isn't just a style of cycling. It's a way of seeing: a practice that involves sizing up topography, judging distances and angles of approach and lines of attack, and generally viewing the streetscape, and the natural landscape, as a giant playground. It captivated preteen Danny MacAskill. In *Chainspotting*, the amateurish camerawork and blaring rock soundtrack added to the video's allure, the sense that the cyclists were staging a guerrilla assault on social proprieties and conventional thinking—on preconceived ideas of what a street was for, what a bicycle could do, how gravity worked.

———

Danny was seventeen when he left Skye. He had finished high school but had no designs on university. His career ambitions had changed. He'd abandoned his plan to work in demolition, deciding instead on a career as a bicycle mechanic. In fact, the two jobs were not unrelated. He'd always liked to tear bikes down and rebuild them from scratch.

He moved to Aviemore, a resort town in the Scottish Highlands. The town had a small but lively trials riding scene. There were lots of places to bike, and things to bike on and over: ski trails, a parking lot full of big boulders, street furniture. He stayed in Aviemore for three years, working at a bicycle shop on the main street and cycling in his off hours. By 2006, he'd ridden the town to death. He left for Edinburgh, where he moved in with a friend and found work as a mechanic at a well-known bike shop, MacDonald Cycles. MacAskill was twenty years old, his cycling skills were prodigious, and Edinburgh offered what seemed to him a dazzling plenitude of shreddable terrain.

MacAskill's perspective on the cityscape was unique. Others in the Edinburgh trials scene gravitated to benches and bollards, the usual targets. MacAskill found his eye drawn to stiffer challenges. Rounded railings. Treacherous stair sets. He taught himself a technique called a hook, which entailed hurling his bike at a high wall and bouncing up onto the wall's narrow lip. His regimen was murder on bicycles. He trashed his wheels and bent his forks. His body suffered, too. MacAskill broke bones and dislocated joints and tore ligaments. His wrists were in constant pain. There were a number of good trials riders in Edinburgh, but it was clear that MacAskill's skills, and will, placed him in a different category.

In the fall of 2008, he began filming a video with a friend named Dave Sowerby, who had a decent video camera and a good eye. The idea was to compile an edit of MacAskill's most audacious tricks. The challenge focused his mind and pushed him to try new stuff. What tricks could he pull off that hadn't ever been conceived of, let alone attempted? Scanning the streets, he sought new places, odd spaces, ledges and protuberances and bits of the built environment that could, if you forced the issue, serve as a riding surface, or at least as a momentary resting place or springboard for one or two bicycle wheels.

Six months later, in April 2009, filming was finished. MacAskill and Sowerby uploaded a five-and-a-half-minute edit to YouTube. Without thinking too much about it, they called the video *Inspired Bicycles*.

The title was well chosen. The film shows MacAskill vaulting his bike from the sidewalk onto ten-foot-high walls and back down again. He hurtles fences and walls, he flies down a twenty-foot-deep pedestrian subway stairwell. He jumps from the roof of MacDonald Cycles to the roof of the copy shop next door, before dropping onto the street below. His tires appear to have superglue on them. He can stop on a dime, sticking perfect landings, on narrow targets, after absurdly long leaps. In one sequence, MacAskill bikes full tilt up an oak tree and twists into a backflip. The video's tour de force showcases MacAskill's vision and imagination, his recognition of cyclable terrain in implausible places: he is shown pedaling across the slender stanchions at the top of a tall wrought-iron fence.

Three days after Sowerby uploaded the video, it had racked up hundreds of thousands of views. MacAskill, who didn't own a computer, found himself fielding dozens of media requests from around the world.

———

In 1896, 113 years before *Inspired Bicycles* appeared online, a Kinetoscope film short, *Trick Bicycle Riding*, was released by the Edison Manufacturing Company, the motion picture arm of Thomas Edison's expanding media empire. The star of the film was a man named Levant Richardson, a skillful cyclist who would go on to be a pioneering manufacturer of roller skates. There is no surviving print of *Trick Bicycle Riding*, but it was the first of several Edison shorts featuring acrobatic cyclists. Two of these, *Trick Bicycle Riding No. 2*

(1899) and *The Trick Cyclist* (1901), can be queued up on the internet today. The camerawork is primitive, but the stunts performed in the films—pedaling backward, 360-degree spins on the front wheel, bicycle rope jumping—are fixtures of trick riders' repertoires to this day, and they are executed with skill.

It is noteworthy that trick cyclists were given starring roles in a handful of the earliest commercial motion pictures. The titles of some other Edison films from the period are instructive: *Lasso Thrower; Trapeze Disrobing Act; Faust Family of Acrobats; Alleni's Boxing Monkeys; O'Brien's Trained Horses; Ching Ling Foo's Greatest Feats; Rubes in the Theatre; Pie, Tramp, and the Bulldog.* The performance of a trick bicyclist fit comfortably alongside circus acrobatics, animal acts, conjurer's tricks, vaudeville knockabout comedy, ethnic burlesque—the raucous variety entertainment popular in the United States and Europe at the turn of the twentieth century. Trick cycling was, in a word, Barnumesque. Like the giant who strode onstage with a dwarf tucked in his breast pocket, a person who executed gravity-flouting, death-defying stunts on a bicycle was a species of sideshow freak.

The emergence of trick cycling as popular entertainment appears in retrospect to have been inevitable. The bicycle is a magnet for show-offs and daredevils; cycling and showbiz were destined to meet and cross-pollinate. Karl von Drais's first ride on his *Laufmaschine* was a kind of theater: a public demonstration, announced with a notice in the press. The crowd that gathered that day in Mannheim was there not just to assess the viability of an invention but to take in a spectacle, and Drais's skill in handling his machine, his ability to stay aboard the thing as it hurtled forward, would surely have struck those viewers as something on the order of a stunt.

P. T. Barnum was among the first showmen to feature trick bicyclists. The most celebrated of these acts was the Cycling Elliotts, a troupe of English siblings, two girls and three boys, ages six to sixteen, who won fame and notoriety in Barnum's circus in the early 1880s. The Elliotts' show consisted of intricately choreographed bicycle "dances" and stunts, executed on custom-sized high-wheeled ordinaries and unicycle "skates." The Elliotts would snake through obstacle courses of lighted candles. They did a cycling version of a Parisian quadrille. They formed a human pyramid atop a single bicycle. They vaulted their bikes onto a rotating table, where they executed elaborate maneuvers without colliding, five bicycles sharing a circular tabletop measuring just six feet in diameter. An admirer lavished praise on the Elliotts in a poem published in *The Sporting and Theatrical Journal:* "Faster and faster, like flashes of light / They ride on their wheels, then fly from our sight / . . . Then up on a table they all spring with ease / With bicycles the Elliotts can do what they please."

In the spring of 1883, during a lengthy run of Barnum's circus at New York's Madison Square Garden, the Elliotts came to the attention of the New York Society for the Prevention of Cruelty to Children (NYSPCC), which obtained a warrant against Barnum, two of his employees, and James Elliott, the Elliott paterfamilias, who managed the troupe. The four men were arrested for violation of New York State's child-endangerment laws, and the case was argued before a three-judge panel. Prior to the hearing, the Cycling Elliotts gave a special demonstration for an audience "of about 4000 invited guests" that included the NYSPCC's president, police officers, and a committee of "a dozen or more leading doctors." It was undoubtedly the first stunt-riding performance that doubled as a legal proceeding. Ultimately the judges ruled in Barnum's favor, and the Elliotts resumed their run in the circus, to wide acclaim. One of the medical experts, the physician Dr. Louis A. Sayre, testified that the regimen of a trick cyclist was "very beautiful and beneficial" to the children's health, stating "if all children took similar exercise, it would be better than doctors or drugs."

There were certain stunts that the Elliotts chose not to perform for the New York magistrate. One of these, "The Revolving Wheel of Fire," featured Tom Elliott, the eldest male sibling, pedaling a bicycle on rollers inside a larger wheel, which shot gusts of flame from tiny valves ringing its exterior. The boy cyclist accomplished this feat while "at the same time spinning a plate making a wreath of fire."

Trick cycling brought together the age-old and the newfangled, marrying the ancient art of acrobatics to the quintessentially modern one of bicycling. Trick cycling was sexy. Riders were graceful and strong, with sculpted physiques. In the pulp novel *Miss Million's Maid: A Romance of Love and Fortune* (1915), a trick cyclist was cast as a sex symbol: "He was [a] . . . small, but beautifully built fellow, supple as a cat."

Trick-cycling troupes were often coed, and, like their male counterparts, these "expert wheelwomen" exhibited their bodies along with their talents. The all-female ensemble Kaufmann's Cycling Beauties appeared onstage in snugly fitted Edwardian dress—tights, shorts, tutus—that accentuated the contours of breasts and thighs and hips. The bicycle was already associated in the public imagination with sexual liberation, and the sensuality of trick cycling, the lithe movements and rippling sinews, added to the frisson. If spectators found their thoughts wandering from bicycle gymnastics to the kind performed in a boudoir, it was only natural.

Trick cycling offered another sort of titillation, showcasing seemingly superhuman skills while holding out the possibility, both frightening and tantalizing, of catastrophic human error. Trick cycling was funny: to watch a stunt rider in action was to witness a series of visual punch lines, and many riders billed themselves as "cycling comedians," donning the costume of a clown or tramp. But at any moment, the slapstick might lurch into unintentional violence. Did spectators want the cyclist to land the jump cleanly, or did they crave the gruesome pratfall? The answer, surely, is that they wanted both, and often enough, that's what they got.

Sensationalism—what Barnum called "humbug"—was the currency of late-Victorian popular culture. Grave danger, high stakes, the Greatest Show on Earth. The stage names and taglines of trick cyclists blared from vaudeville placards like carnival barks:

W. G. HURST, THE KING OF THE WHEEL; ST. CLAIRE SISTERS AND
O'DAY. TEN WHEELS AND NO BRAKES; JOE PAULY, THE HUMAN CAT
AND TRICK CYCLIST; THE ORIGINAL MCNUTTS, THE AERIAL CYCLE
WONDERS; PRINCE WELLS, GREATEST LIVING SENSATIONAL CY-
CLIST. Hundreds of performers claimed to be "The World Cham-
pion Trick Cyclist" or "The World's Trick Cycling Record Holder" or
"The Holder of the United States Championship Medal." These
distinctions were cited in the press, though of course the champion-
ships, medals, and records were entirely fictional.

Which is not to suggest that trick riders were unworthy of super-
latives. They would jerk a bicycle's front wheel into the air and ride
on the rear wheel, pedaling backward, then forward, then backward
again, hurtling at high speed toward the precipice of the stage before stopping, at the last second, and spinning into a figure skater–
style twirl. Trick riders performed stunts with swords and fired
arrows at targets while pedaling hands-free. There were bicycle
sharpshooters. Annie Oakley did a bicycle turn in Buffalo Bill's Wild
West Show, blasting clay pigeons with a Winchester rifle from the
seat of her bike.

Some trick cyclists specialized in contortionist tricks, squeezing
through the center of the diamond-shaped frame and snaking out
the other side, holding their bodies just inches above the ground the
whole time as the bicycle coasted forward. There were trick-cycling
musicians who balanced on two wheels while strumming banjos or
scraping out violin sonatas; a child cyclist, "Hatsley the Boy Wonder," navigated the high wire while soloing on the trombone. Trick
riders rode up and down long staircases that stretched between the
stage and a raised platform, or bunny-hopped up and down those
stairs. The British cyclist Sid Black did a thrilling variation on this
stunt, pedaling at high speed down a sixty-foot-long ladder, arranged
at an angle that sent him shooting off the stage into the theater's
center aisle. Black would complete his descent by whooshing between rows of spectators to the rear of the theater and out into the
lobby, trailing a gust of wind that lifted hats off heads as if in salute.

The essence of the stunt cyclist's art was "equilibrism": balancing one's body on a bicycle in ways that demonstrated creative flair and disdain for the laws of physics. It was dangerous work. At a performance in Bremen, Germany, Minnie Kaufmann, one of the stars of the Kaufmann's Cycling Beauties, attempted a "flip-flap" move—springing from handlebars to the saddle and back again, in a handstand position, on a moving bicycle. But Kaufmann faltered and went flying into the orchestra pit, taking a thirty-foot tumble that ended with a crash into a bass drum.

Trick cycling could be punishing to bicycles too, and riders modified their machines to withstand the beating. They reinforced frames and wheels, carefully calibrated the pressure levels of tires, tweaked gearing systems, and contrived a host of boutique modifications and add-ons. This custom work was generally invisible to all except their fellow stunt cyclists.

But for certain performers, the surgery was the selling point. There were comedy cyclists who specialized in the expert handling of absurdly mutated bikes. Some rode toweringly tall bicycles—the freak bikes of their day—whose saddles sat at giraffe height, fifteen feet above the ground. Riders would mount these machines by climbing ladder-like rungs built into the bike's frame or by swinging into the saddle from a trapeze. There were bikes with square wheels, with triangular wheels, with semicircular wheels. The Villions, a family troupe prominent on English music hall stages, had a unicycle whose wheel looked like a giant egg. The comic effect was heightened by the egg-cycle's rider: a small boy in the getup of a harlequin.

Unicycles, egg-shaped and otherwise, were favorite trick-cycling props. Performers rode them while juggling vegetables or Indian clubs or even bicycle wheels; they rode them across tightropes and up flights of stairs. A widely practiced stunt was to convert a two-wheeler into a unicycle, slowly disassembling the bicycle while riding it, until the rider was left balancing on a lone front wheel. The signature stunt of vaudevillian Joe Jackson was a variation on this gag. Jackson portrayed a tramp whose joyride on a stolen bike goes south when the machine he has stolen starts to fall apart piece by piece—bicycle horn, handlebars, pedals, rear wheel, frame, all dropping away in turn. In Jackson's act, the suave virtuosity flaunted by trick cyclists was ingeniously flipped. It was a pantomime of incompetence: Jackson teetered and swerved wildly but stayed upright and in motion as his bicycle disintegrated beneath him.

Another source of comedy, and wonder, was the spectacle of bicycles under the control of animals, a novelty that gained popularity in the mid-1890s. There were cycling dogs and chimpanzees and bears. There were specially built tricycles piloted by lions and elephants. It is still possible to see a performance by animal cyclists, and these shows can take macabre turns. At the 2013 Wild Animal Olympics in Shanghai, an interspecies race on a circular bicycle track ended badly when one of the competitors, a monkey, swerved his bike into the path of his opponent, a bear, prompting the latter to maul the former, in full view of hundreds. A cellphone video of the incident went viral. It is posted on YouTube under the title "A Bear and a Monkey Race on Bicycles, Then Bear Eats Monkey."

The appeal of four-legged trick cyclists may in part have been a reaction to a glut of the two-legged kind. In the 1890s, trick riding took hold as a recreational pastime. A trick-cycling how-to industry enticed novices by hyping the bodybuilding benefits. Trick cycling, it was said, afforded "exercise to every known muscle." One lavishly illustrated instructional manual claimed (a bit disingenuously) that "graceful, daring, and altogether fascinating feats . . . may be accomplished by any rider possessed of an ordinary amount of nerve" and noted (less speciously) that the mastery of esoteric cycling maneuvers could have practical applications for the bike commuter: "[The trick] rider is naturally *facile princeps* in threading the intricacies of congested traffic in crowded thoroughfares."

There were trick-riding academies, aimed at an upscale clientele. The chief instructor at a popular New York cycling school, an accomplished Black stunt rider named Ira Johnson, would decamp to tony Newport, Rhode Island, during the summer months to service his pupils at their seaside vacation homes. Trick cycling was also in vogue among London's socialites. In 1897, the women's magazine *Hearth and Home* took note of the trend: "Sixty years ago the belles and beaux of the fashionable assemblies qualified for Almack's by attending dancing academies. Nowadays they spend their energies in learning the latest thing in the way of gymkhana tricks on wheels." The teenage Prince Albert, England's future King George VI, was reportedly permitted by his father, George V, to make incognito visits to music halls, where he studied the latest trick-riding turns. The prince would "[emulate] the performances of the professionals" during practice sessions on the grounds of Windsor Castle and Sandringham House.

But the fad for trick riding was not confined to the upper crust. In big cities, see-and-be-seen spots where bikers congregated—the Coney Island Cycle Path in New York, the grounds of the Palais du Trocadéro in Paris—served as public stages for trick cyclists. The riders attracted admiring crowds but came under attack in the cycling press for showboating, a sin of bad form that was thought to bring disrepute to bicyclists. In several American cities and towns, the police cracked down on public trick riding; some municipalities went so far as to pass laws banning the practice. Today, the Code of Ordinances for Memphis, Tennessee, includes an anachronistic prohibition against "all trick and fancy riding . . . in the parks and parkways" on "bicycles, tricycles . . . [and] velocipedes."

As amateur stunt cycling flourished, the ranks of professionals swelled in turn, and market saturation set in. In 1905, the theatrical trade magazine *Broadway Weekly* complained that trick cyclists were "drugs on the market" and that "the ability to do a few saddle tricks will not pay board." The solution, the editorial suggested, was more exciting and dangerous stunts: "to perform tricks that would stagger a horse. . . . If you can ride a bicycle up a wall or across the ceiling, cycle riding will be profitable."

Increasingly, trick riders took on riskier challenges, stunts involving high speeds, steep inclines, and hazardous leaps across chasms. Often these performances found cyclists navigating custom-built structures—rococo contraptions with spirals and ramps that allowed riders to attain high velocity and reach great heights in the confined spaces of theaters and fairgrounds. There were "cycle whirls"—circular velodromes raised dozens of feet above the ground—and vertical loop-the-loops in which cyclists rode upside down. The names given to these acts underscored the peril: "The Loop of Doom," "The Terrible Ring," "La Cercle de la Mort."

There were many accidents and, indeed, deaths. Bicycle wheels got stuck in the slats of aerial velodromes and cyclists were hurled into lethal falls. Riders slid off ramps and dropped out of loops. Concentration flagged, wheels wobbled, gangways collapsed. In 1907, an audience at the Belfast Hippodrome watched a teenage trick cyclist, Hildegard Morgenrott, tumble off a platform and fatally snap her neck. Another young trick rider, Charles Lefault, lost his balance while attempting a turn-of-the-century version of a street trials stunt, steering his bike atop the fortifications near the Porte d'Italie in Paris. "He fell into a dry moat," a newspaper reported, "and was killed on the spot."

Yet trick cycling remained popular, despite and because of the body count. In particular, stunts that turned bicycles into flying machines held fascination for both performers and audiences. There were specialists like Charles Kabrich, a self-styled "bike-chute-aeronaut," who did a kind of airborne ballet on a two-wheeler hitched to a parachute. A trick cyclist named Salvo was a star attraction in the circus troupe of Barnum rival Adam Forepaugh. His act, "The Terrible Trip to the Moon," was hyped with the usual grim sensationalism. ("An Awful Holding of Life as a Pawn. Reaching the Crescent or Dashing to Death.") But Salvo's act was dreamy and romantic, a daredevil's pantomime of space travel by bicycle. Salvo sped his bike down a steep ramp that turned sharply upward like a ski jump, launching the cyclist toward a crescent moon that dangled from chains near the apex of the circus tent. "It is a terrible leap, such as pinches the heart," wrote a reporter in 1906. "The pale, tensely drawn youth shoots into space like the ball from a canon, with nothing between him and dire death but the powerful energy and faith that lifts his wiry body to the reach of the swaying moon."

––––––

The popularity of trick cycling has wavered over the decades, but it has remained a cultural constant. Stunt riders were variety stage regulars until the mid-twentieth-century demise of vaudeville. The swing era brought dance bands mounted on bikes. Ray Sinatra—the elder second cousin of Frank—led a "cycling orchestra" whose sixteen members performed while straddling gleaming Silver King cruisers. In the mid-1930s, Sinatra and his band landed a radio show, *Cycling the Kilocycles,* broadcast weekly on NBC—not the ideal medium, perhaps, for a bicycle orchestra. Presumably listeners took the whole bike thing on faith.

Outside the United States, stunt cycling was recast as a gentrified entertainment, with intimations of ballet and gymnastics. In China, so-called acrobatic cycling emphasizes flashy costumes and ornate configurations of cyclists: a dozen performers balanced on a single bike, fanning out like peacock feathers. "Artistic cycling" competitions, which are popular in central and eastern Europe, feature balancing tricks and fluid gymnastics-style floor routines performed on fixed-gear bikes, with judges awarding points to singles, pairs, and four- and six-member teams.

Today, the most prominent forms of stunt riding fall under the category of sport. Since 2008, BMX racing—motocross-style competitions staged on purpose-built off-road tracks—has been a medal-awarded Olympic event. There are mountain bike and BMX competitions that highlight "extreme" acts of daring, dangerous leaps from ski jump–style ramps, hair-raising flips—all kinds of rad acrobatics. Yesteryear's Loop of Doom and Cercle de la Mort have transmogrified into the ramps and half-pipes of the X Games. The

appeal of a bicyclist zooming through the air and tempting fate is
evidently perennial.

Danny MacAskill is a great athlete, but it would be wrong to
characterize his performances as sport. He is an entertainer. He's
almost certainly the most famous stunt cyclist in history. Since the
release of *Inspired Bicycles,* MacAskill has shot many more videos,
with increasingly large budgets and slick production values, flaunt-
ing an ever more outrageous repertoire of skills, stunts, dangerous
leaps, and journeys to improbable altitudes. These videos have been
viewed hundreds of millions of times. One of the most popular is
The Ridge (2014), which features MacAskill on his home turf: exe-
cuting a series of tricks while cycling a vertiginous knife's-edge trail
up and down various peaks in Skye's Cuillin range. *The Ridge* was
filmed from multiple perspectives. There is footage shot by a crew
that trekked uphill alongside MacAskill, and there are soaring bird's-
eye panoramas captured by drone camera. The hairiest images were
recorded by a GoPro camera mounted on MacAskill's helmet: dizzying verité views of the cyclist's progress as he ascends and de-
scends the rocky path along the ridge, a trail that provides mere
inches of running room and the prospect, with a faulty move, of a
plunge hundreds of feet into a crevasse.

The signature moment of *The Ridge* presents a heroic tableau:
swathed in mountain mist, MacAskill stands with his bike atop the
sheer rock face known as the Inaccessible Pinnacle, one of Skye's
iconic outcroppings. This image, which MacAskill calls "the *Brave-
heart* shot," is both majestic and cheeky, a description that fits
MacAskill's enterprise generally. His videos emphasize feats of
strength, agility, and nerve, but they toss in jokes and slapstick, loud
music, and jaunty asides. In a video called *Imaginate,* MacAskill
performs stunts on a set designed to make him look like a toy bicyclist, frolicking in a landscape of children's playthings. He swoops
up a ramp made of playing cards, hurdles a matchbox car, executes
a bar-spin drop from the gun turret of a toy army tank. In *Danny
Daycare,* he is shown barreling across fields and hills and narrow

ledges while towing a little girl in a children's trailer. (In fact, the "child" in the trailer is a doll.) Often, MacAskill's videos include blooper reels, showing flubs and wipeouts. The aesthetic is quintessentially internet-era and millennial, but it is also a throwback to the fearless, funny stunt-cycling routines of more than a century ago. MacAskill is a digital age vaudevillian.

He spends much of the year on the road, shooting videos and scouting locations for new videos. He has filmed in the Alps and on Kilimanjaro, in Argentina and Taiwan, at the Playboy Mansion, on a barge in the Thames. He does live shows with the cycling team he founded, Drop and Roll. He has corporate sponsorships and a signature bike on the market, but he keeps a low profile, rejecting most of the offers that come his way. He fears any travel that will cut into his cycling time or compromise his credibility in the community of trials riders. He said no thanks to Ellen DeGeneres. He turned down an offer to join a South Korean circus.

MacAskill lives in Glasgow. When I visited him there, in the last weeks of a raw Scottish winter, he was living in a house with several roommates, all serious cyclists. If you catch sight of MacAskill when he's not on a bike, he doesn't look much like a celebrity, or a world-class athlete. He's strong and sinewy but not an awesome physical specimen. He stands five foot nine, has close-cropped red hair and a handsome but boyish countenance. He wears jeans and hoodies and baseball caps. MacAskill has a girlfriend but admits that he spends most of his non-working time on bicycles. "I don't really do much of anything else except ride bikes," he said. When he's not out on the street on his trials bike, he rides a mountain bicycle. Sometimes, he heads out on an electric motocross bike. "I like anything with handlebars," he said.

Over the years, he has suffered injuries that have sidelined him for weeks and months. He has no illusions about the dangers of his line of work. In 2013, Martyn Ashton, a trials legend whom MacAskill hero-worshipped as a kid, fell backward off a ten-foot-high bar, landed hard, and cracked two vertebrae. The accident left him paralyzed from the waist down. Ashton has since returned to mountain biking, using customized bikes. In 2015, he appeared alongside MacAskill and two other riders in *Back on Track*, a video filmed on the Antur Stiniog, a mountain biking trail in North Wales. For MacAskill, overcoming fear is crucial. "Your brain has to do the work. Your body may be telling you not to do something. Your brain has to calm your body and give it a push. You have to make your mind very quiet."

MacAskill himself is quiet. On a bicycle, he appears emphatic and flamboyant, oozing confidence and style. But on those occasions when he's not riding, he is reserved, watchful, laconic. Trials riding—street trials especially—is a cerebral pursuit. It's a form of psychogeography, of cataloging the tiny details of the streetscape. It involves seeking and speculating, measuring and calculating. When MacAskill scans the landscape, he sees broken bits of pavement to use as bumps and kicks. He searches for links between obstacles: a railing that leads to a postbox from which you can ricochet to a bench. He sizes up distances and gaps between targets. Trials riding emphasizes stillness. Though the most eye-popping moments of MacAskill's performances involve bursts of speed, flashes of movement, flights to great heights, the heart of his art is equipoise: finding ways to balance on a bike when the bike is located in a treacherous position and is moving very slowly, or not moving at all.

———

I wanted to see MacAskill in action on his trials bike. I imagined myself following him around Glasgow, sitting on park benches while he catapulted over fences, rode up walls, and generally sliced and diced the landscape. MacAskill had other ideas. He suggested that we go for a ride together, on mountain bikes, in a place called Cathkin Braes, a hilly area southeast of Glasgow's city center with several acres of cycling trails that snake through the woods. I had mentioned to MacAskill that I, too, was a cyclist and that I rode every

day, and he had inferred from the breezy way I imparted this information that I had the basic aptitude required for a mountain bike
outing. So early one weekday we drove up to Cathkin Braes in
MacAskill's van, unloaded a pair of mountain bikes in a parking lot,
and began riding. I followed MacAskill through a fine morning driz-
zle into the woods. It took me less than a minute to discover that my
particular set of cycling skills did not extend to pedaling a two-
wheeler on a beginner's level mountain bike trail.

Bike riding itself is a stunt. Bicycles are unstable: they want to
fall down. An unmoving bike will tip over if it's not propped against
a wall or supported by a kickstand, and if you set a riderless bike in
motion, the unmanned handlebars will eventually turn around the
steering axis and the bike will topple. In essence, cycling is a non-
stop exercise in crash prevention, an unending series of compensa-
tions and corrections to keep the thing upright and rolling forward.
All cyclists master the basic tricks, movements so subtle and intui-
tive that many of us fail to recognize that we are making them at all.
You steer in the direction your bike is tipping to prevent a spill; to
initiate a turn, you briefly torque the front wheel in the opposite
direction. The feats of Danny MacAskill and other stunt cyclists are
beyond the powers of most riders, but they merely underline and
exaggerate the fundamental cycling trick, the balancing act we all
perform when we ride a bike.

History's most consequential lesson in bicycle balance came from
Wilbur and Orville Wright, who, like MacAskill, began their careers
as cycle repairmen. The Wright brothers realized that the same
principles that governed cycling could be applied to aviation: that
a plane, like a bicycle, could be an inherently unstable mechanism.
"The management of our aeroplane, like that of the bicycle, is based
upon the sense of the equilibrium of the operator," the Wrights told
a journalist in 1908. Controlling the aircraft, the Wrights said, "very
soon becomes automatic with the aviator, as does the balancing of a
bicycle-rider." A 1911 treatise on aeronautics, *The New Art of Flying,* compared plane pilots to trick cyclists: "The aviator of the pres-

ent day is somewhat in the position of the bicycle-rider on a slack wire, armed with a parasol." You could say that Danny MacAskill is teaching the same lessons about balance and bicycles and aeronautics as the Wright brothers—only in reverse. In the right hands, with the right pilot, a bicycle can take flight.

Of course, in the wrong hands, an airborne bicycle is a menace, to its rider among others. The trail MacAskill and I were riding wended farther into the woods, and the cycling became more challenging, with steeper drops and sharper turns. Suddenly I was a trick cyclist, and a very bad one, too—clinging frantically to the handlebars while working the brakes like a maniac, as the bike wheels lifted off the ground and the frame slid out from beneath me in various directions. It was dangerous, and scary, but to a neutral observer it would have had a comic aspect, like a slapstick routine. As the downward dips of the trail grew more precipitous, I had the impression that my body was being thrashed around—flapping like a suit of clothes on a drying line as a nor'easter howls through town. MacAskill tried to help, advising me to ballast the bike by shifting my weight backward and hanging my butt over the rear of the saddle. This worked for a while, but I was terrified, and the tension that had seized my body and brain made a crash inevitable. After zigzagging along a relatively flat run of trail, we arrived at a deep drop and I panicked, squeezing the front brake hard. The rear wheel lurched up, and off I went, hurtling over the handlebars—up, up, and away.

I landed hard on my rear end. To be precise: I landed on my coccyx. The injury was less severe than what I could have suffered, but it was insulting, a blow to my dignity as well as my backside. As I staggered back to the bike, MacAskill, a polite person not prone to overstatement, voiced concern. "I'm a wee bit worried," he said, "that you're going to kill yourself."

I said that it might be good if I took a break for a while, and although MacAskill didn't say so out loud, he seemed to agree. We emerged from the wooded trail onto an area of well-landscaped dirt paths, with steep-sided berms and sections that sloped upward like cresting waves. I pulled my bike to the side and watched as MacAskill rode back and forth, whizzing uphill and banking sharply into the berms, making turns that left his body and his bicycle nearly horizontal to the ground.

The mountain bike he was riding was a pretty heavy machine, less conducive to the slickest moves and jumps than a trials bike. Still, watching MacAskill command a bicycle, any bicycle, can bug you out. I knew that the spectacle was the result of expert technique—minute shifts of weight and applications of force, tiny adjustments and improvisations and flickers of intuition that kept the bike cleaved to MacAskill's body and subject to his fancies. But I was unable to discern the technical particulars: to my untrained eye, his cycling presented itself as pure violent beauty, a blur of speed and power and flow.

He rode a fair distance down the trail, turned, and started back again, pedaling smooth and fast. It was clear that if he took the ramped section of the path at sufficient pace, he would get air. And that's what he did. He hit the launch, kicking out the rear wheel and twisting the handlebars in a whip maneuver as the bike shot skyward. The bicycle rose and rose; when I was certain it had reached its highest point, it kept heading up. The trajectory was so preposterous, the flight so prolonged, that for a moment I reached for my cellphone to snap a photo. But I thought better of it: in theory, the law of gravity was still in effect. Before too long, surely, the bicycle would return to Earth.

7

PUT SOME FUN BETWEEN YOUR LEGS

Queen of the Wheel. Studio portrait, 1897.

I want to fuck a bicycle. I want Callisto to take the bicycle apart so I can fuck it. Fuck the frame. Fuck the pedals. Fuck the handlebars. Fuck the front wheel. Fuck the back wheel. Fuck the sprockets. Fuck the spoke. Fuck the saddle. Fuck the seat post. Fuck the hub. Fuck the rim. Fuck the shock ab-

sorber. Fuck the front brakes. Fuck the valve. Fuck the cogset.
Fuck the head tube. . . . I want you to get me a bicycle pump
that will last. Don't get it at Walmart. I want to fuck it. Fuck it
so that I am pumped and pumping and bloated and floaty,
and while I am fucking that bicycle pump, I can feel the gasses
in my body compress. Pump and fuck.

—Vi Khi Nao, *Fish in Exile* (2016)

The heroine of Vi Khi Nao's novel is a woman with the unlikely name of Catholic whose life is thrown into chaos by the
death of her two children and the collapse of her marriage.
Her bicycle fantasy, we are meant to understand, is a symptom of
the larger crisis—not pure fetishism but perversion born of turmoil,
with some perhaps unhealthy masochism in the mix. ("Do you think
if I pumped and fucked long enough my uterus would look like a
thunderstorm?" she asks.) Nevertheless, the lust Nao depicts is a
real thing, a kink that exists in fact as well as in fiction, and it is safe
to say that there are people whose desires in this direction are un-
complicated by spiritual malaise. They simply want to fuck a bicycle.

One afternoon in November 2007, custodial workers at a municipal housing facility in the Scottish town of Ayr walked into a
room and found a man, wearing a white T-shirt but naked from the
waist down, holding his bicycle and "moving his hips back and forth
as if to simulate sex." Robert Stewart, fifty-one, was arrested and
brought before the Ayr Sheriff Court, accused of a "sexually aggra-
vated breach of the peace by conducting himself in a disorderly
manner and simulating sex with an inanimate object." The sheriff,
or judge, Colin Miller, had heard his share of strange cases; in the
early 1990s, he had presided over a special legal proceeding, ex-
haustively covered in the tabloid press, in which he'd reversed the
wrongful conviction of a husband and wife charged with engaging in
child sexual abuse and "satanic rituals." But for Miller, this case was
a novelty. "In almost four decades in the law I thought I had come
across every perversion known to mankind," he said while sentenc-

ing Stewart to three years' probation. "But I have never heard of a cycle-sexualist."

The sheriff apparently hadn't done much research. If you have an internet connection, you are no more than a few clicks away from vivid evidence of cycle-sexuality. Much of what you'll find is, well, porn, the garden-variety kind, photographs and videos in which bicycles serve as plot devices and, often enough, as sexual devices— sex toys with wheels. One popular subgenre features couples on mountain bikes, off-roading to secluded spots in the woods where acts are consummated, incorporating the bicycle in more or less predictable ways. Some bike porn videos are amateur endeavors, captured by the participants themselves using mobile phones. Other videos are clearly the work of professionals, well lit and shot from various angles, starring physically dexterous individuals who are capable of performing sex acts while slung across a bicycle, without pulling a hamstring, or worse. There are videos that follow classic porn narratives, in which the bicycle stuff is mere pretext. ("Young Slut Can't Afford to Have Her Bike Repaired"; "Hottie Rides Bike and Then Rides Cock.") Many scenarios involve nude women and bicycle seats: women pedaling bikes with dildos mounted on the saddles, women masturbating using seats or seat posts, and so on.

There is a distinction to be made between mainstream bicycle porn and a more underground variety. Bike Smut is a loose-knit movement founded in Portland, Oregon, in 2007 by a cyclist and activist known as Reverend Phil. The group bills itself as "a coalition of the horny"; its signature event, the Bike Smut Film Festival, features "a collection of short erotic films made by inspired cyclists from all over the world" that celebrate "the joy and liberation of sex-positive culture and human-powered transportation." The vibe of the films is broad-minded and bohemian, embracing sex that is straight and gay and bi and trans and otherwise. Many of the films are feminist, porn made by women, for women.

The common denominator in Bike Smut films is, indeed, bike smut: the leering camera lenses are directed at chainrings and diamond frames as much as at human limbs and loins. There are video clips in which naked men and women lick and stroke handlebars and top tubes. In other videos, the basics of bicycle maintenance are demonstrated by women in skimpy outfits, armed with Allen wrenches and lubricant. In the film *Fuck Bike #001,* a long-haired, tattooed man is shown pedaling a stationary bike, of a sort: a fourteen-foot-long Rube Goldberg assemblage, composed of bicycle frames and wheels and sundry other bits, whose drivetrain powers a dildo attached to a long metal dowel. At the business end of the contraption, a woman lies on an elevated mattress with her legs spread, writhing and moaning. *Fuck Bike #001* devotes a few seconds of screen time to images of the "couple," the nude cyclist and the nude woman; but the film makes clear that the sexy stuff, the real hot action, is in the kinetic workings of the components, the whirring of cranks and chains and wheels, the play of light on the metal and chrome. Truly, it is bicycle pornography.

————

There are others who look at the bicycle's bits and pieces and see kinky possibilities. Rheta Frustra is a Vienna-based artist and activist whose project Bikesexual aims to "challenge body norms and sexual norms" by creating "upcycled" sex toys using old bicycle parts. On the Bikesexual website, and at workshops conducted across Europe, Frustra offers instruction in the making of butt plugs and bondage gear—handcuffs, whips, cat-o'-nine-tails—from scraps of rubber and metal salvaged from disused bikes. Those who have "always wanted a harness, but . . . were too embarrassed to go into a shop in daylight downtown" can fashion one quickly using a broken bicycle inner tube, bicycle chains, a couple of buckles, and "a used bicycle cog for the dildo."

Like Bike Smut, Bikesexual is subcultural and countercultural, part of the activist underground that regards bicycling as a form of antiestablishment resistance. (Bikesexual, Frustra says, "combines principles of DIY, vegan, ecological, and bicycle culture and queer politics.") But the sexualization of bikes is neither a fringe phenomenon nor a new one. The bawdy caricatures that filled London print shops during the dandy charger's brief heyday—those images of priapic fops and busty ladies groping and humping astride the velocipede—envisaged the bicycle as an erotic machine, or at least an instrument of erotic farce, a sex toy for the Regency's coalition of the horny. During the 1890s boom, while guardians of morality were fretting (and fantasizing) about bicycle seats that "bring about constant friction over the clitoris and labia," studio photographers were capturing images of nude women straddling bikes. (These photos, preserved on cabinet cards, fetch high prices on eBay.)

In this same period, bike smut snuck into mass entertainment under the cover of double entendres. The famous 1892 English music hall hit "Daisy Bell (Bicycle Built for Two)" was said to have been inspired by a royal sex scandal, the affair of Daisy Greville, Countess of Warwick, and Edward, Prince of Wales, the future King Edward VII. The song's lyrics featured suggestive puns about bicycle components ("You'll be the belle / Which I'll ring") and made winking analogies between the titular bicycle built for two and another kind of tandem ride: "You'll take the lead / In each trip we take / Then if I don't do well / I will permit you to / Use the brake."

The bicycle activated the dirty minds of more highbrow artists, including prominent modernist writers. In *Finnegans Wake*, James Joyce writes of a young *"prostituta in herba"* who pedals a "bisexycle." A baldly pornographic scene is found in Georges Bataille's *Story of the Eye* (1928). The novel's unnamed narrator and his lover, Simone, strip nude and go cycling through the countryside. The ride climaxes, literally, with Simone's orgasm, which sends her sprawling off her bike, onto the roadside:

> We had abandoned the real world, the one made up solely of dressed people, and the time elapsed since then was already so remote as to seem almost beyond reach. . . . A leather seat

clung to Simone's bare cunt, which was inevitably jerked by the legs pumping up and down on the spinning pedals. Furthermore, the rear wheel vanished indefinitely to my eyes, not only in the bicycle fork but virtually in the crevice of the cyclist's naked bottom: the rapid whirling of the dusty tire was also directly comparable to both the thirst in my throat and the erection of my penis, destined to plunge into the depths of the cunt sticking to the bicycle seat. . . . I realized she was tossing off more and more violently on the seat, which was pincered between her buttocks. Like myself, she had not yet drained the tempest evoked by the shamelessness of her cunt, and at times she let out husky moans; she was literally torn away by joy, and her nude body was hurled upon an embankment with an awful scraping of steel on the pebbles and a piercing shriek.

It is instructive to compare Bataille's wanton bike ride to the scenarios imagined by the bicycle's turn-of-the-century opponents, who warned that "a long 'spin' in the country" will often result "in sexual embraces." This was classic moral panic, but it may not have been wrong on the facts. For well over a century, the bicycle trip from the city to the country has been viewed as a journey ripe with erotic possibility. (The porn trope of cyclists trysting in the backwoods is merely the latest iteration.) Out on those rustic roads, in those open spaces, the constraints of society no longer pertain; cyclists can taste true freedom and surrender to their wildest desires.

In *Voici des ailes!* (*Here Are Wings!*) (1898), the novelist Maurice Leblanc tells the story of two Parisian couples, Pascal and Régine Fauvières and Guillaume and Madeleine d'Arjols, who undertake a bicycle tour through bucolic Normandy and Brittany. As their journey unfolds, morals loosen, along with corsets, which the women abandon in favor of less constricting clothing. Eventually, Régine and Madeleine discard their blouses altogether, and go wheeling through an Edenic landscape with their breasts bared. For Leblanc, biking itself is a kind of sex. The cyclists, the bikes, the landscape, the elements—all are sexual entities, participants in an ecstatic orgy.

> The road rose and fell over gentle slopes, and in the delirium into which their speed had hurled them, it seemed that the earth was swelling and sagging, like a chest throbbing with the rhythm of breathing. . . . [The cyclists'] arms opened as if for an embrace. The resistance of the air gave the illusion of something moving toward them and nuzzling tenderly against their breasts. The breath of the breeze on their lips was like an ineffable kiss of love. The soft scents of honeysuckle stirred them like secret caresses. . . . Their consciousness vanished, dissolved in things. They became parts of nature, instinctive forces, like the gliding clouds, like the rolling waves, like the floating fragrances, like the echoing sounds.

By the end of the novel, the Fauvièreses and d'Arjolses have swapped spouses, and two new couples pedal off into a future that holds the promise of lots of spicy conjugal activity, and lots of bicycling. The message of *Voici des ailes!* is that cycling represents liberation, and that liberation is by definition libertine.

——————

It's an idea that seems like it would be time-stamped, a remnant of the easily scandalized Victorian age. But it has currency in today's bicycle culture. The World Naked Bike Ride (WNBR) is an annual event in which thousands of cyclists in dozens of cities around the world pedal through the streets in "bare as you dare" states of undress. Conrad Schmidt, the Canadian credited with founding the WNBR in 2004, has characterized it as a return to cycling's roots and a celebration of cycling's essence. "The concept of riding a bike naked goes back to the early days when bikes were first invented," Schmidt has said. "There is just something about bikes and being naked that are meant to go together." Some WNBR cyclists wear body paint or strategically placed socks; others ride fully nude. In spring of 2020, during the first months of the Covid crisis, many WNBR participants wore only surgical masks. A few riders also placed masks over their genitals.

The event has the atmosphere of a countercultural carnival—a boisterous swarm of humanity wending through city streets, letting it all hang out. But the goal, WNBR organizers insist, is not simply to *épater la bourgeoisie*. Philip Carr-Gomm has written that people who protest in the nude "convey a complex message: they challenge the status quo by acting provocatively, and they empower themselves and their cause by showing that they are fearless and have nothing to hide. But at the same time they reveal the vulnerability and frailty of the human being." The WNBR embraces the direct-action tactics of Critical Mass; its rhetoric links nudity and sexuality to environmentalism, safe streets, and anti-automobilism. "By cycling naked we declare our confidence in the beauty and individuality of our bodies," reads the WNBR mission statement. "We face automobile traffic with our naked bodies as the best way of defending our dignity and exposing the vulnerability faced by cyclists and pedestrians on our streets as well as the negative consequences we all face due to dependence on oil, and other forms of non-renewable energy."

The conflict between motorists and cyclists has often been cast in terms of sex and gender. In a world dominated by cars—those turbocharged totems of masculine virility—bicycle riding is regarded by many as emasculating and infantilizing. "It's impossible to feel like a grown-up when you're on a bicycle," wrote dedicated bike-hater P. J. O'Rourke in a 2011 *Wall Street Journal* op-ed. "Search plazas, parks and city squares the world over and you won't find a single statue of a national hero riding a bike. This promotion of childishness in the electorate means that bike lanes are just the beginning. Soon we'll be making room on our city streets for scooter and skateboard lanes, Soapbox Derby lanes, pogo-stick lanes, lanes for Radio Flyer wagons." Hollywood has harped on this theme, portraying male cyclists as sexually stunted man-children: think of Pee-wee Herman pedaling his fire-engine-red Schwinn or Steve Carell's forty-year-old virgin, who doesn't have a driver's license and commutes on a bike to his dead-end job at a strip mall electronics store. These attitudes surface in real-world battles over the right to the road. In traffic altercations, motorists frequently disparage cyclists using homophobic and misogynist language. Social scientists have reported the widespread use of such epithets as "pussy," "cunt," "fag," and the more pointed "bicycle fag." My own field research confirms these findings.

In the face of this hostility, bicycle activists champion a politics of jaunty hedonism. The slogans painted on the banners, as well as the bared torsos, of WNBR riders—PUT SOME FUN BETWEEN YOUR LEGS; I'M BIKESEXUAL: I'LL RIDE ANYTHING; CYCLISTS PUMP HARDER; I CAME ON MY BIKE TODAY; POWERED BY ASS, NOT GAS—picture bicycling as exuberant and debauched. (Driving a car, by contrast, is understood to be unsexy, uptight, normie.) Some cyclists embrace the idea that bike riding is feminine—or, rather, feminist. Adriane Ackerman, a member of Portland's freak bike community, created a head-turning custom two-wheeler: a "double-tall bike adorned with a giant papier-mâché vulva." The bicycle displays what Ackerman calls "the Shock Twat" or "the Cuntraption" in its frame near the front wheel; Ackerman has rigged up a length of plastic tubing, running from a jug filled with red wine mounted on the rear rack, to a spigot in the center of the sculpture. This arrangement allows volunteers, of which there are apparently many, to perform figurative cunnilingus, kneeling before the bike to quaff the Cuntraption's flowing "menstrual blood." As a piece of feminist street theater, it is impressive. ("In my experience," Ackerman says, "there are few testaments to power more striking than hundreds of grown-ass adults waiting in line to get on their knees for a giant hand-made vagina, just to get boxed wine squirted at them from it.")

It is also a witty response to a culture that venerates cars for, as one scholar has put it, their "phallic powers of penetration and thrust."

———

Some may be hesitant to view the culture clash between the car and the bicycle as a proxy battle of the sexes. Still, it's fair to say that automobiles and bikes have contrasting erotic personalities— different kinds of sex appeal. For the writer Jet McDonald, the distinction lies in the way bikes expose riders' bodies to the open air and to the eyes of others: "In northern Europe we save our private bodies for the indoors, the fickle winter polices our flesh. But when the sun finally arrives, the hop from indoors to the bike is small, and we allow a more intimate self out in the open. The car does not do this; the car is a room on wheels. The bodiless driver speeds about in four walls and sexual signals are saved for winks in traffic jams."

We might add that the actions necessary to drive a car demand far less muscle power, and generate far less body heat, than those required to get a bike moving. The analogies to sex are corny but apt. To ride a bike is to enter into an intimate relationship. You swing your thighs across the bicycle, you mount it, you pump the pedals. Your body merges with the body of the bike. Together, you build up a steady rhythm. The bike gains speed in response to your exertions; you push, the bike pulls. And away you go. It hardly seems necessary to note that cycling has so often been described in language suggestive of orgasm—as thrilling, euphoric, ecstatic.

Perhaps these metaphors go too far. Or maybe they don't go far enough. The pangs of gratitude and affection I feel for my bike, and for bikes in general, are deeper than those I harbor for any other inanimate thing and, if I'm being honest, for all but a few animate ones. Henry Miller, one of history's keenest perverts, never recorded any salacious thoughts about bicycles. But in the memoir *My Bike and Other Friends* (1978), he wrote with earnest ardor about the "best friend" of his teenage years in New York City during the first decade of the twentieth century: a two-wheeler manufactured in Chemnitz, Saxony, which he bought after attending a bike race at the old Madison Square Garden. Miller recalls the bike shop mechanic not far from his family home in Williamsburg, Brooklyn, who did his repair jobs for free "because, as he put it, he never saw a man so in love with his bike as I was."

Miller "carried on silent conversations" with his bike. He doted on it, with the tenderness of a young lover in the throes of a first romance. There is a faint hint, perhaps, of the future erotic gourmand, the connoisseur of assignations and caresses and excretions, in Miller's description of his nightly regime of bicycle upkeep. "Every time I returned home," Miller writes, "I stood the bike upside down, searched for a clean rag and polished the hubs and the spokes. Then I cleaned the chain and greased it afresh. That operation left ugly stains on the stone in the walkway. My mother . . . would get so incensed that she would say to me in full sarcasm, 'I'm surprised you don't take that thing to bed with you!'" With bikes, as with humans, the hottest sex acts are often acts of love.

8

WINTER

Braving a snowstorm. Srinagar, Jammu and Kashmir, India, January 2021.

The ship lifted its anchor and moved out to sea, pointing north, toward the top of the world. HMS *Hecla* was a British Royal Navy vessel, 105 feet long, with three masts and a dozen sails when fully rigged. She had seen wartime action in 1816, joining the Anglo-Dutch fleet that bombarded the Barbary pirate stronghold of Algiers. Two years later, the *Hecla* was given a new mission: Arctic exploration. Her hull was reinforced and clad in iron, to withstand the battering of floating pack ice. Between 1819 and 1825, the *Hecla* undertook three expeditions in search of the Northwest Passage. Now, on April 27, 1827, she was setting out from the mouth of the

Thames Estuary on a voyage to the North Pole. The ship carried captain William Parry, a crew of twenty-eight, and, lashed to the deck, a pair of twenty-foot-long "sledge-boats," hybrid craft with iron runners and sails to catch the wind. Parry's plan was to steer the *Hecla* six hundred miles north of the European mainland to Spitsbergen, an island bounded by the Arctic Ocean, the Greenland Sea, and the Norwegian Sea. There, the sailors would switch to the smaller boats, continuing the journey a further six hundred–plus miles over the water and ice.

According to a press report, Parry and his crew had an additional errand to attend to on Spitsbergen Island. Alongside vast stores of guns, ammunition, tobacco, and rum, the *Hecla*'s hold contained some unusual cargo: "several velocipedes." These were to be dropped at Spitsbergen. In an item published prior to the launch of the expedition, London's *Morning Advertiser* imagined the sensation the machines would cause in the frozen north: "When Peruvians first saw a Spaniard on horseback, their consternation was excessive. This no doubt will be the effect when the Esquimaux behold an Englishman on a velocipede."

History holds no further word of these velocipedes. It is possible that the report was erroneous. It's doubtful, in any case, that Eskimos would have laid eyes on the things. Spitsbergen at that time was an outpost under control of the United Kingdoms of Sweden and Norway. It was a whaling mecca and a destination for Norwegian trappers chasing polar bears and arctic foxes. It was also a destination for scientists and naturalists, many of them Swedish. We should imagine a different scene in Spitsbergen: the velocipedes being greeted by quizzical Scandinavians, whose descendants would be counted among the world's most passionate practitioners of travel by two wheels. These bicycles would almost certainly have been the first to reach polar climes.

———

No cyclist can outride the weather. To travel on a bicycle is to experience the pleasure and peril of exposure to the open air, and for a certain breed of rider the pleasure is heightened by the peril of frigid temperatures and landscapes caked in ice and snow. The English cyclist R. T. Lang, writing in 1902, scoffed at the "dilettante who sends his bicycle to winter quarters directly [when] the first brown days of October have come." Winter cycling, Lang said, was his birthright as a Briton, handed down by hardy forebears:

> When . . . the snow [is] whirling and twisting and twirling round the spokes, as I have seen it whirl and twist and twirl in the heart of the Cheviots, over the Derbyshire tors and through the wild fastnesses of the Scottish Highlands . . . it is then that the old Berserker spirit rises in the race, then that it is a fight with all nature as the enemy, a hard unending battle between man and his eternal foe. The sinews strain and every muscle stands out in angry knots as the wind beats down in a wild effort to end all further progress; for a few seconds it is almost a death-struggle, the wheels barely move, the hands grip harder, every muscle of the body joins in the fierce fight; a moment and the battle halts undecided, then the wind gives way, the pedals twist in the exhilaration of victory, only to renew the struggle a few yards further, but with confidence in the power to win. It is a British sport, one in which only the sons of Vikings can revel.

Lang's racialist mumbo-jumbo doesn't quite square with reality: the zeal for wintertime biking is by no means restricted to descendants of Vikings, nor, for that matter, to "sons." But he was right that a sturdy constitution and a high pain threshold are required. As a friend who considers himself an expert at it once told me, winter cycling is a fucking motherfucker. It holds difficulties greater than those posed by other kinds of adverse weather, which can be inconvenient to bicyclists but in all but the most extreme cases are not an obstacle to travel.

Bicycles do okay in rainstorms. A decent set of tires will hug the road even when wet, and a savvy cyclist can pump the brakes frequently to keep the mechanism dry and in working order. Unless you're biking into a typhoon, you can make progress through a strong wind, slowly but surely. Well-hydrated cyclists cross deserts and push through beating tropical heat.

The cold is likewise no impediment to a determined rider. These days, bicyclists can weatherproof themselves comprehensively, sheltering already-gloved hands in mitts that sheathe the handlebars while placing inches of down quilting, neoprene, fleece, and other insulators between the skin and the elements. I saw many such bike riders when I lived in Madison, Wisconsin, a place where the snot in your nose freezes the second you step outdoors on a February morning. On State Street, downtown Madison's main drag, cyclists in snowsuits would glide past, their beards frosted with icicles like a polar explorer's.

The challenge of winter cycling is not low temperatures but bad roadways, which can defeat even the strongest and most skilled riders. Bicycles weren't built to plow through snowdrifts or to navigate skating rinks. Tires with no road to grip can spin out from under you, and snow may stop you dead.

Yet you could say that wintertime is in the bicycle's DNA. The ur-bike, Karl von Drais's *Laufmaschine,* was a kind of winter vehicle, conceived in the "year without a summer" and propelled by that kick-and-glide motion adopted from ice-skating. Ever since, tinkerers have been retrofitting bikes for wintry roads and creating new bikes expressly for seasonal use. The simplest DIY modifications are those made to tires to gain greater traction, wrapping braided chains around the wheels crosswise or studding tires with nails, screws, or other spiky protuberances. There is a 1948 photograph of Joe Steinlauf, an American bike builder, riding what may be the gnarliest, most punk-rock bicycle ever made, a cruiser whose wheels have no tires, just metal rims, each ringed with three dozen three-inch-long spikes. They are the bicycle wheels a medieval inquisition would use to spear a heretic.

In the late 1860s, various species of "ice velocipedes" appeared in the United States and Europe, usually featuring a studded version of the boneshaker's pedal-powered big front wheel, and various skate- or sled-like additions to the frame. "Ice velocipedes are the latest novelty on the Hudson," *The Brooklyn Daily Eagle* reported just after the New Year in 1869. The invention of the safety bicycle brought a new wave of winterized bicycle designs: bikes with greased blades at the front or rear, bikes that approximated the form of giant skis, a bicycle outfitted with "snow shoe attachments." In Holland— prime territory for winter cycling, with its frozen canals and bicycle-mad populace—a clever designer eliminated the front wheel and set a single chain-driven rear wheel between two sets of elegantly looped runners. An American firm, the Chicago Ice-Bicycle Apparatus Co., offered a fifteen-dollar package of add-ons that promised to transform "any style or make of modern safety bicycle" into a winter vehicle that could ride "swifter than summer speed." The company boasted that one of its test bicycles had been clocked on frozen Lake Michigan traveling a quarter mile in twenty seconds.

———

The annus mirabilis of the turn-of-the-century bike boom, 1896, coincided with the discovery of gold in northwestern Canada. Entrepreneurs moved to capitalize on the popular sensations, marketing bicycles to fortune seekers heading north. In the summer of 1897, a New York firm began manufacturing a "Klondike Bicycle," touted as a high-technology godsend for Yukon prospectors. The bike had solid rubber tires and a steel frame that was wrapped in rawhide to protect the rider's hands in low temperatures. It came with an extra pair of wheels that folded down from the middle of the top tube, and there were attachments to the handlebars and seat stays for securing freight.

The idea was that the Klondike Bicycle could serve as both a passenger and a cargo vehicle, allowing riders to haul the one ton of food and equipment that Canadian officials required of each prospector to ensure his survival on the frontier. The owner of a Klondike Bicycle could unfold the machine into four-wheel mode, drag five hundred pounds to the gold fields by foot, then stow the outrigger wheels, mount his bike, and pedal back down the trail to fetch another load. The "stampeders" who carried gear on their backs and relied on pack animals would have to complete several round-trip journeys, covering perhaps twenty-five hundred miles total, before their hunt for treasure could begin. But a cyclist could transport all his supplies in just two trips, stealing a march on the competition.

So said the salesmen behind the Klondike bike. Others were skeptical. A. C. Harris, the author of *Alaska and the Klondike Gold Fields: Practical Instructions for Fortune Seekers*, mocked the "tenderfoot prospectors who have taken bicycles" to the Yukon, unaware of the harsh conditions that would render the machines useless. Proponents of bicycles, Harris wrote, "had overlooked the one thing necessary to country riding besides a good wheel—good roads."

It's true that the terrain was forbidding. To reach the Yukon River headwaters you had to travel mountain pathways like the Chilkoot Trail, with its infamous "Golden Stairs," fifteen hundred steps carved into the snow and ice near the summit of the pass. If you made it over the mountains, you found yourself in treacherous country. Yukon weather was predictable only in its severity. Temperatures dropped to fifty degrees below zero Fahrenheit. Blizzards swept in, blinding fogs wrapped the land, avalanches struck, wind howled. Prospectors suffered frostbite, hypothermia, malnutrition, and starvation. It was rumored that men boiled their boots and drank the broth, for want of anything better to eat.

There were other hazards. When the spring thaw came, travelers could get mired in mud. Summers were brief, hot, and plagued by flies and mosquitoes. Lawlessness and violence reigned. Bandits ambushed prospectors along the trail; suicide was said to be epidemic. The commissioner of the Yukon wrote to the Canadian minister of the interior in the fall of 1897, reporting gruesome scenes: "The heartbreak and suffering which so many have undergone cannot be imagined." Soon word began to filter south that the whole enterprise was a fool's errand, that all the gold-rich territory had been claimed, that the only people getting wealthy in the Klondike were the early stakeholders and entrepreneurs who had established businesses catering to the gold rush hordes. One of these was Frederick Trump, Donald Trump's grandfather, an immigrant who had dodged the draft in Germany, fled to the United States, and made a small fortune opening hotels in the Yukon riverbank towns of Bennett and Whitehorse.

Still, hopeful prospectors pilgrimaged north, and hundreds of them, perhaps thousands, brought bicycles. In 1901, the *Skagway Daily Alaskan* estimated that 250 cyclists were heading up the trail to Dawson City, the boomtown that had sprung up at the confluence of the Yukon and Klondike rivers, near the site where gold was first discovered. Photographs from the period capture images of men, including Inuit natives, astride bicycles that had been modified to suit the Arctic. There were handmade four-wheelers, two bicycles that had been fused into one by soldering iron crossbars to connect the frames. Many cyclists loaded cargo on sleds or toboggans, which they harnessed to their bikes and dragged behind. Occasionally, bikers brought small dog teams with them, reversing the usual equation by riding in front of the dogs rather than mushing them along from a trailing sled.

But a benefit of traveling by bicycle was that it freed a prospector from the need for draft animals, which were costly to feed and difficult to care for, and were prone to dropping dead. The White Pass Trail, the entry point to the Yukon from the Alaskan tent town of Skagway, earned the nickname Dead Horse Trail because of the thousands of horses and mules that perished there, tumbling from cliffs or lying down to die in the snow, having been driven too hard and fed too little. Dogs often fared no better. One cyclist recorded a macabre sight as he pedaled the trail along the south bank of the Yukon River: "A red short haired dog frozen hard as stone. Someone had stood him on his nose on a little snow mound, his tail straight up and his feet in a trotting position. He looked like a circus clown doing his trick."

Klondike cyclists claimed another advantage over horses and dog teams: speed. If the weather cooperated, bicycle riders could travel faster than anyone, up to one hundred miles per day on flat stretches of trail, about twice the distance covered by prospectors with dog teams. When the trail turned steep, cyclists dismounted and humped their bikes uphill, but they made up the time on the downward slopes. The tracks left by the dog sleds, generally about eighteen to twenty-four inches wide, proved to be serviceable bike paths. A cyclist would hold his wheels in the narrow grooves and churn forward, over ice-shackled earth and frozen rivers, tracing a ribbon across a world of murky, milky white.

Of course, cycling in the Yukon came with a special set of miseries. Learning to steer in the dogsled tracks was not easy, and the trial-and-error process could be painful. A bicyclist reported that he "took about 25 headers into the snow" on his first day on the trail. When the trail ran out at the edge of a river, with no ice bridge leading to the opposite bank, riders forged the freezing water on foot, battling strong currents and dodging ice floes while carrying their bikes overhead. Often cyclists found themselves in wastes of rough ice, with no sled paths to ride. Horses were responsible for some of the rough ice: their heavy tread and weighty sled-borne tow loads chopped the trail to bits. The jagged ice would slice the hooves of the horses, and the dog teams that followed would suffer in turn, leaving toenails and flesh behind when their feet caught on the edges of the horse tracks. Cyclists were left to navigate a shattered landscape, slickened by the blood of horses and dogs.

Almost no cyclist was adequately clothed. Those who lacked protective eyewear succumbed to snow blindness. Some learned to ride one-handed, using their free hand to rub their nose in an effort to stave off frostbite. The cold wounded bicycles, too. Tires stiffened and cracked in the low temperatures; bearings froze solid. A spill could cripple or behead a bike, shattering pedals or snapping handlebar stems in two. Repair work was often called for, and those who lacked the necessary parts and tools were forced to improvise. When inner tubes punctured, cyclists stuffed tires with rope and rags. Ed Jesson had to contrive several makeshift fixes during his thousand-mile bicycle journey from Dawson City to Nome, where gold had been discovered in late 1898. While Jesson was wheeling through Rampart Canyon, in the Yukon's Sawtooth Mountains, a strong wind picked him up and flung him onto a serrated chunk of ice. The accident skinned Jesson's hands and badly bruised his knee; a portion of his bike's handlebars broke clean off. Jesson limped to a campsite, where he performed surgery: "I split a nice straight grained piece of spruce and with my knife made 2 nice pieces to tape on each front fork of the wheel, letting them extend high enough to fasten a cross stick to them, to act as a handlebar. I made a real good job of it."

———

Another cyclist who followed the stampede to Nome was Max Hirschberg, a nineteen-year-old from Youngstown, Ohio. Hirschberg had arrived in the Klondike during the first wave of the gold rush and spent a couple of years running a roadhouse outside Dawson City. Just after the New Year in 1900, he sold his share in the ..adhouse, cashed in some small mining claims, and secured a dog team for the trek to Nome, where it was said that gold was so plentiful you could scoop it straight off the beach for miles along the Bering Sea coastline. On the eve of his scheduled departure, a fire broke out at the hotel where he was spending his last night in Dawson City. Hirschberg escaped the burning building, but he stepped on a rusty nail and contracted blood poisoning. By the time he recovered, it was March, and the spring thaw was setting in. Hirschberg realized he was facing a ticking clock. It was too late in the season to travel by dogsled—the dogs would go nowhere on a trail turned to slush and mud. The best route to Nome was over the frozen Yukon, but the river ice would soon start to melt. And Hirschberg knew that news of the Nome gold strike was bringing boatloads of fresh prospectors north. To beat the mob, he would have to find his way to Nome quickly. He bought a bicycle.

Hirschberg pedaled out of Dawson City on March 2. The skies were clear, and the temperature was thirty degrees below zero. He was better dressed for the weather than most, leaving little skin exposed. He wore a fur hat that covered his ears, a fur nosepiece, and fur gloves that stretched to his elbows. A robe fastened to the bike's handlebars provided extra insulation for his arms and hands. His high-top shoes, made of felt, were laced tight over two pairs of woolen socks. He pulled a drill parka over a mackinaw coat, a pair of fleece-lined overalls, and a flannel shirt. It was a wonder that Hirschberg could move his body, with all the layers. Otherwise, he traveled light. A sack fixed to the springs of his bike seat held a change of clothes, a watch, a penknife, matches, pencils, and a diary with a waterproofed cover. Hirschberg also had a "poke," a small bag, containing gold dust worth $1,500 and several gold and silver coins. There was another $20 in gold coins next to his skin: Hirschberg's aunt in Youngstown had stitched them into a belt, which he'd strapped tight around his waist, beneath his overalls.

It was a difficult trip. Hirschberg was an experienced cyclist, but he took many tumbles while acclimating to the two-foot-wide paths left by sled runners. Storms blew in, dumping snow that obscured the trail. Even when the skies were clear, Hirschberg faced the danger of losing his way. The trail meandered north and west, across the frozen Yukon and alongside it, following the river's bends; in spots, the river fractured into many channels, and Hirschberg was uncertain which path to follow. His bike took a beating. About six hundred miles into the journey, Hirschberg skidded on river ice and busted a pedal. He fashioned a wooden pedal, but it wore down quickly and had to be replaced every seventy-five miles or so. He solved the problem with the help of a Jesuit priest stationed in the trading post town of Nulato, who built a sturdy replacement out of galvanized sheet metal and copper rivets.

Hirschberg saw great sights along the way. His route took him past herds of caribou. Cycling on a crystal-clear day near the mouth of the Tanana River, he looked to the south and spied the silhouette of Mount McKinley. In an account of the trip written years later, Hirschberg recalled crossing the border from Canada into the United States near the Yukon town of Forty Mile: "A thrill shot through me as I caught sight of Old Glory waving." Technically he was in the United States, but he was traveling through the homelands of far more ancient civilizations. Many nights, he slept in indigenous villages. When Hirschberg reached the northernmost point of the Yukon River, Fort Yukon, about a mile above the Arctic Circle, he was retracing the path taken decades earlier by the first settlers to enter the territory of the Gwich'in people. Fort Yukon had been home to Robert McDonald, an Anglican priest and missionary who married a Native woman, had nine children, and established an alphabet for the Gwich'in language. McDonald translated the Bible, the Book of Common Prayer, and various hymns into the local tongue. Just outside town, Hirschberg cycled past a cemetery holding tombstones dating to 1850 and 1860, the graves of some of the first white people to die in Alaska.

The greatest obstacles Hirschberg encountered on his ride were the literal ones, barriers and death traps formed by alternately thawing and refreezing water. When the Yukon River froze, it tossed up a gauntlet of icy walls, some standing straight up and down, others sloping across the trail. Temperatures fluctuated; creeks along the riverbanks froze, melted, and froze again. Often, the creeks overflowed their banks, creating doubly slippery conditions as water sloshed over a floor of glassy ice. The terrain could trick the eye. Once, Hirschberg pedaled from a bank of the Klondike onto what he thought was glare ice, only to find himself submerged in fast-running river water. He grew accustomed to riding with sodden socks and shoes encased in frost.

As March turned to April and the air warmed, travel over the frozen waterways grew perilous. Hirschberg could hear ice cracking beneath his wheels as he rode. Sometimes he had to brake abruptly to stop his bicycle from tumbling into a blowhole or a section of open water that had materialized in front of him. One day, while cycling across the thawing Shaktoolik River en route to the Bering Coast, Hirschberg broke through the surface and found himself trapped between a floor and a ceiling of ice, floating in frigid water beneath the surface ice and above the still frozen bottom of the Shaktoolik. He managed to break through the surface and clamber his way over the floes, bicycle in tow, to the opposite shore.

The last mishap of Hirschberg's adventure came as he was closing in on his destination. While he was wheeling over an icy trail just east of Nome, his tires lost their hold, sending bicycle and rider flying. Hirschberg picked himself up but discovered that the bike's chain had snapped in two. Ingenuity was called for. A stiff breeze was blowing east to west, so Hirschberg stripped off his mackinaw, pinned a stick between his back and the garment, and let the tailwind fill the coat like a spinnaker. It was by this means that Hirschberg and his chainless two-wheeler reached Nome, on May 19, 1900. He was no longer a teenager: his twentieth birthday had come and gone during the trip. It's unclear how much gold Hirschberg found in Nome, or if he found any at all. The undertaking may well have proved a net loss: Hirschberg's poke, holding the $1,500 in gold dust, had disappeared when he'd plunged into the Shaktoolik. But he came away with another kind of prize, his story, an epic that climaxed with that headlong final push into Nome. It was a spectacle likely never before seen, in Alaska or anywhere else: a man gusting across an ocean of ice and snow on a bicycle that had become a sailboat. "Without my chain I could not control the speed of my bicycle," Hirschberg recalled. "At times the wind was so strong that I was forced to drive into some soft snow to stop my wild flight."

———

The deeds of Klondike cyclists may never be matched. Nor may their particular brand of foolhardiness. But more than a century later, there is a global subculture of "extreme" winter cyclists, and their exploits, it's fair to say, are of a magnitude more insane than Max Hirschberg's. Their heroism is recreational, with no desperate quest for treasure driving it, no impetus behind it besides the purest pursuit of thrills and glory.

The most thrilling and glorious form of winter cycling—which is to say the most death-defying—is based on a simple calculus: if you manage to keep yourself upright, you can ride a bicycle very fast down a hill whose surface is tightly packed with ice and snow. In the Yukon, the coaster brakes of prospectors' safety bicycles grew white hot, even in frigid weather, when riders jammed their pedals backward while braving long, steep descents. (Cyclists tossed their bikes into snowbanks to cool them down.) These days there are "downhill bikes" intricately engineered to handle the stresses of high-speed descents. And there is a class of skilled athletes who specialize in steering these machines down snow-coated mountains. In events like the Megavalanche and the Glacier Bike Downhill, riders face off in breakneck races on Alpine ski slopes. The holder of the world record for bicycle speed is a Frenchman named Éric Barone, a former skier and movie stuntman. In 2017, when he was fifty-six, Barone piloted a mountain bicycle down one of the fastest ski tracks in the world, the Chabrières slope in Vars, in the French Alps, breaking his own record by reaching a blinding top speed of 141.499 miles per hour.

There is a video of the historic ride on the internet. Barone's bicycle has the bulk of a small motorcycle; he wears a helmet fit for an astronaut and a flame-red suit of stiff skintight rubber, designed both for aerodynamics and to "hold his body together in a crash." You watch as Barone's bike is tipped by assistants down the starting ramp, rolling onto the Chabrières slope at an elevation of 8,850 feet. For a second, a drone-mounted camera holds a shot just above and to the left of Barone, and you view the track more or less from the rider's perspective: a sheer drop into a white void. It's a terrifying sight, even for those bicyclists who will never face a descent more fearsome than the dip at the end of the driveway.

The distance between Barone's feat and the Sunday cyclist's leisurely spin is vast, but we fool ourselves if we imagine that they do not occupy points on a continuum. All bike rides are dangerous. Cycling advocates rightly blame alarming rates of injuries and deaths on systemic inequities, on traffic laws and infrastructure that favor cars over bikes. But even under ideal conditions, the riskiness of riding a moving vehicle is inherent, and the vulnerability of cyclists is in various respects unique. There will always be a touch of daredevil in anyone who chooses to push a bicycle out onto a road. Tricky weather raises the stakes and shifts the odds toward the possibility of a catastrophe, which may explain why certain cyclists derive such bliss from winter riding. The thrill is keener when the threat is greater.

For some, the thrill of winter riding is sensual: the blood-quickening, skin-palpating rush of a bicycle ride is intensified by the snap and bite of cold air. Then there's the macho aspect. R. T. Lang may have been pushing it with his bluster about the Berserker spirit, but I've spent nearly every winter of my adult life riding bikes in New York City and can attest that a freezing February morning is the time when cyclists are, or imagine themselves to be, at their most swashbuckling. There is a particular feeling of haughtiness and power that comes over you when you're moving swiftly across snow-dusted streets, sweating while others shiver or cower in cars. Your legs churn and you go slicing through the headwind, watching your vaporous breath billow for an instant before you vanish into it and burst out the other side, like a god gusting through clouds. The temperate seasons offer no such tonic to a cyclist's ego, or id.

———

There are places, of course, where winter cycling is a nearly year-round activity. If you spread out a map of the world and scan its uppermost section, moving east from Alaska across the northern reaches of Canada, across Greenland, and over a number of icy seas, you eventually spot a blob marked Spitsbergen, the polar island where William Parry and his crew either did or didn't deliver several velocipedes in 1827.

Today, Spitsbergen is the largest and only permanently populated island in the Norwegian archipelago of Svalbard. It is no longer the whaling and hunting ground it was nearly two centuries ago, although people who wander beyond Spitsbergen's main settlement, Longyearbyen, are required to carry a gun in case of polar bear attack. A Norwegian state-owned coal-mining company operates on the island. And Spitsbergen remains a magnet for scientists. A snow-covered mountainside outside Longyearbyen is the home of the Svalbard Global Seed Vault, a climate-controlled subterranean bunker designed to house millions of seeds, from all over the world. At the University Centre in Svalbard, researchers specialize in Arctic biology, geology, geophysics, and technology. Course offerings include "Arctic Marine Zooplankton," "Air-Ice-Sea Interaction," and "Frozen Ground Engineering for Arctic Infrastructures."

The university's students and faculty make up about 20 percent of Longyearbyen's population of twenty-one hundred. Longyearbyen is known as the world's northernmost town, the only settlement at its latitude with a permanent population of over one thousand. The place is also a tourist destination. Visitors come to soak up the stark Arctic beauty, to hike, to go snowmobiling, to take dogsled rides, to view the northern lights. Hardier eco-tourists camp overnight in ice caves. I stayed on Spitsbergen for a week several winters ago. I arrived in mid-February, the waning period of the polar night, when the sun was beginning to appear above the horizon for the first time in months. The days weren't dark, but they weren't bright, either. The quality of the light was similar to dusk at lower latitudes, as if a scrim of somber deep blue had been stretched across the sky. It was beautiful and melancholy.

Certain vaguely worded emails may have given friends the impression that my Arctic trip had an Ernest Shackleton aspect to it. In fact, I stepped off a plane into the Svalbard Airport's sleek terminal and took a taxi into Longyearbyen, where I was dropped at the Radisson Blu Polar Hotel Spitsbergen. There was seal and whale on the menu in the hotel restaurant, and picture windows that gave onto a vista of tundra ringed by snow-mantled mountains. But in terms of comforts and amenities, it might well have been a Radisson in Orlando, Florida. Longyearbyen has a small commercial area, a couple of streets where a visitor can replicate the routines of a bourgeois urban existence. There's a café that serves espresso in the morning; there are several bars that pour cocktails in the evening. Shoppers at Longyearbyen's supermarket are greeted in the entranceway by a taxidermied polar bear, posed on its hind legs with its teeth bared. Inside, there is fresh produce flown in from the Norwegian mainland, much of it labeled *økologiske,* organic.

Also, Longyearbyen is full of bicycles. Day and night, residents can be seen pedaling at a stately pace through the town center. In the mornings, a procession of parents tow their children to the elementary school on sleds hitched to bikes. There are bicycles parked in front of shops, the public library, the university. You'll also find bikes leaning against snowbanks outside nearly all of the houses, which are scattered along the hillsides just beyond the commercial strip. When storms blow through, local newspapers remind residents to bring their bicycles inside, lest they be whipped by the wind into dangerous missiles.

Winter cycling technology has advanced in recent decades. The hotbed, so to speak, of winter biking is Alaska, which has given the world a new kind of bicycle, the fat bike, whose wide forks hold tires that spread up to four inches across, twice the width of the typical mountain bicycle tire tread. The oversized tires permit riding on both soft and rough ground, through deep snow and over slippery ice, and you can ride with far lower than normal tire pressure, allowing more rubber to squash down and grip the ground. Fat bikes look silly, like cartoon crossbreeds of a bicycle and a monster truck, but they do the job, rolling smoothly over terrain that once stymied all but the most resolute.

There are a handful of fat bikes in Longyearbyen. (One local business offers fat-bike tours of scenic spots.) Mostly you see mountain bikes, of varied makes and price points, nearly all looking worse for wear. Longyearbyen isn't easy on bicycles. The town sits in a little valley that appears to have been dug out of the surrounding mountains by a giant ice cream scoop. Much of the year, the valley floor is slathered in snow and ice. It is very cold. Temperatures in the winter can drop to thirty degrees below zero, and even in July and August rarely reach fifty. Residents wear heavy clothing and big lumbering snow boots, hardly ideal gear for bike riding.

But Longyearbyen's cyclists know how to handle themselves. During my stay, I saw dozens of cyclists, and witnessed just one accident. It wasn't the cyclist's fault or the bicycle's; the snow and ice weren't to blame, either. It was a mishap peculiar to the Arctic: the culprit was a reindeer. In Longyearbyen, reindeer have the run of the town, as pigeons and squirrels do in Manhattan. They wander the residential streets, and they pitch up outside the Radisson, grazing on the grasses that poke through the snow near the hotel's driveway. Occasionally, the reindeer get in the way of automobiles and bicycles. One afternoon, as I set out for the coffee place, I saw a reindeer dart into the path of a woman who was pedaling her bike briskly past the hotel. I watched it happen as if in slow motion: the rider's eyes widening as she jerked her handlebars hard to the left; the wheels flying out from under the bike's frame; the cyclist's long torso listing and then slamming down, like the mast of a sailboat whose keel has broken the surface of the sea. I jogged over to make sure that she was okay, but she waved me off wordlessly, with a look that said she was both embarrassed and annoyed. It was a minor spill, and she would have preferred that it had gone unwitnessed. So I turned away and watched the reindeer, which had bolted uphill: a grayish figure moving across a blue-and-white landscape, shrinking as it scampered farther into the distance until it disappeared altogether, swallowed up by the permanent gloaming of the polar night.

9

UPHILL

A cyclist riding the highland trails near Thimphu, Bhutan, 2014.

I n Bhutan, there is a king who rides a bicycle up and down the mountains. Like many stories that are told in this tiny nation, tucked in among the southern slopes of the eastern Himalayas, it sounds like a fairy tale. But it is hard news. Jigme Singye Wangchuck, Bhutan's fourth *druk gyalpo,* or "dragon king," is an avid cyclist who can often be found pedaling trails in the steep foothills that ring the capital city, Thimphu. Everyone in Bhutan knows about the king's passion for cycling, to which he has increasingly devoted his spare time since December 2006, when he abdicated, relinquishing the crown to his eldest son. In Thimphu, many will tell you about close encounters or near misses—the time they spotted the king, or someone who looked quite like him, on an early-morning ride, churning uphill or darting out of a fog bank on the road near the Great Buddha Dordenma, the enormous statue that looms over the southern approach to the capital.

The statue, which is gilded and nearly two hundred feet tall, was built to commemorate the king's sixtieth birthday. He is beloved in Bhutan, perhaps the most revered figure in the country's history, with a biography that has the flavor of myth. He became head of state in 1972, when he was just sixteen years old, following the death of his father, Jigme Dorji Wangchuck. Two years later, he formally ascended to the throne. It was a heady moment in Bhutanese history. For millennia, Bhutan had been isolated: a land of devout Buddhism and pristine natural beauty cradled by the Himalayas, which served as a bulwark against both military aggressors and modernity. It was only in the late 1950s that the country opened to the outside world, abolishing serfdom and slavery and undertaking the difficult task of reconciling its medieval infrastructure, politics, and culture to twentieth-century life. Now the burden of that transformation fell on the shoulders of the teenage king. Under his leadership, electricity and modern medical care reached Bhutan's hinterlands. The country harnessed the potential of its many fast-flowing rivers to establish a hydropower industry, and navigated the perilous geopolitics that come with its geography. Bhutan is tiny, landlocked, and wedged between giants. There are just eight hundred thousand Bhutanese citizens; the country is bordered by the two most populous nations on earth, China and India. In 2006, the king shocked his subjects by unilaterally ending Bhutan's absolute monarchy. He led an effort to draft a constitution and institute democracy. In 2008, the country held its first general election.

Outside Bhutan, the fourth king is best known for his contribution to what might be called political philosophy. It was he, the story goes, who formulated the concept of Gross National Happiness, Bhutan's "guiding directive for development," an ethos of holistic civic contentment based on principles of good governance, environmental conservation, and the preservation of traditional culture. Gross National Happiness, or GNH, has made Bhutan a fashionable name to drop in international development circles and a tourist destination for well-heeled, usually Western, New Age seekers.

Somewhere along the way, the king took up cycling. It is rumored that he learned to ride when he attended boarding school in Darjeeling, about seventy-five miles from Bhutan's western border. His education continued in England, at the Heatherdown School, in Berkshire, whose stately campus was crisscrossed by pupils on bikes, commuting between dormitories, classrooms, and cricket greens. Eventually, the Bhutanese royal family imported a bicycle to Bhutan. According to one story, it was a Raleigh racing bike, manufactured in Hong Kong, which arrived in parts and was assembled "upside down" by servants. The defect was spotted by Fritz Mauer, a Swiss friend of the royal family, who personally rebuilt the bike. The now-functional bicycle became a favorite possession of the young crown prince, who often took cycling trips in the dense forests abutting various royal family residences. He became famous—infamous, in the circles of nervous courtiers—for riding "along mud trails at perilous speed."

The royal family's bicycle was possibly the first bike in Bhutan, and Bhutan may well have been the last place on earth the bicycle reached. Prior to 1962, the country had no paved roads. Today, Bhutan remains, by the usual standards, inhospitable to cycling. It is, almost certainly, the world's most mountainous nation. The average elevation in Bhutan is 10,760 feet. According to one study, 98.8 percent of the country is covered by mountains. Its roads twist through daunting climbs and hairy descents. Its rugged off-road trails, mottled with rocks and caked in mud, pose a challenge to the sturdiest bicycle tires and suspension systems.

Yet today there are thousands of bicycles in Bhutan, and the number is growing. In Thimphu, a city of about one hundred thousand with no traffic lights, bikes scramble up the hilly streets, navigating the one major intersection, where smartly dressed police officers direct traffic from an ornate gazebo that stands in the center of a roundabout. Meanwhile, government officials are increasingly voicing the aim "to make Bhutan a bicycling culture." The idea is not altogether surprising, given Bhutan's commitment to environmentalism and sustainability. Still, the idea of a "bicycling culture" taking root in the Himalayas is by definition eccentric. It is no coincidence that the societies that have most successfully integrated cycling into civic life are in northern Europe, where the countries are, as the saying goes, low.

The cycling fad in Bhutan is also noteworthy because the story begins with a king and his bike. We know this is not unprecedented: if we riffle the pages of history, we find various places in which bicycles first reached sovereigns and the sovereign-adjacent. But in the twenty-first century, at least, cycling fever does not typically spread from palaces to the people. "There is a reason we in Bhutan like to cycle," says Tshering Tobgay, who served as Bhutan's prime minister for five years, from 2013 to 2018. "His Majesty the fourth king has been a cyclist, and after his abdication, he cycles a lot more. People love to see him cycle. And because he cycles, everybody in Bhutan wants to cycle, too."

———

Each year, Bhutan holds a kind of national bicycle holiday, a celebration of the unique pleasures and rigors of Himalayan cycling. The Tour of the Dragon is a 166.5-mile road race that stretches from Bumthang, in central Bhutan, to Thimphu, about sixty-five miles from the country's western border. It is a spectacular journey, following a route through unspoiled forests and fields, across rolling river valleys, and, of course, up and over the great big hills, touching a few tiny villages along the way. The ride is absurdly strenuous. Cyclists must tackle four mountain passes, which range in height from just under four thousand feet to nearly eleven thousand feet. In places, the road grade reaches 15 percent, and one uphill climb stretches on for nearly twenty-four miles. Tour organizers boast that it is the most difficult one-day bicycle race on earth.

The year I visited, the race was held on a Saturday in early September, at the tail end of Bhutan's three-month-long monsoon season. In the morning, in Thimphu's Clock Tower Square, a central gathering place in the city's downtown, builders were assembling a stage for the presentation of medals. The sky was cloudy, but no rain was forecast: good cycling weather. Nearby, workers for the Bhutan Olympic Committee, which oversees the race, milled around the finish line, wearing orange uniforms with matching baseball caps. Several workers had pin-back buttons with photos of a dashing couple: Jigme Khesar Namgyel Wangchuck, the current Bhutanese king, and the queen, Jetsun Pema. Like his father, the king is a passionate cyclist. In the weeks prior to his coronation in November 2008, he journeyed across Bhutan to "meet his people." He made much of the trip by bicycle, occasionally staying overnight in the homes of locals. The king is known to take his bike out for spins in Thimphu. He has been photographed pedaling a tandem with his wife on roads adjacent to the royal palace.

It was eleven A.M. A banner posted in Clock Tower Square read, EXCELLENCE THROUGH SPORTS FOR ALL. At the rear of the big stage was a larger sign. It showed a silhouetted cyclist hunched over handlebars, riding in the slipstream of a fiery red dragon. The Bhutanese name for the nation is *Druk yul*—*druk* means "thunder dragon," and *yul* means "land." The national anthem, "The Thunder Dragon Kingdom," has a searching melody based on an old folk song, but the lyrics are emphatic and grandiose:

In the Drukpa Kingdom of Dharma sovereign
The teachings of enlightenment flourish
Suffering, famine, and conflicts disappear
May the sun of peace and happiness shine forth!

The sun did shine on race day, breaking through the scattered cloud cover around noon. A short while later, the first cyclist showed up in Thimphu: a short, slight man perched on a mountain bike spattered with mud. His bright-hued Lycra shirt and shorts were emblazoned with the word "NEPAL." It was Ajay Pandit Chhetri, the five-time Nepalese national racing champion, who was riding in the Tour of the Dragon for the first time. He broke the finish-line tape ten hours, forty-two minutes, and forty-nine seconds after the race's two A.M. start time, besting the previous record by seventeen minutes.

The Tour of the Dragon is not quite the Tour de France. That day, just forty-six riders, mostly amateurs, took part. Only twenty-two racers made it to the end, most of them straggling in hours after the winner. One of the most vigorous riders was an unofficial partici-pant, a man often referred to in Bhutan by the nickname "H.R.H.": His Royal Highness Prince Jigyel Ugyen Wangchuck, the crown prince and heir presumptive to the Bhutanese throne. The prince is the president of the Bhutan Olympic Committee, and the Tour of the Dragon is his brainchild. He spent several hours that day on his bike, pedaling alongside the racers, offering pep talks, tracing and retracing his path along the mountain passes. Eventually, he jumped off his bike and got into a chauffeured car, speeding ahead of the pack so he could greet the winner in Thimphu.

In the evening, the Tour of the Dragon racers assembled in a tent facing the stage in Clock Tower Square, before a crowd of a few thousand that had gathered to watch the medal presentations. The riders made their way to the dais, where they were congratulated by the crown prince and other dignitaries. When the ceremony was

over, I caught up with Chhetri, the race winner. Did he plan to return to Bhutan the following year to defend his title? Chhetri said
he wasn't sure yet. How did the Tour of the Dragon's course compare with those of other races in which he'd competed? The mountain passes were challenging but the scenery was beautiful, he said.
Chhetri wore a big smile and spoke with the studied smoothness of
a man who had fielded questions from journalists before and knew
how to say very little, even when holding forth at length. His main
agenda, evidently, was to express gratitude to the host nation, and
his words seemed tailored to the land of GNH. "I'm just so happy,"
he kept saying. "I'm so happy that I was able to come to Bhutan."

———

The subject of Gross National Happiness comes up often in Bhutan. GNH is both an emblem and a conundrum—a point of pride
but also a subject of disquisition, debate, and confusion. Many in
Bhutan find it hard to articulate exactly what GNH is. Many contend that the concept is misunderstood. Some observers of Bhutanese politics suggest that GNH is not so much profound as it is
nebulous—less a philosophy than a brand or a slogan, vague enough
to appeal to all comers, notably tourists with excitable Orientalist
imaginations and ample spending money.

Kinley Dorji is one of the people most often asked to explain
GNH. For years he worked as a journalist—he is the former editor-
in-chief of *Kuensel*, Bhutan's national newspaper—and there is still
a hint of ink-stained wretch in his gruff manner. But by the time
I met with him, he had moved on to a different job, as the head
of Bhutan's Ministry of Information and Communications, working
out of a pleasant office in a Thimphu compound that houses many
government ministries. "Here is the key point on GNH," he said.
"Happiness itself is an individual pursuit. Gross National Happiness then becomes a responsibility of the state, to create an envi-

ronment where citizens can pursue happiness. It's not a promise of happiness—it's not a *guarantee* of happiness by the government. But there is a responsibility to create the conditions for happiness."

Dorji said: "When we say 'happiness,' we have to be very clear that it's not fun, pleasure, thrills, excitement, all the temporary fleeting senses. It is permanent contentment. That lies within the self. Because the bigger house, the faster car, the nicer clothes—they don't give you that contentment. GNH means good governance. GNH means preservation of traditional culture. And it means sustainable socioeconomic development. Remember that GNH is a pun on GDP, gross domestic product. We are making a distinction."

To visitors from practically anywhere else on earth, Bhutan presents itself as a startlingly different place. It's a country of shocking beauty: soaring peaks, verdant valleys, centuries-old rope bridges that stretch across white-water rapids. There are monasteries nestled on clifftops. The terminal at Paro International Airport resembles a monastery, as does Changlimithang Stadium, a forty-five-thousand-capacity arena in Thimphu that hosts soccer matches and archery tournaments.

Bhutan is the only nation whose state religion is Vajrayana Buddhism. Its official language, Dzongkha, is spoken in no other country. Television and the internet arrived in 1999, but Bhutan's embrace of twenty-first-century life remains tentative and ambivalent. The law mandates that all buildings be constructed using "classical" Bhutanese designs and methods. Government workers and schoolchildren are required to wear traditional dress, the kimono-like garments called *gho* (for men and boys) and *kira* (for women and girls). Bhutan's success in combating the Covid-19 pandemic—only three Covid deaths, through the end of 2021—has been ascribed to geography and topography: the Himalayas are great social distancers. But the efficiency with which the government vaccinated nearly the entire adult population underscores another kind of Bhutanese exceptionalism, the bureaucratic competency and social cohesion that shield a small developing nation from the pathogens, and the pathologies, plaguing the theoretically more sophisticated wider world.

The most exceptional thing about Bhutan is the land itself. A majority of Bhutan's citizens still live off the land, practicing subsistence agriculture and animal husbandry. The country's tropical lowlands, pine forests, and alpine heights are bastions of biodiversity, populated by creatures found in few other places on the planet: the clouded leopard, the one-horned rhinoceros, the red panda, the sloth bear, the serow, and Bhutan's national animal, a stocky ungulate called the tankin, which looks a bit like a goat that's been doing a lot of barbell work at the gym.

The preservation of these ecosystems is a top priority in Bhutan, which has been called "the world's greenest nation." Almost all of Bhutan's electricity comes from hydropower. Bhutan's constitution mandates that 60 percent of its land remain under forest cover; currently, forests cover nearly three-quarters of the country's approximately fifteen thousand square miles. All those trees have helped to make Bhutan a carbon sink: it absorbs three times as much CO_2 as it emits, and is one of only two carbon-negative nations. (The other is Suriname.) An additional 4.4 million tons of annual CO_2 emissions are offset by hydroelectricity exports, mostly to India, and Bhutan projects that the figure will rise to more than 22 million tons by the year 2025. The government has set ambitious goals for further progress. By 2030, Bhutan intends to reach net zero greenhouse gas emissions and produce zero waste. By 2035, 100 percent of Bhutan's agriculture will be organic.

All of this has earned Bhutan a reputation as an earthly paradise, the last unsullied place. (*The New York Times* has called Bhutan "the real Shangri-La.") Bhutanese officials dismiss this notion—yet they trade on it. Once, Bhutan admitted only twenty-five hundred tourists each year; today the number has swollen to one hundred thousand, with luxury resorts springing up in remote regions to lure eco-tourists. Bhutan's official tourist slogan makes a bald appeal to the *Eat, Pray, Love* crowd: "Happiness is a place."

The realities of Bhutan are, of course, more complicated. On the streets of Thimphu, there are drug rehabilitation clinics and pizza joints, and when children get out of school, they discard their *ghos* and *kiras* for hoodies and skinny jeans. In 2020, the Bhutanese parliament passed a bill that decriminalized homosexuality, but gay, lesbian, and transgender Bhutanese are still stigmatized and subject to widespread prejudice. Gender equality is a work in progress. Few of the country's elected officials are women. A 2017 study found that more than 40 percent of Bhutanese women surveyed had experienced physical or sexual partner violence and never told anyone or reported the incident.

Gross National Happiness itself is entangled with troubling history. According to the official narrative promoted by the government, GNH has been national policy since the 1970s. But the scholar Lauchlan T. Munro has argued that GNH is an "invented tradition" that originated with a quip by the fourth king in a 1980 *New York Times* interview, and was only elevated to the status of "organizing ideology of the Bhutanese state" years later.

This change, Munro says, was part of a "skillful and hard-nosed" response by the Royal Government of Bhutan (RGOB) to a series of domestic and geopolitical crises in the 1980s and early '90s. During that period, a wave of Buddhist nationalism arose in Bhutan in reaction to the country's rapid modernization and opening to the outside world. In an effort to appease traditionalists, and to address the social fracturing brought on by Bhutanese youth's embrace of Western values and popular culture, the government began pushing a slew of new laws and reforms under the rubric "One Nation, One People." These included the institution of a national dress and behavior code based on Bhutanese and Buddhist norms. At the same time, the RGOB enacted draconian measures against the population it refers to as *Lhotshampa* ("people from the south"), a mostly Hindu, Nepali-speaking minority in southern Bhutan. The government banned the use of Nepali in schools, forced the *Lhotshampa* to wear traditional Buddhist Bhutanese clothing, and conducted a census that was designed, critics assert, to delegitimize a population that had lived in Bhutan for centuries, designating thousands of Nepali Bhutanese as "migrant laborers" and illegal immigrants. According to one human rights report, "thousands of Nepali-Bhutanese were arrested, killed, tortured and given life sentences" during this period. In 1990–91, Bhutan's army expelled an estimated one hundred thousand Nepali-speaking citizens, forcing them into refugee camps in eastern Nepal. Human Rights Watch has deemed these expulsions "ethnic cleansing"; Bhutan has been called the "world's biggest creator of refugees by per capita."

It was in the aftermath of these events that Bhutan began touting Gross National Happiness as its official doctrine, promoting "the image of a small, landlocked, plucky country" following an "alternative path to development based on happiness, not material consumption." It's clear that Bhutan's commitment to sustainable development is profound and unique; it's clear that the antimaterialist ideals of GNH are deeply held by many in Bhutan. But it is also true that GNH has functioned as propaganda, giving a gauzy New Age spin to a policy of ethno-religious nationalism. In Bhutan as elsewhere, happiness is a goal, an ideal. A place? Perhaps not.

A place where you can reliably find happiness—or, at least, boisterous high spirits—is a residential section of Thimphu, northwest of the city center, where children gather to play on the hilly backstreets. No one is quite sure who created the pastime that youngsters in Thimphu call "bearing." The name derives from the metal roller bearings that are attached to a wooden plank to create a vehicle, of a sort: a rudimentary conveyance that combines elements of skateboard, furniture dolly, go-kart, and sled. Some variations have a single wheel in the front and a pair of wheels on an axle in the rear; others have four wheels. There is also a wooden hand brake, nailed to the main plank. They are homely machines, but they serve their purpose. A kid can march up the steep roads of the city, crouch on the plank, and go zipping downhill.

As a child growing up in Thimphu, Sonam Tshering would go out in the evenings to play bearing with his friends. It was fun, and treacherous, and the vaguely illicit nature of the activity enhanced the excitement. As you barreled downhill, the scraping metal wheels would throw sparks into the night sky—a fireworks show that accompanied your headlong journey. Sonam learned to work the hand brake to vary the pace of his descent, but he preferred to move fast. He loved the speed and the danger, the feeling of the cool air rushing over his body, and the sound of the roller bearings shrieking across the pavement. "I have always been very much attracted to wheels," he says.

He was born in Thimphu in 1988, the sixth of eight children in a devoutly Buddhist family. When he was a young child, Sonam imagined that he would grow up to be a monk. (A family friend, an astrologer, told Sonam that he was drawn to the monastic discipline because he had been a monk in a previous life.) As he reached his teens, more worldly interests took hold. He studied geography at Royal Thimphu College. When he graduated, he took a civil service exam and landed a clerk's job in a government office in Thimphu.

It was an outcome that pleased Sonam Tshering's father, who had worked for the government as a tax collector. But for Tshering, the allure of wheels would prove decisive. He had learned to ride a bicycle as a child, knocking around Thimphu a bit on bikes borrowed from neighbors. Shortly after his graduation from college, in 2010, a friend told Tshering that the Bhutan Olympic Committee was sponsoring a day-long bike race from central Bhutan to Thimphu. This was the inaugural Tour of the Dragon—not a race, per se, but a trial run to assess the feasibility of staging a competitive event. The Olympic Committee had provided five bicycles to be used by young Bhutanese interested in cycling, and one bike was still up for grabs.

Tshering's brother-in-law, a Bhutanese national raised in Germany, was a serious mountain cyclist. He had taught Tshering a thing or two about bicycles, including the basics of maintenance and repair. But Tshering had never cycled in the mountains, and he had never ridden a bicycle with gears. He was given a Trek mountain bike, a jersey, cycling shorts, and sunglasses. He received two days of training in Thimphu. On a Friday in September, Tshering was driven to the town of Jakar, in Bumthang, a district of lush mountain valleys in north-central Bhutan. The following morning, at two A.M., Tshering and a couple dozen other participants gathered on a mud road and set out on the ride.

The sky was black, the air was cold, and the terrain was forbidding. The riders followed a winding river road for about a mile before heading uphill, embarking on a nearly four-mile climb through soupy fog to the Kiki La Pass, at an elevation of ninety-five hundred feet. The bikes issued to Tshering and the other riders had reflectors but lacked proper headlights. The cyclists had been given cheap Indian-made LED bike lights, which they'd taped to their handlebars. The tape didn't always do the job: one of Tshering's fellow cyclists had to hold his light between his teeth for the length of the arduous climb to Kiki La. As the riders rode back down the pass, winding through the vaporous blackness around tight switchbacks, the flickering LED lights reminded Tshering of the sparks kicked up by roller bearings on the hills of Thimphu.

In that first Tour of the Dragon, Tshering gave out after 112 miles. But he was hooked. The Olympic Committee allowed the riders to keep their donated bikes, and Tshering spent the following year training and educating himself, learning about seat positioning, gearing strategies, and other technical aspects of mountain biking, while building up his speed and stamina. In 2011, Tshering again entered the Tour of the Dragon. This time, he won.

A few weeks before his civil service job was slated to begin, Sonam's brother-in-law came to him with a proposal. The brother-in-law had developed a relationship with a French bicycle company and had decided to open a bicycle dealership in Thimphu, stocked with French bikes and mountain cycling gear. Did Sonam want to run the shop?

It was an easy decision. Wheels for Hills was the second bike store in Bhutan. When he wasn't minding the shop, Tshering was out on his bike. He competed in international events, including several races across the border in India. He traveled to the United States to take part in the 24 Hours of Moab, a major mountain biking event held each autumn in the Utah desert.

I met Tshering early one evening at a spot well known to Thimphu's cyclists, a high mountain road dotted with fluttering Buddhist prayer flags on the city's southern side. Tshering had his bicycle in tow: a Commencal Meta SX, a spiffy French mountain bike with twenty-six-inch wheels and a hot pink aluminum frame. He was wearing a black T-shirt and fluorescent yellow shorts. On his lower left leg there was a tattoo of a grinning skeleton on a bicycle.

Tshering is one of the Bhutan cycling scene's favorite sons. After his Tour of the Dragon victory in 2011, he was invited to ride with the prince, H.R.H. "The moment I entered the palace gate," Tshering said, "I prayed from inside: 'Let not this be my last time here.'" That winter, Tshering spent two weeks with the royal family at their vacation compound in Manas, in southern Bhutan. There, he met another mountain biking adept: His Majesty the fourth king, who Tshering, like many in Bhutan, often refers to by the nickname K4. Tshering told me that the rumors were true: K4 always wears his *gho* when he rides, and he is an exceptionally strong cyclist. "He is one of the toughest riders in Bhutan I've ever met," Tshering said. "He's not a very technical rider, and downhill isn't his specialty. But climbing uphill—I don't think anyone can top him."

Tshering has never entertained the belief that he can be a top international racer. His goals are more modest and community-minded. He coaches a local cycling club whose dozen riders range in age from ten to nineteen. He envisions a time when the club will have a state-of-the-art training facility and can compete at the international level. As for his own cycling: he finds the kind of fulfillment on a bike that you might expect of an erstwhile aspiring monk. "The feeling that you get when you're riding on the trail, alone in nature, surrounded by all those nature sounds, it is one of the greatest feelings you can ever have," Tshering said. "My happiness—my own personal GNH—is the mountain bike and the forest."

————

Tshering is not the only person who links cycling to Gross National Happiness. One day I met with Tshering Tobgay, the former prime minister, who is now Bhutan's most prominent international advocate for environmental and sustainability issues. He is also a cyclist who has raced in the Tour of the Dragon. "GNH is about wholesome development," Tobgay told me. "And cycling is about wholesome development. You cannot love cycling and not be an environmentalist. It is one of the reasons we must encourage more cycling in Bhutan."

We are used to hearing such talk from bicycle activists in the traffic-shackled metropolises of the West. It is odder to find the same ideas circulating in the world's most pastoral and environmentally progressive nation. Yet if you gaze down on Thimphu from the mountain roads where Sonam Tshering, the fourth king, and other cyclists like to ride, you take in a familiar spectacle: a landscape steadily being mutated by car culture and urban sprawl. Thimphu's population has more than doubled in a generation. Everywhere you look, there are automobiles chugging up newly constructed roads and buildings rising behind bamboo scaffolding on land that, a few years ago, was a vast rice paddy, stalked by peasants and livestock.

But Bhutan's bike boom is also based on a primal impulse, one we can trace through history, long before the automotive age. It is the desire that has compelled riders to meet the stiffest cycling challenge there is. Before mountain bikes hit the market with their fine engineering and gear ratios tailored to both grueling climbs and rapid descents; before the Repack racers souped up their old Schwinns and rode the slopes of Tamalpais; all the way back into the depths of the nineteenth century, when the bicycle was a novel and, in relative terms, primitive contraption—from the start, there have been cyclists who've had the urge to push their two wheels skyward, up and over the peaks that tilt toward the heavens.

The American author and adventurer Elizabeth Robins Pennell was the first woman to cycle over the Alps, in 1898, on a safety bicycle with just a single gear. "I was scorched by the sun, stifled by the dust, drenched by the rain," Pennell wrote. "Long kilometers of climbing were the price paid for every coast." Why did Pennell undertake this great trial and endure its afflictions? "I wanted to see if I could cross the Alps on a bicycle" was Pennell's answer. Most people ride bikes simply to get around or to get exercise. Others have loftier ambitions. "I did not think I was very original," wrote Pennell. "Other great people have crossed the Alps: Hannibal on elephants, Caesar in a litter." The cyclist who summits a mountain gains glory; the world will gaze up at her in admiration. She also beholds glory, looking down on the world from such a high perch. For some, those great sights from great heights may also bring insight—wisdom to which those at lower altitudes, with their endorphins in a less riotous state, will never be privy.

Riding a bike in the Himalayas is, by definition, the most arduous cycling on the planet. But in Bhutan, the attitude toward pedaling uphill is, understandably, less awed, more insouciant, than in other, flatter lands. In Bhutan, all biking is mountain biking.

Tshering Tobgay, for one, doesn't see Bhutan's topography as an impediment. "In fact, our terrain in Bhutan is bicycle-friendly," Tobgay said. "If it's all flat, it's no fun." Outsiders have a bad habit of discerning Buddhist parables in even the blandest Bhutanese policy pronouncements. Yet it is tempting to find a deeper message in

Tobgay's words, a metaphor for happiness or, at least, contentment—Gross National, spiritual, personal. Tobgay said: "Here in Bhutan, with our landscape, there are ups and there are downs. Wherever there's an up, there's a down. Both parts are necessary. Both parts are fun. In that sense, I think Bhutan is perfect for bicycling."

10

NOWHERE FAST

Passengers pedaling stationary bikes in the gymnasium of RMS *Titanic*, 1912.

Apair of exercise bicycles are resting 12,500 feet beneath the North Atlantic Ocean, about 370 miles south-southeast of Newfoundland. In 1912, these same bikes sat alongside rowing machines, an "electric camel," and other pieces of state-of-the-art equipment in the gymnasium of the RMS *Titanic*. The bicycles had a single flywheel and were mounted in front of a large dial whose red and blue arrows marked the rider's progress toward the distance of 440 yards, a quarter mile. There is a famous photograph of a man and a woman using these machines, taken by a photographer for a London newspaper in the hours prior to the ship's departure from Southampton, England. Their clothing is prim— proper attire for Edwardian travelers on a luxury ocean liner. The woman wears a black woolen overcoat and a veiled hat topped with flowers; the man has a tweed suit and a shirt with a white, presumably starched, collar. It is eerie to imagine these cyclists, or others like them, pedaling in place while the big boat speeds toward the crash that will send it to the bottom of the ocean.

The last passengers to ride the bikes were Charles Duane Williams, fifty-one, an American lawyer based in Geneva, and his twenty-one-year-old son R. Norris Williams, a Harvard student and champion tennis player. The Williamses repaired to the gymnasium to pedal as the ship foundered, sportsmen to the end. When it was clear that the *Titanic* was going down, they made their way onto the deck, where the elder Williams was struck by the ship's collapsed funnel and swept overboard to his death. R. Norris Williams was also washed into the sea, but he swam to an inflatable lifeboat. He suffered severe frostbite, overruled doctors who announced their intention to amputate his legs, and went on to win men's singles titles at the U.S. National Tennis Championships in 1914 and 1916.

It is unclear where in the *Titanic*'s two-square-mile debris field the stationary bicycles ended up. Underwater photographs reveal that the walls of the gymnasium were crushed inward—the result, experts hypothesize, of a massive column of water that blasted the *Titanic* when her bow hit the seabed. The bikes, or the remnants thereof, are probably still in the gym—eaten by rust, encrusted with anemones, circled by fish.

It has been suggested that the stationary bicycle predated the locomotive kind. Proponents of this theory point to the Gymnasticon, a
machine patented in 1796, which had a pair of flywheels powered
by wooden treadles and bore some resemblance to today's recumbent exercise bikes. As with most questions of bicycle genealogy,
your opinion will depend how elastic your definition of a bike is, and
how long and hard you squint. In any case, it is certain that by the
late 1870s, various devices were in use that allowed cyclists to pedal
a bike indoors, without moving forward an inch.

Many of the earliest machines were so-called rollers. Typically
these had rectangular frames made of metal or wood that held three
free-spinning cylinders a few inches above the floor. A cyclist would
place his bicycle on the cylinders, straddle the bike, and pedal as a
"cyclometer" connected to a conveyor belt ticked off the distance
covered. Rollers were quickly adopted by professional cyclists for
training purposes; they are widely used to this day by serious riders,
amateur and pro. Less successful were efforts to turn roller-cycling
into a spectator sport. In 1901, two world-famous cyclists—the pioneering Black racing champion Marshall "Major" Taylor and the
record-setting speed demon Charles "Mile-a-Minute" Murphy—
competed in a series of one-on-one roller-bike contests in vaudeville theaters. But even these stars could not sell audiences on a race
that lacked forward motion.

The first rollers required cyclists to balance their bikes as they
pedaled, but modified versions appeared with components that held
the bicycle firmly in place. Manufacturers also began to produce
true stationary bikes, freestanding apparatuses equipped with handlebars, an adjustable seat, and, almost always, a single spinning
wheel. These "home trainers" had various mechanisms to simulate
loads and apply resistance, allowing riders to adjust the difficulty of
their indoor ride. This customization—the fact that you could replicate the rigors of every genre of bike ride, from the lazy spin down
a flat road to the onerous uphill climb—was an impressive novelty.
"The use of a home trainer gives the best sort of indoor exercise,"

wrote the cycling activist Luther Henry Porter in 1895. "It can be taken in every stage from the most charming moderation to the utmost severity."

The arrival of home trainers marked an evolution in the way people conceived of bicycles and bicycling. To ride a stationary bike was to embrace the notion that exercise—the pure physical exertion of pedaling—was an end in itself, separate from the experience of bicycle travel. Stationary bikes recast cycling as "training," and construed the bicycle first and foremost as a fitness machine, a device for building stamina, growing muscles, shedding pounds. It was an esoteric idea at a time when the health benefits of cycling were still a topic of public debate. To some, the act of pedaling an unbudging bike, indoors, made no sense. "We may expect to find some idiot advertising, in the very near future, a stationary bike for home use," sniffed a British journalist in 1897, unaware that such machines had been invented years earlier. "He will declare [a ride on a stationary bike] to furnish all the benefits of a spin along country roads into the heart of nature."

Some stationary cyclists went to lengths to simulate outdoor conditions. Riders were advised to situate their home trainers by open windows or to direct electric fans toward the bikes to produce wind resistance. In 1897, an ambitious home cyclist, a scene painter by trade, created a pastoral panorama in his London living room. The man painted "two long country views" on large strips of canvas, which he arranged on rotating spools on either side of his roller bike. These canvases were connected by slender wires to the rim of the bicycle's rear wheel; when the wheel revolved, the scenery was set in motion, and the man's indoor ride was transformed into a bucolic one, a cruise through "fields, villages, towns . . . the realism of which left little to be desired." Four circular fans, set at the top of each of the spools, enhanced the effect, shooting a stiff breeze across the two-dimensional downs and dales.

For those wishing to simulate outdoor bike riding today, technology has of course advanced. These days a cyclist can download an app, strap on a headset, and undertake a virtual-reality journey on a home trainer. In January 2017, Aaron Puzey, a software engineer in Scotland, completed a nine-hundred-mile bike ride using a VR app he designed himself. Puzey's software siphoned data from Google Street View to assemble a 3D version of the roads from Land's End, in Cornwall, to the village of John o'Groats, in northeastern Scotland—the storied lengthwise crossing of the British mainland undertaken by generations of wet and wind-lashed cyclists. Puzey traveled the route on his stationary, in his living room.

But stationary bicycling can't, and needn't, substitute for the standard kind. Pedaling in place is its own kind of cycling practice. We can describe the contrast between a stationary bike and a traditional one in terms other than "training versus travel." In the classic nineteenth-century formulation, the bicycle is an annihilator of space—making the big world small, propelling the scene painter from the ersatz English countryside in his London flat out into the real-life green and pleasant land. The exercise bike, by contrast, is a devourer of time. When you pedal a stationary you are literally going nowhere; the point is how long you pedal for, and at what pace. Spinning, the "studio cycling" sport that originated in the late 1980s and has become a global fitness phenomenon, pits cyclists against the clock: spin classes are tests of endurance, challenging cyclists to keep the pedals pumping without pause for forty-five or sixty or seventy-five minutes at a stretch. You could say that a stationary bike is a clock with pedals. Most models are equipped with digital displays that flash numbers back at the cyclist, tallying the time elapsed down to the tenths of a second, along with other crucial statistics: speed, pedal rotations per minute, calories burned.

A stationary bicycle is a versatile machine. It has often been repurposed and reimagined, adapted for ends that have little or nothing to do with biking per se. Exercise bikes are favorite tools of sports therapists, who prescribe regimens of stationary cycling to patients recovering from leg and lower torso injuries. Stationaries are also used for diagnostic purposes. Cardiologists employ specially designed exercise bicycles to conduct electrocardiograms, cardio-pulmonary examinations, and other tests of heart, lung, and muscle function. Doctors say that this method yields more accurate results than traditional cardiovascular stress tests conducted on treadmills, because bicycles engage so many muscles and body systems. A patient gets on the bike and is wired up: electrodes are pasted to her chest and midriff, pulse oximeters are clipped to her fingertips or earlobes, a breathing mask is fitted over her face. Trussed in this fashion and propped on the saddle of an upright stationary or the reclined seat of a recumbent, the patient may look less like a bicycle rider than a bicycle component—the node of a gonzo gearing system co-designed by Rube Goldberg and Google.

Stationary bikes were put to use in unlikely ways long before the digital age. Beginning in 1899, a research team led by Professor W. O. Atwater of Wesleyan University conducted a celebrated series of experiments to gauge the efficiency of "the human engine." The scientists placed a stationary bike inside a large metal-lined wooden box and used magnets and a small dynamo to convert the action of the bike's chain-driven rear wheel into an electrical current. The guinea pig for this research was a male cyclist who pedaled the stationary, at staggered intervals, for several days and nights. The rider was not permitted to leave the box, which was outfitted with a folding bed, a chair, and a table. The man's food, drink, and "excretory products," as well as the bicycle's electrical output, were measured and analyzed "with the greatest accuracy." By this means the scientists were able to calculate the ratio of the "fuel" consumed by the cyclist to the energy generated by his pedaling. The findings, Atwater announced, left no room for doubt. A human being was the world's most economical energy source, "much better . . . than a locomotive, yielding twice as much power for a given amount of fuel. . . . In fact no kind of engine yet contrived—steam, gasoline or electric—is equal to the human engine as a producer of energy."

A different set of conclusions might have been drawn from the same data: that riding a bicycle is an exceptionally efficient means of turning human exertion into energy, and that stationary bicycles in particular can be utilized to convert that energy into power sources like electricity and to run machines and tools of various kinds. Over the decades, the pedal power of stationaries has been harnessed to run dentists' drills in New Deal Civilian Conservation Camps, to activate the air-conditioning in a subterranean Roman bunker built for Benito Mussolini, to light a giant Christmas tree in Copenhagen's City Hall Square, and to work the film projector in a movie theater in Vilnius, Lithuania. In 1897, a whimsical inventor in St. Louis began marketing a "shower-bath bicycle" whose arrangement of pumps and pipes and a watering can–like nozzle, arcing up and over the rider from the bike's rear sprocket, permitted a cyclist to exercise and bathe simultaneously, while regulating the water pressure with the vigor of his pedaling. Today the same principle is applied in southwestern Colombia's Nashira Eco-Village, a planned community of single women and children, where a lone stationary bicycle provides the pumping power that runs the communal showers serving a population of four hundred.

The promise of exercise bicycles as alternative energy sources has excited the imaginations of environmentalists. Stationaries have been utilized on small farms and communes to grind flour and thresh wheat, and some cycle advocates have dreamed grander dreams of pedal-driven agriculture and industry, of putting stationary bikes to work on a vast scale in fields and factories and homes. These ideas were elaborated in one of the more fascinating artifacts of 1970s bicycle utopianism, *Pedal Power in Work, Leisure, and Transportation,* a manifesto, history, and how-to co-authored by a group of scholars and activists and published in 1977 by Rodale Press, which specialized in books about sustainability. *Pedal Power*'s rhetoric combined technophobia and machismo, a familiar mix among bicycle activists, assailing "this age of lasers and deep space probes" in which "much of the muscle in the industrialized world hangs like a rag doll." The solution, the authors wrote, was to foster a "climate of bikology," exploiting the "full human potential inherent in the use of bicycles for work."

The book made the case for the "Energy Cycle," a low-tech pedal-driven contraption developed by engineer Dick Ott and the "Research and Development Department of Rodale Press." The Energy Cycle consisted of a stripped-down bike frame, the seat of a typing chair, a work bench, and a variety of cranks, sprockets, and pulleys. It could be combined with any number of tools to perform a range of jobs, from farm work and light manufacturing to basic household tasks. It could power lathes and drills and stone polishers and potter's wheels; it could pull weeds and winch a plow and irrigate a field; it could clean grain, shell corn, roll oats. It was also a kind of jumbo Cuisinart, an infinitely adaptable kitchen appliance. It was capable of opening cans, sharpening knives, kneading dough, beating batter, churning butter, plucking feathers, skinning fish, slicing meat and cheese, pureeing fruits and vegetables, making sausages and ice cream and applesauce. By delegating the heavy-duty labor to the legs and feet, the Energy Cycle freed a user's hands to do other things: "Researchers report that when working with cherries, a person can sort, pluck, and feed with the hands while the feet do the pitting." But the authors of *Pedal Power* imagined a headier future for pedal-driven machines:

> As the bicycle in a sense "liberated" people at the turn of the century, pedal power can liberate millions again. Women, who throughout the world must daily perform difficult tasks by hand, can benefit. . . . If pedal power extends beyond class and economic lines, we have put geography to rest.

More than four decades later, this vision sounds both naïve and prescient. "Bikology" has not emancipated millions nor rendered geography obsolete. But the use of pedal-driven tools is on the rise, particularly in rural communities of the developing world, to help ease the burdens of manual labor and bolster economic productivity. (In Latin America, where pedal-powered contraptions are popular, a new word has entered the vernacular: *bicimáquinas,* "bicycle machines.") Aid workers are increasingly turning to devices such as pedal-driven water purifiers, which harness the power of stationary bicycles to bring potable water to impoverished regions and disaster zones.

In the West, the bicycle machine remains a scruffy pet of the activist left. During the two-month-long Occupy Wall Street standoff in the autumn of 2011, demonstrators at Manhattan's Zuccotti Park charged batteries and powered laptops by pedaling stationary bikes rigged with generators. It was a cheap, practical way to supply energy to the Zuccotti Park tent city. But for protesters decrying, among other things, an unholy alliance of politicians, Wall Street, and the fossil fuel industry, the power of those whirring bicycle wheels was above all symbolic: a low-tech rebuke to Big Oil capitalism.

———

Wall Street, for its part, does not view stationary bicycles as engines of the revolution. They are commodities whose value has been trending upward for two decades. Today, the global stationary cycle market is valued at nearly $600 million, and is expected to grow to almost $800 million by 2026. High-design flourishes and hefty price points have reached the humble world of pedal-driven food-prep gizmos. What would the dreamers behind the Energy Cycle make of the Fender Blender? It is a stationary, available in various Day-Glo hues, with a pedal-activated blender that rests on a platform above a twenty-eight-inch flywheel. Designed and marketed by Rock the Bike, an Oakland-based "event technology" company specializing in pedal-powered novelties, the Fender Blender is "good for thousands of smoothies with minimal hassle and maximum fun." The bikes retail for about $2,700.

The driving force behind stationary bicycle sales is fitness, a craze for indoor cycling that has elevated the sport to the level of step aerobics and yoga as a workout-industry mainstay. Today, consumers who purchase exercise bikes for use in the home make up the largest sector of the market. I wonder how many of these machines will meet the fate of the stationary I remember from childhood visits to my grandparents' house: a lime-green Schwinn "Exerciser" that migrated over the years from living room to guest bedroom to a mildewing corner of the basement, where it languished next to an unloved ping-pong table, as lost to the world as the bikes that went down with the *Titanic*. Surely legions of stationary bicycles are sunken in cellars, relics of forsaken New Year's resolutions, of fitness regimens that hit the shoals.

Then again, for millions today, exercise cycling is a more serious pursuit than in the past. The origins of the current boom date to 1987, when Jonathan Goldberg, a South African–born professional bicycle racer, narrowly averted a deadly crash while road training at night near his home in Santa Monica, California. Goldberg welded together a homemade stationary and switched to training in his garage. Soon he began to contemplate the entrepreneurial prospects of indoor cycling.

Goldberg, who goes by the nickname Johnny G, had a head for business and a flair for bromides. The result was a new form of exercise, or at least a shrewd reformulation of an old form of exercise, which Goldberg christened "Spinning." (Goldberg quickly trademarked the term, along with "Spin," "Spinner," and "Johnny G Spinner.") Spinning was modeled on aerobics: high-energy classes, held in gyms and fitness centers, with thumping music and instructors exhorting cyclists to pedal harder and longer. Goldberg's innovation was to give the enterprise an overlay of spirituality and self-help. "The stationary bike, potentially the most boring piece of equipment imaginable, can be brought to life, but only if you have a true urge to imbue it with energy," Goldberg wrote in *Romancing the Bicycle: The Five Spokes of Balance* (2000), a memoir and mission statement. "The Spinning program is . . . about surrendering to the Universe, freeing the mind, opening the heart and creating personal parameters." In publicity portraits, Goldberg, a wiry man with peroxide-blond hair, was cast as a kind of Zen master: photos showed him practicing martial arts on a windswept beach and seated in the lotus position in a garden beside a Buddha statuette. If the imagery was "Eastern," Goldberg's self-actualization credo was, unmistakably, American. "The gift of the Spinning program," he wrote, "can be synthesized into one vital message: You are the most important person in the world. Never stop believing in yourself."

In recent years, a new generation of moguls has transfigured studio cycling, pumping it up with new technology and higher decibel music, while reformulating the spin class as an "extreme" athletic endeavor and a "tribal" rite. The company most responsible for the shift is SoulCycle, which grew from a single location on Manhattan's Upper West Side to a juggernaut with studios in more than a dozen American states and Canada, and a valuation of hundreds of millions of dollars. SoulCycle was founded in 2006 by three New Yorkers, Elizabeth Cutler, Julie Rice, and Ruth Zukerman. These entrepreneurs recognized that affluent, fitness-conscious young urbanites wanted a more social experience in the gym. They pitched SoulCycle as a "cardio party," with "rockstar instructors" leading riders who "move in unison as a pack to the beat." SoulCycle's studios combine elements of the nightclub and the wellness spa. The music is up-tempo, rhythmic, loud. The studios are lit by candles and have walls emblazoned with slogans and beatitudes: WE ASPIRE TO INSPIRE. WE INHALE INTENTION AND EXHALE EXPECTATION. WE COMMIT TO OUR CLIMBS AND FIND FREEDOM IN OUR SPRINTS. THE RHYTHM PUSHES US HARDER THAN WE EVER THOUGHT POSSIBLE. ADDICTED, OBSESSED, UNNATURALLY ATTACHED TO OUR BIKES. HIGH ON SWEAT AND THE HUM OF THE WHEEL. CORE ENGAGED, WE RESHAPE OUR BODIES ONE RIDE AT A TIME.

The language is drivel—even rockstar instructors must find it difficult to inhale intention—but it is undoubtedly drivel by design.

There is no denying SoulCycle's marketing savvy, which begins with its clever brand name. Like Johnny G, SoulCycle sells stationary biking as a spiritual practice, a means of personal enlightenment. This idea is increasingly a part of bike culture, circulating online and in cycling's version of inspirational literature. (Sample titles: *The Bicycle Effect: Cycling as Meditation*; *The 100 Most Powerful Affirmations for Cycling*; *Mindful Thoughts for Cyclists: Finding Balance on Two Wheels*; *Pedal, Stretch, Breathe: The Yoga of Bicycling*.) A tenet of the spirituality marketed by SoulCycle is that inner peace brings outer beauty: the enlightened cyclist, it is strongly intimated, will also be a hot cyclist with a rockin' bod, like SoulCycle's toned and tatted instructors.

SoulCycle has endured financial setbacks, and weathered the Covid-19 shutdown of its studios, in part by holding "indoor cycling" classes outdoors. But it was the SoulCycle studio ambience that gained the company its cult, and that can't be replicated in broad daylight. The lights are dim. The music thuds and booms. The candles flicker like constellations. The words on the wall read: TAKE A JOURNEY, FIND YOUR SOUL. Seventy cyclists are pedaling their unmoving bikes to a distant place, an illimitable territory not found on any map. They travel the boundless roadways of the self.

———

The stationary bicycle has reached other frontiers. Peloton, the subscription media and exercise-equipment service, attracts thousands of riders at a time to its livestreamed cycling classes. The slick design and high price tags of Peloton's proprietary bikes, equipped with touchscreens that allow members to join both live and on-demand classes from the comfort of home, have further elevated the stationary bicycle to the level of luxe status symbol. The company launched in 2013, but its apotheosis came in 2020, when Covid drove millions of fitness buffs into quarantine. In April 2020, in the early weeks of the crisis, a record twenty-three thousand Peloton members streamed a single live class. A good number of them, it's safe to assume, were refugees from SoulCycle. Peloton cannot simulate the sweaty camaraderie that devotees of SoulCycle cherish, in what I suppose must now be characterized as IRL stationary biking. Instead, Peloton's members—a few million strong at this writing, though the company has vowed to grow the number into the hundreds of millions—have merged the old-fashioned act of bicycling with that quintessential twenty-first-century experience: staring at a screen, alone and yet not alone, in the spectral company of countless others. If Peloton meets its membership goals, it may yet lay claim to the largest mass bike rides in history—a virtual phalanx of millions, pedaling together through cyberspace.

At least one exercise bicycle has departed this earthly plane altogether. Some 220 miles above the earth's surface, in the International Space Station, there is a machine called a Cycle Ergometer with Vibration Isolation and Stabilization System, or CEVIS. Missions on the space station usually last six months. While in orbit, astronauts experience microgravity, floating and drifting in the air, never using their legs to support their own weight. These conditions take a toll on the human body. Astronauts lose bone density and muscle mass, and they must maintain an intensive exercise regimen to ensure that their legs will still work—that they will be able to stand upright and walk—when their feet again touch terra firma.

The CEVIS is located in the space station's Destiny Laboratory. It has been called "NASA's stationary bicycle," but it is not exactly stationary, and it doesn't look much like a bike. It has neither handlebars nor a seat. It consists of a set of pedals that drive a small flywheel through a planetary gear set. The flywheel is contained inside a small rectangular box, from which the pedals protrude; this apparatus is attached to a larger metal frame, which, in turn, is bolted to the wall of the laboratory by isolation mounts. To operate the CEVIS, astronauts simply clip their shoes into toe clips and pedal. There is a back pad to support the upper body, and riders can further secure themselves with a belt and shoulder straps. But the toe clips are sufficient to keep a cyclist moored to the bike, and many astronauts choose to simply balance their bodies atop those pedals, which gives a ride on the CEVIS the appearance of a magic trick. The pedals turn; the bike and the cyclist hover in dreamy microgravity. The thing looks like a levitating unicycle. "Cycle Ergometer with Vibration Isolation and Stabilization System" doesn't capture the effect.

Astronauts can adjust the resistance level of the CEVIS. They can do scaled training and interval training. A computer monitor mounted at eye level, like a screen on a Peloton bike, allows cyclists to listen to music or watch a movie as they pedal. The CEVIS is also a data device. Its computer collects information on riders and transmits the numbers back to planet Earth, so NASA doctors can create cycling protocols tailored to the fitness needs of individual astronauts.

The CEVIS does not quite fulfill the old fantasy of bicycles in outer space. No one will mistake the pedaling astronaut for the nymphs in those old advertising posters, zigzagging their bikes through an obstacle course of moons and stars. But a spin on NASA's bicycle holds other wonders. Astronauts are often required to ride for ninety minutes at a stretch, during which time the space station passes over two sunrises, completing an orbit of Earth. At NASA they like to joke that the riders of its exercise bike are the fastest cyclists in history, capable of circling the globe in a single workout. ("Lance Armstrong, eat your heart out!" wrote the astronaut Ed Lu in a blog post.) A cyclist clicks his shoes into the CEVIS and goes wheeling above clouds, deserts, jungles, oceans full of islands and icebergs, the Himalayas, the Amazon, Newfoundland, New York, Antarctica, Africa, Asia—crossing the heavens at 17,150 miles per hour, and going nowhere at all.

11

CROSS COUNTRY

Barb Brushe's and Bill Samsoe's Bikecentennial
ID cards, 1976.

We will go tandem as man and wife . . .
Ped'ling away down the road of life
> —HARRY DACRE, "Daisy Bell (Bicycle Built for Two)"
> (1892)

T he Old Pali Highway climbs over the mountain that sepa-
rates downtown Honolulu from the northeastern side of
Oahu. It is a legendary road, which looms large in Hawaiian
history and myth. The highway runs across ancient footpaths and
passes near the site of a pivotal battle in King Kamehameha's wars
to unify the Hawaiian Islands. That battle, in May 1795, concluded
when Kamehameha's men drove hundreds of Oahu warriors off the
edge of Nu'uanu Pali, a precipice that drops more than a thousand
feet into the valley below. The ghosts of those soldiers are said to
haunt the Old Pali Highway. In the early 1960s, tunnels were bored
through the mountainside and a new motorway, Hawaii State Highway 61, opened. The old road was closed to motor vehicles and became a favorite route for hikers and cyclists.

When Barb Brushe was a young woman working as a nurse in Honolulu, she knew the Old Pali Highway well. She would go for bicycle
rides there, pushing the pedals of her ten-speed alongside her friend
Cliff Chang. It was a friendship, not a romance, but Barb admired
Cliff's striking looks, long hair, and free spirit. And she liked that Cliff
liked to ride bikes. On her days off, Barb would meet up with Cliff and
bike the Pali: battling the steep grade and the howling wind on the
ride up the mountain; pedaling past avocado groves and the lookout
where King Kamehameha is said to have claimed his victory; zooming
around hairpin curves on the way downhill.

One day in the winter of 1975 while they were crossing the Pali
on the way back to Honolulu, Cliff asked Barb if she had heard
about a mass bicycle ride that was planned for the following summer on the U.S. mainland, timed to coincide with the bicentennial
celebration of the Declaration of Independence. Groups of cyclists
would embark on a cross-country journey, following a route of
mostly rural two-lane highways, from Oregon to Virginia.

BARB: Cliff said, "It's called Bikecentennial." Right away, I thought,
"I'm going to do that." It was a snap decision. We rode over the Pali

to a bike shop where they had information about it, and I signed up
to do it. I bought a Fuji road bike. And in the spring of '76, I went
home and I trained for it.

Barb had grown up in Roseburg, Oregon, a city of twenty thousand that squats on the banks of the Umpqua River, about 170 miles
south of Portland. For decades, Roseburg billed itself as "The Timber Capital of the Nation," a boast that may have stretched the
truth, but not by much. In the 1960s, when Barb was a child, there
were still some three hundred timber mills in town, most of them
devoted to cutting Douglas fir lumber, the "green gold" reaped in
the dense forests of the surrounding mountain ranges. Barb's mother
worked in the library at Umpqua Community College. Her father
was a timber cruiser for the Bureau of Land Management.

BARB: My dad was six foot four. He was a big guy who worked out
in the woods. He taught me how to ride a bike. As a kid, the bike
was my means of transportation. It was my way of getting around
Roseburg. I'd bike to school. I'd bike around the neighborhood.

For six weeks in the spring of 1976, Barb rode hard to prepare
for the Bikecentennial. She built her stamina and toned her muscles
on long rides in the Hundred Valleys of the Umpqua, along the river
roads and across mountain passes that reached steeper grades and
greater heights than the Nuʻuanu Pali back in Honolulu.

BARB: I was in good shape in those days. The hills were tough. It
can be hard on your knees. But I was pretty strong. I got stronger.

Barb celebrated her twenty-fourth birthday on June 12, 1976.
Two days later, a Monday morning, she strapped her sunflower-
yellow Fuji to the roof of the family car. Barb and her mother were
heading seventy-five miles northwest, to the coastal city of Reedsport, one of two West Coast trailheads for the Bikecentennial.

BARB: Right before we left Roseburg, my father said: "Any daughter of mine can do this." I thought to myself, "Oh, gosh, there's no
backing out."

When Barb and her mother arrived in Reedsport, they found a
bustling scene. Reedsport was a conservative town, but it had
opened its doors to the Bikecentennial, and its streets were filled
with men and women of a vaguely countercultural cast—lots of
lanky hair and scraggly beards—readying themselves and their bicycles for the long road ahead.

They milled around the Welcome Hotel, a three-story Art
Deco–era building, which served as both the trailhead office and a
hostelry where riders bunked down for a night or two before embarking on the trip. (The rooms were too small to accommodate
beds for all the cyclists, so the hotel pulled the furniture out of a few
rooms and riders slept on the floor in sleeping bags, up to seven per
room.) Barb was issued a Bikecentennial ID card and an orientation
packet. At a local public library, she gathered with other riders to
watch *Bike Back into America,* a twelve-minute-long inspirational
film featuring scenes of the forty-two-hundred-mile-long cross-
country route: picturesque small towns, rolling plains, purple mountains' majesty. The movie's finale was set to John Denver's "Sweet
Surrender," a maudlin folk-rock ballad whose lyrics evoke the romance of the open road and the freedom of young adulthood: "Lost
and alone on some forgotten highway / Traveled by many, remembered by few / Lookin' for something that I can believe in / Lookin'
for something that I'd like to do with my life."

Barb spent the night at the Welcome Hotel, in a room with several other young women. The next morning, June 15, she woke up,
had breakfast, and joined a group of cyclists outside the hotel to
prepare for departure. She had thirty-five pounds of gear, which she
bungeed to her bike's rear rack and packed into panniers. She had
an extra tire, a patch kit, and various tools for repairs. She had a
sleeping bag and a foam mattress she had bought at a fabric store.

She had a few changes of clothing, including warm clothes that she planned to send home once she'd made it over the Rockies.

Certain riders—more experienced cyclists and those who coveted adventure but not a social scene—undertook the trip solo. But most Bikecentennial riders joined groups of ten to fifteen, headed by a tour leader. There were two types of Bikecentennial groups. The cyclists who signed up for so-called Camping Groups opted to rough it, pitching tents in campgrounds or on farmland or, occasionally, laying out sleeping bags under the stars. The cost for Camping Group riders was $580 for the eighty-two-day cross-country journey, about seven dollars per day, meals included. Barb had signed up for a Bike Inn Group, whose members paid about four dollars more per day to sleep indoors—in church basements, school gymnasiums, college dorms, VFW Halls, Lions Club libraries, and other subluxury accommodations along the route.

On that morning, June 15, outside the Welcome Hotel in Reedsport, Barb's Bike Inn Group briefly crossed paths with a Camping Group that was starting its journey the same day. The group's leader caught Barb's eye. He was strong and lean, with an air of calm and confidence about him. He looked to Barb like he was about her age, probably in his early twenties. He was wearing a white bicycle helmet.

BARB: At that time, few people wore bike helmets. It was an unusual thing. The guy had reddish hair and a pretty full beard. Not long hair—but longish. He looked athletic. It's just one of those flash memories: I can picture him there with the helmet on. That's the first time I saw Bill.

———

BILL: My parents met when they were both working for Simmons, the mattress company. My mother was a secretary. My father worked for Simmons for forty-four years, as a packing engineer.

Bill Samsoe was born in 1953 in Kenosha, Wisconsin. A few years later, the Samsoe family moved to Chicago Heights, Illinois, a working-class suburb about thirty miles south of downtown Chicago.

BILL: I must have been five or six when I learned to ride a two-wheeler. My dad had had a heart attack, so our neighbor from across the street helped me learn. He would run behind me and keep the bike steady. The first time I took off on two wheels—it was fantastic. There's an incredible feeling of independence and liberty.

Bill graduated from high school in 1970 and enrolled at Illinois Wesleyan University in Bloomington, Illinois. After college, he took an entry-level job at an insurance agency.

BILL: I lasted a month in that job. That winter, I went up to northern Wisconsin, to this small ski area. I became a ski bum. I didn't really have any direction in my life at that time. I made some friends up there, fellow ski bums. One of them suggested I take a leadership training course with American Youth Hostels so I could lead bicycle trips. I went through the training course and I was able to lead a trip, in 1975, called the "Yankee Explorer."

The trip followed a circuitous route, beginning in Connecticut, wending through Massachusetts, upstate New York, Vermont, New Hampshire, and Maine before looping south to Boston.

BILL: The kids were pretty young. They'd just finished the eighth grade. It was my first time in a leadership role. It was my first time on a long-distance bicycle ride.

Two of Bill's friends from the American Youth Hostels training course had moved to Missoula, Montana, to run leadership training for a new organization, which was planning an ambitious cross-country bicycle ride for the following summer. When the Yankee

Explorer trip was over, Bill called them up and they urged him to come west, to Missoula, to work for Bikecentennial. He figured he had nothing else better to do. He moved in with his friends, sleeping on the floor of their apartment in downtown Missoula. During the days, he worked at the Bikecentennial office, doing whatever was asked of him. He put together tool kits and first aid kits. He made hundreds of ID cards for Bikecentennial participants. When he was offered the opportunity to do the cross-country ride himself as the leader of a Camping Group, he jumped at the chance.

BILL: I really didn't know what I was getting into. It was a lot of responsibility, being a leader on an eighty-two-day bike trip. When you're young, those things don't occur to you. You go with the flow.

Leading a Bikecentennial group was hard work. You had to be a strong cyclist. You had to be good in a crisis. Group leaders were responsible for the safety and welfare of all those in their charge. The job called for people skills. Adults were thrust together in close contact for two months, and conflicts arose. A cool head and a sense of humor helped. You had to know your way around a bicycle tire patch kit, and a first aid kit. If you knew how to cook, that was good, too.

BILL: The first day, we left Reedsport and rode only about forty miles. It was a shakedown ride. Pretty simple. It was my job to carry the cookstove. We all were supposed to take turns cooking. I did the honors that first night—I think we had macaroni and cheese and hot dogs. That night, we determined that I would not be doing much more cooking.

Bill's group quickly settled into a routine. A strenuous day of biking would end at a campsite. They'd set up camp and take turns

helping to get the meal ready. They would read, write in their journals, and attend to their bikes, cleaning their chains or switching out
a patched inner tube for a new one. Every ten days, mail drops
would bring news from family and friends. Bill often received letters from his older sister, Marge, who was also working as a Bikecentennial group leader, traveling the same route.

BILL: She was exactly two weeks ahead of us from Oregon all the
way to Yorktown, Virginia. She would send postcards about what to
expect on the trip. She sent along tips about good camping sites. I
remember she wrote to warn me about a black-and-white dog in a
particular spot that was attacking cyclists. Sure enough, we saw the
dog come running out when we got there.

Bill's Camping Group followed a snaking route east. Across the
Oregon border to Idaho. North into Montana. They spent the night
of July 4 in the tiny town of Wisdom, Montana, sleeping inside for a
change, in a run-down house donated by a local. There was a black-
and-white TV, and some of the cyclists tuned in to live coverage of
the Bicentennial celebrations in Washington, D.C., and New York,
watching the fireworks light the sky over the Washington Monument and the Statue of Liberty. Several members of the group ventured into town, where they lit sparklers and firecrackers with local
children.

From Wisdom they headed southeast to Dillon, Montana. Then
Virginia City, Montana. Then on into Wyoming. They passed
through Yellowstone, skirted the Grand Tetons, and pedaled south
over the Colorado border. Big sky. Big mountains. Big, beautiful
country. Bill's group had fallen into sync socially. Sometimes they
synced up out on highways, too.

BILL: Once, our whole group got into a pace line riding out of
Pueblo, Colorado, on the way to a place called Ordway. This was

unusual. We almost never rode in formation all together like that. It was just a slight downhill, but we were moving pretty fast. We passed a police cruiser that was pulled over on the side of the road, and as we rode by, his voice came crackling over the speaker on the top of his car: "You're doing eighteen miles an hour. Way to go."

They kept rolling east. Ordway, Colorado; Eads, Colorado; Tribune, Kansas; Scott City, Kansas. As the cyclists moved from the mountains into the Great Plains, the weather turned sultry. On the morning of July 31, Bill's group broke camp in Newton, Kansas, twenty-five miles north of Wichita. Their destination was Eureka, Kansas, about seventy-five miles southeast. As group leader, Bill normally brought up the rear, but that morning he asked his assistant leader to run anchor. It was a sweltering day, hot and sticky, with barely a breath of wind. A long ride lay ahead, and Bill was eager to get going. So he took off early, on his own. He rode hard for about forty miles, then decided to stop for a bite in Cassoday, a tiny farm town that bills itself as "The Prairie Chicken Capital of the World."

BILL: There was a little restaurant, and I thought it seemed appropriate to have an egg in the Prairie Chicken Capital. I went in, I had an egg. Then I got back on the bike and headed out again. I wasn't too far out of Cassoday when I caught up with Barb and Les.

Barb Brushe and her friend Leslie Babbe had also spent the night in Newton and were making their way to Eureka that day. Barb's Bike Inn Group frequently crossed paths with Bill's Camping Group. Back in Baker City, Oregon, both groups had stopped for the night at a YMCA. (The Bike Inn cyclists slept inside the building; the Camping Group pitched tents outside.) Before dinner that evening, the Bikecentennial riders descended on the Y's volleyball and racquetball courts. Bill and Barb wound up playing on opposite sides in a doubles racquetball match. It was then that Bill began to take an interest in Barb.

BILL: I was impressed by how athletic she was. She knew how to handle a racquet. She was a really strong rider. Also, I have to be honest, she had great legs.

Now Bill and Barb were out on the road together—under the baking sun, in a vast prairie, somewhere close to the exact geographic midpoint between the coasts. They fell into conversation, riding more slowly than they otherwise might have.

BILL: Les had the good sense to bike ahead and kind of leave me and Barb alone.

They talked about their families, their hometowns, their plans. The weather was scorching, and a haze hung over the long, flat roadway. All at once, the color and texture of the sky seemed to change. Strange noises rose to their ears.

BARB: We were riding along and we started to hear this crunching sound.
BILL: It was like we'd entered a different weather system. Suddenly there were invaders coming out of the sky.

Various climatic conditions can produce the phenomenon known as a grasshopper swarm. The swarms typically appear in the aftermath of periods of rain that are followed by drought. Rainy conditions cause grasshopper populations to explode; drought diminishes their food supply and pushes the insects into smaller and smaller areas to search for nourishment. A grasshopper swarm is an event on a biblical scale. (Locusts are a species of grasshopper.) Grasshopper swarms darken the sky and blanket the land. Sometimes the infestations are so large that they are picked up by weather radar detectors. During the "great grasshopper plagues" of the 1870s, millions of Rocky Mountain locusts descended on the plains stretching from Texas to the Dakotas, devouring crops, stripping the wool from live sheep, eating through wooden tool handles and leather horse saddles, and halting the progress of locomotives that failed to gain traction on railroad tracks buried inches deep in insects. For humans on the ground when a swarm strikes, it is like getting caught in a sudden squall.

BARB: They're flying in your eyes, your nose, your mouth, your ears. They're all over the place, all over your body.
BILL: There were probably hundreds of thousands of 'em. Maybe millions. All over the road. Squish, squish, squish.
BARB: It went on for miles and miles. It was surreal.
BILL: A memorable day.
BARB: Bill and I had kind of been circling around each other during that trip. But we got to know each other a little bit, out there with the grasshoppers.
BILL: I thought to myself, "Man, Barb's just at the top of the human being list."

One afternoon in April 1973, a man named Greg Siple was sitting at an outdoor café in a tiny village in northern Mexico when a curious image surged up in his mind: he pictured a huge group of bicyclists, riding in unison across the United States, like a giant swarm of insects. Siple, a twenty-seven-year-old from Columbus, Ohio, was in Mexico with his wife, June, and another American couple, Dan and Lys Burden. The Siples and Burdens were ten months and nearly seven thousand miles into a bicycle journey that Greg had dubbed "The Hemistour," an epic eighteen-thousand-mile trip that ran the length of the Americas, from Anchorage, Alaska, to Tierra del Fuego at the southern tip of Argentina. That day, the two couples had covered forty more miles, biking from a campsite on the outskirts of the Chihuahuan Desert city of Torreón to Chocolate, a town so small it was barely a town at all. But now, as they sat chatting on the café porch where pork stew, not chocolate, was simmering in iron kettles, Greg's thoughts drifted back to the other side of the border. What would it be like, he wondered, to undertake another bicycling odyssey, across the U.S. this time, traveling in the company of thousands from the Pacific to the Atlantic? Wouldn't an event like that be popular and, what's more, powerful, sending cyclists in droves out into the great land on a journey of discovery?

"My original thought was to send out ads and flyers saying, 'Show up at Golden Gate Park in San Francisco at 9 o'clock on June 1 with your bicycle,'" Siple told an interviewer years later. "We were going to bicycle across the country. I pictured thousands of people, a sea of people with their bikes and packs all ready to go, and there would be old men and people with balloon-tire bikes and Frenchmen who flew over just for this. Nobody would shoot a gun off or anything. At 9 o'clock everybody would just start moving. It would be like this cloud of locusts crossing America."

Greg was a graphic artist by trade. But long-distance cycling was his passion, and his mission. In July 1962, when he was sixteen, Greg and his father, Charles, took a two-day trip, biking south from their home in Columbus to the Ohio River city of Portsmouth. It was a "two-century" journey: one hundred miles per day. Charles found the ride exhausting, but Greg wanted more.

The following year, Greg found three companions to bike with him, and he repeated the Columbus to Portsmouth round trip. In 1964, six cyclists took part; in 1965, the number jumped to sixteen. The year after that, forty-five people joined the ride, including Greg's childhood friend Dan Burden, and June Jenkins, the future June Siple, a keen cyclist who had led bike tours for the Columbus chapter of American Youth Hostels. By this time, the ride had gained a sponsor, and a clunky acronym, TOSRV (Tour of the Scioto

River Valley). Within a few years, it grew into one of the largest annual bike touring events in the United States.

In 1973, 2,200 riders took part in the TOSRV. As for Greg: he—
along with June and Dan and Lys—was thousands of miles from
Ohio, heading south through Mexico. That afternoon at the café in
Chocolate, Greg shared his big idea with the others. He wanted to
stage an event that would "combine the best features of the TOSRV
and Hemistour into a summer-long ride across America." The Bicentennial was just three years away; a massive cross-country ride
would be a perfect way to commemorate the occasion and to celebrate bicycling.

Right away, June and the Burdens said they wanted in. They got
it. They could *see it*. It was one of those heady, giddy moments when
a group of like-minded individuals experiences a collective epiph-
any, and the way forward becomes instantly clear, like a ribbon of
road that's revealed when the fog lifts. For the four friends, there
was no doubt about the cause to which they would devote themselves for the next three years. Some weeks earlier, June had purchased a cyclometer, a little gizmo you attach to the hub of a bike
wheel that ticks off the miles as you ride. That evening, when they
arrived at their campsite on the road outside of Chocolate, June
checked her cyclometer reading, the tally of the total miles she'd
traveled since acquiring the device. It read: *1776*. Everyone took
this as a good omen.

———

It was nearly two years later that Greg and June Siple completed the
Hemistour, rolling into Ushuaia, Argentina, on February 25, 1975.
They'd taken five months off in the fall and winter of 1973, but had
spent the better part of three years on the road. For Dan and Lys
Burden, the Hemistour had ended early, in Salina Cruz, on Mexico's
Pacific Coast, about one thousand miles south of Chocolate. Dan

had contracted hepatitis while back home in the United States for a visit, and the Burdens never returned to the road.

But planning for the Bikecentennial shifted into high gear. The promotional efforts had begun, guerrilla style, with a series of cryptic classified ads placed in cycling magazines. ("BONETINGLING, Kaleidoscopic, Multitudinous adventure from brine to brine, backroading it for seventy days—BIKECENTENNIAL 76.") Dan and Lys settled in Missoula, where they established a headquarters for the operation out of their apartment. They collected grants and donations—one thousand dollars here, five thousand dollars there—and acquired 501(c)(3) tax-exempt status. Posters were printed up; fliers were distributed to bike shops. Word started to spread. Letters arrived in Missoula seeking more information and offering support. (Some letter writers were less encouraging: "A rolling Woodstock that will be a permanent destructive black mark on bicycling. My only hope is that you will fail before it gets started.") A friend had a Volkswagen Microbus, and he and June took a trip across the country, armed with topographic maps, to plot a coast-to-coast route along the backroads.

That route—the TransAmerica Bicycle Trail—would take cyclists through ten states: Oregon, Idaho, Montana, Wyoming, Colorado, Kansas, Missouri, Illinois, Kentucky, and Virginia. The trail passed through more than two dozen forests and touched five mountain ranges. It stretched over grasslands and sections of desert; it took in hundreds of small towns. Bikecentennial riders could choose to ride all or part of the trail, in either direction, from west to east or the other way around.

In 1976, the idea of bicycling four thousand miles across the United States struck most people—including, quite possibly, some of the people who had signed up to do it—as an odd and perhaps even foolish thing to do. But prior to the automotive era, stories of epic journeys by bicycle were mainstays of American popular culture. A bicycle was not considered a practical means of long-distance travel for the average person. (There were railroads and steamships for that sort of thing.) A long-distance ride, a bike tour, was an undertaking for special individuals, for adventurers and athletes and other seekers of glory. It was a means of demonstrating your physical strength and stamina, and also your character—your moral mettle and spiritual fortitude. It was a way to be a hero.

In the Victorian era, the exploits of bicycling voyagers—mostly but not exclusively American and British, mostly but not exclusively male—were chronicled in newspapers and magazines and in some of the earliest and most popular bicycle books. Bicycle races evolved to take the form of grand "tours": competitions that covered vast distances, traveled between cities, and followed paths up and down tall mountains. The most famous of these long-distance races, the Tour de France, was the creation of a newspaper: a publicity stunt designed to boost circulation, cooked up in 1903 by the Parisian sports daily *L'Auto*. Newspapermen understood that serialized coverage of great treks on two wheels was good for business.

The literature of bicycle "expeditions" had an unseemly side. In these swashbuckling narratives, the bicycle was pictured as a colonizing and civilizing force, bringing enlightenment to primitive corners of the planet. The most famous bicycle travelogue, *Around the World on a Bicycle* (1887), the American cyclist Thomas Stevens's account of his global trip on a penny-farthing, typifies the breezy racism of the genre. The "natives" that Stevens encounters in the Indian country of the American west, the Middle East, and Asia, are portrayed as savages and simpletons, who greet Stevens's bicycle with wonder, terror, and incomprehension. In Stevens's account, the bicycle is both an instrument of empire—a means of reaching the "darkest" and remotest corners of the world—and a justification for it: people who couldn't understand bicycles, whose cultures did not produce the bicycle, deserved to be subjugated.

But there was another side to the Victorian cult of bike touring. In novels and songs and popular lore, the long-distance bicycle trip was a metaphor for conjugal bliss. Whether riding a tandem, or rolling side by side on his-and-hers two-wheelers, lovers traveled on a vehicle that was—as in the chorus of the famous hit—"built for two." The bicycle brought couples together, sealed their bonds of love, and bore them on the greatest of all long and winding journeys: down the road of life, as man and wife.

The romance of the bicycle tour faded with the arrival of the automobile and the airplane, modes of transport capable of carrying people far greater distances at incomparably faster speeds. But around the time that Greg Siple and his father were taking their first two-hundred-mile round-trip bike ride, a resurgence of bicycle touring—and a huge new bicycle boom—was gathering force.

In the late 1950s and early '60s, a new kind of bicycle, manufactured in Britain, found favor among American adults who, for years, had dismissed bikes as children's toys. These British imports were different from the balloon tire behemoths that had dominated the American market for decades. They were lightweight, equipped with derailleur gears, and came in three-, eight-, and ten-speed models. They were easier to ride, and speedier, and they held appeal for adults who were seeking new ways to exercise, in a country that was growing more fitness conscious.

The new bikes were luring cyclists back to country roads and open spaces. "In summery locales like Florida and Southern California, grown-ups began taking ten-speeds on day trips and multi-day vacations," writes the historian Margaret Guroff. The bikes were marketed in advertisements that showed attractive, physically fit couples pedaling in bucolic settings. In the '60s and early '70s, an American bicycle touring industry arose to meet the growing demand for rustic adventures on two wheels.

Other advertisements revived the imagery of airborne bicycles from the 1890s. (An ad for the AMF Roadmaster, a popular ten-speed model, bore the tagline "Flying Machine.") In fact, the new bicycle craze was far larger than the great turn-of-the-century boom.

A 1972 federal government report found that there were now eighty-five million cyclists in the country, fully half of all Americans between the ages of seven and sixty-nine. Some of them were urban commuters and college students, who put the bicycle to everyday use. A greater number were recreational cyclists: fitness bikers and adventure bikers, who rode to get exercise or to get away from it all. In any case, they were buying a lot of bikes. For three straight years—1972, 1973, and 1974—bicycles outsold cars in the United States.

Geopolitics played a role. During World War II, fuel rationing prompted the biggest surge in cycling by Americans in half a century; in 1973, the OPEC oil embargo once again brought fuel shortages and price increases, leading many Americans to seek alternatives to travel by car. But a different kind of politics—a changing political consciousness—was also at work. This was the period of rising ecological awareness, the era of Rachel Carson's *Silent Spring* (1962), of the inaugural Earth Day (1970), and of landmark legislation: the Clean Air Act of 1970, the Clean Water Act of 1972, the Endangered Species Act of 1973. Young Americans, disillusioned by the Vietnam War debacle, were looking skeptically at their country's institutions, patterns of consumption, and vaunted "way of life." Automobiles— which for decades had shaped the country's economy, built environment, and mythology—were coming under attack.

For many, the car was no longer an American dream machine. It was the foul Leviathan of the roadways, a polluter and a poisoner. (The term "gas guzzler" gained prominence in this period.) In the winter of 1970, students at San Jose State College held a weeklong "Survival Faire," a series of rallies to call attention to environmental issues. On February 20, students staged a ritual interment of an automobile: they pooled their money, purchased a brand-new 1970 Ford Maverick, and rolled the car into a twelve-foot-deep pit. With mock-somber gravity, they conducted burial rites. "As the local citizenry looked on from the sidewalks," the *San Francisco Chronicle* reported, "the students marched by at a slow funeral pace set by the band which played a selection of songs in dirge styles."

Meanwhile, a new bicycle politics was emerging. In Amsterdam, the anti-automobilism message of the Provo movement was taken up by middle-class citizens, who were distressed by the number of traffic deaths in residential neighborhoods. They swarmed the streets in protest, demanding a safer, more bicycle-friendly, more sustainable city. Bicycle activists were asserting themselves in North America as well. In 1971, in Los Angeles, fifteen hundred cyclists joined a "Pollution Solution" ride organized by the group Concerned Bicycle Riders for the Environment. In mid-'70s Montreal, Le Monde à Bicyclette, a Provo-like affiliation of anarchists and artists, began staging direct action happenings that called attention to the toll of car culture and promoted the "poetic velo-rutionary tendency."

It was in this atmosphere of changing values and generational disaffection that promotional literature began circulating in fifty states, touting "the biggest bicycle touring event in world history." "Let 1976 be the year to bring before America its need to celebrate and keep alive the forests, farms, folk and fellowship of rural America," read one of the earliest Bikecentennial fliers. The Bikecentennial was novel, but its tendency wasn't quite velo-rutionary. It sought a compromise between old-fashioned patriotism and post-'60s counterculture. It gave a vaguely hippie spin to the archetypal American trek to the frontier; it was a bureaucratized journey Back to the Land. It was a classic thing, and a brand-new thing.

BILL: There were some people on the trip that I guess you might call hippies. But the atmosphere wasn't really political.
BARB: The Bikecentennial had a unique feeling. It was a mood very particular to that time.
BILL: I felt like I was a straight arrow. I had a beard and long hair—long for me, at least. But I guess I was somewhat conservative. Not

politically conservative. Just kind of a straitlaced guy. Most of the people in our Bikecentennial group were like that. They were just people
that wanted to ride a bicycle from coast to coast.

Four-thousand-sixty-five cyclists took part in the Bikecentennial. About two thousand rode the full-length TransAm trail; others
had signed up for shorter journeys, or dropped out before completing the trip. Most of the riders were white and middle-class. There
were only four Black Bikecentennial riders. Some three-quarters
of the cyclists were between the ages of seventeen and thirty-five,
but there were a number of riders of retirement age, and a few
children. The oldest person to complete the cross-country trek was
sixty-seven, the youngest were two nine-year-olds. Cyclists from all
fifty states took part. There were 329 riders representing fourteen
countries outside the United States, including Holland, France,
Germany, Japan, and New Zealand. In a survey conducted after the
Bikecentennial summer, a majority of the riders said the most enjoyable aspect of the experience was "seeing rural America close-up."

BILL: The Bikecentennial took you into nature and small towns. It
was an education. You learned a lot about the beauty of the land.
You met a lot of people.
BARB: It was quite a sight when a bunch of bicyclists rolled into
your town.
BILL: People would come running out to tell us we could sleep on
their farms. They'd take us out to ice cream, invite us to swim in the
lakes on their property, invite us to use their phones to call home.

For the Bikecentennial cyclists, every day brought unexpected
encounters, surprising sights, adventures and misadventures. Days
could be long and hot. (Occasionally, they were long and cold.) But
invariably there were pleasures out on the road and rewards waiting
at the end of the day: a dip in a municipal pool, a drink at a small-
town soda fountain, a local offering a plate of homemade cookies. At

the Bike Inns and the campsites, they played cards and chess. Bridget O'Connell, a nineteen-year-old who began the trek as an independent rider but was "inducted" into a Camping Group, would perform flute concerts for her fellow riders each evening. Some Bike Inn cyclists became familiar with every frame of *Bike Back into America*, the promotional film, which was shown and reshown, since there were often no other entertainment options. The audience would boo and hiss when ill-paved roads appeared onscreen.

The cyclists formed fast friendships. There were unforgettable characters in their midst. Wilma Ramsay, the forty-nine-year-old proprietor of a roadhouse in Buchan, Australia, rode nearly the entire TransAm trail wearing a knee-length skirt, a girdle, pantyhose, and shoes with heels. Wilma was joined on the trip by her older brother, Albert Schultz, a prospector and mechanic from Alice Springs, Australia. He had the beard of a biblical patriarch and pedaled the trail wearing heavy work boots. He smoked a pipe; often, he smoked it while cycling. He carried a wooden mallet to ward off dogs and a bottle of Everclear grain alcohol, which he added to the tea that he brewed nightly in his "billy pan," or cooking pot. Prior to the Bikecentennial, the siblings had not seen each other in twenty-five years. Wilma invited her brother on the trip so they could get reacquainted.

Every rider experienced triumphs and setbacks. They endured headwinds, sunburn, saddle sores. Spokes snapped. People were always catching flats. There were food- and weather-related calamities. A Camping Group had a Chinese meal at a restaurant in a tiny Kentucky town, and half the group ended up at a local hospital with IVs in their arms. Riders got caught in thunderstorms and, sometimes, snowstorms. On June 13, when a freak blizzard hit portions of Wyoming and northern Colorado, several Bikecentennial riders found themselves pedaling on a mountain pass through fifteen inches of snow.

Many riders had never slept in the open air before and they learned how to scout out the best spots: in fragrant pine forests, next to babbling brooks, in cornfields where the sound of the wind soothed you to sleep. They spent the night in tipis in Idaho and lean-tos in Kentucky. When bad weather struck, they took cover where they could: in church pews, in abandoned houses, in caves. The members of one Camping Group sought shelter from an over-night rain shower in a pigsty, where they slept among grunting hogs.

They encountered wildlife, although not all of it was alive. One day, Lloyd Sumner, a Camping Group leader, saw a prairie chicken get mowed down by a passing car. Sumner scooped up the carcass and carried it with him to that night's camp, where he plucked it, cleaned it, roasted it over an open fire, and ate it for dinner. Riders pedaled past snakes, bear cubs, herds of cattle. On a road in western Kansas, cyclists slalomed between turtles that were making their way, slowly, to the other side.

For many riders, time seemed to dissolve as the real world, the world off the TransAm trail, grew more distant and fuzzy. They were on bicycle time. They were moving fast, covering fifty miles per day on average. Yet they were moving slow, in the way that bikes do: slow enough to notice a flower bending in the breeze on the road-side, and the bumblebee that was joyriding on that swaying flower. Sometimes they rode really slow, when the road turned vertical.

BARB: My most vivid memories are the mountains.
BILL: We rode some tough hills. We went over the Hoosier Pass, which is like eleven thousand five hundred feet. There were times when you didn't think you could make it.

The most notorious climb on the TransAm trail was in Rockbridge County, Virginia. For weeks before arriving, riders had heard dread-ful stories about the hill in the Appalachians that seemed to go straight up. Its nickname was the Vesuvius.

BILL: There's a town at the bottom of that hill called Vesuvius, so we all called the hill Vesuvius. It was brutal.

BARB: I do not know what the grade would have been for that mountain, but if you told me it was eight or nine percent grade, I'd believe you. It was just switchback, switchback, switchback.

BILL: It took at least an hour, maximum effort. We couldn't have been moving faster than three miles an hour.

BARB: You really couldn't do anything except think: "Get one revolution, get another revolution. Just one more pedal stroke."

BILL: The guys who were the really fast riders got up there first and came out on the Blue Ridge Parkway, where there was an incredible view of the Shenandoah Valley. Every time another rider reached the top, a huge cheer went up.

August turned to September. Bill's and Barb's groups were closing in on the trip's endpoint, Yorktown, Virginia.

BARB: Of course, I was eager to reach that goal. But I really didn't want it to end. You had that feeling like, "How will I go back to real life?"

BILL: One day, toward the end of the trip, I was at this little country store with a couple of the other group leaders. We were standing outside the store and Barb went riding past. I actually said it out loud: "I think I'm in love."

Bill and Barb's Bikecentennial groups reached Yorktown on the afternoon of September 6, 1976. They marked the occasion by dipping their wheels in the Atlantic Ocean. That night, a group of the cyclists, including Bill and Barb, biked a dozen miles inland to Williamsburg, where they celebrated with a steak dinner.

BILL: It was a place called the Peddler. They had these big roasts. The waiter would put the knife on the roast and say, "How thick do you want it?" They'd cut it off and they'd weigh it. There were, I think, fourteen of us for dinner. The bill came to less than a hundred dollars. Those were the days.

After dinner, the cyclists stuck around to drink and dance. Sometime late in the evening, Barb asked Bill to join her on the dance floor.

BARB: It wasn't really my style. I'm not the kind of person to ask a man to dance. But for some reason it seemed like the right thing to do.
BILL: It was a slow dance. It was really, really nice.

———

And then it was over.

BILL: It was very abrupt. Disorienting. You'd just spent all this time with these people, taken this incredible journey. And suddenly everyone dispersed. The next day some of us rode our bicycles up to Washington, D.C. Others flew home. We had some Dutch guys in our group, and I remember they had to take an early bus to the airport to fly back to Holland. I didn't really know what to do, so I headed to Colorado. I went back to being a ski bum.

Bill took a job at the ski-rental shop in a resort near Dillon, Colorado. That Christmas, he sent holiday cards to everyone in his Camping Group and a handful of people in Barb's Bike Inn Group.

BARB: The truth is, I was really floundering.

For a couple of years, Barb had been in a relationship with a Coast Guard officer. She had originally planned to stay on the East Coast after the Bikecentennial ride, to be with him.

BARB: After the bike trip, I was a different person. I had just had the grandest adventure of my life. I realized that my relationship was not what it should be. Something was missing.

Barb moved back to her hometown, Roseburg. But she felt rest-less, and after a few months, she returned to Hawaii, and to her old job as a nurse.

BARB: And then I got the letter.

Bill had sent his Christmas card to Barb's home address in Rose-burg. Barb's mother forwarded it along to her daughter in Hawaii.

BARB: I can remember where I was sitting at the Kapiʻolani Library in Honolulu. I knew right then that my life had changed. It was just a simple, friendly letter. But it hit me like a bolt of lightning.

Bill and Barb began corresponding and talking on the phone. When ski season ended in the spring of 1977, Bill went to Dallas, where his parents were living. While he was there, he applied for a job as a flight attendant with Braniff International Airways.

BILL: I began working at Braniff in May 1977. Lo and behold, we had a training flight over to Honolulu, with a quick two-hour lay-over. Barb and I arranged to meet each other at the airport.

But when Bill got off the flight, he couldn't find Barb any-where.

BILL: I went to a pay phone and called her apartment. No one home. I was kind of shell-shocked. So I walked around the Hono-lulu airport for a while and went to have a drink with my fellow flight attendants. I got back to the gate about fifteen minutes be-ʿore we were supposed to take off. I looked up, and there was Barb.

Somehow, the two friends had missed the connection. Barb had spent more than an hour wandering the terminal, searching for Bill.

BILL: We talked for a few minutes, and then I had to go. She gave me this big hug. That was it—she had me.

They wrote many letters. Sometimes Barb dashed off a note during her breaks at work, writing on letterhead marked "Queen's Medical Center Patient Progress Notes." Bill replied on hotel stationery from the Ramada Inn in Kansas City or Dunfey's Royal Coach Motor Inn in Dallas. They discussed books they'd read: *Watership Down, On Death and Dying, The Inner Game of Tennis.* The wrote about bike riding, about their roommates, their jobs. They often wrote about God and religion. Sometimes, more esoteric questions were pondered. In one letter, from the summer of 1977, Bill mentioned a *Newsweek* cover story he'd read about the possibility of life on other planets: "We beamed a message towards a star cluster estimated at 24,000 light-years from here. We can expect an answer in 48,000 light-years—*if* there is life there. The author proposes this: 'Older civilizations, whirling around second- or third-generation stars, would possess technologies so advanced that to earth eyes they would appear indistinguishable from magic' . . . What do you think about that, Barb?"

That fall, Bill visited Barb on a few occasions, for a couple of days at a time. They spoke on the phone as often as they could afford. In December, Bill went to Honolulu for an extended stay.

BILL: I'd worked at Braniff for six months, which meant that I'd earned a week's vacation and full flying-pass privileges. I flew over to Hawaii and spent a week with Barb.

BARB: December sixteenth was the day that Bill proposed.

BILL: It was the day before I had to leave. We went out to dinner that night. I'd waited until the sixteenth because that's my birthday. I was hoping that if I proposed on my birthday, she'd take pity on me and say yes.

BARB: I'd just gotten out of the shower. I had an old robe on. I had a towel around my head. Bill got down on one knee and everything.

What a scene. I told him, "You know, if you hadn't proposed to me, I would have proposed to you."

———

Bill and Barb were married on June 17, 1978, almost exactly two years to the day after they'd first crossed paths at the Bikecentennial trailhead in Reedsport. It was a small wedding, held at Barb's parents' home in Roseburg.

BARB: The minister from the church I grew up in performed the ceremony, right there in the backyard.
BILL: There were maybe thirty-five guests.
BARB: This was before the time of these lavish weddings. We had a couple of salads. And a cake, of course.
BILL: There was a half-keg of beer.
BARB: My best friend from childhood played the autoharp and sang "Whither Thou Goest." Our neighbors from a couple of blocks away crashed the wedding. Homer and Betty Oft. What an appropriate last name. They were an eccentric couple—they were a little bit off.
BILL: The weather was perfect. It was just a great wedding.
BARB: It was a great wedding.

They moved to Dallas, where Barb found a nursing job and Bill continued to work as a flight attendant. They weren't rich, but they had what they needed. They were happy. They were the kind of couple whose happiness inspires admiration and maybe a little resentment among friends and family members whose relationships are more troubled. They never seemed to fight. Disagreements, minor domestic disputes, were always resolved quickly and without raised voices. Barb gave birth to a son, Erik, in 1980.

There were stresses—times when money got tight. On May 12, 1982, Bill was sitting in a plane on the tarmac at Dallas/Fort Worth International Airport, waiting to take his fourth flight of the day.

BILL: I had flown to Washington, D.C., that morning, then to Memphis, then back to Dallas. We were supposed to end up with a layover in Kansas City. There were big thunderstorms in the area and flights started getting canceled out of Dallas. And then, suddenly, all the flights were canceled.

Braniff International Airways had filed for bankruptcy.

BILL: We were on the plane, at the gate, with a full load of unsuspecting passengers. Braniff had just died, but we had not been officially informed. I forget the sequence of events, but somehow what was happening became apparent. The passengers left the plane. I left the plane through a back staircase that exited to the tarmac. I avoided the terminal and walked out to my car. I had to drive home and tell Barb, who was seven months pregnant.

In June, Barb gave birth to a girl, Kelly.

BILL: It was a scary time for us. There was a moment when we were down to our last two hundred dollars. I scrambled and created a little business. I did lawn care and landscaping in the summer. I had a chimney sweeping business in the colder months. I did this for ten years. Shortly after Kelly was born, Barb continued her nursing career. We managed.

The Samsoes liked Dallas. They lived in a small house on the northeastern edge of the city. The kids were happy and had full lives with great friends. Bill and Barb liked the racial and ethnic diversity of Dallas. Erik and Kelly attended public schools where white kids were in the minority. Their classmates were the children of immigrants from Latin America and Southeast Asia. The Samsoes liked eating in Mexican restaurants and they savored the cultural richness of life in the big city. But both Bill and Barb loved the great outdoors, and they longed for a different kind of day-to-day existence.

BARB: We wanted our children to have a rural way of life. We wanted them to be out in nature, where they could plant and hike and kayak. Even at ten years old, our daughter was starting to say things like, "I want the best clothes, Mommy." Of course, we couldn't give her the best clothes. We didn't have that kind of money. Also, I really missed the mountains. I just desperately missed the mountains.

Bill and Barb had friends who lived in Ravalli County in southwestern Montana. The Samsoes learned that fourteen acres of land were for sale near where their friends lived, in a scenic valley, fringed with forest, that spreads out in the shadows of the Bitterroot Mountains. They took a trip to see the property.

BILL: It was the dead of winter. There was snow on the ground. Very austere, very bare. But so beautiful.

The family moved to Montana in 1992. They lived in Missoula with Bill's sister, Marge, for nine months while their house was being built. It's a two-story wood-frame house, with cedar siding and a deck on two sides.

BARB: We have two acres for our house. We left the animals in charge of the other twelve acres.

The Samsoes' home sits about three-tenths of a mile from a bend in the Bitterroot River, in what once had been the territory of the Bitterroot Salish, or Flathead, people. Lewis and Clark's expedition passed by the river bend on September 9, 1805, and Meriwether Lewis made a note in his diary: "A handsome stream about 100 yards wide and affords a considerable quantity of very clear water." There are otters in the river, and various species of trout. The surrounding land is home to deer and elk and black bears and mountain lions. Bald eagles swoop overhead. Vultures roost in trees, and when an animal dies, they descend to do their work, picking the remains bare and leaving nothing behind, not even a bone. In this wild place, Bill and Barb found the life they wanted. But the early years in Montana posed challenges.

BARB: We left everything behind when we moved. When we got here, we didn't have work lined up. Being a nurse, I was able to find a job pretty quick. But Bill didn't have a job for a couple of years. It tested us.

BILL: I worked for a radio station for a short period of time. I worked for almost a year trying to start a business, but that didn't happen. I wound up with two possibilities. I could go to work for a small solar energy company or a health club. I ended up at the health club. I did that for ten years. Eventually, I got a job as the membership director at the Chamber of Commerce in Missoula. That fit me like a glove.

It sometimes seems to Bill and Barb that time has raced past, decades disappearing in a blink. Over the years, they've planted more than seventy trees on their property, and they've watched those trees grow tall. They raised their kids and saw them get married and have kids of their own. In the early 2000s, shortly before Kelly's wedding, her aunt Marge pulled her aside for a private chat. Marge just wanted to make sure that Kelly had realistic expectations. Did she understand that marriage was hard, that most marriages weren't as good her parents', that most couples were not so well-matched?

Bill and Barb have traveled as much as they can afford and have spent as much time as possible outdoors, swimming and kayaking, hiking and exploring nature. And riding bikes. When they lived in Dallas, they participated in an annual hundred-mile bike ride in

Wichita Falls, Texas, called the Hotter'N Hell Hundred. For years, Bill competed in triathlons, racking up thousands of miles in the saddle.

In 2018, to celebrate their fortieth wedding anniversary, Bill and Barb decided to cross the country by bicycle again.

BARB: It seemed like the perfect way to mark the occasion.

Theoretically, it was less strenuous than the Bikecentennial: a fifty-nine-day "Southern Tier" trek from San Diego to Saint Augustine, Florida. The trip was run by the Adventure Cycling Association, a fifty-thousand-member organization, co-founded by Greg and June Siple and Dan and Lys Burden, that evolved out of the Bikecentennial. The Southern Tier route covered 3,100 miles, a journey some thousand miles shorter than the one in 1976. Forty-two years earlier, Bill and Barb had carried their own gear; this time, a support van with a trailer towed the cyclists' luggage from place to place. Although they spent most nights in campgrounds, there were occasional overnights in hotels—far posher accommodations than the Bike Inns of the Bicentennial summer. But the Samsoes were in their sixties now.

BARB: You get pretty exhausted when you're going over mountains in the West. I really, really wanted to quit. We had purchased insurance just in case an injury occurred. I started thinking, "If I fall over and I break my collarbone, then we can use the insurance, and this trip can be done." And then, after two weeks on the road, it just kicked in: "Oh, I can make it."

On the Southern Tier trail, the sights and sounds were different than those on the Bikecentennial. The route rolled through the Arizona desert, Texas hill country, the Louisiana bayou. As in 1976, the route stuck mostly to backroads that led through small towns. But the mood this time was different.

BARB: There's an ugly face of America right now. And of course you see it out on the road.

BILL: We saw a lot of Trump signs. "Make America Great Again."

BARB: I'm not proud of myself for it, but I jump to conclusions when I see a Trump sign on someone's lawn. I assume that the people are either very stupid or very hateful. Maybe both.

BILL: There was a real pride that you felt out there in '76. It was a patriotic year. The so-called patriotism that people express today—to me, it's not patriotism at all. Right now, we would never fly an American flag outside our house. It's a symbol that has been taken over by elements in this country that we don't want to be associated with.

BARB: Here in Montana, you see pickup trucks, with gun racks, and they're flying two American flags. And they'll have a Trump bumper sticker. Bill still rides his bike around here sometimes, and he's had some bad experiences out on the road, with big trucks.

BILL: As they pass by, they'll blow a plume of exhaust in your face. I've heard that they have a special button which activates it. I don't know if that's true—but it's obvious that it's done deliberately.

BARB: I know there's a goodness in this country. In so many people. To me that's the real face of America. But it's hard to see it now. That's the America that needs to come back.

———

Bill and Barb aren't the only couple who met on the Bikecentennial in 1976. There were a number of Bikecentennial marriages. There were many flings.

BILL: I know that there were some temporary liaisons. Some hook-ups, here and there.

BARB: You were totally clueless at the time.

BILL: It's true. Much later I found out that there were two members of my group that hooked up. They were together the whole way across the country. I suppose they kind of snuck off sometimes. They tried to make a go of it after the trip.

BARB: It didn't last long.

BILL: I think it lasted a week.

One day back in July 1976, Barb's Bike Inn Group made a seventy-five-mile trip from Missoula to Darby, Montana. Barb was about a third of the way through the journey that day, riding as she often did with Les Babbe, when the two friends pulled over to admire a breathtaking view. They were on the Eastside Highway, a two-lane road that offered a lofty vantage point on the scenery. Off to the west was a picture-postcard tableau of mountains and valley.

BARB: I can remember stopping at the top of the hill and looking out and thinking, "Wow, this is beautiful." That's where we live now.

The Samsoes' house sits just steps from the Eastside Highway. Barb had pulled her bike off the road a stone's throw from the spot where, years later, she and Bill would build their home.

They've spent more time at home than usual in recent years, because of Covid. For the first year of the pandemic, they almost never left their property. Erik and his wife live just twenty-three miles away in Missoula; Kelly and her husband and their two children live just six miles down the road. Barb's mother lives in Missoula, too. But during those long pandemic months, Barb and Bill got used to visiting with their loved ones on Zoom.

BARB: We really didn't want to see anybody. We were focused on trying to keep ourselves and our loved ones safe. We're lucky, because we enjoy each other's company. We played board games. Bill read.

BILL: There's something my father used to say: "I wake up with nothing to do in the morning and by the time I go to bed, I haven't finished half of it."

BARB: We can go quite a way on a nice walk without leaving our fourteen acres.

BILL: You never get tired of the scenery out here.

BARB: It sounds corny, but the sunsets are the best.

BILL: It's incredible to watch the sun go down over the mountains. To watch that last light catch the clouds and make gorgeous reds and pinks. We've seen a lot of this country, and I'm pretty sure there's not another spot where we'd prefer to have a house.

The house is well lived-in.

BILL: It's a house filled with love. Also, filled with lots of junk.

In many American homes, the flotsam of life—the trash and the treasure—has a way of washing up in the garage. In the Samsoes' garage, there are gas cans and gardening supplies, tools and tarps, bags of fertilizer and charcoal briquettes. Tacked to the back wall, there's a burlap sack from the Pakalolo coffee company—a souvenir of Barb's years in Hawaii—and a large map of the United States. There's a Pink Floyd poster on the wall, too, and a Led Zeppelin poster with lyrics from "Stairway to Heaven." ("And as we wind on down the road / Our shadows taller than our soul . . .") Bill's old white bicycling helmet, the one that caught Barb's eye on that day in Reedsport, hangs on a coat hook nearby.

There are also bicycles in the garage—nine of them altogether, suspended from hooks in the ceiling. There are three mountain bikes, and a couple of Bill's triathlon bikes. (Bill calls these his "Go Fast" and "Go Faster" bikes.) There are a pair of his-and-hers Fuji touring bicycles, which the Samsoes bought for their fortieth-anniversary Southern Tier trip. The bikes cost $725 each.

BILL: That was about the price of the most expensive bike on the market at the time of the Bikecentennial. Nowadays, you can spend thousands of dollars on a bike.

There are two more bikes hanging from the ceiling in the garage: a yellow Fuji S10-S and a black Sekai 2500. These are the bicycles that Bill Samsoe and Barb Brushe rode across America in the summer of 1976.

BILL: Neither of us has been on those bikes in quite a number of years. I used mine for triathlons for a while, but it's not really a triathlon bike. It's a touring bike.

BARB: We'll probably never ride them again, but I don't think we'd ever get rid of them.

BILL: They're museum exhibits, you know? But I bet if I put in a little bit of work, they'd ride fine. They say if you treat it right, a bicycle will run for a hundred years.

12

BEAST OF BURDEN

Rickshaws on the traffic-plagued streets of Dhaka, Bangladesh, 2007.

I was in Dhaka, which is to say I was stuck in traffic. The proposition might more accurately be phrased the other way around: I was stuck in traffic, therefore I was in Dhaka. If you spend some time in Bangladesh's capital, you begin to look anew at the word "traffic," and to revise your definition. In other cities, there are vehicles and pedestrians on the roads; occasionally, the roads get clogged, and progress is impeded. The situation in Dhaka is different. Dhaka's traffic is traffic in extremis, a state of chaos so pervasive and permanent that it has become an organizing principle. It is the weather of the city, a storm that never lets up.

Dhakaites will tell you that the rest of the world doesn't understand traffic, that the worst congestion in Mumbai or Cairo or Lagos
or Los Angeles is equivalent to a good day for Dhaka's drivers. There
is data that supports the claim. In the Global Liveability Index, a
quality-of-life report issued annually by the Economist Intelligence
Unit, Dhaka routinely ranks at or near the bottom of the 140 cities.
Its infrastructure rating has been the worst in the survey for a decade running.

Dhaka is home to nearly twenty-two million people. Yet it almost entirely lacks the amenities and rule of law that make big cities
navigable. Just 7 percent of the city's land is covered by roads. (In
places like Paris and Barcelona, models of nineteenth-century urban
planning, the number is 30 percent.) There are too few sidewalks in
Dhaka, and those that exist are often impassable, occupied by vendors and masses of poor citizens who make their homes in curbside
shanties. Pedestrians are forced out into the roadways to march
alongside vehicles, exacerbating the congestion. Dhaka has only
sixty traffic lights, and they are more or less ornamental—few drivers heed them. Intersections are manned by traffic cops, who gesture halfheartedly, like dancers running through desultory hand-jive
routines.

Fundamentally, traffic is an issue of density: it's what happens
when too many people try to squeeze through too small a space.
And density is the great Bangladeshi affliction. Bangladesh is the
twelfth most densely settled nation on earth, but with an estimated
164 million citizens, it is by far the most populous of the countries
at the top of the list. (The places that rank higher in density are
small, affluent city-states and island nations: Macau, Monaco, Singapore, Bahrain, Gibraltar, Hong Kong, Vatican City, etc.) To put
the matter in different terms: the landmass of Bangladesh is 1/118th
the size of Russia's, but its population exceeds Russia's by more than
20 million.

Bangladesh's density problem is magnified in Dhaka—in part
because, practically speaking, Dhaka is Bangladesh. Nearly all of

the country's government, business, healthcare, and educational institutions, and most of its jobs, are concentrated in Dhaka. Larger global and geopolitical forces are also to blame. Erosion from rising sea levels is devastating coastal Bangladesh and the Ganges River delta, driving an exodus of rural Bangladeshis to Dhaka's slums. The fact that Bangladesh itself emits just 0.3 percent of the greenhouse gases that are causing climate change is an academic point. The nations most responsible, like the United States and China, have shown little interest in one of the world's largest unfolding climate refugee crises. Each year, four hundred thousand migrants arrive in Dhaka—a relentless tide of humanity flooding the already inundated capital.

Those new Dhakaites find themselves in a city of contradictions and extremes. Dhaka's vitality—its thriving manufacturing sector, its growing middle class, its lively cultural and intellectual scene—is offset by misery and misrule: poverty, pollution, disease, crime, violence, municipal corruption and incompetence, and, at the level of national politics, a zero-sum battle between the ruling Awami League and the opposition Bangladesh Nationalist Party (BNP), a rivalry, commentators assert, that has forced Bangladeshi voters to choose between authoritarianism and extremism. The city is suffering—wilting—from the effects of climate change. A 2021 study by American researchers, published in the *Proceedings of the National Academy of Sciences,* determined that Dhaka is the world's worst affected city by "extreme heat exposure from both climate change and the urban heat island effect."

Yet it is traffic that has sealed Dhaka's reputation as a symbol of twenty-first-century urban dysfunction. Traffic has made Dhaka a surreal place, a town that is both frenetic and paralyzed, and has altered the rhythms of daily life. In 2015, a Dhaka newspaper published an article titled "5 Things to Do While Stuck in Traffic." Suggested activities included "catching up with friends," reading, and journaling.

My own journal begins on the Dhaka-Mymensingh Highway,

which runs south from Hazrat Shahjalal International Airport into the center of town. If you do a web search for this stretch of road, you may come across a Facebook page titled "Highway to Hell, Airport Road." Photographs posted online reveal the nature of the hell, aerial shots capturing a scrum of automobiles strewn at odd angles across eight lanes of road.

These images had me prepared for the worst. Yet on my flight to Dhaka I was told that traffic in the city would be unusually light. For weeks, Bangladesh had been gripped by a *hartal,* a nationwide general strike and "transportation blockade." The *hartal,* called by the BNP to protest the policies of the Awami League, had disrupted the capital, with street demonstrations and sporadic violence causing Dhaka's denizens to curb their normal routines. It had accomplished the seemingly impossible, breaking the logjam on Dhaka's streets. A Bangladeshi on my flight explained the situation. "In Dhaka, you have either horrible traffic or really horrible traffic," he said. "But with the *hartal,* there will be almost no traffic. Traffic will be okay."

Horrible traffic, really horrible traffic, almost no traffic, okay traffic. It takes just a few minutes in Dhaka to realize that these are not scientific terms. When my plane touched down I caught a taxi, which exited the airport into a roundabout before making its way onto the highway. There, unmistakably, was traffic: cars and trucks as far as the eye could see, stacked in a configuration that bore no clear relationship to the lane lines painted on the blacktop. My cab edged into the convoy and a crawl began.

The traffic rolled south for twenty seconds. The traffic stopped. We idled for a couple of minutes. Then, for mysterious reasons, we crept forward again. Occasionally, the traffic would run unimpeded for a minute or so, reaching a clip of perhaps fifteen miles per hour. But soon we would lurch to a halt again. It was the kind of stop-and-go routine I'd experienced on American interstates—the bumper-to-bumper conditions that traffic reporters detail on the radio, shouting something about a jackknifed tractor trailer over thumping helicopter blades. But there was no accident here. There was simply the inscrutable, indomitable phenomenon that everyone in Dhaka describes with an English monosyllable: a "jam."

In fact, Airport Road may be less plagued by jams than anywhere else in Dhaka. It is one of the city's best-maintained roadways, and one of the most shrewdly planned, with interchanges and overpasses that help ease the flow of traffic. It is when you leave the highway and gain the city proper that the bedlam of Dhaka presses in.

There are Dhaka's municipal buses, London-style red double-deckers of ancient 1970s vintage, which shudder along, spouting exhaust, looking like they might at any moment emit a last wheeze and topple over. There are privately owned bus coaches, too, so crammed with passengers that many are forced onto the exterior, clinging to open doorways or half-ejected through windows. Buzz-ing all around are the small vehicles that Dhakaites call CNGs, be-cause they run on compressed natural gas. They're auto-rickshaws of the kind you find across urban Asia: small metal boxes propped atop three wheels and divided into two tiny compartments, one for the driver and another, slightly larger but still a tight squeeze, for passengers. CNGs are painted forest green, nearly all of them are dirty and dinged up, and they make a lot of noise, snarling through the streets like junkyard dogs. They're ornery little machines, the barbaric cousins of golf carts.

I watched as my cabbie maneuvered through the swarm. It was an impressive performance, with a distinct vernacular flavor. Dha-ka's drivers may be the most aggressive on earth. They may also be some of the best, if your idea of skillful driving is expansive enough to include the lawlessness that Dhaka demands. The novelist K. Anis Ahmed, an acclaimed chronicler of life in Dhaka, has described the tricks practiced by local motorists:

> Juts and jags to fill up any bubble of navigable space that opened up, lane-cutting and lane-straddling, bivouacking through sup-posed shortcuts, light-bumping non-motorized vehicles, threat-ening to run over peddlers and pedestrians with a set of tires

rolled onto pavements, turning without signals into one-way streets, running red lights, and ignoring the sign language of the ill-paid traffic cops. . . . All the while one tried to drown out the protests of all competitors with the dumb, brutish, incessant bleating of their electric horns.

Some claim that Dhaka's name derives from the *dhak*, a big drum with a clattering sound. There's no mistaking the pounding that the city gives to your auditory nerves. Studies have determined that street noise in Dhaka on working days vastly exceeds the 70 decibels that the World Health Organization considers "extreme sound." Traffic is Dhaka's inescapable music, a theme song of groaning engines, braying horns, and bellowing motorists. Perhaps the cry most often heard from Dhaka's drivers is the Bengali word *aste*. "*As-tay, as-tay, as-tay!*" they shout, leaning on horns, shaking fists, pressing the gas pedal and plowing forward. Rough English translation: "Gently."

———

There is one form of transportation in Dhaka that might be deemed gentle, at least by the city's hard-as-nails standards: the three-wheeled, pedal-driven cycle rickshaw. Dhaka has been called the rickshaw capital of the world. The claim is probably justified, but the particulars of the matter are sketchy. There are about eighty thousand licensed rickshaws in Dhaka, but most of the rickshaws on Dhaka's roads are not officially accredited. Conservative estimates have put the number of rickshaws, legal and not quite, at around three hundred thousand; a 2019 study by the Bangladesh Institute of Labour Studies gave an estimate of 1.1 million. The sociologist Rob Gallagher, the author of a comprehensive study, *The Rickshaws of Bangladesh*, addressed the conundrum by invoking an Indian parable in which an adviser to the king, asked to identify the number of crows in the royal city, replied, "Well, sir, there are exactly

999,999." The courtier explained that if someone were to count the crows and find fewer than 999,999—that would mean that some crows had recently flown away. If, on the other hand, the figure were to come out to more than 999,999, the reason would be obvious: some crows are visiting from out of town.

There are lots of rickshaws in Dhaka, in other words, and to calculate the total is an impossible task. If we extend the count to encompass all the people who work in the rickshaw trade, the numbers grow astronomical, taking in well more than 999,999 souls, in a variety of satellite industries. (The Bangladesh Institute of Labour Studies report estimated that three million citizens of Dhaka subsist on income gained from rickshaw industry work.) There are the men who pedal the rickshaws, the so-called rickshaw pullers—in Bengali, *rickshawallahs*. There are the tradesmen who build and maintain and decorate the vehicles. There are roadside rickshaw mechanics and tire repairmen, and the other vendors who service rickshaw pullers from street corner stalls, ladling out cheap food and cups of sweet tea. There are the middlemen and the moneymen: the garage owners who rent out rickshaws and operate depots, and the low-level political bosses, police officers, and other bureaucrats who get a cut of the action, taking bribes and protection money at various levels of the rickshaw food chain.

In short, the Dhaka rickshaw game is a big business, and an essential one. The cycle rickshaw is by far the most popular form of public transport in Dhaka, a service patronized by nearly everyone in town, with the exception of the very rich and the desperately poor, a category that includes the *rickshawallahs* themselves. In 1992, Gallagher estimated that there were seven million passenger trips taken by rickshaw in Dhaka each day, covering a distance of eleven million miles. These totals, Gallagher noted, "nearly double the output of London's underground railway." In the decades since, Dhaka's population has more than tripled, and the statistics have surely spiked accordingly.

But numbers cannot convey how rickshaws dominate the cityscape. They are omnipresent—rarely out of sight and never out of earshot, even when unseen, their bicycle bells pealing above Dhaka's din like crazed songbirds. They move through the congested avenues and alleyways in multitudes, jostling and pitching alongside motorized traffic. The manner and extent to which rickshaws contribute to Dhaka's transport crisis is hotly disputed, but no one denies their iconic status—they are universally recognized as symbols of Bangladesh. They are simple, gearless machines, with a single wheel at the front and a chain drive that loops under a rear subframe to turn two rear wheels. The accommodations for the passenger are spartan: a cushioned seat, an adjustable hood, a footrest. Yet the rickshaws' colorful, elaborately adorned frames give them a queenly appearance.

There is another kind of cycle rickshaw in Dhaka, the cargo vehicles that locals call "rickshaw vans." These are tricycles, mounted with large wooden platforms, which transport towering piles of anything and everything: metal pipes, stalks of bamboo, watermelons, huge spools of cloth, cartons of eggs, propane tanks, jugs of water, garbage, live animals, groups of children commuting to and from school, day laborers heading to a work site. To the extent that Dhaka can be said to function at all, it is propelled by pedal power. When people or things travel from point A to point B in Dhaka—when a university student or a dozen two-hundred-pound sacks of rice make it through the gridlock and arrive at their destinations—you will usually find a man bent over the handlebars of a cycle rickshaw, hauling the load.

———

The bicycle is a beast of burden. For as long as bikes have existed, people have been stacking things on top of them and carting stuff around. In Karl von Drais's original 1817 design, the *Laufmaschine* had both a rear-mounted "luggage board" and fittings for panniers akin to those slung over the backs of packhorses. The various *Laufmaschine*-derived two-wheelers that appeared in the years immediately following Drais's invention likewise all featured cargo racks. The same is true of nearly every bicycle manufactured in the two centuries since. Bikes have front racks and rear racks and beam racks; cargo boxes and baskets; panniers and saddlebags; horizontally and vertically oriented carriers; trailers and sidecars that hitch to frames; holdalls that attach to the handlebars or mount in the back; seats and carts and platforms for transporting children. Of course, there are many varieties of bikes expressly designed as freight vehicles—"cycle trucks," *porteurs,* Long John bicycles, and other bikes whose frames, drivetrains, and wheelbases are engineered to accommodate payloads. The more remarkable fact, from an engineering standpoint, is that even the spindliest conventional bicycle will support a load of many times its own weight, assuming the stuff is properly balanced and secured. Bikes are built to schlep.

History has turned on this principle. On February 2, 1967, Senator William Fulbright of Arkansas convened a special hearing of the Senate Foreign Relations Committee on the state of the American intervention in Vietnam. The star witness was Harrison Salisbury, the assistant managing editor of *The New York Times,* who had recently returned from a trip to Hanoi. It was no secret that American forces were struggling in Vietnam, but Salisbury's testimony startled the committee. The United States was losing the war, he said, and it was being beaten by bicycles.

Salisbury told the senators that the North Vietnamese Army's supply chain—the munitions and matériel that flowed from north to south along the Ho Chi Minh Trail—was largely conducted using bicycles. The bikes were single-speed roadsters, manufactured in China. But the Vietcong reconfigured them. They widened the handlebars, welded broad platforms to the frames, and reinforced the suspensions, transforming the bicycles into rolling cargo pallets capable of bearing loads of several hundred pounds. They also wreathed the bikes in leaves, for camouflage. Traveling in teams of dozens, the bicycles could transport the same volume of supplies as trucks, and they were stealthier, nimbler, more maneuverable. American forces strafed the Ho Chi Minh Trail with Agent Orange to strip away the jungle cover; they bombed roads and bridges. But the bikes were hard to spot, and unlike larger vehicles, they could negotiate the narrow bamboo footbridges that the Vietcong had thrown up to replace those the Americans had destroyed. "I literally believe that without bikes [the North Vietnamese Army] would have to get out of the war," Salisbury told the Foreign Relations Committee. Senator Fulbright was incredulous: "Why don't we concentrate on bicycles?"

In fact, bicycles had been utilized as military supply vehicles since the nineteenth century. More widespread still was the commercial and industrial use of cargo bikes. "The corps of bicycle newspaper carriers in London, slipping, heavily loaded, with enormous rapidity and eel-like dexterity through the London traffic, is a never-failing source of wonder," wrote a British journalist in 1905. Such sights were becoming commonplace in the cities of Europe and North America at that time. It was another instance of bicycles taking over work previously done by horses: although a horse-drawn cart had greater freight capacity than a cargo bicycle, the difference in maintenance costs—the fact that bicycles were cheap and easy to store and didn't need to be fed—made them a good bargain for movers of low-bulk commodities like newspapers.

In Europe and the United States, the cargo cycle's heyday lasted some four decades, reaching a peak in Europe in the 1930s. This was the period of the butcher's bike and the baker's bike, of mail and milk deliveries by bicycle, of bicycle-borne fruit stands and patisseries, of knife sharpeners and glaziers pedaling around town towing mobile workstations. The trend was encouraged by the development of the cargo tricycle, whose extra wheel afforded greater stability. To ride these bikes and trikes required strength and stamina, and a culture of machismo developed among the tradesmen. In

France, newspaper-delivery cyclists faced off in events like the Critérium des Porteurs de Journaux, an annual competition in which "riders raced cargo tricycles loaded with up to 40 kg of ballast."

The use of cargo bicycles declined with the rise of motorized alternatives, first in the United States and then, after World War II, in Europe. Changes in commercial culture and the patterns of goods distribution also contributed to the cargo cycle's demise. But some freight bikes stuck around, even in those places most in thrall to automobiles. To this day, street vendors in American towns and cities sell ice cream, hot dogs, and other foodstuffs out of *triporteurs*, carrier tricycles with squat rectangular carts that sit between two front wheels. In the cycling meccas of northern Europe—especially the Netherlands and Scandinavia—cargo bikes remain a popular means of household transport.

The cult of Dutch- and Danish-style "cargo cruisers" has spread in recent years to city dwellers in the United States and western Europe. Cargo cruisers have two or three wheels, with long wheelbases and containers roomy enough to store all sorts of freight, including, often, child passengers. In the United States, especially, these cycles make a political statement: to choose a cargo bike as a family vehicle is to signal skepticism about car culture and an inclination toward progressive "European" values. Of course, the bikes are also markers of social class. Cargo cycles are expensive and, with their bulk, a bit ostentatious. They are status symbols, in other words, favored by the kinds of bourgeois bohemians who inhabit gracious urban neighborhoods lined with bike lanes. The history of the cargo cycle is a parable of gentrification: the manual laborer who hauled loads through the industrial city has become a knowledge worker pedaling genteel streets with a storage hold full of kids and kale.

But this is just part of the story. Elsewhere on the planet, commercial-freight cycling continues on a staggeringly vast scale. In South and East Asia, in Africa, in Latin America, millions of cargo bikes and trikes transport billions of pounds of goods and raw materials each day. The vehicles vary widely in type and design, according to local traditions, available materials, and the whims and improvisations of individuals. A common trait of all these bicycles and tricycles is their ability to hold loads of extraordinary size, which, invariably, is what they are called upon to do. The spectacle is familiar across the developing world: a solitary cyclist dwarfed by a payload of boxed goods or lumber or metal or textiles or you name it, piled to the height and breadth of a two-story house. It's a marvel and a sight gag. It is also an indelible image of human toil: a man moving a mountain.

The economics of cargo cycling are not well understood. It is clear that cargo bikes are woven into the informal economies of some of the world's largest cities, a crucial link in the proverbial "last mile" journey of consumer goods. But statistics point to a larger story. According to a recent estimate, there are "between 40–60 million working tricycles" in China alone. This astonishing figure exceeds by many times the combined worldwide tally of all other freight vehicles—trucks, trains, ships, and airplanes. The sheer number of cargo bikes, and their prominence in countries with large export markets such as China, India, and Bangladesh, suggests that the humble cycle may be playing a more integral role than we realize in the mechanics of global trade. Certainly the existence of a massive cycling workforce, pedaling for their bread on the streets of the Global South, exposes the provincialism of bicycle discourse in places like the United States, calling into question our quaint First World assumptions about bikes and biking. For millions in Dhaka and Chengdu and Lima and Kampala and elsewhere, the bicycle signifies labor not leisure, livelihood not "lifestyle" or "quality of life."

By some accounts, the most widespread form of freight cycling is the one devoted to human cargo. "The passenger-carrying cycle—in its various passenger rickshaw forms—is almost certainly the most numerous type of working cycle in existence today," wrote the scholars Peter Cox and Randy Rzewnicki in 2015. Cycle rickshaws serve vital public transit roles in several African nations; they can be found in large numbers in Latin America and the Caribbean, in places like Peru and Cuba. In recent years, cycle rickshaws have become a presence in European and American cities, mostly as a novelty aimed at sightseers. But Asia is the rickshaw heartland. Some rickshaws are configured like those in Dhaka, with the puller in front and the passenger seated behind; others have the opposite setup or situate the passengers beside the puller in a sidecar. They go by various names: *bikecab, pedicab, velotaxi, beca, becak, trishaw, trisikad.* Madagascar's rickshaw is the *cyclo-pousse*, Mexico's is the *bicitaxi*, Thailand's the *samlor.* The bicycle taxis of Malawi— technically not rickshaws at all but two-wheeled bikes with padded longtails that passengers straddle or ride sidesaddle—are called *Sacramentos*, an ironic moniker taken from the name of a bus company that is famous in Malawi for its comfortable coaches. The word "rickshaw" derives from the Japanese *jinrikisha*, "man-powered carriage," which cuts to the crux. All rickshaw passengers must reconcile themselves to the stark inhumanity of the arrangement, the fact that their comfortable travel inflicts strain and, often, suffering on another human being.

The rickshaw was invented in Japan, probably in 1869. It may initially have been conceived as a kind of wheelchair, a device for invalids, but it took hold as a means of transport. Early designs were primitive: a sedan chair resting on an axle, large wooden wheels, a pair of handles that the puller gripped to lug the contraption over the roads. The addition of ball bearings, rubber wheels, and other features improved the functionality, and by the late nineteenth century, rickshaws were features of urban life throughout East Asia and India.

From the start, they were controversial. They represented democracy, of a sort. In earlier times, elites were borne through the streets on litters; now the rickshaw made a nobleman of anyone who could afford a modest fare. Of course, that taste of luxury came, literally, on the back of the rickshaw puller, a fact that troubled consciences even in harshly class-stratified societies like British India and late Qing dynasty China. The development of the cycle rickshaw in the 1930s revolutionized the trade and made the puller's job less physically onerous. But it is still punishing work. For some critics, human-rights concerns trump all others: rickshaws are simply an anachronism, they insist, a vestige of the Age of Empire and of antiquated caste systems, with no place in the twenty-first century.

In Dhaka, the rickshaw's history tracked the larger historical pattern: hand-pulled rickshaws first reached the city in the late nineteenth century, and the pedal-driven kind arrived in the 1930s. Today, arguing about rickshaws is nearly as popular a pastime in Dhaka as riding them. Some contend that rickshaws are the machines best suited to negotiate the city's traffic-choked roads, and the most environmentally friendly. Others say they are inefficient, pointing out that four rickshaws rolling abreast take up the square footage of a bus while transporting just eight passengers. There are the familiar moral questions. Is rickshaw-pulling dignified work, a path out of abject poverty for some of Dhaka's most downtrodden? Or is it an abomination, a job that turns men into mules who bear crushing weight across blighted streets?

There have been various proposals to ban rickshaws in Dhaka, but these efforts have always been beaten back. Some intriguing arguments have been advanced in the rickshaw's favor. The researchers Shahnaz Huq-Hussain and Umme Habiba make a populist and feminist case, arguing that Dhaka's poor and middle class "are highly dependent on non-motorized transport" and that women especially "would be immobilized if it were not for the convenience, safety, security, and privacy afforded by the rickshaw." The rickshaw is often defended on sentimental grounds. Rickshaws are deeply entangled with the history and mythos of Dhaka, and they hold poignant associations for Dhakaites. For many, rickshaws are romantic: countless love affairs have blossomed, unnumbered furtive kisses have been shared, beneath the dropped hoods of cycle rickshaws.

Dhakaites also romanticize the men who pull the rickshaws,

which is curious given the intensity of the pity and disdain *ricksha-wallahs* inspire. The workforce is exclusively male and largely composed of migrants from the countryside. There are pullers as young as twelve years old, not surprising in a nation with an estimated five million child laborers. Many *rickshawallahs* work in Dhaka between the sowing season and the harvest, return to their home villages to work the land, and migrate back to Dhaka to repeat the cycle. Rickshaw pullers' living conditions are generally abysmal. Their health is often poor, and rates of drug abuse among *rickshawallahs* are high. The Covid pandemic brought new, deeper miseries, as Dhaka locked down and fares dried up, leaving *rickshawallahs* with virtually no income for months on end. The city came back to life in 2021, but competition got fiercer as thousands of new migrants, rural Bangladeshis who had lost their jobs during the pandemic, arrived in Dhaka and took to rickshaw-pulling. Ask a *rickshawallah* about the difficulties of the job and he will relate a woeful catalog: traffic accidents, bad weather, pollution, crime, police brutality, verbal and physical abuse by customers and passersby, low earnings—the list goes on.

The *rickshawallah* looms large in the Bangladeshi imagination. He is a heroic and pathetic figure, a perennial protagonist for writers and poets, and a ready all-purpose metaphor. The rickshaw puller is to Dhaka what the dockhand and the factory worker were to Victorian London: a proletarian everyman, embodying the dream and the nightmare, the ambitions and the degradations, of city life. In "Hafiz and Abdul Hafiz" (1994), the poet Mahbub Talukdar portrayed the *rickshawallah* as an Odysseus of Dhaka—a doomed nomad, traveling everywhere and going nowhere, stuck in an existential traffic jam.

> *I ply a rickshaw in the city of Dhaka,*
> *From Sadarghat to Nawabpur, Bangshal Road,*
> *Chawbazaar . . .*

The wheels of the rickshaw revolve along with the wheel of
time.
Time passes, but I remain in one place.

———

Mohammed Abul Badshah is not a poet, and I suspect he would put the matter differently. Badshah does not complain about remaining in one place, no matter how long he spends mired in jams. His problem is the opposite one: too much moving, too many miles, too many hours under the scorching sun and the lashing rain. Badshah has been pulling a rickshaw in Dhaka since 2008. He has crisscrossed the city thousands of times and reckons that he can picture nearly every road in his mind. When he sleeps, the streets, sights, and riotous traffic of Dhaka invade his dreams. He sometimes kicks himself awake at night, when his feet reach to turn phantom pedals.

Badshah was already forty-four years old when he began working as a *rickshawallah*. Now in his fifties, he is an old-timer, decades older than most of the men who pull rickshaws in Dhaka. His age tells, he says, in sore muscles. He says his legs are stronger than they have ever been, but they are wearier, too. His calves cramp; his back seizes up. When this happens, he does some stretching exercises and pushes through the pain. Sometimes, out on the road in bad traffic, tempers flare and coarse words about Badshah's age are thrown his way. Once, he had a confrontation with a young *rickshawallah* outside a medical center, where dozens of pullers were jostling in a queue, awaiting customers. The young man called Badshah "father-in-law," a grave insult. More curses were exchanged; there was a scuffle, and the young *rickshawallah* sank his teeth into the older man's right hand. The bite left a scar that Badshah displayed to me like a trophy. "I punched him and I slapped him," he said, grinning. "He stopped biting."

The first time I laid eyes on Badshah, he was in another queue of rickshaw pullers, this time in the busy Kawran Bazar district, in a little triangular area delineated by traffic barriers where the top of the Sonargaon Road meets a roundabout. It's a place that *rickshawallahs* referred to as "the Tigers," because of the large sculptures of a Bengal tiger and a tiger cub that stood there, on a raised platform. One August morning at 4 A.M., the larger of the two tigers, twenty-five feet long and made of concrete, came crashing down on top of a rickshaw van puller, pinning him to the ground and killing him. In the days following the accident, recriminations flew. The Dhaka South City Corporation, the local government body, cast blame on the company it had contracted to mount the statues, while the press and the public raised a hue and cry: the statue had been shoddily engineered and improperly maintained, and what's more, the tigers were hideous; they didn't look anything like real tigers. It was a textbook Dhaka kerfuffle—both tragedy and opéra bouffe.

But on the March day that I met Badshah, that mess lay months in the future. The monument was intact and, I thought, beautiful, in a garish way. The tiger sculptures looked like gigantic folk art tchotchkes, brightly painted and lavishly lacquered, with bared teeth and wild cartoon eyes. Below these creatures, a crowd of *rickshawallahs* milled around in the heat, attempting with varying degrees of aggression and apathy to scare up fares.

Badshah was one of the laid-back types. When I first saw him, he was sitting motionless on his rickshaw's passenger seat, impassive and regal. He might have passed for a statue in his own right. A translator I had hired to assist me with my reporting asked him to take me to Old Dhaka, and the two engaged in a gentle version of the ritual haggling that precedes all rickshaw rides. Visitors to Dhaka are often unaware that they're expected to bargain or perhaps are daunted by the prospect; but the failure to do so is a breach of etiquette and may be met by *rickshawallahs* with disdain, even though they stand to benefit, receiving their full asking price. As for Badshah: he handled the negotiation with a sense of ceremony, squinting into the distance while revising his rate as if calculating according to a precise system, which he may well have been. A price was settled on, I climbed into the rickshaw, and Badshah steered south toward Old Dhaka.

It was the first of many trips I took in Badshah's rickshaw. While we rode, I asked about his job and his life. Every so often, a trace of irony would steal into his tone and a hint of annoyance would flash in his eyes. It was clear that I'd asked him something dumb. If the conversation pointed in a direction even vaguely sentimental— a subject that seemed to demand some expression of piety or self-pity on Badshah's part—he would chuckle and wave it away. He didn't go in for that sort of thing. One day, Badshah pulled his rickshaw over to offer charity to a group of imams who were seated at curbside stands, soliciting funds for their mosques. When I inquired about his own religious practice, Badshah shrugged. "I am a Friday Muslim," he said.

The trip to Old Dhaka that morning was slow going, a two-mile-long creep in tight traffic. Badshah picked his way through jams on main arteries—Sonargaon Road, Shahbagh Road, Kazi Nazrul Islam Avenue—before moving onto narrow streets that were hemmed in on either side by five-story buildings. Overhead, criss-crossing electrical wires and laundry lines sliced the skyline. We were in Old Dhaka now. It is a historic place, the core of the city that arose during the period of the Mughal Empire and was proclaimed the capital of Mughal Bengal in the early seventeenth century. Today it is a maze of roads and alleyways that wend along the northern banks of the Buriganga River. The area retains a medieval flavor: bustling marketplaces, wafting scents of chilies and fish and raw meat, pedestrians everywhere darting and yelling, clanging sounds from storefront workshops. Horse-drawn "tomtom" carts roll in the streets, and untethered dogs, goats, and cows wander freely. Along the Buriganga waterfront are more scenes of commotion and commerce, thousands of passengers boarding and disembarking from ferryboats on the wharves of Sadarghat, one of the world's largest and busiest river ports. In Dhaka, waterways offer no relief from traffic.

In recent years, Dhaka has instituted regulations barring non-motorized vehicles from certain thoroughfares. While these rules are often ignored, they have reduced the number of rickshaws on some of the city's most traveled streets. But 85 percent of Dhaka's roads are too small to accommodate large motor vehicles, and rickshaws predominate. In the labyrinths of Old Dhaka, there are legions of them. They jockey for running room in conditions more clotted than anywhere in the city.

Rickshaw-pulling is rugged work, a contact sport. On Dhaka's chockablock streets, rickshaws knock and scrape; a newly built rickshaw that sets out, gleaming, will end its first working day scuffed like a jalopy. Pullers develop repertoires of moves, dips and swerves and quick stops, to avert crashes. But they also learn to collide on purpose, aiming their wheels at other vehicles to bash their way through. Badshah's means of gaining clearance in packed conditions resembles an American football stiff-arm: a reach and a shove, executed instinctively and fluidly, while his legs pump the pedals. I saw him do this several times in the gauntlet of Old Dhaka, stretching to push back at rickshaws that had veered too close for his liking or were inhibiting his progress. Once, on a road near the Chawk Bazar, a famous Mughal-era market, Badshah performed this maneuver on the hindquarters of a cow that had taken up a languid position in the middle of the road, indifferent to the traffic seething on all sides.

As rickshaw pullers go, Badshah is mild-mannered. He does little yelling or mouthing off and generally shies from conflict, the occasional brawl outside a medical center notwithstanding. His bursts of aggression are tactical and professional. Once, in central Dhaka, we found ourselves in a frustrating jam, marooned for several minutes in an unmoving column on a side street called Garden Road. At last, the jam dissolved and wheels began to roll, but the rickshaw directly in front of us remained motionless. This would not do. So Badshah bulldozed forward, ramming his front wheel several times into the rickshaw's rear bumper, delivering a series of vehement jolts. It was a collegial gesture: one guildsman telling another to get with the program, to look alive.

Even when rickshaws aren't crashing into each other, there are no smooth rides. In Old Dhaka and in the city's vast slums, the roadways are poorly paved or unpaved. Rickshaws must navigate rutted dirt paths and streets strewn with garbage and broken concrete. In the monsoon season, roads become lakes; when the floodwaters recede, feet-deep mud is left behind. Often, pedal power isn't sufficient to produce momentum, and rickshaw pullers are forced to dismount and, indeed, pull—dragging the vehicle by the handlebars through slop, up inclines, across potholes, over rubble.

But even the most immaculate road would pose difficulties for a *rickshawallah*. The Dhaka rickshaw is a lemon, an engineering disaster. Experts have concluded that the machines are "overweight yet lacking in strength and reliability, poorly braked, unstable, difficult to steer and, because they have no gears, hard work to propel." Elsewhere in Asia, cycle rickshaws that make use of small motors and battery power are reducing the physical torment of rickshaw-pulling. But Dhaka is lagging behind. There are thought to be thirty or forty thousand battery-powered "easy bikes" on the city's streets, but they are operating in defiance of a ban imposed in 2015 by Bangladesh's High Court, and authorities have seized and destroyed thousands of them. In June 2021, Asaduzzaman Khan, the Bangladeshi Home Minister, redoubled the government's anti–easy bike stance, announcing a new ban on the machines on the grounds that they are "very risky" and cause accidents. The rickshaw capital of the world is a bastion of rickshaw traditionalism, to the detriment of its *rickshawallahs*.

Badshah performs the grueling routines of pedaling and pulling, dismounting and remounting, with impressive spryness. When he isn't riding the rickshaw—when he stops at a roadside stall for a cup of tea or a plate of food—his eyes cloud over, and his body goes limp with exhaustion. But on the road, he is a picture of keenness and efficiency. Once, as we entered a small roundabout in fast-moving traffic in Old Dhaka, Badshah swerved violently to an outside position, a lurching lane change that shot us laterally through a tiny opening between two hard-charging rickshaws, with maybe an inch to spare on either side. A second later, the reason for this move became clear: a cop was stationed in the center of the traffic circle, urging *rickshawallahs* along by swatting at them with a wooden baton. I must have let out a gasp, because Badshah started laughing and threw me a glance over his shoulder. He was amused by my greenhorn ways. I was an American and a journalist, in theory far worldlier than Badshah, an uneducated man who almost certainly will never set foot outside Bangladesh. But Dhaka had made my eyes go wide. "It's a crazy city," Badshah said. "It's a crazy job."

———

He was born in the countryside, in a small village in the Barisal District of what was then East Pakistan, where his family had a small patch of land. His father worked in a rice mill. In 1971, Badshah's family was among the forty million Bengalis displaced by a cataclysm: the Pakistani military junta's genocidal crackdown on Bengali nationalists, a campaign that led to the Bangladesh Liberation War. The Badshahs fled to Dhaka. The city was hardly a safe haven. It was the site of some of the worst violence of the war, including the event that had instigated the conflict, the massacre of students and staff at Dhaka University on March 25, 1971. But it was preferable to settle in among Dhaka's crowds than to sit vulnerable in the sparsely settled countryside. Young Mohammed Abul Badshah was seven years old when the family arrived in the city. Today, Badshah still speaks Bengali with an accent that betrays his Barisal origins. But the decades he's spent in Dhaka distinguish him from the recent rural migrants who pull rickshaws, and must in part account for his cool in the face of the city's maelstrom. When Bangladesh gained its independence, on December 16, 1971, Dhaka's population was just over one million. Badshah grew up along with Dhaka, watching its transformation from backwater to megacity. His internal metronome long ago fell into sync with Dhaka's antic tempo.

His schooling ended at age seven, with the move to Dhaka. He went to work, earning small sums as an errand boy in street markets and scaring up other odd jobs when possible. In his late teens, Badshah found work on an assembly line in a ballpoint-pen factory, a job he kept for several years. At twenty-five, he married Shahnaz, a teenage girl from his home village whose family had recently arrived in Dhaka. They soon had a daughter and moved south, to the coastal city of Chittagong, where Badshah scrapped out a living hawking clothes. He disliked the work and missed Dhaka. After five years, the couple returned to the capital, now with three daughters in tow.

It was then that Badshah first began pedaling rickshaws. For several years, he sold ceramic items, mostly plates and bowls, off the back of a cycle van. It was a good experience, but not good business. "I learned to pull the rickshaw, I learned some roads," Badshah said. "But there is no money in selling these things."

Badshah is a handsome man with lively dark eyes. He has thinning brown hair and a neatly trimmed white mustache that arcs over his upper lip. His smile reveals several missing teeth. He typically wears a *lungi,* the traditional sarong-like cloth wrap that is knotted at the waist, and a loose-fitting oxford shirt. When Badshah rides the rickshaw in the midday heat, he ties a cotton scarf over his head to keep cool.

He is gaunt, as nearly all *rickshawallahs* are, a testament to the cruel mathematics of the job, the lopsided ratio of calories expended to calories taken in. Effectively, rickshaw pullers earn a starvation wage: an insufficient amount to meet their costs of living while maintaining a healthy body weight. The problem is widespread in Bangladesh. Billboards and television advertisements in Dhaka tout the professional and romantic benefits of "weight gainer" supplements. (GAINED WEIGHT . . . GOT MY SOULMATE! THANK YOU,

ENDURA MASS!) The ubiquity of cycle rickshaws ensures that abject poverty is never out of sight in Dhaka, even in the upscale neighborhoods—Uttara, Lalmatia, Gulshan, lake-front Baridhara—where the city's well-to-do retreat to fine homes. Everywhere, always, there are *rickshawallahs,* presenting a feudal spectacle: convoys of the emaciated, struggling and straining while healthier, better-fed passengers sit back at their ease. Writers have likened the bodies of *rickshawallahs* to skeletons and vultures. "We eke out our living in this country / Men laboring like cows and horses," wrote the poet Dilip Sarkar in "The Rickshawallah's Song." "We pull this human burden on our backs, / To calm the burning in our stomachs / To get two square meals a day."

Badshah rides the rickshaw from ten in the morning to eight at night, every day but Friday. He averages between fifteen and twenty fares per day, earning about four hundred Bangladeshi taka, roughly five dollars. His spends fifty-five taka a day on food and drink at roadside stalls: forty for a simple meal of rice, vegetables, and fish, and an additional fifteen on three teas, one revitalizing cup every few hours, at five taka each. On especially good days, he can net six hundred taka, a bit more than seven dollars. It's very little money, but it's the best living he's made. Badshah doesn't know how to read, and the only word he can write is his family name. He remembers enjoying his first day as a *rickshawallah,* but has liked the work less each day since. He continues at it, he says, because he has no better options. "I will pull the rickshaw for many more years," he said. "It is the best job I can do."

Workdays end with a crawl home. Badshah lives in Kamrangirchar, a peninsula on the Buriganga River that holds Dhaka's largest concentration of slums. An estimated four hundred thousand people inhabit an area of just over one and a half square miles. Many live in conditions akin to those in refugee camps, crowded into shacks that sit atop dirt floors, with walls and roofs patched together from corrugated metal, wood, thatch, pieces of linoleum, plastic tarps. Rates of malnutrition and infant mortality in Kamrangirchar are high; skin afflictions, diarrhea, and respiratory ailments are rampant. In 2014, a spokesman for Doctors Without Borders called Kamrangirchar "one of the most polluted places on the planet."

The neighborhood was formerly a public landfill, and when you cross the bridge that links the southeastern end of the peninsula with Old Dhaka, the stench of garbage and sewage hovers heavily. Along the Buriganga banks, huge dumping grounds remain. Ragpickers—women and children, mostly—sort through the rubbish, scavenging plastic recyclables and other scraps for resale. Acrid trash fires burn in the riverside dumps and in the streets and alleys of Kamrangirchar, where residents cook meals over open fires kindled with whatever flammable stuff is at hand, wood or paper or plastic.

The water that sloshes the Kamrangirchar shoreline is filthy. From the river's edge you gaze down on a toxic goulash: vast flotillas of garbage riding a viscous brown-green current. Nevertheless, many people in Kamrangirchar wade into the river to bathe and to wash their clothes. For decades, a main source of contamination were the dozens of leather tanneries situated just downriver from Kamrangirchar, which disgorged hundreds of gallons of pollutants into the Buriganga everyday. The government finally intervened in the spring of 2017, forcing the tanneries to relocate to a suburb northwest of the city. But industrial pollution is still a scourge in Kamrangirchar. The neighborhood is home to hundreds of small-scale factories—plastics and electronics recyclers, aluminum casters, smelters, manufacturers of car batteries and PVC drums and balloons. These businesses operate virtually unregulated, exposing workers to hazardous conditions while spilling poisons into the air and the groundwater. In many factories, the workers are children as young as six. Kamrangirchar's blight is a local problem, but its causes lie far away. Like the billions of dollars' worth of garments made by workers toiling in Dhaka's sweatshops, many products manufactured in Kamrangirchar's factories, like balloons, are shipped overseas. Meanwhile, a large portion of the toxic e-waste and plastics that are recycled in Kamrangirchar flows into Bangladesh from distant places, including the United States. Dhaka is where the world does much of its dirty work.

Badshah's living situation is better than most in Kamrangirchar. His home is in Boro Gram, a dingy but vibrant market area in the center of the peninsula. To reach his house, you slip through an arched entrance on a busy shopping street and head down an alleyway that tapers, fifty yards on, to a passage flanked on either side by small one-room dwellings. Space here is tight. There are seven homes in total, and those seven households share a single toilet, a shower, and a stove, open to the air. The passage separating Badshah's home from his neighbor's facing door is just a couple of feet across; when residents heading in opposite directions meet in the passage they must flatten their bodies against the walls to slide past. It isn't easy living, but it's not squalid, and the atmosphere, for Kamrangirchar, is serene. In the alley, Dhaka's clamor fades to a faint background howl, giving way to local sounds, homely domestic music: clanking pots; children shouting and singing; family arguments; someone hammering on metal, repairing a broken chair.

The buildings in the alley are decently built. Badshah's home has concrete floors and walls and a sheet-metal roof that rarely leaks, even during the monsoon season. The house is wired for electricity and cooled in hot weather by a ceiling fan. It is a tiny place, a windowless box of about 150 square feet. Most of the space is occupied by a large bed. In one corner there is an old-fashioned sewing machine, powered by a foot treadle. (Shahnaz, Badshah's wife, brings in extra money by working as a seamstress.) On a cabinet at the foot of the bed sits a fifteen-inch television that flickers at all hours, showing Indian soap operas or cricket matches or whatever else happens to be on. There are a couple of shelves, packed with clothing and kitchen implements. The walls are painted a pretty shade of light green. The rent costs 3,000 taka per month.

The family has lived in this home for eighteen years. There was a time when the room was home to six people, but now Badshah's three eldest daughters, all in their twenties, have married, freeing up elbow room and easing Badshah's financial burden. One child remains in the house: Faima, a shy, bright girl of twelve. Faima is a good student and has progressed further in school than anyone else in her family. (Her sisters all dropped out after grade five, at age eleven.) In another year, when Faima is thirteen, she will finish grade eight, and it is a foregone conclusion that her schooling will end then. I asked Badshah what Faima will do when she stops attending school. He said that she will probably help out at home and then go to work, perhaps in a garment factory, as her sisters had prior to their marriages. In all likelihood, he said, Faima, too, will marry before long. I asked if there was any chance that Faima would continue her studies. She had already defied the odds. In recent decades, Bangladesh has made progress in public education, increasing rates of primary and secondary school enrollment, especially among girls. Yet more than half the children in Dhaka's slums never attend school. With persistence, Faima could go on to complete her secondary schooling and might even attend a university. But such possibilities seemed to Badshah too remote to entertain. Maybe his grandchildren would be able to go to a university, he said.

He has five grandchildren, and counting. His eldest daughter, twenty-five-year-old Yasmin, lives nearby in Kamrangirchar with her husband and three children; two others, Nazma, twenty-three, and Asma, twenty-two, live just outside Dhaka. Badshah does not conceal his pride in his children. His daughters are intelligent, he says, and hardworking, and sensible. He takes a dimmer view of his sons-in-law. Yasmin's husband, in particular, is a sore point. For years he worked at a factory making wall clocks, but for the past few years he has pulled a rickshaw. It hasn't gone well. Badshah said: "He isn't really a working type guy." On two occasions, Badshah gave him money to buy used rickshaws, but each time the son-in-law wound up reselling the machines when he ran short of cash. He currently pulls a rented rickshaw, and he complains bitterly about the hardships of the job. "It's not a good job for him," Badshah said. "He should go back to clocks."

Badshah's own rickshaw was a gift from his daughter Asma, who bought it used, for 7,000 taka, with money she had saved from her job at a garment factory. It is by far the most valuable piece of property Badshah owns. Rickshaws are expensive and highly coveted. A new rickshaw costs 25,000 taka, well beyond the means of most pullers, who purchase used machines or, more often, rent them from garages for 100 taka per day. There is a brisk black-market trade, and *rickshawallahs* must remain alert to the risk of theft. A puller who wanders a few steps too far from his parked machine may look up to see three wheels disappearing in the distance. Rickshaws have been hijacked at knifepoint in broad daylight; the weapon of choice for some thieves is Tiger Balm, the chili-based muscle rub, which they smear on their victims' eyes to disable them. To have a rickshaw stolen can be ruinous. Badshah found this out a few years ago when he picked up a crook posing as a plainclothes police officer. When Badshah pedaled past a traffic cop, the passenger politely asked him to pull over and run twenty yards back down the street to fetch his uniformed "colleague." By the time Badshah reached the traffic cop, the impostor had moved from the rickshaw's passenger seat to its saddle and pedaled away, vanishing into the throng. Suddenly, Badshah had no rickshaw and a monstrous debt— the cost of the stolen vehicle, which he had to repay, at an extortionate rate, to the garage owner from whom he'd been renting.

It was then that Asma emptied her savings to buy her father the used rickshaw. Badshah has been pulling that rickshaw ever since. He keeps the machine at a garage in Kamrangirchar, not far from his home. Dhaka's thousands of rickshaw garages function as depots, safeguarding vehicles for a fee. (Badshah pays 200 taka per month.) Nearly all garage owners maintain their own fleets of rental rickshaws. Some garages offer lodging to *rickshawallahs*. These accommodations, called *tongs*, are crudely constructed scrap boxes, often set on bamboo pilings above the rows of parked vehicles. Here, *rickshawallahs* sleep wall to wall in what amounts to an urban campsite. Typically garage owners provide this housing gratis, in exchange for a puller's rental business. For a garage owner, the arrangement carries a fringe benefit: the lodgers serve as a security service, guarding against thieves, who are known to strike rickshaw depots overnight.

The garage where Badshah stows his rickshaw is on the smaller side, a ramshackle rectangular lot that provides storage for fifty or so vehicles, including its home stable of a dozen. I went there with Badshah on a sultry afternoon when temperatures in the mid-nineties pressed down on dusty, malodorous Kamrangirchar and the whole neighborhood seemed to be drooping. The exception was the owner of the rickshaw garage, who was so spirited that the heavy air around him practically pulsated. He was a middle-aged man, about Badshah's age, with a potbelly, close-cropped salt-and-pepper hair, and a sprouting of stubble on his cheeks and chin. He wore a sweat-stained brown shirt unbuttoned halfway down his torso; his fingers were caked in bike-chain grease. The only time he stopped smiling, oddly, was when I asked him to pose for a photograph.

He's a decent man, Badshah told me, more honest than other garage owners. This didn't mean he wasn't a bullshitter. He was slick, in the manner of a politician on the stump, greeting each new visitor to the garage like a long-lost relative. It's the kind of exaggerated bonhomie that warms some people's hearts and prompts others to keep a hand on their wallets. He was a businessman, in other words, and a successful one, by Kamrangirchar's standards. Like many garage owners, he was a former *rickshawallah* who had purchased one used rickshaw, then another, and eventually graduated from wage slave to entrepreneur.

Seated to his left under the sheet-metal roof that covered the front half of the garage lot was a *rickshawallah* with a full beard and a grave countenance who appeared to inhabit his own spiritual microclimate. He was a man enveloped by black clouds. He looked physically stronger than most *rickshawallahs*, huskier and better fed. But his shoulders slumped, and his whole being seemed to have been dragged downward by melancholy. Badshah settled in alongside the two men, and they fell into conversation. They made an odd trio. The garage owner was garrulous and upbeat; the bearded man, brooding and lacerating; Badshah, a mostly silent observer, offering little more than the occasional grunt or head shake. I asked them about the state of the rickshaw trade. "It's a good business," the garage owner said. "It's not so bad. For years I pulled a rickshaw. And now look. I own many rickshaws." I asked about the public image of *rickshawallahs*, about the way they are treated by their customers. The garage owner said, "The customers are not so bad. They are usually respectful. We are respected. The day that there are no more rickshaws—everyone knows, on that day there will be no more Bangladesh."

But the bearded man was having none of it. Most rickshaw riders are middle-class people, sometimes very rich people, and they look at pullers as the lowest of the low, he said. Passengers hurl insults and call names; sometimes they even beat *rickshawallahs*, knowing there are no consequences for doing so. Often the riders stiff *rickshawallahs* for their fares, refusing to pay the amount they had negotiated at the beginning of the trip.

The bearded man was reciting a litany now. The work is too dangerous. The roads are in terrible shape, there are accidents all the time, traffic is horrible, rickshaw pullers are injured and killed. A bus driver, a guy in a CNG, they will run over a rickshaw and drive away without thinking twice. Dhaka is full of crime—muggings, hijackings, bombings, murder. Nothing you see in the street surprises you. The police are corrupt. They'll beat you, they'll puncture your tires, they'll rip out the passenger seat of your rickshaw so you cannot work. There is no legal place to park your rickshaw in Dhaka, and at any time the police can decide you've pulled over in the wrong spot and impose a fine, or worse. In fact, they'll fine you for any little thing; if you've done nothing wrong, they'll make something up. It's terrible. You can't make a living like this.

The bearded man's voice had risen; he was thundering like a prophet. The garage owner let out a laugh and threw up his hands in exasperation. Badshah just sighed and shook his head, and it was impossible to tell who or what he was disagreeing with, or if he was disagreeing at all.

———

Dhaka's rickshaws are known around the world as objets d'art. Their frames carry colorful paintings and elaborate ornamentation; they have been called "moving museums." Nearly all the rickshaws you see in Dhaka are battered, with chipped paint and fraying appliqués. But their mystique is inseparable from their weather-beaten appearance, and from the way they rattle and judder as they travel. They have a funky majesty.

Dhaka's rickshaw-building mecca is Bangshal Road, a slender strip that runs east to west through the commercial heart of Old Dhaka. There, you can catch a rare glimpse of rickshaws in pristine condition and view the various phases of rickshaw construction: workers welding the iron chassis, bending bamboo to hold the hoods that shield passengers from the sun and the rain, fixing tinsel and tassels to handlebars. There are little workshops where artisans wrap plywood seatbacks with bright plastic, hammer decorative nails, sew hood coverings, and festoon the hood coverings with beads and sequins.

And there are the rickshaw painters, whose work covers the frames. Observers of the rickshaw business will tell you that frame painting is a dying art: before long, they say, cycle rickshaws will bear mass-produced images and signage. But for now, painters still ply their trade on Bangshal Road. Their specialty is back-plate work, paintings in lurid shades that are fixed to the vehicles' rear bumpers. These take on a variety of themes. There are portraits of Bollywood movie stars and other celebrities, like Barack and Michelle Obama. There are images of beautiful women whose drowsy, half-lidded eyes stare back seductively—or is it indifferently? There are historical panoramas. A popular subject is the 1971 Liberation War: battle scenes, heroic freedom fighters on the march, grisly depictions of Pakistani army officers assaulting Bangladeshi women and girls. There are images of animals, avian and floral motifs, slogans and religious maxims rendered in ornate Bengali script. There are pastoral tableaux—soaring mountains, idyllic villages, swans drifting on lakes spangled with moonbeams. And there are pictures of cities. The back-plate painting on Badshah's rickshaw shows a dreamy cityscape, with a sunset blazing above turreted towers and an enormous domed building that resembles the Taj Mahal. Beneath these edifices is a road unlike any you'll find in Dhaka. It is tidy, tranquil, and entirely traffic-free.

One day I climbed into Badshah's rickshaw and he pedaled to the University of Dhaka, where I had an appointment with a man named Syed Manzoorul Islam, a novelist and a critic who is an English professor at the university. He is a shrewd observer of Bangladeshi politics and culture, and he has written perceptively about rickshaws and rickshaw pullers.

For a student of *rickshawallahs* and their folkways, Islam's office is well located. The university sits in the center of town, in the Shahbagh district, a kind of borderland between Old Dhaka and the newer parts of the city. The traffic situation here is not bad. On Nilkhet Road, Shahbagh's main east-west thoroughfare, the procession of rickshaws and motor vehicles flows thick, but it flows; the streets rarely jam up. Most rickshaws pass over these roads a couple of times a day. The university campus itself is pleasant and quiet, shaded by massive trees. It is a popular *rickshawallah* gathering spot, a place to eat, socialize, and rest. There are rickshaw repairmen here, and food and tea vendors. Badshah told me that he sometimes detours to the campus to take a nap, and when we turned off Nilkhet Road and came to a stop just inside the university's main gate, I saw a half dozen sleeping *rickshawallahs*. They had pulled their rickshaws to the side of the campus driveway and draped their bodies across the vehicles: heads resting on the passenger seats, legs stretched over saddles, feet propped on handlebars.

Chaos can intrude in Dhaka's most peaceful places. Just five hundred yards east along Nilkhet Road lay the traffic circle where, in 2015, the Bangladeshi-American writer Avijit Roy was murdered by militants from the Islamic extremist group Ansarullah Bangla Team. Roy, an atheist and a free-speech activist, was sitting with his wife in a cycle rickshaw when he was ambushed by men armed with machetes. On our ride to the university, Badshah pointed out the site of a memorial that had sprung up after the attack. But now, inside the campus gates, the wildness of the city seemed remote. The day was sweltering, but the campus had its own weather. Mahogany, tamarind, and rain trees stretched overhead to form a cooling canopy. Their boughs bent in the breeze, waving above the dozing *rickshawallahs* like the wings of gigantic, beneficent birds.

Badshah had no plans to nap that day. An afternoon's work lay ahead of him. Later he might make his way back to the university area and stop for a cup of tea. Perhaps we would run into each other then, he said. For now, it was goodbye. He shook my hand, gripped the handlebars of his rickshaw, and walked the machine back through the university gates, onto Nilkhet Road.

Once a rickshaw has come to a standstill, it is not easy to get the thing moving again. To start the wheels rolling, Badshah lowered his back and shoved, like a man launching a rowboat from a muddy riverbank. He then swung his right leg over the saddle, stood upright on the pedals, and began pedaling. Slowly, the rickshaw gained speed. I watched Badshah glide into the traffic, and I kept my gaze fixed on him for another thirty seconds or so, until I could no longer pick out his slender form and striped shirt among the rickshaws and *rickshawallahs* that had enveloped him, six hundred or so wheels turning beneath two hundred or so men, streaming east on Nilkhet Road. They were moving toward the intersection of Kazi Nazrul Islam Avenue, exiting the relative calm of the university zone and heading back to some of Dhaka's unruliest streets, a river emptying into a roiling sea.

————

I found Syed Manzoorul Islam's office up two flights of stairs in the Faculty of Arts building. Islam is one of Bangladesh's most esteemed intellectuals. He looks and sounds the part. He is a small man with sparse salt-and-pepper hair, a mustache, and searching eyes framed by wire-rimmed glasses. He's one of those preposterously erudite people who seem to have inhaled all history and literature, and mastered countless more arcane subjects as well. He can whip from a disquisition on Dickens to a discussion of bicycle mudguards. His office was crammed with books, stacked in teetering piles, which appeared to have been introduced to the room by a bulldozer.

One of Islam's favorite topics of conversation is Dhaka and its discontents. In this, he is not alone. "Nowhere else do people talk as much about their city," Islam said. "Everyone in Dhaka discusses Dhaka endlessly. Everyone finds faults. There are many faults to find." When Islam looks at Dhaka, he sees shocking depths of governmental ineptitude and venality. He sees the legacy of colonialism and war, and the cruelty of the global economy. He sees a city that visits indignities on the daily lives of its most privileged citizens and afflicts its least fortunate with intolerable suffering.

But Islam also looks at Dhaka and sees a new world coming into view. "Of course Dhaka is a mess. But there are great changes happening here. Women are putting behind the shackles of family obligations and patriarchal considerations. Everywhere, women are working. They are taking charge of their own lives and their own bodies. In fact, I'm not so worried about the messiness of the city. I'm more worried about what people are doing with their lives. How are they taking stock of their lives? Are the people of Dhaka becoming stakeholders in the city? Are they simply passing shadows? No, these people are owners of the city, and they are clamoring. I see Dhaka as a restless city. A city of vitality. This is a place where the future lies."

Whether that future will include rickshaws is one of the questions Dhakaites debate ad nauseam. The garage owner had his opinion: the day there are no more rickshaws, there will be no more Bangladesh. Islam takes a different view. Eventually, more efficient mass transit will arrive in Dhaka, immeasurably improving the lives of the city's citizens. What will be lost when the rickshaw goes, Islam says, is a talisman. "Rickshaws embody tradition," he said. For the millions who labor in the garment factories and on the construction sites of the globalized "new Dhaka," rickshaws are comforting relics. They are reminders, Islam has written, of the "form of life threatened by the chaos and alienation" of the twenty-first-century megacity. The *rickshawallah* tows two hundred pounds of wood, rubber, and steel, and hundreds more pounds of human cargo. And he carries the weight of collective nostalgia.

Nostalgia is inscribed in the images that adorn the vehicles themselves. Like rickshaw pullers, most rickshaw painters are migrants from rural Bangladesh, and their artworks—those blooming flowers and verdant fields and tender scenes of village life—hold visions of a world left behind. More curious are the urban panoramas, like the one on Badshah's rickshaw, with its elegant towers and improbably orderly streets. Islam has published studies of rickshaw painting. He told me that the image on Badshah's back plate is typical of rickshaw cityscapes.

He said: "When you look at these pictures, you have to ask yourself: What city is this? Usually, it's a city that looks a bit like Singapore, a very beautifully designed city with tall buildings. Often, the paintings will also show a plane, either taking off or landing. The roads are absolutely quiet, without any transport. Maybe one or two cars. It's a city with fantastic traffic regulations, a city with discipline. Rickshaw pullers, more than anyone, realize the importance of discipline on the roads. They are the victims of indiscipline, of a city with an insane traffic system, where no municipal rule exists. And so these paintings show a fantasy city, a soft city, a disciplined city. It is the imaginary city that everyone carries in their mind when they migrate to Dhaka."

Islam said: "I think this also explains the images of planes. That's the highest level of transport, isn't it? In the mind of the rickshaw puller, maybe, that represents a different kind of fantasy. It is an aspiration, a dream of the future. *If I do this backbreaking work—if I pull this rickshaw in this unyielding, insane city—perhaps then someday my children will fly in that plane.*"

13

PERSONAL HISTORY

The author and his son. Brooklyn, 2018.

I. First Ride

A cycling life begins in a blaze of glory. For hours or days or weeks, you still don't know how to ride a bicycle. You wobble and lurch and wipe out, locked in a pitiful struggle with the pull of gravity and the weight and waywardness of the obstreperous metal machine. Then, suddenly, you are breezing along a road that stretches toward a limitless horizon. Or maybe, more likely, you're pedaling in circles on a schoolyard blacktop. In any case, you're riding a bike. There are few transitions in life more abrupt and definitive: you're not a cyclist, then you are. The skill that eluded you moments earlier is now magically assimilated, and nothing short of blunt brain trauma or a neurological disaster will shake it loose.

In recent years, researchers have gained a greater understanding of the processes that guide our mastery of bike riding. Scientists have identified a nerve cell, the molecular layer interneuron, that controls signal output from the cerebellum, which translates a newly learned motor skill like cycling into a code that is engraved as memory elsewhere in the brain. It is an example of so-called procedural memory: like walking or talking or tying your shoelaces, bike riding is a motor function that, once learned, we can perform automatically, without recourse to conscious thought. In fact, cycling is the most famous example of procedural memory. "It's just like riding a bike," we say, describing something that becomes second nature, an activity we can pick up where were left off, no matter how much time has elapsed.

Most people learn to cycle when they are young. Just as "you never forget how to ride a bicycle," you never forget your first bicycle ride, or so we are told. Proverbially, a child's first bike ride brings an exhilarating taste of freedom and autonomy, a preview of the great escape that lies a dozen or so years further down the road. The first ride enacts the flight from the clutches of adult caretakers, when the kid pedals away from the grown-up who has been steadying the bike with a grip on the underside of the saddle. The French writer Paul Fournel, one of the bicycle's most lyrical chroniclers, described the thrill of his first ride: "One morning I no longer heard the sound of someone running behind me, the sound of rhythmic breathing at my back. The miracle had taken place."

Dramatizations of this "miracle" are familiar from movies, television, and advertisements, which for decades have portrayed the bicycle as an emblem of childhood. In the postwar United States, the historian Robert Turpin has written, "so pervasive was the idea that bicycles and children belonged to each other that there was little room for anyone else." The notion that learning to ride a bike was a rite of passage akin to learning to walk or read was promulgated by the bicycle industry, which, having lost adult cyclists to automobiles, recast bikes as a mandatory purchase for parents, essential to the physical and moral growth of children, especially boys. As one California bike merchant put it: "Nothing equals the bicycle as a developer of sturdy bodies, strong lungs, ruddy cheeks, bright eyes, and self-reliance in your growing boy."

There is a famous *Saturday Evening Post* cover illustration that captures a wholesome scene. *Bike Riding Lesson* (1954), by the artist George Hughes, shows a young boy on a bicycle careening down a leafy residential street while his father grips the handlebars and seat, struggling to keep the bike upright. Around the boy's waist is a leather holster with a toy six-shooter: he's a cowboy, riding a bucking bronco. That *Saturday Evening Post* archetype—bright-eyed children, bicycling through idyllic suburbs—is still part of pop culture, having passed through successive cycles of nostalgia and revivalism. In *E.T. the Extra-Terrestrial*, Steven Spielberg's BMX-riding California kids gave the '50s suburban imagery an exurban '80s update. More recently, *Stranger Things*, the Netflix series set in '80s suburbia, winked at *E.T.*, putting its plucky protagonists on Schwinn Sting-Rays.

Today, across the globe, teaching children to ride bicycles is both a social convention and a policy priority. Governments from Colombia to Australia have instituted youth cycling instruction programs at the federal and local levels. In New Zealand, children receive cycling education in school and through government-trained instructors in local municipalities. France's ambitious Cycling and Active Mobility Plan includes a program to ensure that every schoolchild in the country knows how to ride a bike by age eleven.

Meanwhile, the milestone of the first bicycle ride remains totemic. On the internet, proud parents upload videos documenting the triumphs—first rides in playgrounds, on front lawns, along driveways, on shady Norman Rockwellian streets with porches and picket fences, in Steven Spielbergian cul-de-sacs. These days, many children begin learning to ride on a balance bicycle, a bike with neither pedals nor chain nor freewheel, which you sit astride and scoot forward by pushing your feet off the pavement—a *Laufmaschine*, in other words. To teach a novice how to keep a bike stable and moving forward, Karl von Drais's invention turns out to be far preferable to a bicycle rigged with training wheels. History's original bike has returned as a starter bike.

———

My own first ride is uncommemorated. There's no home-movie footage, not even a snapshot. I'm reasonably certain of when it happened: I was five years old. I know where it happened. It was on Claremont Avenue, a few blocks from my childhood home in Morningside Heights, a quiet neighborhood, by Manhattan standards, that abuts the campus of Columbia University on the Upper West Side. Claremont Avenue is a particularly sleepy stretch of street, notable mainly for the looming neo-Gothic cathedral of Riverside Church and for a handful of grand prewar apartment buildings that serve as faculty housing for Columbia and Barnard College professors. I'm pretty sure it was neither my dad nor my mom but my "other mother," my mom's partner, Roberta, who was present at the illustrious moment—who jogged along the sidewalk with a steadying hand, and with a gentle push launched me into a biking life.

Beyond that, I draw blanks. I'm middle-aged: the memories are receding along with the hairline. Or it could be that my first ride wasn't especially memorable. There have been a lot of bike rides: revelatory rides, humdrum rides, great rides, lousy rides, last night's ride, this morning's ride. As a kid, I rode up and down the block on West 121st Street. Our building stood on the north side of the street, almost exactly halfway up a hilly stretch of sidewalk that sloped down on either end to meet teeming avenues, Amsterdam to the east, Broadway to the west. I was under strict instructions to stop well before I got to the corner, and I enjoyed making the little bike skid when I jammed the pedals backward to activate the coaster brake. Years later, when I moved with my mother to Brookline, Massachusetts, a Boston suburb, I would ride around the neighborhood, a place called Coolidge Corner. And I'd ride my bike down Beacon Street into Boston proper, to explore the streets and go shopping for weird records and vintage clothes—the talismanic possessions that were, along with the bicycle itself, essential armature, the stuff that distinguished me and, I imagined, made me cool, or at least offered some protection against the many slights and humiliations life held for a teenage boy.

I was crazy about bikes, but I was no expert. I knew gearhead kids who hung around bike shops and wielded Allen wrenches like switchblades—who were always revamping their bikes, making them badder and radder. I wasn't like that. To this day, I can barely patch an inner tube. I wasn't a masher who went on long rides and hammered up hills. I wasn't a BMX kid who popped wheelies and shredded half-pipes. I rode to get my mind right. It was as if there was a vent in my skull, and as I pedaled and built up speed, the wind would whip through, clearing out the muck. It's not that biking around made me sharper-witted or smarter. On the contrary, I was, like many males my age, confused about nearly everything important yet certain I had the world figured out, or could at least bluff my way through by affecting a certain swagger. I'm sure that bike riding made me more confident in these misapprehensions, a more self-possessed dolt. It definitely calmed me down and bucked me up. I could get on my bike in a fog of neurosis and dismount a while later feeling all right—brave enough, at least, to pick up a phone and call a girl.

I've always paid attention to the way bicycles look, so it's odd that I can call to mind only hazy images of the bikes I owned as a child and young adult. I know that the bicycle I rode that day on Claremont Avenue was a banana-seat wheelie bike of some sort, a fitting first ride for a '70s kid. The bicycles of my younger years rather neatly align with period trends. Sometime in the early '80s, I got a ten-speed with dropped handlebars; in the late '80s, I got a mountain bike. Along the way, there were other bikes, of varied makes and looks. Bikes came; bikes went. I must have had six or seven between the ages of five and twenty-five. I outgrew certain bicycles and wore out others—or, rather, mistreated them, locking them up overnight on the street all year long, even in the winter.

I love bikes, but I'm not precious about them. I've never owned an expensive bicycle. I don't doubt that a splendid high-end machine would ride like a rocket ship, but I've never felt the impulse to splurge on one. As a kid, I admired my neighbor's fancy Cannondale road bike, which looked like it had been assembled from bits of sky and cloud: gleaming cobalt frame, white handlebars, white saddle. But I also envied the piratical battered BMX Mongooses that kids zipped around on, with ratty tennis balls wedged between the spokes. Then as now, I was no connoisseur. I was, I am, something more along the lines of a bicycle glutton. If the pedals turn, I'll ride it.

Not that I haven't drawn certain lines. When I was young, I often spent weekends in Connecticut, at the family homestead of my father's second wife, a big house on a hill above a bend in the Connecticut River. For decades, the house had served as an open-door retreat for my stepmother's family, a large WASP clan, and for various satellite clans of friends and friends of friends. The place was packed with relics of past inhabitants and visitors, including, in the garage, a number of old bicycles of uncertain provenance. One of these was a vintage child's cruiser, probably an early 1960s model. There was rust on the fire-engine-red frame, but someone must have done some maintenance work, greased the chain and trued the wheels, because the thing rode great. It was perfect for tooling around the roads that wound through the nearby woods.

It's possible that the bicycle was formally bequeathed to me by some adult in a position to do so. One way or another, I claimed it:

it was *my bike* on those weekends in the country. Technically speaking, it was a girl's bike, with a step-through frame, but that didn't bother me. There was a problem, though: the red, white, and blue plastic streamers on the handlebars. These struck me as goofy and shameful. Flapping around frantically as you rode, the streamers turned the dignified business of a bike ride into madcap child's play. An alteration was called for. I can't remember if at first I tried and failed to yank the things out of the handlebar grips. In any event, I wound up performing a more violent surgery. I found a big pair of garden shears hanging on a pegboard above a workbench in the garage, and I clipped the streamers clean off, *snip, snip,* like a groom docking a show horse's tail.

II. Messenger Boy

July 1988. I had just turned nineteen and was spending the summer in Boston. I was living with my mom, who, now that I had (in principle, at least) reached young adulthood and (again, in principle) flown the nest, was enrolled at Boston University, pursuing a long-deferred dream of advanced degrees. My dreams were more banal, and more ridiculous. I was growing my hair long. INXS, the Australian pop-rock group, was at the peak of its international fame, in heavy rotation on the radio and MTV. I wasn't crazy about the band—I liked them just okay—but I loved the looks of their lead singer, Michael Hutchence, with his big dark eyes and falling tresses and slithery dance moves. I decided that if I wore my hair like Hutchence's, his Dionysian charm would rub off, and girls would start swan-diving into my bed.

By July, my hair had reached the length where I could pull it back into a stumpy ponytail. I had four piercings in my left ear, including one, jammed through the hard cartilage at the top of the ear, that was always getting infected. I had a guitar I didn't really know how to play, but that didn't stop me from bashing at it. I couldn't sing, either, but I didn't know that at the time, and I was

convinced, dead certain, that I was a great songwriter, destined for
stardom—more precisely, for niche stardom, the best kind of stardom. I didn't covet the mundane global popularity of Michael
Hutchence; I pictured myself as a cult hero, an artiste, showered
with love by critics and a small but rabid audience that recognized
my genius. I moved through my days with my head in a haze: that
was one of my couplets, scrawled in the notebook I carried with me
everywhere in case the muse struck. It wasn't one of my better lines,
but it was accurate. My mind was misted over with dreams and desires and grandiosities, with melodies and lyrics, with visions of fame
and acclaim and girls and glory—all the triumphs to come. In the
meantime, though, I was a middle-class kid, a college student heading into sophomore year, and I needed a summer job. So I got one,
as a bicycle messenger.

In the 1980s, New York's bike messengers were legendary, a
new species of urban superhero: daredevils who threaded heaving
Manhattan traffic at top speed. The difference between bike mes-
sengering in New York and in Boston was the difference between
New York and Boston. New York is the big time, the matchless metropolis, huge and frantic and thrilling. Boston, by comparison, is
the sticks. On a bicycle you can cross the town from north to south,
from Charlestown to Mattapan, in about an hour. As a Boston bike
messenger in the late '80s, you spent at least half of your workday
riding around in the same area of about two-tenths of a square mile:
the downtown Financial District, a labyrinth of just a few dozen
streets that twisted between Chinatown and City Hall Plaza. Some
jobs sent you farther afield: west to Back Bay and Kenmore Square
and Allston-Brighton, south to the South End, across the Charles
River to Harvard and Central and Porter Squares in Cambridge.

It took just a few days on the job for these points to link up in
your mind and for the mental map to snap into focus. Which is not
to say that once you knew the streets, you knew the town. With its
deep history, its tribal neighborhoods and neighborhoods within
neighborhoods, its political progressivism, its profound racism, its

festering town-versus-gown antipathies, its deranged sports culture, its unfathomable accents, Boston was and is fascinating and baffling. As a bike messenger, you were immersed immediately in the beauty of Boston, the graceful streets and sight lines and buildings, especially in posh Back Bay and Beacon Hill. You also learned quickly about the virulence of Bostonians, who—when driving automobiles, at least—were angry people, angrier than seemed possible or comprehensible in such a quaint setting. Boston's traffic doesn't rage quite like New York's, but the drivers rage. The presence of bicycles on the road was viewed by drivers as an affront, and any hint of insufficient deference—any suggestion that some patch of road should be ceded, even momentarily, by the motorist to the cyclist—could provoke a vehement response. A driver's side window would roll down to reveal a livid face, with veins as thick as mooring ropes bulging from the forehead. The words would pour out in Bostonese: *cawksukkah, arhhshole, qwee-yah.* You had to stay alert, ready to take evasive action when a psycho turned his wheels in your direction and floored it.

Despite these hazards, I loved the job. The bike I rode that summer was a Ross ten-speed. It wasn't a great bike in the first place, and it had taken a beating under my care. But it wasn't a jalopy; it rode. I'm sure I had to sign some paperwork indemnifying the courier company against injuries I might suffer in the line of duty. In exchange, I got a black messenger bag, a pager that I attached to the bag's shoulder strap, a clipboard, and a sheaf of delivery logs to keep track of my jobs and collect signatures on pickup and drop-off. I kept a bunch of pens in my bag and a plastic baggie full of dimes, so I could call into dispatch from a pay phone when the pager buzzed or when I completed my run and needed a new assignment. You could start and finish work whenever you wanted, within reason. I usually began at nine sharp and knocked off around six. I'm not sure how many miles I covered in a day, but it was enough to leave me sweat-soaked and weary in an agreeable way— the kind of weariness a nineteen-year-old washes away with a shower before heading back out to meet friends and drink beer. It was the most time I'd ever spent on a bicycle, and it confirmed my suspicion that I didn't really want to be off a bicycle.

The job was straightforward. You picked up a package from one place of business and delivered it to another. In those days before email—before fax machines, even—bike courier business was brisk. If a letter or memo or report needed to get across town fast, you called a messenger service, and within minutes a sweaty, smelly, disreputable-looking person showed up in your office to pick it up. Often the hauls included oversized manila envelopes or architectural blueprints, rolled up in bulky cardboard tubes. You'd collect the items and a signature, stick the cargo in your bag, head back outside, unlock your bike, and whisk the package to its destination as quickly as possible—the quicker the better, so you could move on to the next job. Bike messengers were paid a flat hourly rate plus a commission for every delivery. The more jobs you did, the more cash you earned. So you rode hard.

That was the idea, in any case. My MO was different. No way around it: I was slow. It wasn't that I was lazy; it's that I had another agenda. I was busy enjoying the ride, drinking in the atmosphere, and trying to write songs in my head. Sometimes I'd detour down an unfamiliar street because it looked interesting. There were other distractions: a shop window, a plaque marking a historical event, a fight in the street, a pretty girl in a crosswalk. If a particularly good lyric popped into my head, some great gift from the gods of song, I'd pull over to write it down. I might find a bench and stay there for a while. A financial services firm could endure a delay of a few minutes before receiving a notarized contract. But Art could not wait.

My leisurely approach to the job didn't go unnoticed. Once, when I called into dispatch after a drop-off, the voice on the line had a harsh edge. "Don't you want to make money?" the dispatch guy asked. "Yeah, of course," I said sheepishly, but I lied. I had no rent to pay; my college tuition and living expenses were covered by my father. My bike messenger earnings provided some walking-around cash and maybe a little extra to stick in the bank. It was plenty.

Other messengers were more serious. For them, it was a career, or at least a real job, something they did while they figured out what their career would be. It was also a way of life, a subculture. I had heard that there were a couple of bars in Jamaica Plain where messengers hung out, but I was not sufficiently dialed in to know where they were, nor brave enough to inquire. I did know another spot where messengers congregated after hours. It was a little stretch of sidewalk on a small street not far from South Station, just steps from the dispatch office where I would go to drop my manifests and pick up my paltry paychecks. Every weekday at around six P.M., the block would fill up with messengers leaning on their bikes, sitting on the curb, talking shop, drinking cheap bottled beer, and smoking cigarettes and pot.

The scene was alluring but intimidating. I'd head over there after work sometimes and kind of linger on the fringes, in a spot where I could observe but not be observed. I'd flip my bike over, set it on the sidewalk so that it rested upside down on its seat, and pretend to be scrutinizing a wheel or attending to some other minor repair. If anyone noticed me, they didn't care enough to acknowledge my existence or to be irked by it. Nearly all of these messengers were in their twenties, and most of them looked like punk rockers, like outlaws, with spiky hair and pierced ears and pierced noses. It was clear that these people were out of my league, both older and wiser. They knew more than I did about bikes and, undoubtedly, about most other things, too.

New York's bike messenger corps was largely Black and Latino. But Boston being Boston, the messenger scene was very white, and very male. There were exceptions. One of the messengers who was always hanging around on the block after work was a young woman, probably in her early twenties, whose name I never learned. She had very blue eyes, a shaved head like Sinéad O'Connor's, and an air of implacable cool. I found her fascinating. I didn't have a crush on her, exactly. I didn't want to be her boyfriend; I wanted to be her, or someone quite like her. Also, I wanted her bike. It was the ugliest bike I'd ever seen, and the most magnificent, a postapocalyptic junker—a fixie I think—that looked like a prop from a Mad Max movie. It was black—or was it? It was impossible to tell, since the frame was wrapped in layers of black tape and festooned with stickers from bands whose names I didn't recognize. It seemed possible that the tape and the stickers were holding the bike together. There were scrapes and dents—scars that testified to untold feats of badassery. The bike looked like it had taken fire, zigzagged through war zones. As for the bike's owner: she was a strong cyclist. When she rode off after having a beer and a cigarette, her wheels seemed to singe the pavement.

The effect of this scene was so powerful that for a time I considered buzzing my hair, maybe getting a nose ring, going full punk-rock pirate. I didn't cut my hair, though. I kept growing it out. By August, I had a more substantial ponytail and was letting a long tendril or two fall in front of my face—a louche Hutchencean touch. The hair didn't work its magic on any girls that summer, but I figured my luck would soon turn. In the meantime, I biked around, delivered some packages, and daydreamed. While I rode, I wrote my songs. The unhurried cycling tempos, the languid spinning of the pedals and wheels, the trees, the breeze, the way my breathing fell into time with the respirations of the bike and the surrounding scenery—it was musical, rhythmic, and it lent itself to the composition of tunes and lyrics.

After work one night, I went out with friends in Cambridge and stayed out late. It was well after midnight by the time I set out for home, but I didn't go home. I kept riding around town, retracing routes I rode during my workday. Over the Mass. Ave. Bridge. Through the pretty streets of Back Bay: Beacon Street, Marlborough Street, Commonwealth Avenue, Berkeley, Clarendon, Dartmouth, Exeter. Up and down Beacon Hill, punishing climbs followed by dreamy descents. Into the nearly empty Financial District. The night was warm and windy, I'd had a few drinks, and the muses, it seemed to me, were belting out an astral chorale. As I rode, I wrote a song. It wasn't a great song, but it was the best I'd written or ever would write. It had a good title: "I Love Romance." Usually my lyrics were fussy and florid, clogged up with what I thought was clever wordplay. But in this case I tried to keep the words as simple as possible.

> *Ten thousand cars*
> *Ten million stars*
> *In the sky above*
>
> *Shining bright*
> *Oh what a night*
> *I want to fall in love*
>
> *May I have this dance?*
> *I love romance*
>
> *Down this road*
> *A man once strode*
> *With a coat and cap and cane*
>
> *Beneath these stones*
> *His yellow bones*
> *Are wrapped around the water main*
>
> *May I have this dance?*
> *I love romance*

Typing out these lyrics today—seeing the young poetaster's lines spread out on the cold white slab of the laptop screen—I'm struck by both their solid craftsmanship and their overcooked ambition. I can't recall exactly what I thought I was saying in 1988, but it's clear

that I was after something grand, straining to make a wry and knowing and artfully elliptical Big Statement about Love and History and
Memory and Death—stuff like that. I set the lyrics to a slow swing
beat and some minor seventh chords that I scratched out on the
guitar, in my crude way. I was going for a moody and ominous and
sophisticated vibe, Kurt Weill Weimar cabaret by way of Tom Waits,
whose records I was listening to a lot in those days. "I Love Romance" was, I knew, destined to be track number four on my debut
album. A hidden gem, beloved by the cognoscenti. A deep cut.

Today, I realize that the song is really about bicycling. It's about
the thoughts that flood your mind when you ride through city streets
under a night sky—the sense of wild possibility, the *Ah! Sweet mystery of life!* epiphanies, which convulse the soul of a naïve, sentimental, pretentious, comprehensively self-absorbed young white
dude—all enhanced by the steady cadence of the rotating pedals
and the thrill of whooshing through the dark beneath a brooding
skyline.

I kept "I Love Romance" in what passed for my repertoire for
years. I wasn't a very good bike messenger, but I was a better bike
messenger than I was a musician. I've definitely never had a more
pleasurable job. In late August, I headed back to school, at the University of Wisconsin–Madison, and moved with five close friends
into a house in an off-campus student ghetto. I left the Ross ten-
speed behind in Boston, but the day after I arrived in Madison, I
went into town and bought a used bike for, I think, forty bucks.

III. Crash

When I was maybe nine or ten, I steered a bicycle over some pebbles, felt the front wheel catch, wrenched the handlebars, and
tipped over, falling onto my left side and tobogganing across the
blacktop. This was in the summertime, on a drizzly morning in Connecticut, on the old red bike whose streamers I'd lopped off. I was
riding near my step-grandparents' house, on a thickly wooded road

which, at that time of day, was empty of any other human presence. The surrounding woods were deep and twisty, scenery I associated with the fantasy novels I was reading—a place you could imagine containing a colony of hobbits or a den of Narnian lions. I may have been daydreaming about something along those lines; in any case, I'd been moving fast, and it was a hard spill. When I hit the ground, I took a long slide, bumping and skidding on a diagonal course, leaving skin behind on the rain-washed pavement. I didn't knock my head or break a bone, but the scrapes on my arm and thigh burned as if the flesh had been pan-seared. "Road rash" is what cyclists call it. My bike lay capsized about fifteen yards behind me, and on the stretch of road in between, the asphalt was painted with smears and spots of blood, like abstract expressionist drizzlings on a black canvas.

That may or may not have been my first bike accident. I've had a fair number, possibly more than the average cyclist, and, again, these memories tend to blur. Some mishaps have left marks. When I was sixteen or so, I went flying off my bike and broke the knuckle on my left ring finger. To this day, that finger is misshapen, with a bulbous swollen joint. (When I got married, I had to buy an extra-large wedding band to fit over the knuckle; a jeweler soldered metal stabilizer balls on the inside of the ring so it wouldn't slip off my finger.) Another accident, in college, left me with a lump on my shin the size of a ping-pong ball. I have no memory of the crash itself, but I do remember sitting with that leg up in a friend's off-campus apartment, icing the swelling with a bag I'd grabbed from the freezer: Birds Eye mixed vegetables.

My wife says that I'm accident-prone, and while the stats may support this thesis, I don't quite believe it. It seems to me that the law of averages is at work: if you bike around a lot, you're liable to bump into things now and then. This is especially true if you do most of your biking in New York City. Over the past couple of decades, the city has created hundreds of miles of bike lanes; there are plans, supposedly, to add hundreds more, and to increase the num-

ber of lanes that are protected from motor vehicles by barriers. But
for now, New York's bicycle infrastructure is inadequate, and cyclists are forced into roaring traffic on streets where motorists operate with something close to impunity.

Thousands of bike riders are injured by automobiles in New
York each year, and only in rare instances do drivers face legal re-
percussions. The same is true of cases in which cyclists are killed.
New Yorkers have grown accustomed to seeing ghost bikes, memorials to lost cyclists that pop up at the locations of fatal accidents.
Ghost bikes are painted entirely white; often, they are adorned with
flowers or a laminated photograph of the deceased. A glimpse of
one of these shrines never fails to deliver a throb of dread. It reminds you, as you pedal past, of your total vulnerability. The cars
and trucks growling on all sides have the power to deliver swift judgment; no matter how seasoned and cautious a city cyclist you are, it
may merely be dumb luck that determines whether you reach your
destination. Should you meet a violent end, a ghost bicycle will arise
where you fell; otherwise, New York will greet the news with a
shrug. Occasionally, city leaders squeeze out a few crocodile tears in
response to fatal bike accidents. But it is clear that these deaths are
viewed, by New York's officialdom and by a large proportion of its
citizenry, as unfortunate but inevitable—a predictable outcome of
doing something as foolish, as illicit, as riding a bike on streets that
belong to automobiles. "Is It O.K. to Kill Cyclists?" was the question
posed in a 2013 *Times* op-ed. The answer, the article's author, Daniel Duane, concluded, is yes: in the United States, we have a "justice
system that makes it de facto legal to kill people, even when it is
clearly your fault, as long you're driving a car and the victim is on a
bike and you're not obviously drunk and don't flee the scene."

New York, in other words, is a very American place. The car is
the great unifier, one of the last shared passions that bind a fractured body politic, just as the Interstate Highway System binds
Portland, Maine, to Podunk to the Golden Gate, from sea to shining
sea. New York is often thought of as the exception to America, a

city-state that floats off the coast of the continent and operates according to its own, vaguely "European" rules. The city's relationship to automobiles would seem to be a case in point. New Yorkers own 30 percent fewer cars than residents of other large American cities. Driving a car in New York is presumed by many to be impractical and inapposite—antithetical to the spirit of the town.

But cyclists know that New York is as car-centric as anyplace west of the Hudson. Car culture bridges New York's political chasms. The Upper West Side liberal whose hatchback sports a THINK GLOBALLY EAT LOCALLY sticker, the Staten Island Trump supporter who flies a thin blue line flag from his roof rack—these natural foes are united by a belief in free curbside parking, by opposition to congestion pricing, and by disdain for the human gnats that buzz around on bikes. Car culture is written into the city's statutes and the columns of its newspapers, notably the Murdoch-owned *New York Post,* which is relentlessly anti-bicycle, portraying bikes as a safety hazard, to pedestrians in particular. The tenor of the coverage does not differ greatly from that of 125 years ago, when the diabolical scorcher slalomed through the columns of Hearst's and Pulitzer's scandal sheets. This may explain why so many New Yorkers regard cyclists as a great threat to their peace of mind and their persons, when both data and common sense demonstrate that the real danger comes from the three-thousand-pound hunks of steel that have the run of the streets. New Yorkers are, of course, far more likely to be hit by a car or truck than a bike, and with far graver consequences.

To ride a bike in New York, in other words, is to face both peril and hostility, and many residents who under other conditions might happily pedal around town will never dare. But more than a million do ride, and the number is growing, thanks in part to Citi Bike, New York's popular bicycle-sharing program. A New York cyclist rides warily, defensively, strategically, and picks up the little tricks of the game: how to ease off on pedaling and surf through the jolt when you hit a big divot in the pavement; how to scan the sideview mirrors of parked cars, in order to spot a driver who is about to pull out or fling a door open.

A certain mind-set is called for. You cultivate a breezy fatalism, telling yourself that you, as a bike rider, are merely more aware of the doom that lurks everywhere—more wised up than the boulevardier who might at any moment stroll under a falling piano or stray into the path of a car that has jumped the curb. It's certainly true that cyclists understand automobiles better than anyone, especially those who drive them. "Cars make you stupid, the way wealth makes you stupid," writes the essayist Eula Biss. "They are like important men in conversation with other important men. Bicycles are sometimes kindly accommodated by cars, often ignored, occasionally respected, sometimes nervously followed, and frequently not even seen. In this sense, riding in traffic is not unlike being a woman among men."

The conditions faced by bicyclists in New York are therefore a blessing as well as a bane. They bestow upon the cyclist gifts of insight and acuity that are unavailable to those who strap themselves into rolling boxes and face the world from behind a windshield. On a bike, wrote the journalist Bill Emerson, "Dogs become dogs again and snap at your raincoat; potholes become personal." It might also be said that a city becomes extra-cityish, more seething and carnivalesque, from the vantage point of a bicycle. Danger is a sensory intensifier, supercharging the scenery, making everything appear volatile and alive. Viewed from the saddle of a bike, New York reveals its old ungentrified face, mutating back into the decrepit, volcanic city of yore: old-school hip-hop New York, punk-rock New York, jaunty but menacing Damon Runyon New York. That may not be a great argument for steering a bike through the lethal rush-hour flow on Queens Boulevard. But for those of us who have bicycling in our bones, the arguments against it are worse. Bike riding can kill you, but to trudge through your days without biking—that's no way to live.

So I ride on, and occasionally trouble veers into my path or charges up from behind. In the mid-1990s, while pedaling on Tenth Avenue in Chelsea, I was rear-ended right in front of a church: the Church of the Guardian Angel, no less. The driver took off, and two nuns came running out of the church's parochial school. I was scraped up but not seriously hurt—*Deo gratias.* About a decade later, in June 2006, I was struck from behind again, this time by a rip-snorting SUV on Cadman Plaza West in Brooklyn Heights, a busy roadway packed with vehicles moving on and off the Brooklyn Bridge. It was the worst accident of my life. The force of the fall severely dislocated my left shoulder; the labrum, the ring of cartilage surrounding the shoulder socket, was shredded to bits. An engine company from the nearby firehouse was the first on the scene; one of the firefighters told me, "Your arm's not where it should be, my friend." A few days later, a surgeon screwed the shoulder back into place and reconstructed the macerated labrum using tissue grafted from elsewhere in my body. Today the range of motion in my left arm remains impaired, and an ache in my creaky glenohumeral joint forecasts changes in barometric pressure.

I can't blame all of my accidents on city streets. There was the spill in Connecticut when I was a kid and that pratfall with Danny MacAskill in the Scottish forest. But some crashes are definitionally urban. The city cyclist's archenemies are car doors, those monstrous heavy-metal appendages that swing out to clothesline pedalers as they pass. I've been doored several times, most grievously on Eighth Avenue near Fiftieth Street in midtown Manhattan, when a man burst out of a yellow taxi just as I rolled level with the passenger-side rear door, delivering a brutal knock to my left kneecap. How I limped away from that scene without broken bones I'll never know, but it took several weeks, and half a dozen trips to an acupuncturist named Dr. Chan, to get me off crutches. My main memory of the event is the sound. I heard the accident before I felt it—a nanosecond before the sensation sped up the superhighway of the spinal cord to register in the brain as pain. First came the squeak of the door rotating on its hinge. And then an appalling crunch, like a pecan splintering in a nutcracker.

IV. Locking Up

There are other misfortunes that can befall a bicyclist in the big city. In the summer of 1999, I stepped out of the building in the East Village where I'd been living and saw that my bike was gone.

It was six A.M. The previous night, I'd locked up in my usual fashion. I threaded a steel link chain through the spokes of the front wheel; I twisted the chain around a green sheet-metal pole that held a parking sign; I snaked the chain back through the center of the diamond frame and wound it around the top tube. Then I pulled the chain taut and dropped a solid steel padlock through two of the chain links, cinching the bike to the pole. This was on Avenue B at the corner of East Tenth Street, opposite Tompkins Square Park, just steps from a twenty-four-hour bodega. That morning, when I discovered the bike was missing, I asked one of the bodega's employees, who was stocking bins outside the store with bouquets of cheap flowers, if by any chance he'd seen someone steal a bicycle that had been locked to a pole—to that pole, right over there.

Yes, he told me; yes, he had. Two hours earlier, at around four in the morning, a couple of guys had pulled up to the curb in a truck with an open flatbed. When they stood on the flatbed, the men were at a height where they could reach out and touch the parking sign at the top of the pole. One of the guys took out a wrench and unbolted the sign. His colleague then lifted up my bike, whose front wheel was still chained to its frame, and together the men shimmied the machine up and over the pole, some twelve feet off the ground. They put the bicycle on the flatbed and they drove off.

The bodega guy reported these facts in a straightforward but weary manner. It was clear that the incident had aroused only mild interest on his part. It certainly wasn't an event he'd felt moved to interrupt on a technical point—e.g., that driving around town stock-piling bikes that don't belong to you is neither nice nor, strictly speaking, legal. In fact, the thieves were more civic-minded than the witness. The man who had removed the parking sign bolted it back in place before leaving the scene.

Bicycle theft is a worldwide epidemic. Tens of millions of bikes are stolen each year. In the United States, stolen bikes account for approximately 5 percent of larceny-theft cases, and those numbers only begin to tell the story—most bike thefts go unreported. To steal a bike does not take much in the way of skill or cunning. Bicycle locks can be sawed or whacked or clipped; they can be pried open with pliers or frozen with compressed air from a spray can and then smashed with a hammer. In most cases, the police are ineffectual, viewing stolen bikes as too minor a problem to warrant the allocation of manpower and resources. In short, bicycle theft is a crook's dream: easily accomplished and almost completely shrugged off by law enforcement. It's crime without punishment.

This is one of the reasons I've never bothered to invest in an expensive bicycle. If thieves will patiently dismantle street furniture to swipe a piece-of-shit cruiser, how long will a pricey beauty last in the wilds of Gotham? A few years before that theft on Avenue B, my new bicycle was stolen, just hours after I'd picked it up at the shop. It was a Trek 800 Sport, an unlovely mid- to low-end mountain bike that cost just $250. But it was brand-new, with an unblemished shiny green frame. That evening, I rode uptown from my apartment in Chelsea to visit my mom, who by that time had moved back to New York and was living in Morningside Heights again, just west of Broadway on 114th Street. I found a pole on the end of her block, near Riverside Drive, and hitched up the bike with a Kryptonite U-lock. This was dumb: U-locks are notoriously easy to crack. (On the internet, you can watch instructional videos demonstrating how to pop one open with a ballpoint pen.) I had dinner at my mom's, and when I came downstairs—*poof.*

Easy come, easy go. Tonight I'll lock up outside my apartment building, looping a hardened manganese steel chain around the wheels and the frame and padlocking the bike to a streetlamp. It's a heavier-duty, theoretically more thief-proof version of the setup I used on Avenue B. But if some enterprising scoundrel with the right set of tools and the nerve to see the job through comes along, the lock will not hold. Tomorrow I may wake up to find the bicycle where I left it, or it might be long gone: stripped for parts, or re-painted and pawned off to a fence, or totally intact but now some-one else's bike, its pedals rising and falling under a stranger's shoes.

V. Cycleur

And yet. For all the hazards and aggravations of cycling in New York, there are those of us for whom cycling is the essence of a New York existence, who know that to live in New York without a bike is to only half-experience the city—to view it at a blurry distance, as if peering through the glass of a snow globe that has been given a good shake. It's not just that bike riding is the most efficient and, mortal peril notwithstanding, most enjoyable commuter option, the best way to beat the gridlock and go about your business. It is also the best way to comprehend and imbibe New York, to make sense of the place, to gulp the town down.

A bicycle teaches you the lay of the land, apprising you of basic topographical facts. Four hundred years of digging, dredging, and excavating have reshaped and flattened out the landmasses of the New York City archipelago. But many streets in the five boroughs still rest atop the slopes and peaks of glacial moraines and slabs of Triassic crust. "It is by riding a bicycle that you learn the contours of a country best, since you have to sweat up the hills and coast down them," wrote Ernest Hemingway. A bike reveals the terrain behind the names—Brooklyn Heights shows you its heights, Murray Hill its hill. A New York cyclist, laboring up and whizzing down the gradients pedestrians and motorists may barely notice, connects to the immemorial past, before this place was Dutch, before it was Lenape land, before mastodons roamed. Your two wheels tell you a New York story that unfolds on a geologic time scale.

But biking is also the best way to penetrate the mysteries of today's town. The Mexican-born writer Valeria Luiselli, now a New Yorker herself, coined the term "cycleur" to describe a bicycling flaneur, one who moves through the cityscape with purposeful purposelessness, on a free-flowing *dérive*. "[The cycleur] has discovered cycling to be an occupation with no ultimate outcomes," Luiselli writes. "He possesses a strange freedom that can only be compared with that of thinking or writing. . . . Skimming along on two wheels, the rider finds just the right pace for observing the city and being at once its accomplice and its witness."

What is just the right pace? Once upon a time, the bicycle promised blazing speed. (The first name to gain wide currency, velocipede, comes from the Latin *velox pedis,* "swift of foot"; the meaning is preserved in the French *vélo*.) Today, many prize the bicycle for its slowness, espousing "slow cycling" alongside other decelerated lifestyle choices ("slow food," "slow sex"), while championing the bicycle as an antidote to the warp-speed information age.

But for a New York cycleur, the ideal pace is neither fast nor slow. It's a stately in-between tempo that allows you to scan the landscape, in Luiselli's phrase, "as if through the lens of a movie camera." Your trip to the grocery store becomes cinematic, a tracking shot that sweeps the skyline and street and sidewalk. You catch sight of the office tower stacked against the horizon, a pair of Chuck Taylors slung by their shoelaces over a telephone wire, a squirrel scampering out of a trash can with the remains of a bagel. You vacuum up shopfronts and signage, advertising slogans, graffiti, hundreds of faces, and hundreds more faceless heads bent over cellphones. A bicycle ride offers the best of travel by foot and by motor vehicle. You can take in the panorama in its blurry breadth or slow down to consider the details.

To put it another way: the seat of a bicycle is a fine perch from which to watch the world slide by. Sitting on a bike seat, you reach

the altitude of LeBron James. I tend to raise myself up even higher:
I do a lot of standing up on the bike, balancing on the motionless
pedals as the freewheel spins. This puts you at a height from which
you can gaze down on the roofs of passing SUVs. Unless you're on
stilts or a pogo stick or piloting a pedal-activated biplane, it is impossible to gain as lofty a view while traveling under your own power.
New York looks good from up there.

VI. Turkey

As for how I look up there: it may not be pretty. In a technical sense,
I don't know how to ride a bike. An expert cyclist—a sport cyclist
who cares about riding fast and well—might look on my form and
render a harsh judgment. In cycling slang, a clumsy rider is a "turkey." Undoubtedly, I'm one of those. I've never been concerned
about correct posture, proper pedaling technique, or even optimal
frame size. I set my saddle height according to a remedial formula,
placing the pedal in the six o'clock position and making sure that my
knee is more or less straight. That's the extent to which I attend to
technical matters.

When I face hills or headwinds, my performance turns grace-
less. There is a good deal of unpleasant wheezing and grunting. I've
been known to put off visits to the mechanic, and eventually my
bicycle, too, begins to cry out: the gears grind, the chain rattles, the
brake pads let out a stuck-pig squeal. So much for the silent steed.

Yet these niceties are beside the point. My biking practice—
year-round, all-weather urban commuting and wayfaring—is its
own kind of rude art, and I'd put my skills up against anyone's. I'm
adept at slipping and sliding through congested streets. I know how
to work with, and against, the flow of traffic. Shortcuts; gas station
rights; quick lurches into the narrow gap between the fenders of
parked cars, then up and over the curb onto the sidewalk—I exe-
cute these and other maneuvers without thinking, with a master's
resort to pure instinct.

It may not make an aesthetically pleasing spectacle. But who's watching anyway? A bicycle, says Valeria Luiselli, "allows the rider to sail past pedestrian eyes and be overlooked by motorized travelers. The cyclist, thus, possesses an extraordinary freedom: he is invisible." That's not quite true; but it feels true, and that's good enough. On a bike, you escape the surveillance of others and the withering gaze you turn on yourself, especially if you're the kind of person prone to staring down his reflection in every other shop window. When I ride my bike, petty vanity fades. I reach that Zen state, that place of grace, where I don't care if I look like crap.

VII. Phantom Limb

Bikeless days are a bummer. They do happen. Rain drowns the city, or snow dumps down. You have appointments to keep, and you have to show up looking more presentable than you would after an eighty-block bike ride. Maybe your bicycle is in the shop. Maybe your bicycle has been stolen. When you're used to traveling by bike, the condition of bikelessness is disorienting and debilitating. Without wheels, you feel like an amputee.

In the subway, you're cooped up, shifty, bored. In a taxi, you stare resentfully at the bikes sliding past. On foot, you may have the feeling that you are fording a river of quicksand. Travel by bicycle reveals hidden New York truths, but it also lies about the city, giving mistaken impressions of distances and dimensions. Trips you make in a flash on your bike become epic schleps when you have to walk or rely on public transportation. Off your bike, New York is larger but less magnificent, a place designed to frustrate and defeat. The scenery looks duller. Your mind feels duller.

The consolation comes at night. In your dreams, you're on your bike again, cruising familiar streets. Or perhaps those streets have turned psychedelic and you're pedaling a flying bicycle through a sci-fi city, a New York that has levitated into the Milky Way, where stars roll out like a carpet under your tires and planet Mars is speared on the Empire State Building's spire, like a cherry on a cocktail toothpick. In 1896, H. G. Wells wrote about the way a cyclist keeps biking through the night: "A memory of motion lingers in the muscles of your legs, and round and round they seem to go. You ride through Dreamland on wonderful dream bicycles that change and grow."

VIII. Meet You at the Corner

My older son learned to ride one weekend afternoon. That morning he had heard the news: his closest friend had been seen riding a bike around the neighborhood. My boy had been slow to take up biking, but the idea that his friend had reached this milestone first was too much to bear. He learned to ride that day. He was six.

For years, he had been a bike rider, but not a cyclist. He was a passenger on my bike, my traveling companion on rides around town. For a while I towed him in a trailer, one of those little chariots you hitch up behind your bike and drag through the street. Later, I switched to a child bike seat that put him mere inches behind me. We went all over the place: to school and to the park, north to Williamsburg and Greenpoint, over the bridges into Manhattan. Uptown, downtown. As we traveled, we'd chat: about New York, history, school, Chinese food, bicycles. Once, I mentioned an article I'd read about a long-distance cyclist who had set the goal of biking the equivalent of a trip to the moon and back. My son wondered if we could do the same: How many journeys from home to his elementary school would equal a round trip to the moon? We crunched the numbers and came up with a rough figure: about five hundred thousand commutes. We decided to set a more manageable goal.

But then he learned to ride himself, tasting freedom and danger. On our new journeys around town, I rode in the street and made him stick to the sidewalk. The idea was that he would ride parallel to me, mirroring my progress from the safety of car-free terrain. But he had no patience for this routine. He would outrun me, gunning along the sidewalk and reaching the end of the block before I did, while I sat stalled behind cars. "Meet you at the corner," he'd say and then, zoom, he was out of sight. For a while I insisted that he stop at the corners and wait for me before crossing the street. But soon it became clear that this was pointless. He was careful, he said; he wasn't going to get hit. Besides, I was too slow. Why should he have to wait around for me?

Today he's a big, handsome teenager, nearly my height. He's graduated to a retro-style BMX bike with a slick white frame and twenty-six-inch wheels. He's taught himself to wheelie and pogo and do other tricks. More often, he simply bikes around the city, seeing friends, hanging out, doing who knows what, who knows where, all over town, at all hours of the day and night. He's reached that stage of adolescence where he's here but not here, a spectral presence who drifts into the house, eats, sleeps, maybe does a little homework, exchanges a few words, and then drifts out again—hops back on the BMX and heads off to parts unknown. The anxiety of parenting a teenager is intensified when your kid likes to scream around New York on his bike. But I'm in no position to tell him not to do it, and besides, it could be worse. He could be driving a car.

Recently, I had the strange experience of bumping into my son on his bike. He was riding alongside a friend, about a dozen blocks down the street from our home. It was a novelty, a rare sighting of the teenager in the wild. My wife and I were out for a walk with our younger son, and then, suddenly, there he was, steaming up in the crosswalk: my big boy, looking more like a young man than ever. It was a brief encounter. "Hey guys," he said. And then, after a few pleasantries: "We gotta go." And they went, my son and his friend, zipping up the street and out of sight.

We still bike around together, sometimes. There are occasional family rides: my son leading the way, my wife and I trailing behind. We'll caravan like this, across Brooklyn, to a bookstore or an Asian restaurant. There is still a child's bike seat behind me, but it has a different occupant now: my younger son, who hasn't yet mastered his own bike. He's been hesitant about learning to ride, but he's getting too big for the child seat; it's just a matter of time. Soon he, too, will be on his way, heading for the corner.

IX. Graceful Aging

I saw a news item not long ago about a woman in rural Chile named Elena Galvez. It was one of those inspirational stories that goes shooting around the internet. Galvez, who is in her nineties, bikes hundreds of miles a week, transporting her hens' eggs to a market. The eggs are her only source of income; her sole means of transportation is a beat-up cruiser that Galvez calls her "companion and friend." "I am nothing without her," Galvez says. She maintains that cycling is the secret to longevity. If she makes it to one hundred, she insists, credit must go to the bicycle.

You can grow old on a bike. Many older people stay active by taking up genteel sports like golf. But those pastimes pull you away from life. A golf course is a sham Elysium, a walled garden cut off from the wide world. A bicycle can help keep an aging body fit. But more importantly, it keeps that body *out there,* where the action is.

When I fantasize about my life as an elderly person—when I conjure an idealized picture of my so-called golden years—I return to the same soft-focus images, which run through my mind like a montage in a cheesy movie: me and my wife, biking together in the twilight through placid New York streets. It is mortifying to recall the vainglorious visions I held in my head as a young man. But I have to admit that not so much has changed: today, more or less the same stuff kick-starts my daydreams. I no longer crave rock stardom—a good thing, for me personally and for the community at large. But bicycles still loom front and center, and, I guess, I still love romance. A great city; a decent bike; a body spry enough to work the bike; my wife, on her bike, pedaling alongside. That's the ride into the sunset I want. If my luck holds, if I'm not flattened by a cornering truck or sideswiped by a driverless Uber or I don't suffer some other misfortune on or off two wheels, I may yet become that great and noble—or maybe it's humble but dignified—creature. An old man on a bicycle.

14

GRAVEYARDS

A bicycle in the muck of the drained Canal Saint-Martin. Paris, 2017.

Every decade or so, the city of Paris drains the Canal Saint-Martin. The nearly three-mile-long waterway, which runs south across a swath of the Right Bank, was originally constructed to keep Paris clean, supplying fresh water to a city plagued by cholera and dysentery. But for the two centuries of the canal's existence, it has often served a different—in fact, opposite—function. It is a dumping ground, a big liquid trash can. The periodic draining is therefore also an unveiling. The water recedes, and the stuff kicked or heaved or furtively dropped into the canal over the preceding few thousand nights is revealed.

When the canal was emptied in 2016, crowds gathered on footbridges and along the *quais* to watch cleaning crews trudge through the mud and clear out the junk. There was lots of it. Mattresses, suitcases, street signs, traffic cones. A washer-dryer, a tailor's mannequin, tables and chairs, bathtubs and toilets, old radios, personal computers. A number of vehicles, none of them designed to travel on water, were pulled from the mire. There were baby strollers, shopping carts, at least one wheelchair, and several mopeds.

Today, the streets abutting the canal in the Tenth Arrondissement are among Paris's trendiest, lined with chic cafés and restaurants. But late at night the area retains some of the dank atmosphere of bygone years, when it was a scruffy *quartier populaire* and often served as the setting for noir films and hard-boiled detective novels. In those pulp fiction tales, dark secrets emerge from the Canal Saint-Martin murk. The murder mystery in Georges Simenon's *Maigret and the Headless Corpse* is set in motion when the police dredge up a dismembered body near the Quai de Valmy. No human remains were discovered during the 2016 cleaning, but workers did find a handgun in one of the northernmost locks. Later, officials announced that a rifle had also been found.

The most plentiful items in the canal—other than wine bottles and cellphones, that is—were bicycles. Nine years earlier, in 2007, Paris had launched a bike-share scheme, Vélib', and as the waters were drawn off, the skeletal forms of dozens of Vélib' cruisers could be seen half-buried in the sludge on the canal floor. There were scores of other bikes, too, of various makes and vintages, some of which appeared to have been maimed before being sent to the watery grave. There were bikes with bent and twisted wheels, or no wheels at all. There were bikes whose wheels and frames were intact but whose stems and handlebars were missing: headless corpses.

Some of the bikes may have ended up in the canal by accident.

There are numerous scenarios that can result in the unintentional depositing of a bicycle in a body of water, and mishaps of this sort do occur. Cyclists lost in the dark or disoriented by fog steer bikes off towpaths into canals. Drunk cyclists fall from bridges. Thieves fleeing police by bicycle swerve into the river. The luckier victims manage to pull themselves—and, sometimes, their bicycles—back to dry land, but these incidents can have calamitous outcomes. A scan of newspaper archives turns up grisly stories with vivid headlines: "Tumbled into Dock: Cyclist Drowns at Port Talbot," "Body Attached to Bicycle in River," "Friend Saw Girl on Bicycle Drown," "Boy Drowns in Canal: Found with His Bicycle," "Woman Cyclist Drowned: Blown Over Parapet of River Bridge," "Rode into Canal in Black-out: Gloucester Man Drowned Cycling to Work," "Cyclist Drowned, but How?" Some despondent souls have deliberately pedaled into the depths. In the fall of 2016, a thirty-eight-year-old transgender woman left a suicide note in her apartment in DeWitt, New York, not far from Syracuse. The woman then went to a nearby state park, where she handcuffed herself to a mountain bike and rode into a lake. Her body, still manacled to the bike, was found a week later.

As for the bikes in the Canal Saint-Martin: it seems safe to assume that most of them wound up in the water neither by accident nor under tragic circumstances. People enjoy mischief-making, and a bicycle is a good thing to make mischief with. There are lots of bikes around, and you can steal or sabotage them without consequence. For those disposed to random acts of hooliganism—who, perhaps, sublimate the compulsion to do violence to sentient beings by trashing insentient stuff they happen across—a bike presents an inviting target. It may be that the bicycle, whose quasi-animate "iron horse" quality has unnerved and enticed for two centuries, stirs deep urges in certain vandals. The growth of share schemes like Vélib' has put more bicycles on the streets of the world's cities, and these bikes may strike saboteurs as fair game, since they are not owned by individuals. The introduction of dockless share bikes, which sit on sidewalks rather than secured in docking stations, has removed an impediment to such forms of self-expression as wheel bashing, frame mauling, and brake-cable clipping. Some people take a more whimsical approach: dangling bikes from wrought-iron fences, perching them atop traffic lights and bus shelters, sticking them in high tree branches to roost like nesting pterodactyls.

Throwing a bicycle into the water is a specialized sport, one that offers its own peculiar set of frissons and satisfactions. On the internet, there are homemade videos of pranksters rolling bikes down embankments into lakes, tipping bikes over quayside railings, tossing bikes into rushing whitewater. In one clip, a teenage boy faces the camera holding a weather-beaten blue BMX. "Mike, this is your bike," he says. "It's been in my garage, and I don't really want it. So I'm gonna throw it off the jump in the pond. I hope you don't mind." With a running shove, the boy sends the riderless bicycle somersaulting off a wooden plank into the water. Whoops and laughter can be heard in the background as the jittery camera captures the bike's quick demise, the rear wheel bobbing briefly above the surface before vanishing into the gulping pond—a slapstick murder. I won't lie: it looks fun.

———

Clearly, for many, it is fun. In some places, it's an epidemic. An Englishman who grew up in the city of Peterborough, in Cambridgeshire, recalled that in the 1960s local boys would steal bicycles and go joyriding; the escapades would end with the ritual dumping of the bikes in the River Nene. This practice was discovered when "a boat snagged on . . . an underwater mountain of bicycles." In Amsterdam, drowned bikes were at one time heaped so high in the city's 165 canals that they scraped the underside of flat-bottomed barges. The solution was *fietsen vissen*, "bicycle fishing." In the old days, this task was accomplished by freelance scavengers who plied the canals in rowboats, using hooked poles to extract bikes, which were sold for scrap. In the 1960s, Amsterdam's water agency assumed responsibility for bicycle fishing. These days, a corps of municipal workers trawl for drowned bikes on boats equipped with cranes attached to hydraulic claw grapples. The problem is not as severe as it once was, but fishermen still pull fifteen thousand bicycles from the canals each year. It is a unique Amsterdam spectacle that never fails to draw a crowd of onlookers: the big metal claw rising out of the water with a dripping haul of wheels and frames and handlebar baskets. The bikes are dropped into garbage scows and transported to scrapyards for recycling. It is said that many of the recycled bikes are turned into beer cans.

In Amsterdam, as in Paris, no one is quite certain why or how so many bicycles wind up in the water. City officials ascribe the problem, vaguely, to vandalism and theft. Alcohol surely plays a role, and there could well be a kind of ecosystem at work: a bicycle is pulled from the canal and recycled into a beer can, whose contents are guzzled by an Amsterdammer, who, weaving home at the end of a dissipated night, spots a bicycle and is seized by an impulse to hurl the thing into a canal. The writer Pete Jordan, in his charming book about Amsterdam and cycling, *In the City of Bikes*, devotes several pages to bicycle drowning, linking the practice in part to the city's tumultuous political history. In the 1930s, Communists pranked fascists by tossing their bicycles into the Prinsengracht, the "Prince's Canal"; during the German occupation in World War II, resistance leaders called on Amsterdammers to dump their bicycles into canals to keep them from falling into the hands of the Nazis, who were confiscating bikes. Jordan also cites the 1963 Dutch novel *Fietsen naar der maan* (Cycling to the Moon), which depicts bicycle drowning as an elaborate form of theft: a bicycle fisherman secretly knocks bicycles into an Amsterdam canal at night; he returns the next morning to retrieve the bikes, which he sells to a fence.

The situation in Amsterdam is perhaps best explained by simple math. There are an estimated two million bicycles in the city and thirty miles of canals, and logic dictates that there will be some spillover of one into the other. When an Amsterdammer needs to get rid of an old bicycle, a waterway will often provide the most convenient dumpster. The Dutch newspaper *Trouw* once characterized Amsterdam's canals as "those traditional garbage cans where we take our visitors on boat trips."

But this is not just a Dutch custom. In 2014, the Tokyo Parks Department became aware that nonnative fish had been introduced into the large pond that sits in the center of Inokashira Park, in the city's western suburbs. The fish, which were thought to have been put in the water by former owners, were causing environmental damage; officials decided to drain the water to remove the fish. But when the pond was emptied, another kind of invasive species was found: dozens of bicycles. The discovery took many in Tokyo by surprise. Sanitation workers had long complained about the abandoning of unwanted bikes in streets and alleys and parking lots. But the dumping of bicycles in bodies of water was a largely unknown— by definition, hidden—folk custom. How many more bicycles are covered by the world's waters, concealed by ponds and lakes and canals, by the Danube, the Ganges, the Nile, the Mississippi?

———

A lot, it is reasonable to surmise, and the numbers appear to be growing as bike-sharing schemes proliferate. During the first year Vélib' was in operation, Paris police officers fished dozens of bikes out of the Seine. A bike-share company stopped doing business in Rome after too many of its bicycles were thrown into the Tiber. "Dockless Bikes Keep Ending Up Underwater," reported the *Boston Globe* in 2018, soon after the arrival of bike-share firms in Boston and its suburbs.

The same problem has been reported in Melbourne, in Hong Kong, in San Diego, in Seattle, in Malmö, Sweden, and in many other cities. In Britain, share bikes have been pulled from canals in London and Manchester, and from the Thames, Cam, Avon, and

Tyne rivers. (The Canal & River Trust, which holds the guardian-
ship over waterways in England and Wales, released underwater
video footage showing fish drifting lazily along the floor of a canal,
past bicycle wheels fringed with algae.) In February 2019, in New
York, a Citi Bike cruiser that had evidently spent some time in the
Hudson River appeared overnight at a docking station on Manhattan's Upper West Side. The bicycle was blistered with barnacles and
mollusks; its spokes were covered in seaweed. A Hudson River con-
servancy expert was asked by the website *Gothamist* to assess the
length of time the bicycle had been underwater. "Based on the oysters on the handlebar, we'd say [the Citi Bike has] been in the river
since at least August, potentially since June," the expert said.

The most dramatic reports of bicycle dumping and dredging
have come from China. In the years 2016 and 2017, the then-largest
bike-sharing companies in the world, Ofo and Mobike, salvaged
thousands of their dockless rental bikes from rivers in southern
China. One widely circulated video showed a man on a busy pedestrian footbridge tossing Mobikes into Shanghai's Huangpu River.
Other viral clips captured such spectacles as the demolishing of
share bikes by a group of children and a share bike being battered
by a hammer-wielding elderly woman. Share bikes in China have
been stolen and stripped, thrown under automobiles, buried in construction sites, and set on fire. In China, the wave of vandalism
prompted soul-searching. "It is common to hear people describe
bike-sharing as a 'monster-revealing mirror' that has exposed the
true nature of the Chinese people," *The New York Times* reported
in 2017.

Or perhaps that mirror reflects larger truths about our times.
The man who was filmed throwing bicycles into the river in Shanghai was a migrant from Hong Kong who told journalists he had destroyed an additional nine Mobikes with a hammer. The man said
that he was infuriated by the company's violation of users' privacy:
"The chips in Mobikes are unsafe and disclose users' personal information, such as their locations."

He is surely not the only person whose acts of bicycle sabotage are motivated by political rage. Theoretically, a bike-sharing program is an initiative that makes city life not only more convenient and more pleasurable but more ecological and more equitable, fairer and freer. In fact, many bike-share schemes are public-private partnerships, sponsored by multinational banks whose logos emblazon the bicycles' mudguards. The dockless bike-share industry is dominated by tech companies that have flooded streets and sidewalks with bikes, often before regulations or infrastructure are in place. Most dockless programs are app-based and offer a familiar digital age trade-off: ease and convenience at the expense of privacy. The apps collect a rider's personal data, and the bicycles use built-in GPS chips and wireless connections to transmit that rider's location as frequently as every few seconds. A bicycle that spies on its rider—it's quite a plot twist for the machine that, once upon a time, promised a previously unimaginable kind of personal freedom.

In China, more than seventy dockless bike-share start-ups, backed by more than $1 billion in venture capital, pushed millions of bikes into cities in 2016 and 2017. Supply swamped demand, and the bikes, quite literally, piled up. On the outskirts of Beijing, Shanghai, Xiamen, and other cities, tens of thousands of impounded share bikes, many of them brand-new, filled vast vacant lots, towering dozens of feet above the ground in enormous agglomerations. These places have been called "bicycle graveyards," but in overhead photos and videos captured by drone, they often look more like fields of flowers: the bright yellow and orange and pink hues of the bike frames stretch out for acres, like a lurid carpet laid over the land. History-minded viewers of these images might think of that archetypal speculative bubble: the "tulipmania" that captivated the Dutch Republic in the seventeenth century. In any event, the share bike that is heaped on a junkyard mountain—or torched, or trashed, or chucked into a river—tells a story about the twenty-first century, though the meaning of that tale, and its denouement, are at this

point far from clear. Whatever fate the future holds, it comes with a
bicycle body count.

———

Of course, there have always been bicycle graveyards. If you walk
down a desolate street in an industrial neighborhood, you might
happen upon a scrap-metal facility, and if you look hard enough, you
will probably spot bikes and bike components, scattered amid heaps
of detritus. There is a large scrapyard one block from my Brooklyn
apartment. All day, huge grapple excavators hiss and snort over
mounds of metal, loading and unloading barges in the adjacent
Gowanus Canal. The scrap is placed into balers and compressed
into five-hundred-pound blocks. Sometimes I've caught sight of bicycle parts in those big rectangular bales—frames and wheels and
other bike bits, flattened out like fossilized remains. Several years
ago, the scrapyard was fined $85,000 when the New York State De-
partment of Environmental Conservation discovered more than
one hundred instances of "metal spillover," in which the company
had dumped debris into the canal. Perhaps the slimy Gowanus—
like the Canal Saint-Martin, like the picturesque *grachten* of old
Amsterdam—holds hidden troves of bikes beneath its waterline.

For all I know, one of my old bicycles could be in the canal. It
occurs to me that of all the bikes I've owned, twenty or so at least,
the only one whose whereabouts I can account for is the black
cruiser that at this moment is locked to a streetlamp, a block and a
half from that noisy scrapyard. Naturally, I don't know what became
of my bikes that were stolen. But I also have no memory of having
ever given a bike away, or of selling a bike; nor can I recall throwing
a bike into a dumpster. I'm sure I must have left a bike or two behind in a basement when I've moved house.

As for the rest: beats me. Where do bicycles go when they die?
A bicycle is a durable good, but it's also a disposable one: it's an easy
thing to get rid of, if you don't mind being a little antisocial about

it. In the affluent developed world, at least, a bike can be bought cheap, and when it breaks down, or when a new bike is purchased, an owner will often expel the old one—leave it somewhere outdoors to be claimed by a passerby or scooped up by the sanitation department.

Then there are those bicycles that are ditched in lonelier locations, where they lie around in increasingly abject states as time and the elements take their toll. In cities, you often see bikes that are abandoned but locked up, fastened with old chains or U-locks to poles and fences. Usually, buzzards swoop in to pick at the carcasses, making off with whatever they can—a wheel, or two wheels, or a set of handlebars. These pillaged bikes can be sad sights to behold. Chains droop from battered chainrings, smashed reflectors litter the ground, spokes and brake cables splay out like the haywire hairdos in George Booth cartoons. I think of the great Tom Waits song "Broken Bicycles": "Broken bicycles / old busted chains / with rusted handlebars / out in the rain . . . / laid down like skeletons / out on the lawn." The lyrics are metaphorical—it's a song about ruined romance—but it works as reportage. If those broken bicycles on the lawn are like most bikes, they are made largely of either steel or aluminum alloy, which means they originated underground, as ore or sedimentary rock that was pulled from a mine. Now little bits of the bikes are returning to the earth: the flakes of rusted steel and the fine chalky particles that coat the surface of oxidized aluminum may be scattered by the wind and washed down the sewer in a rainstorm.

Some derelict bikes get a second life. The scrapyard down the street from my home ships its metal bales off to recycling facilities. There, the scrap is cleaned and sorted, placed in furnaces and heated to a molten state, and submitted to purification processes. Eventually, the metals are cast or rolled into sheets and put back in circulation. Steel and aluminum are among the most widely recycled materials on earth. Sometimes, as in Amsterdam, a scrapped bicycle frame may be reborn as a beverage can, or as food packaging of another sort. Recycled steel and aluminum are also used in the building of airplanes and automobiles and, indeed, bicycles. They are used in the construction of street furniture and houses and apartment buildings. The mystic in me likes to imagine a cityscape formed from old bicycles: cyclists riding bikes reincarnated from earlier bikes, pedaling past skyscrapers supported by girders and beams and rebar made of recycled bike frames, while jet planes patched together from scrapped bicycles soar overhead. Metal recycling produces environmentally damaging waste, but some by-products can be recycled and put to use. The dross or slag that results from aluminum casting is sometimes utilized as a filler in asphalt and concrete mixtures. In certain places, therefore, the road itself is a sort of bicycle graveyard, and cyclists out for Sunday rides are rolling their wheels across a landscape of reconstituted bones.

15

MASS MOVEMENT

Bicyclists at a Black Lives Matter rally. Brooklyn, June 2020.

O n June 4, 1989, the people of Beijing awoke to find a bicycle graveyard in the heart of the ancient city.

Overnight, tanks had rolled in, and People's Liberation
Army (PLA) troops had shot their way through the streets, killing
hundreds, possibly thousands, of their fellow citizens, including
pro-democracy demonstrators who had occupied the vast plaza of
Tiananmen Square for fifty days and nights. The indelible images of
the Tiananmen crackdown are the photographs, taken on the afternoon of June 5, of "Tank Man": an unidentified lone protester facing
down a column of tanks on Chang'an Avenue, on the northern edge

of the square. Today, those photos are suppressed in China, as are virtually all references to the events of June 4. But in the spring and summer of 1989, TV viewers in China became familiar with a different scene.

When the army retook Tiananmen Square, its first order of business was erasure. The pillows and blankets and tents, the placards and banners, the thirty-three-foot-tall papier-mâché statue that protesters had named the *Goddess of Democracy*, virtually every trace of the occupation, which, at its height, had seen one million people, mostly students, assemble in the square—all of it was reduced to rubble, plowed into piles, and either burned or airlifted away by helicopters. The footage broadcast on television in the succeeding days and weeks showed a spectacle of order restored: sweeping views of the now pristine and vacant square. Or almost vacant. At least one reminder of the protest and its violent end remained, and was caught in the slow camera pan across Tiananmen Square that aired over and over again. It was a picture of carnage: dozens of bicycles, mangled and flattened by army tanks, and left behind in a heap.

There could be no question that the government wanted the Chinese people to see that wreckage, and to heed the message it sent. The Tiananmen protesters had been a cycling army. The uprising was touched off by the death of Hu Yaobang, the former Chinese Communist Party (CCP) general secretary, who had been forced to resign in 1987 due to his support for pro-democracy activists. Hu was a hero to reform-minded Chinese citizens, and when news of his fatal heart attack reached Beijing's university campuses on April 15, 1989, students began gathering for impromptu demonstrations. A Beijing Normal University student reportedly "took a bicycle and a loudspeaker to organize the chaotic crowd," and soon they were marching together toward Tiananmen Square. One of those protesters, Zhang Boli, was a thirty-year-old journalist who was attending a training program for writers at Beijing University.

Zhang realized that the students "needed to propose something to the government." So he stopped marching, took out pen and paper, and jotted down a list of demands—including calls for democracy, for freedom of the press, for an end to corruption—which became the basis of the movement. "I wrote down seven requests," Zhang recalled, "and rode a bike to catch up with the others."

Over the next several days, thousands more made the journey to Tiananmen Square, pouring into the plaza that held the Great Hall of the People, the Mausoleum of Mao Zedong, and other symbols and citadels of party power. A huge portrait of Hu was installed on the Monument to the People's Heroes, the ten-story obelisk that rises above the square. On April 22, more than one hundred thousand students gathered outside the Great Hall of the People, where Hu's memorial service was being held, demanding an audience with the Chinese premier, Li Peng. In the Politburo, a debate was raging. Demonstrations had spread across the length and breadth of China. Li and other hard-liners were pressuring Deng Xiaoping, China's paramount leader, to take aggressive steps to repress the protests. On April 26, an editorial in the state newspaper the *People's Daily* denounced the movement as "a well-planned plot" designed to "throw the country into turmoil."

But demonstrators still flooded into Tiananmen Square, and many came on bicycles. Most pedaled single-speed roadsters. Others rode tricycle rickshaws with cargo flatbeds. The cyclists carried flags and banners emblazoned with handwritten slogans, which streamed behind them in the breeze. One observer compared the procession to a fleet of tall ships—a bicycle regatta, sailing down the avenues and alleyways of the city. Some of the protesters linked arms while riding, a kind of trick-cycling stunt that doubled as a display of solidarity and might.

On May 10, students held a massive "bicycle demonstration" in support of journalists who had issued demands for press freedoms. More than ten thousand cyclists joined the twenty-five-mile circum-

navigation of Beijing, which followed the line of the old city wall en
route to Tiananmen Square. Philip J. Cunningham, an American
student living in Beijing, was among the legions who set out that day
from the campus of Beijing University. In a memoir, *Tiananmen
Moon* (2009), Cunningham recalled the climax of the ride, a triumphant surge into the square in violation of police orders:

> The mad dash across Tiananmen Square was the high point
> of the day. A defiant burst of energy propelled us clear across
> the forbidden ground in a giant, diagonal slash. . . . From the
> vantage point of a gliding bicycle, it was a magnificent scene.
> Before us and behind us, red flags and school banners lashed
> the air and unfurled in the jet stream of rushing cycles. This
> gave the illusion that flags and banners, some strapped to bi-
> cycles, others held aloft by skilled cyclists, were flying above
> the crowd under their own power, like the magical brooms of
> the sorcerer's apprentice.

It is no exaggeration to say that bicycles and tricycles kept the
Tiananmen occupation going. In the square, bikes were used to
mount flagpoles and to support tents. People slept on and underneath cargo tricycles. Bikes and trikes ferried supplies and suste-
nance into Tiananmen Square. They were used as food and beverage
stands. When more than three thousand protesters went on a hunger strike, volunteer doctors and nurses attached homemade red
crosses to their handlebars and biked to Tiananmen. Cargo tricycles
were converted into field hospital beds to treat the ailing.

Bicycles became even more essential after May 20, when martial law was declared in Beijing and public transit ground to a
standstill. Protesters rode bikes between university campuses to
convey messages and share intelligence. The *Goddess of Democracy* sculpture was delivered to the square from the Central Academy of Fine Arts, arriving piece by piece on the back of tricycle
rickshaws. The students erected the statue just opposite the Tian-

anmen Gate, where it stood facing the iconic twenty-foot-tall portrait of Chairman Mao.

On the night of June 3, as PLA tanks rumbled across Beijing on the way to Tiananmen Square, citizens tried to thwart the advance by piling bicycles in the streets to create barricades. When the troops moved into the square in the early-morning hours of June 4, some protesters used their bikes to flee for their lives. Some stayed and fought as best they could, thrusting their bicycles at the enormous armored vehicles. Witnesses have said that riders of bicycles and tricycles saved many lives that night. Brave cyclists pedaled into the teeth of gunfire, retrieving the wounded and speeding them to hospitals as bullets whizzed past. Others were unlucky. They were shot down or crushed beneath the treads of tanks, and died amid the ruins of their bikes.

———

Three years later. About six thousand miles across the North Pacific. One evening in October 1992, a few dozen people were gathered in San Francisco's SoMa district, in a narrow street lined with small apartment buildings, garages, and light industrial businesses. The ground-floor space behind the roll-up door at 498 Natoma Street was home to Fixed Gear, an underground bike shop and "bicycle salon" that was a magnet for the city's bike messengers and cycling activists. That night, the crowd had come to view a screening of *Return of the Scorcher*, a documentary by a local filmmaker, Ted White, that celebrated "radical bike history" and advocated a bicycling renaissance as a remedy for social and ecological ills.

The previous year, White had traveled to China with a friend, a New York bicycle designer named George Bliss, to chronicle bike culture in the world's most populous nation. The Tiananmen crackdown had crushed China's bicycling insurgents. But when White and Bliss arrived in Guangzhou, a port city of 3.5 million on the banks of the Pearl River, they found another bicycle brigade: the great masses of Chinese citizens, commuters and children and the elderly, who swarmed the streets on two wheels, every day, everywhere.

China was the *Zixingche wang guo,* the "Kingdom of the Bicycle," the nation that had embraced cycling on an unprecedented scale. It has been suggested that the country's affinity for bicycles has roots in its agricultural traditions: for centuries, farmers in the rice-growing regions of central and southern China had "pedaled" the treadles of water wheels to irrigate fields. But the bicycle itself first entered Chinese consciousness in reports from diplomats who had encountered the exotic "self-moving cart" on missions to Europe. "On the avenues people ride on a vehicle with only two wheels, which is held together by a pipe," wrote an envoy from the court of the Tongzhi emperor who traveled to Paris in 1866. "They dash along like galloping horses."

In the 1890s, the safety bicycle arrived in China, finding niche popularity among a small group of elites and expats in cosmopolitan Shanghai. The failure of the bicycle to gain wider acceptance may in part be explained by its status as a Western import. In an era marked by the rising anti-imperialist fervor that culminated in the Boxer Rebellion (1899–1901), the association of bikes with missionaries and colonial officers was a black mark. But other factors—in particular, cost—kept the bicycle from reaching the masses. The most famous cyclist in early-twentieth-century China was none other than Pu Yi, the teenage last emperor of the Qing dynasty, who ordered the removal of the doorway thresholds in the Forbidden City so he could bike unimpeded through the palace complex.

History would soon sweep away the vestiges of China's old ruling order; Pu Yi was expelled from the Forbidden City in 1924 and sent into the first of many exiles. Bicycles, though, would remain and proliferate. In the 1930s and '40s, China's politics were tumultuous, but its industrial economy boomed. The development of a domestic bicycle industry brought prices down, and cycling became a favored form of transit among the Republic of China's modernizing middle classes. By 1948, there were about 500,000 bicycles in use across the country, including 230,000 in the city of Shanghai.

And then: 1949 and revolution. From the start, the People's Republic of China promoted the bicycle as a tool for everyday use and a spur to the economy. The first Five-Year Plan, Chairman Mao's sweeping economic-development initiative, laid out an ambitious vision for the growth of China's bicycle industry. In the decade that followed, small manufacturers were consolidated into large ones, and bike producers were given access to rationed raw materials. Like other necessities of daily life in China, bikes were allocated to citizens through a coupon system, but the government encouraged cycling by prioritizing coupons and providing subsidies for workers who needed to commute to their places of employment. China's streetscapes and landscapes—from Beijing's narrow *hutongs* to the paths that wound through fields and paddies in the agrarian hinterland—were already conducive to cycling. The state went a step further, creating new infrastructure in cities, including wide bike lanes, which were segregated from automotive traffic on broad Soviet-style boulevards.

Within a decade, the number of bikes in China had doubled. The bicycle had also attained new cultural status. It was an emblem of the nation itself, a symbol of "an egalitarian social system that promised little comfort but a reliable ride through life." Eventually, the bicycle would become something close to compulsory: along with a watch and sewing machine and radio, it was one of the proverbial "three rounds and a sound," the must-have possessions for all Chinese adults who wished to get married and start a family. New bicycles rolled off the factory floors of state-owned manufacturers. They were simple, sturdy bikes with a single gear and unadorned black frames, but their brand names had a mythic chime, suggestive of majesty and durability: Phoenix, Pheasant, Red Flag, Flying Arrival, Golden Lion, Mountain River, One Hundred Hills.

Most hallowed of all were the "Ford and GM of China," the Shanghai-based firm Forever (*Yongjiu*) and the de facto national bicycle, the Flying Pigeon (*Fei Ge*), a hefty machine modeled on the 1932 British Raleigh Roadster. The Flying Pigeon Company was headquartered in the northeastern city of Tianjin, in a former munitions plant that Mao ordered converted to bicycle production in 1950. When Deng Xiaoping came to power in 1978, in the aftermath of the Cultural Revolution, he promised "a Flying Pigeon in every household": the Chinese people's journey into an era of reform was to be made aboard the hard-wearing two-wheeler. During this period the Flying Pigeon was said to be the most popular mechanized vehicle on the planet.

Statistics appear to support the claim. In the 1980s, Flying Pigeon produced four million bicycles per year and employed a workforce of ten thousand. By the end of the decade, China's annual bicycle sales had topped thirty-five million, surpassing global sales for motor vehicles. There were more than eight million bicycles on the streets of Beijing alone; 76 percent of the city's road space was occupied by bikes. Yet the throngs who cycled to the Tiananmen Square protests represented just a tiny fraction of China's unfathomably immense bicycle fleet: in 1989, there were some 225 million bikes on the nation's roads. The numbers bespoke a cultural attachment, a sense of the centrality of bicycles to China and "Chineseness," that penetrated the realm of national myth. The bicycle, writes Paul Smethurst, "was so absorbed into the state-sponsored culture in the 1960s that most citizens believed (and still believe) that it was a Chinese invention."

———

This was the bicycle kingdom to which Ted White pilgrimaged, with his movie camera and his friend George Bliss, in the autumn of 1991. White, twenty-eight, and Bliss, thirty-seven, were bike lovers and bike advocates, part of an activist vanguard that aimed to revive cycling in American cities. They knew that once upon a time, in the 1890s, it was the United States whose streets had teemed with millions of cyclists. White and Bliss dreamed that those bicycling armies could be revived, and urban America could be wrested from the grip of car culture. Both men had spent time in the Netherlands, Denmark, and other northern European bastions of cycling. In China, they were sure, they would find more inspiration—another vision of the bike-friendly society they longed to build, or rebuild, back in the States.

But when White and Bliss set foot in Guangzhou, disembarking from a ferryboat that had carried them to the mainland from Hong Kong, they beheld a cycling culture of another order. There were bicycles in every direction, rolling through the city in columns too vast for the eye to take in. The traffic carried a blur of young and old, male and female, riding those famous black roadsters. There were load-bearing bikes and tricycles too, with goods battened onto racks and cargo beds. Moments after arriving, White watched as a paraplegic man swept by on a hand cycle. White had long championed the ideal of "velodiversity," of streets that made room for all kinds of bikes and bike-like devices. Guangzhou itself appeared to be a kind of vast pedal-operated machine, powered by human sinews and by the whirring of countless cranks and chains and wheels.

It was this spectacle that White captured on film that day and in the days following, stalking the streets with a camera on his shoulder. A year later, in October 1992, at Fixed Gear on Natoma Street in San Francisco, an audience of a few dozen watched Guangzhou's bicycle parade pour past on-screen. The crowd that gathered that night to see *Return of the Scorcher* were Ted White's people: bicycle people, messengers and artists and young parents with child seats mounted on their bikes, the kind of urban bohemians for whom cycling was both a daily routine and a political cause. A number of those in attendance were part of a new movement that aimed to increase the visibility of San Francisco's cyclists by staging a group ride through the city on the last Friday of every month.

A few weeks earlier, on September 25, 1992, about sixty cyclists had gathered in Justin Herman Plaza, near the San Francisco Bay waterfront, for the first of these rides, a journey that flowed south-west on Market Street, one of the busiest thoroughfares in town. "Aren't you sick & tired of having to fight for your life on city streets?" a flyer advertising the event asked. There were precedents, of course, for protest rides that championed bicycles over cars. But the San Franciscans had a sharp political critique, a keen awareness of how the system was rigged against bicyclists and a strong sense of indignation about it: "Why are we treated like cars by the law, but like obnoxious and unwelcome obstructions by people in cars?" The ride's organizers held up a vision of strength in numbers, of bicyclists asserting their right to the roads by converging on them, en masse: "Imagine 25, 500, or even 1000+ bikes heading up Market together!"

Now, at the *Return of the Scorcher* screening, the crowd at Fixed Gear saw images of another kind of bicycle armada: the cycling commuters of Guangzhou, rolling over bridges and fanning across avenues as they went about their daily business. This footage was intercut with an interview with George Bliss, the New York bicycle designer. In China, Bliss said, he'd learned "how it feels to get up in the morning and get on a bike and go to work with a million other people, riding with jingling bells." The film, Bliss added, could not do justice to the experience of cycling in Guangzhou: "It's not the same as being in it, and being swept along by it, and feeling it pour around you and coming at you from every direction simultaneously." Bliss was especially impressed by the unwritten rules of the road, the systems that had developed organically on streets where motor vehicles had to yield to bikes, which far outnumbered them. Describing the way cyclists would navigate busy intersections with no traffic lights, Bliss said, "It was a kind of critical mass thing where all the cyclists would pile up and then go."

That phrase, "critical mass," struck a chord with the audience at Fixed Gear. The organizers of the monthly group ride had initially called it a "Commute Clot"—catchy enough, perhaps, but it cast the ride in negative terms, as a thrombosis impeding the flow of the city's lifeblood. "Critical mass" sounded a different note, suggestive of both protest and power. Within days of the *Return of the Scorcher* screening, new flyers appeared, inviting cyclists to "Join the Critical Mass." In November, Chris Carlsson, a writer and activist prominent in San Francisco bike circles, printed up a pamphlet, *Critical Comments on the Critical Mass*, hailing the nascent movement as "a *public space* where real politics between real people can unfold" and envisioning a radically altered San Francisco, a future in which "wild eco corridors," laced with bike paths and walkways and restored creeks, would crisscross the city. "We can be proud of our choice to bicycle, and we can and should flaunt it," Carlsson wrote. "Our CRITICAL MASS should be a mass and it should be *critical!*"

———

What does the future hold for the bicycle? What does the bicycle's future portend for the wider world? Will our cities move to the thrum of millions of bikes, as Beijing and Guangzhou did three decades ago? Or will cyclists find themselves, as they did in San Francisco in 1992, unwelcome on the streets, and in a fight for their lives?

No easy answers present themselves. History twists and turns in peculiar ways. The cyclists who pedaled along Market Street on those first Critical Mass rides, a confederacy of just several dozen, could not have anticipated that their local protest would launch a global movement. In the years since, thousands of Critical Mass rides have been staged, in more than six hundred cities, on six continents. Yet Critical Mass has not strayed far from its roots. Critical Mass isn't an organization; it's an idea. There is no leadership or membership. In San Francisco in the early '90s, participants established the tradition of "xerocracy," whereby anyone could take the initiative to plot routes for the rides and distribute photocopied maps—a decentralized approach that worked both strategically, to stymie police who might intervene to stop the protests, and ideologically, as an expression of nonhierarchical principles.

Over the years, other tactics have evolved and spread from city to city. Critical Mass participants often employ the maneuver known as "corking," stationing cyclists at the intersections of cross streets to block traffic and allow the Mass to roll through red lights. There is the "bike lift," when riders dismount and raise their bicycles overhead. An even more arresting piece of street theater is the "die-in," where riders lay their bodies and bicycles down on the street, in a group simulation of a massacre. The tactic appears to have first been used in Montreal in the 1970s by the proto-Critical Mass group Le Monde à Bicyclette; it is intended to evoke the injuries and deaths inflicted on bicyclists by cars and to suggest the peril we all face in an age of ecological collapse. But the die-in calls to mind other terrors—including, of course, the bicycle graveyard in Tiananmen.

Nearly everywhere Critical Mass rides have been staged, they have met resistance from law enforcement, motorists, and government officials. But there is no doubt that Critical Mass has made its mark. To the extent that cities across the globe have taken steps in recent years to adopt policies favorable to cycling—to the extent that even in those places where few changes have taken place, the question of bikes, cars, and safe streets is now a topic of debate— some credit must go to the activists who have taken to the roads in numbers and pressed the point.

Most Critical Mass rides are modest in size: a few dozen cyclists, maybe a couple hundred. Some are far larger. In Budapest, two Critical Mass rides held annually, on Earth Day (April 22) and International Car-Free Day (September 22), draw tens of thousands of riders, transforming the elegant avenues and bridges of that city into bicycle-mobbed terrain that calls to mind the streetscapes of China. To be precise: the streetscapes of yesteryear's China. Here we must take account of another momentous historical twist. Over the past three decades, while activists and policy makers around the world have pursued the dream of building a cycling culture like

China's, China itself has made a drastic move in the opposite direction—embracing automobility and clearing its roads of the bike-riding masses that were, seemingly, as organic and omnipresent as the earth underfoot and the sky overhead.

It's a change that can be traced back to Tiananmen Square and the spring of 1989. In the aftermath of Tiananmen, the Chinese government moved to suppress all vestiges of the pro-democracy movement and to purge those factions within the CCP that had advocated political liberalization. At the same time, Deng and other party leaders recognized that a new social compact was called for. In the 1990s, China instituted Deng's program of economic "reform and opening," casting aside the old Maoist ideal of collectivism in favor of competition and consumption. The government dissolved the people's communes and shuttered the state-run factories, instituting a new form of market-economy socialism that welcomed foreign trade, direct investment, and private enterprise. The system rested on a Hobbesian bargain: Chinese citizens gained unprecedented personal prosperity while abjuring basic rights and freedoms, leaving politics and governance under the CCP's unchallenged control. The result was "the Chinese miracle," the supercharged economic expansion that unfolded through the '90s and into the new millennium, and will culminate—around 2028, experts estimate—when China overtakes the United States as the world's largest economy.

Cynicism about the government runs deep in China. Many citizens quietly disdain the CCP's corruption, propaganda, and repression of dissidents. They resent the censors who expunge "subversive" material from the internet, and the facial-recognition systems and surveillance drones that cast a digital dragnet over the population. In private, they may roll their eyes at Xi Jinping, China's president and paramount leader, who has promoted a Mao-like cult of personality and sought in recent years to tighten ideological adherence to "Xi Jinping Thought" at all levels of society.

But in a nation with a history of shattering political violence, deprivation, and famine—where the traumas of the Great Leap Forward and the Cultural Revolution still loom in collective memory—the trade-offs are widely judged to be worth it. By most measures of safety, security, and material comfort, the Chinese people are vastly better off today than they were at the time of the Tiananmen uprising, or anytime before. In 1989, China's GDP per capita was $310, a figure lower than that of such nations as Sri Lanka, Guinea-Bissau, and Nicaragua. Three decades later, the per capita GDP reached $10,216, and hundreds of millions had been pulled out of poverty, into the largest middle class any nation has ever known.

That new middle class, 400 million and counting, enjoys not just a baseline standard of living unimaginable to previous generations— ample food, decent housing—but also disposable income and nice stuff: the wares and trappings of the consumerist good life. There are an estimated 1.6 billion cellphone subscriptions in China, a figure that exceeds the country's population; a reported 1 billion Chinese have internet access. (At least a third of them use a VPN to circumnavigate the government's Great Firewall.) They purchase name-brand clothing and upmarket household commodities. And more than 200 million are owners of the luxury good that has come to epitomize individual ambition, success, and freedom in the new China: a car.

This may be the most miraculous—or, at least, the most consequential—development associated with China's economic miracle. Until 1984, it was illegal for Chinese citizens to purchase a passenger car; at the time of the Tiananmen uprising, only 1 in 74,000 Chinese commuters owned a motor vehicle. In a series of directives issued in the early '90s, the government designated the auto industry a "pillar" of China's new economy, laying out heady plans to ramp up domestic motor vehicle production and seek joint ventures with foreign manufacturers, with the goal of producing 3.5 million cars by 2010. From today's perspective, that figure seems laughably modest. In 2009, the year China surpassed the United

States to become the world's largest automobile producer and consumer, nearly 14 million cars were built in the nation's factories.
Four years later, China set a record for the most passenger cars sold
in a country in a single year, 20 million.

Car culture expresses itself architecturally. To make room for
motor vehicles, China has shapeshifted, altering its landscape and
built environment at a rate, and on a scale, without analogue. Today,
China's network of expressways covers nearly one hundred thousand miles, more than twice the size of the U.S. Interstate Highway
System. Those roads tie together a nation of sprawling cities, urbs
and suburbs and exurbs, many of them brand-new places, populated by millions who have relocated from the countryside in recent
decades. (China now boasts more than one hundred cities with
more than one million residents.) These new urban settlements
were constructed for automobiles, on a scale inhospitable to traditional patterns of city life and traditional means of city transit.

Meanwhile, China's older cities have been retrofitted for cars.
China has pulled down and built up, razed and refigured, bulldoz-
ing residential districts and demolishing ancient urban cores to construct multilane roads, overpasses, and highways. Many cities have
been so comprehensively overhauled that lifelong residents find
themselves disoriented—lost in their own hometowns or convinced
that the towns themselves have been lost. "So many past events and
recollections that were once clearly inscribed in cityspace are now
all gone," a native of Kunming, the capital of Yunnan Province in
southwestern China, told the anthropologist Li Zhang. "I can only
trace them by looking at . . . faded black-and-white photographs in
archives." Since the 1990s, an estimated 90 percent of Beijing's
eight thousand *hutongs*—the famous courtyard alleyways where
residential life thrived for centuries—have been destroyed, replaced by high-rises and ring roads carrying eight lanes of traffic. To
appreciate the magnitude of China's urban transfiguration, the
scholar Beth E. Notar has written, you must imagine a scenario in
which "most of the old neighborhoods of Boston, New York and

Washington, D.C. were demolished and rebuilt within ten years, along with those of Chicago, Atlanta, Dallas, Houston, Denver, Phoenix, Seattle and San Francisco."

As the old streets vanished, so did the cycling multitudes that had filled those streets. The numbers tell a tale of astonishing change. In 1996, bicycle ownership in China reached an all-time high of 523 million, or 1.5 bicycles per household. But with the onset of "automobile frenzy," bike usage went into a precipitous decline. Within ten years, more Chinese people were traveling by car than by bicycle, and bike riding had become a marginal activity even in China's oldest and most traditionally bike-thronged cities.

This was, among other things, a measure of the CCP's awesome ability to wield centralized power and engineer grand social transformations. Just as China's unparalleled cycling culture had been a creation of the state, the product of meticulous planning and investment under the regimes of Mao and Deng, the bicycle's demise was a policy achievement. It is noteworthy that China's huge automobility push was accompanied by lavish investment in alternative forms of transit, including the construction of the world's most extensive high-speed rail network and the creation of new subway and bus lines in cities. China's devotion to cars, in other words, was not monomaniacal—but the government's promotion of car culture was based on ridding the roads of bikes, and that commitment was absolute. It pursued a program of, as it were, de-bikeification, conceived in Beijing and implemented at the municipal level.

China's Road Safety Law, enacted in 1994, included a provision permitting local authorities to reclaim road space previously allocated to non-motorized transport. Cities across the nation moved swiftly, converting bike lanes to car lanes and parking spaces for cars. Planners set ambitious goals for moving cyclists off the roads. Guangzhou, whose bicycling critical mass so thrilled George Bliss and Ted White, formulated a transport master plan in the early 1990s that aimed for a 40 percent reduction in bicycle commuting by the year 2013. (That target was met, and eclipsed, a decade early:

by 2003, bicycle usage in the city had decreased by about 60 percent.) Other cities took more draconian steps. In the early 2000s, Shanghai declared a total ban on bike riding in certain busy downtown areas. In the same period, the bustling city of Dalian, in the northeastern coastal province of Liaoning, pronounced itself a "non-bicycle city."

The changes were especially dramatic in the great cycling city of Beijing. In 1996, there were an estimated nine million bicycles in the capital, roughly 2.5 bikes per household, and nearly two-thirds of all trips in the city were made by bike. Within fifteen years, the number of bicycles on the roads had fallen to under four million, and travel by bicycle accounted for just 16.7 percent of Beijing journeys. In part, this was a reflection of the city's steroidal growth. Today, the urban area of Beijing is more than ten times the size it was in 1990, covering an expanse larger than the state of Rhode Island. Under the old Communist work unit system, citizens lived close to their workplaces and could easily cycle to work. But for millions in sprawling twenty-first-century Beijing, life without a car is untenable.

As car culture tightened its grip, conditions on Chinese streets began to resemble those that had prompted cyclists in San Francisco to found Critical Mass. The roads were congested, wreathed in exhaust fumes, and dangerous. Bikes were frequently struck by cars, and often, blame for the accidents was attributed to the cyclists. Bicycles were also said by critics to be a cause of the traffic epidemic, a judgment that led to the closure of more bike lanes. The hostile conditions compelled more cyclists to forsake bikes for cars or, in the case of those who couldn't afford cars, to opt for mass transit. In Beijing, this development was commemorated, the researchers Glen Norcliffe and Gao Boyang Gao noted in 2018, by a new feature of the landscape: discarded bicycles, which were "abandoned by the thousands" and lay "in neglected piles outside apartment buildings and elsewhere." They were monuments, you might say, to the lost bicycle kingdom.

They were monuments, also, to a change of heart—an emotional and ideological alteration as profound as those proscribed in policy papers and laid down in asphalt. The Chinese had fallen out of love with bikes. It wasn't just that a nation of motorists now regarded bicycles, like San Francisco's drivers did in 1992, as "obnoxious and unwelcome obstructions." Anti-bicycle sentiment in China ran deeper and was more inflected by stigma and shame. In a society where the car had become the ultimate status symbol—the holy grail for untold millions of middle-class strivers, and for millions more striving to join the middle class—the bicycle was viewed as embarrassing, old-fashioned, "for losers," "for the poor." Bikes were anathema to a modern lifestyle, to the ambitions and aspirations of the young and upwardly mobile. Fashion-conscious Chinese women were now "choosing skirts instead of pants [and] giving up their bikes"—a mirror-image inversion of the 1890s boom, when women on the cutting edge paraded their modernity by forsaking dresses for bloomers and bikes. And where the bicycle had previously been an indispensable asset in the Chinese marriage marketplace, one of the essential "three rounds," it was now an impediment to romantic success. On a 2010 episode of a popular TV dating show, *If You Are the One*, a twenty-year-old contestant was asked by a suitor to go for a bicycle ride on a date. Her response became a much-memed viral catchphrase. "I'd rather cry in a BMW," she said, "than smile on a bicycle."

———

If you want to begin wrapping your mind around global car culture—if, for that matter, you want to ponder the gnarly complexities of life on planet Earth in the globalized twenty-first century—a good place to start is Wuhan, the city of eleven million in Hubei Province, in China's industrial heartland. Like so many Chinese cities, Wuhan was once a biking town, but most of its millions of cyclists long ago ditched their two wheels. Today, Wuhan is a car city par excellence. It is one China's "Detroit," a major production base for the automobile industry. Each year, millions of cars, approximately 10 percent of all those manufactured in China, are built in Wuhan's factories. Wuhan is the headquarters of the Dongfeng Motor Corporation, one of China's "Big Four" auto companies. Several foreign car makers—Honda, Nissan, Peugeot, Renault, and General Motors, among others—have plants in Wuhan. The city is also home to hundreds of automobile parts suppliers, which export their products across the world.

In the winter of 2020, Wuhan gained notoriety as a different kind of global origin point. The first known case of the novel coronavirus, SARS-CoV-2, was identified in Wuhan in December 2019. The precise nature of the virus's origins was unknown, and is still the subject of heated debate. But the manner in which Covid-19 became a pandemic, rampaging across China and spreading to virtually every nation on earth, is no mystery. It moved at speed, in a world that moves at speed. It followed the same pathways as the spark plugs and catalytic converters and steering-gear components that are assembled in Wuhan and dispatched across the planet. It rolled out of town on the Shanghai-Chongqing Expressway. It made ocean passages on the container ships that ferry goods out of China. It zoomed above the seas in Boeings and Airbuses.

And then, as Covid took hold in one nation after another, everything slowed down and stopped moving. In cities great and small, a hush fell over the streets. Cars largely vanished from roads, buses and subways ceased operation, the skies were emptied of airplanes. Everyday existence had taken on a surreal and terrifying texture. But amid the dread and death, new, and very old, forms of life appeared.

Quarantining city dwellers looked out their windows and beheld arcadian scenes. Animals were wandering into abandoned city centers. Boars roamed in packs through Haifa, Israel; pumas appeared on the streets of Santiago. In Istanbul, where marine traffic had dwindled and a fishing ban was in place, dolphins were spotted in the Bosporus, far closer to the city's shoreline than they normally ventured. There were similar spectacles in India, where hundreds of thousands of migrating flamingos turned Mumbai wetlands into a sea of pink, and herds of buffalo strode untroubled down empty highways in New Delhi.

Photos and videos of rewilded cities shot around the internet, including many that were clearly fake. (No, dolphins were not frolicking in the canals of Venice.) But the images, real and phony alike, offered a ready metaphor, and a degree of comfort, to those seeking meaning in the madness of the pandemic. Perhaps things were returning to the way they should be; perhaps a better existence was possible, one where we recalibrate our rhythms to match those of the natural world and life moves at a statelier, saner pace.

Changes were already taking place. There were other creatures roving cities. Bicyclists were repopulating the roads. With options for public transit reduced, and urbanites compelled to put distance between themselves and their neighbors, the rusty three-speed in the basement had new allure. As lockdown restrictions eased, millions began hauling out old bikes or buying new ones. "What do bikes and toilet paper have in common?" asked *The Washington Post* in the spring of 2020. "Both are flying out of stores amid the coronavirus pandemic."

Between March 2020, when the lockdown began in the United States, and April 2021, year-over-year bicycle sales rose nearly 60 percent nationally. Lines stretched down sidewalks outside bicycle shops. Many shops ran out of bikes, and additional inventory was slow to arrive, as manufacturers struggled to keep up with orders and supply chains were disrupted. Bike theft skyrocketed. (The owner of a Brooklyn bike store told a journalist that the best way to avoid having one's bicycle stolen under the current conditions was to "sleep with it next to you.") Many of those buying bikes were recreational riders, seeking a socially distanced kind of exercise. In the early months of the outbreak, a nonprofit group that promotes the conversion of defunct railway lines into paths for biking and walking reported record ridership on American cycle trails. But there was also an explosion of bicycle commuting in such unlikely places as Houston and Los Angeles, where only a tiny percentage of the population traveled by bike in normal times. A study conducted in the first weeks of the outbreak found that one in ten American adults had recently ridden a bicycle for the first time in a year or longer, and a majority said they planned to continue cycling after the crisis passed.

America's pandemic-provoked "transit upheaval," as CNBC put it, was only one part of a much larger phenomenon—a global "Great Covid-19 Bicycle Boom." In Santo Domingo, Lima, Milan, Moscow, Dubai, Beirut, Abidjan, Nairobi, Singapore, Seoul, and hundreds of other cities, cyclists were amassing on roadways. In many places, they took advantage of existing infrastructure, converging on bike lanes and patronizing cycle-share systems in unprecedented numbers.

But cities were assembling new infrastructure on the fly. "Corona cycleways" arose across the globe. Emergency funds were appropriated, programs were fast-tracked, incentives and subsidies to bolster biking were introduced. Pop-up bike lanes appeared in Mexico City and Bogotá, in Kampala and Cape Town, in Jakarta and Tokyo, in Sydney and Auckland. In the Philippines, temporary cycle lanes, installed in central Manila after Covid hit, were expanded into a permanent network covering two hundred miles and passing through twelve of Metro Manila's sixteen cities. India's Ministry of Housing and Urban Affairs, citing the "cycling revolution" that had taken over the country during the pandemic, launched the "India Cycles4Change" initiative, calling on municipalities to "transform . . . into havens for cycling" with new infrastructure, the establishment of open streets, outreach to women riders, and other measures.

Some of the most aggressive moves to remake roads and claim space for bikes were undertaken in the United Kingdom and Europe. A study published in the spring of 2021 found that new cycleways had been installed in 106 European cities since the onset of the pandemic. Under the leadership of Anne Hidalgo, its zealously pro-cycling mayor, Paris added hundreds of miles of bicycle "*coronapistes*" in the first months of the crisis and banned cars from the Rue de Rivoli, transforming one of the city's most famous thoroughfares into a two-mile-long cycling cavalcade. The following year, Hidalgo introduced a more dramatic plan to ban through traffic in several arrondissements, a scheme that would turn much of central Paris into a virtually car-free zone.

These changes were testaments to the depth of the Covid crisis, how it had reordered priorities and unlocked political possibilities, emboldening policy makers and citizens to take action. Or maybe "emboldening" is exactly wrong; perhaps it was simply fear, the blind terror incited by Covid, that was the real driver of change. Commuters, scared of contracting the virus in buses and trains and taxicabs, gravitated to bicycles, a means of transit that put breathing space between themselves and the neighbors who had suddenly become nemeses, potential vectors of disease. These new cyclists rode on routes delineated by traffic cones, plastic bollards, and police sawhorses, the pathways that authorities patched together in panicky haste, desperate to get people moving again and to jolt moribund economies back to life. The result, in any case, was the realization of long-held hopes. The cycling cities dreamed of for decades by Critical Mass riders and other activists were—despite and because of a historic catastrophe—coming into view. The paradox was noted in a BBC interview with Will Butler-Adams, the managing director of Brompton, the English bicycle manufacturer famous for its folding bikes. Pedaling through a world gripped by sorrow and trepidation, cyclists found themselves in something like idyllic conditions—in clean air, on safe streets, riding free and easy. They were experiencing, Butler-Adams said, "the joy of . . . cities as they could be."

———

New York was one of the places whose roadways, and folkways, were in the throes of transformation. The city's first case of Covid-19 was documented on March 1, 2020. (Later research revealed that the virus had begun circulating in the five boroughs as early as January.) Soon, New York was the global epicenter of the pandemic. By April 6, there had been more than 72,000 confirmed Covid cases in the city, and at least 2,400 of the infected had perished. On April 7, 774 New Yorkers died. On April 8, there were 810 more deaths.

New Yorkers were learning that a plague brings a macabre logistical problem: lots of corpses that need to be disposed of. Morgues and cemeteries had run out of room, as the city faced what one official called "the equivalent of an ongoing 9/11." The dead were piling up in refrigerated trucks parked on street corners outside hospitals. On April 9, an Associated Press drone camera captured video of bodies being lowered into a mass grave on a patch of land off the coast of the Bronx. This was Hart Island, a 101-acre strip in Long Island Sound, which for more than a century had been home to New York's potter's field, the city's burial ground for the indigent and anonymous.

The footage, which circulated widely online, induced a shiver. For New Yorkers, Hart Island was a place out of sight and out of mind, a necropolis within the metropolis, cut off from the living population geographically and psychically. The island had been uninhabited for decades, was almost entirely closed to the public, and could be accessed only by the ferries that periodically made the Stygian voyage to deliver the dead and transport the crews, drawn from the city's prison population, that were tasked with burying the bodies. The AP video showed workers in protective gear arranging coffins in a wide, muddy trench. The bird's-eye vantage point lent the scene a chilling impersonality. When the burial crew shoveled dirt over the plain wooden boxes, they did so with the unceremonious diligence of a street repair team scooping asphalt into a pothole. It was a glimpse into the abyss.

Death was never out of earshot now. Day and night, sirens

howled on the other side of the walls where millions were holed up. From my living room windows, you could see two levels of nearly empty roads. Down below, the Brooklyn streets; above them, resting atop huge steel pillars, a long, loping span of the Gowanus Expressway. Normally, both the streets and the highway were crammed with cars, but the traffic had thinned to a trickle, mostly those wailing ambulances speeding the stricken to hospitals. When the sirens faded, the quiet of the city was startling. You could hear birdsong, and the wind in the trees, and, now and then, lonely footfalls in the street. The silence was broken, each night at precisely seven P.M., by a callithumpian eruption, as New Yorkers leaned out of windows or stepped onto apartment balconies to rattle pots and pans with kitchen utensils, paying noisy tribute to the doctors, nurses, ambulance drivers, and other essential workers who were toiling on the front lines while the rest of us stayed inside.

You could hear another sound, too, if you listened closely: the high-pitched hum of electric bicycle motors. The riders of these bikes were deliverymen, carting food orders to quarantining residents. They were frontline workers, too, deemed "essential" by the government. It's doubtful, though, that many of those who hailed the heroes of the pandemic by banging on kitchenware were thinking of the guy who had just dropped off their dinner of pizza or pad thai.

The delivery workers were mostly immigrants from Latin America: from Mexico, Guatemala, Ecuador, Venezuela, and elsewhere. The machines they rode were not fancy e-bikes but hybrid bikes rigged with rechargeable e-bike attachments. Even in non-pandemic times, their jobs were among the most difficult in the city. They faced physical danger from motorists and adverse weather conditions; they were frequent victims of bike theft, often at the point of a gun or knife. Like many gig economy laborers, they were not entitled to a minimum wage, overtime, health coverage, or other benefits, and they complained that portions of their tips were being illegally garnished by the restaurants and the delivery app companies themselves. Most restaurants refused to let them use the bathroom when they came to pick up orders.

The neighborhoods where the delivery workers lived, in Brooklyn and Queens and the Bronx, had some of the highest Covid rates in the city. The deliverymen were keeping the restaurant industry afloat, feeding hundreds of thousands of New Yorkers, and many of them were winding up in coronavirus wards. New York City, it seems, is not so very different from the megacities of the Global South. Dhaka has its *rickshawallahs*; we have our *deliveristas:* an underclass of working cyclists, tens of thousands of them, who keep the city going while enduring hardships, hazards, and abuse.

The *deliveristas* were not the only cyclists riding in the locked-down town. Other essential workers were commuting by bike to avoid Covid exposure on public transportation. In May, with the curve finally flattening, New Yorkers began to emerge from their homes. The pattern established in other cities around the world played out: bike lanes were jammed; share-bike usage was sky-high. And then, in the last week of the month, events more than a thousand miles away drew legions more New Yorkers, and their bicycles, out of lockdown and into the streets.

———

On the evening of May 25, George Floyd was murdered by Minneapolis police officer Derek Chauvin after allegedly using a counterfeit twenty-dollar bill to buy cigarettes. In the days and weeks that followed, an estimated 15 million Americans joined an uprising that has been called the largest protest movement in the nation's history. In New York, demonstrators swarmed the city, marching and chanting. Over the weekend of May 30–31, the unrest got wilder. Protesters smashed windows and looted high-end retailers; they tossed Molotov cocktails and torched police cruisers. On Monday night, June 1, Mayor Bill de Blasio imposed a citywide curfew in an effort to restore order.

On the night of June 3, police officers were seen confiscating bicycles from Black Lives Matter demonstrators who were continuing to march in defiance of the eight P.M. curfew. In one widely shared video clip, a jittery camera captured a cop wheeling an apparently commandeered bike; a woman could be heard screaming at the police, asking why bikes were being taken and how protesters were supposed to travel home. Another piece of viral footage showed three policemen clubbing a cyclist with batons on a Manhattan street. It was unclear whether the man was arrested or what became of his bicycle.

In the days that followed, the NYPD's anti-bicycle actions continued. The *Daily News* reporter Catherina Gioino tweeted that the police had been ordered to "focus on the bicyclists." Other social media posts documented arrests and violent attacks on cyclists, including journalists with press credentials. The city's first curfew since the Second World War had been imposed, according to Mayor de Blasio's executive order, to curb "assault, vandalism, property damage, and/or looting." New Yorkers were left to wonder how scenes of cops beating protesters and snatching their bikes—or, in some cases, leaving the bikes littered on the street—squared with the stated objectives.

These incidents were not exactly surprising. The NYPD has a long history of hostility to cyclists, especially cyclists who are also protesters. For years, the police used aggressive, sometimes violent tactics to sweep up participants in Critical Mass rallies. In 2008, an NYPD officer body-slammed a Critical Mass rider; the cop later received a felony conviction for this action and for filing a false criminal complaint in an attempt to frame the cyclist. In 2010, the city agreed to pay a settlement of nearly $1 million to eighty-three Critical Mass riders who had been wrongly detained or arrested between 2004 and 2006.

In the de Blasio era, the NYPD engaged in sporadic crackdowns against bicyclists, issuing tickets, levying fines, and confiscating bikes. (Cycling advocates have characterized these "ticket blitzes"—

which often follow incidents in which cyclists are maimed or killed by automobiles—as a form of institutionalized victim blaming.) For years, de Blasio and the NYPD waged "war on e-bikes," seizing hundreds of bikes, a campaign that almost exclusively hit the city's *deliveristas*.

The conflict between law enforcement and cyclists played out nationwide. In Los Angeles, San Francisco, Portland, Chicago, Atlanta, Miami, and dozens of other cities, protesters pedaled and marched with their bicycles, facing off with police officers who, in many cases, were also mounted on bikes. Bicycle cops have become fixtures of police forces over the past few decades. But in the 2020 protests, Americans saw something new: militarized bicycle police, using violent riot-control tactics against demonstrators who weren't rioting.

Bike cops unleashed tear gas, shot pepper spray, tossed flash grenades, and pummeled protesters with nightsticks. The officers wielded their bicycles like weapons, using them as shields and battering rams. BikeCo., the North American distributor for Fuji Bikes, issued a statement announcing that it was suspending the sale of police bikes after seeing its products deployed in ways "that we did not intend or design them to be used."

In New York, the NYPD's own "elite" unit of bike-mounted officers emerged, wearing uniforms that split the difference between storm trooper, hockey goalie, and Teenage Mutant Ninja Turtle. This was the NYPD Strategic Response Group (SRG) Bicycle Squad, which specializes in crowd control. On June 4, the squad participated in police interventions and mass arrests at a Black Lives Matter demonstration in the Bronx, using their bicycles to strike, push, and help to confine, or "kettle," protesters. Human Rights Watch characterized the NYPD's actions in the incident as a "planned assault" and "police brutality."

The SRG Bike Squad's "Instructor Guide," a 173-page manual made public by the muckraking news site *The Intercept*, details the unit's duties. These include serving as a "force multiplier" at pro-

tests and gathering intelligence by monitoring "crowd[s], ring leaders, and/or organizers." The manual offers examples illustrating the
difference between "peaceful" crowds ("Parades or details such as
New Year's Eve") and "violent" crowds ("Occupy Wall Street, BLM
movement, Anti-Trump Demonstrations"), and provides instruction in a number of "aggressive" cycling maneuvers (the "Power
Slide," the "Dynamic Dismount") that bike officers use to control
and subdue. The dystopian trend of American life has not, it seems,
spared the bicycle.

———

The high-profile presence of bicycles in the Black Lives Matter
uprising was perhaps surprising to some. But transportation issues are social justice issues. The toll of bad transit policies and
worse infrastructure—trains and buses that don't run well and
serve low-income neighborhoods inadequately, vehicular traffic
that pollutes the environment and endangers the lives of cyclists
and pedestrians—is borne disproportionately by Black and Latino
communities. Researchers have found that the fatality rates in road
accidents for Black and Latino cyclists are, respectively, 30 percent
and 23 percent higher than for whites.

Studies also confirm that police pull over, harass, and arrest non-
white cyclists at drastically higher rates than whites. A survey in
Oakland, a city with a 28 percent Black population, concluded that
sixty percent of the cyclists pulled over by police were Black. Studies of tickets issued to bike riders by police in Chicago and Tampa
found even more pronounced disparities. In New York, 86 percent
of all cyclists ticketed in 2018 and 2019 for riding on the sidewalk
were Black and Latino, and nearly half were twenty-four years old
or younger.

These statistics reflect the truth that, in many American cities,
bike riding by people of color is de facto illegal. For the police, the
presence of a bicycle serves as a pretext to engage in racial profiling

and employ stop-and-frisk tactics that—institutionally, officially—
they claim to have abandoned. A *Los Angeles Times* investigation
analyzed more than 44,000 bicycle stops by the L.A. County Sheriff's Department (LASD) between 2017 and July 2021. A majority
of the stops occurred in low-income neighborhoods with large non-
white populations, and seven out of ten stops involved Latino cyclists. The *Times* reported that LASD sheriffs apprehend cyclists
"for minor violations such as riding on the sidewalk" and "search
85% of bike riders they stop even though they often have no reason
to suspect they'll find something illegal. Most bicyclists were held in
the backseat of patrol cars while deputies rummaged through their
belongings or checked for arrest warrants." Bicycle traffic stops can
have tragic outcomes. On August 31, 2020, ninety-eight days after
the death of George Floyd, LASD deputies shot and killed Dijon
Kizzee, a twenty-nine-year-old Black man, who they had attempted
to apprehend for "riding a bicycle on the wrong side of the road" in
the South L.A. community of Westmont. An autopsy found that
Kizzee was struck by sixteen bullets, suffering wounds to his hands,
arm, shoulder, chest, chin, back, and back of the head.

In New York, the summer and autumn of 2020 were seasons of
bicycle protest. *Deliveristas* staged demonstrations outside NYPD
station houses to decry the department's indifference to an epidemic of e-bike thefts and assaults on delivery workers. In October,
hundreds of *deliveristas* converged on City Hall, demanding better
wages and working conditions. New movements were emerging.
Street Riders NYC, formed in June by six Brooklyn-based Black
activists, drew thousands of cyclists for protest rides that wound
through the city. These were Black Lives Matter demonstrations,
with calls for racial and economic justice, defunding the police, and
the dismantling of the American carceral state. But the protests also
addressed the politics of race and mobility, celebrating the ecumen-
ical "freedom of cycling" while—tacitly, at least—critiquing a white
bicycle activist establishment that for years had ignored issues of
transit equity and the unique burdens faced by cyclists of color.

Perhaps the most revolutionary new form of bicycle protest is one that does not claim to be a protest at all. The term "bikelife" originally referred to "gangs" of motocross dirt bikers and four-wheeled ATV riders from cities like New York and Baltimore who gained fame with videos showcasing the wheelies, donuts, and other wild stunts they executed on urban streets and highways. In the early 2010s, Darnell Meyers, a Harlem bicycle deliveryman then in his early twenties, began posting online videos of his bikelife-inspired moves, performed not on motor vehicles but on an old-fashioned So Cal Flyer: a retro-style BMX bike, manufactured by the legendary company SE. The bike's large but lightweight aluminum frame, big wheels, chunky tires, and pegs served as a sturdy platform for tricks, and Meyers's repertoire was awesome. He could stand atop the seat or handlebars as the bike coasted forward at high speed; he could tilt the bike over so that it hovered, just inches above the pavement, and slide along on the side of the rear wheel, as if riding a surfboard or a magic carpet; he could yank his front wheel up, to a nearly ninety-degree angle, and pedal, balanced on his rear wheel, while reaching backward to let his hand brush the ground, like a boater skimming a lake with his fingers.

The most striking thing about Meyers's brand of trick cycling wasn't what he did, but where he did it: on the streets of New York, often while weaving through traffic. He prided himself on his wheel-ieing prowess, traveling with the front of his bike raised skyward for block after block, and gave himself a nickname that celebrated the practice: DBlocks. He garnered a large Instagram following, and began to post notices inviting fellow cyclists to meet up for group rides across the city. This wasn't exactly a novelty. DBlocks had first caught the bicycle bug at age eleven when he saw groups of neighborhood kids pedaling through Harlem in packs. But DBlocks's "ride-outs" quickly grew large, and then larger: squadrons of BMX cyclists, mostly young and Black and male, surging along the avenues by the dozens or the hundreds, with their front wheels raised off the pavement, performing dangerous, flashy tricks for mile after mile, and chronicling their exploits on social media feeds.

Today, the movement known by the hashtag #bikelife is a global phenomenon. Ride-outs have reached six continents and achieved pop prominence through their appearance in rap videos. Like drag racing and skateboarding, #bikelife is an example of the kind of anarchic thrill-seeking that captivates teenagers and young adults of certain dispositions, in no small part because it outrages authority figures. In New York, the police have targeted #bikelife events, confiscating participants' bicycles and reportedly breaking up ride-outs by ramming mopeds into cyclists. (The SRG Bike Squad manual leaked to *The Intercept* includes the policing of "Bicycle Ride Outs" in a list of the squad's achievements.)

But #bikelife is not just teen rebellion for its own sake. To behold a ride-out—to watch hundreds of Black kids, a dozen abreast, wheelieing across bridges, down highways, and along other roads where bicycles are forbidden—is to witness as radical a display of bike riding as freedom and resistance as any in the bicycle's two-century-long history. Like prior generations of bicycle activists, #bikelife riders stake claim to the commons of the public roadways—but they do so with an aggressiveness and flamboyance that makes a Critical Mass rally look quaint by comparison.

Of course, #bikelife represents a larger politics. Black Lives Matter is in part a moral crusade about mobility and who is at liberty to go where. It decries a system that surveils and circumscribes the movement of Black people—that construes the mere presence of Black people in public spaces as trespassing, a crime punishable by imprisonment or even death. In #bikelife ride-outs, members of America's most demonized and overpoliced population assert their right to absolute freedom of movement. Ride-outs dramatize the vulnerability of Black bodies, placing speeding riders in rowdy traffic, on thirty-two-pound bikes, amid vehicles one hundred times heavier. But ride-out cyclists enact defiance and fearlessness, transforming dangerous commutes into virtuoso performances while scorning the authorities by self-surveilling: documenting their putatively illegal activities on cellphone cameras and posting the evidence online. Thundering through the city with their front wheels aloft, like a cavalry on rearing stallions, #bikelife riders celebrate the joy, style, and audacity of biking while Black.

———

The bicycle's foes have greeted the new American bike boom with old-fashioned vituperation. The culture wars are raging, and jabbing rhetorical thumbtacks into bike tires is a time-honored way to own the libs. In the first year of the pandemic, anti-bicycle invective resounded in the usual precincts of social media and the right-wing press. But it also rumbled down from the Olympus of the Supreme Court. In a November 2020 decision, *Roman Catholic Diocese of Brooklyn, New York v. Cuomo*, the court barred restrictions on religious services that New York's governor, Andrew Cuomo, had imposed to combat the spread of Covid-19. In a concurring opinion, Justice Neil Gorsuch derided the inclusion of "bicycle repair shops" in a list of essential businesses and included bicycles in a catalog of "secular" lifestyle adornments, alongside wine and acupuncture treatments. "According to the Governor, it may be unsafe to go to church, but it is always fine to pick up another bottle of wine, shop for a new bike, or spend the afternoon exploring your distal points and meridians," Gorsuch wrote.

It was familiar rhetoric, and there was more of it to come, especially when Joe Biden defeated Donald Trump in the 2020 presidential election and appointed the sharp-witted and ambitious wonk Pete Buttigieg to the post of secretary of transportation. Buttigieg made sensible statements like "I don't think a lot of Americans are aware . . . how far behind we are on bicycle and pedestrian safety" and "We're better off if our decisions revolve not around the car but around the human being." This was red meat for right-wing pundits, and they chomped at it, wringing a couple of news cycles out of the proposition "Democrats are coming for your cars." When cameras caught Buttigieg commuting by bicycle to a cabinet meeting, right-wing media falsely reported that Buttigieg had "faked" the bike ride, exiting a chauffeur-driven car "to ride his bike a few feet" for the paparazzi.

Boorish American car culture and incipient American fascism were natural allies. In the spring of 2021, Republican-controlled legislatures in Oklahoma and Iowa had passed bills that grant immunity to drivers who strike protesters with their cars. The second summer of the pandemic was upon us, and the mood in the United States was intensely, almost comically, ominous. Everywhere you looked, it seemed, there were scenes of decadence and portents of decline and fall. Covid vaccines had arrived, but so had the Delta variant. While billions around the world waited in desperation for their first vaccine dose, half of eligible Americans were spurning these readily available medicines based on lunatic conspiracy theories. Presumably there was significant overlap between the population of anti-vaxxers and those who claimed that the January 6 white nationalist insurrection at the U.S. Capitol was a false-flag hoax perpetrated by antifa.

Meanwhile, tycoons were leaving the planet. On July 20, 2021, the wealthiest person on earth, Jeff Bezos, went hot-rodding in sub-orbital space for ten minutes aboard a phallic rocket ship called New Shepherd. The design of this spacecraft so closely resembled the silhouette of a penis and testicles as graffitied on the wall of a junior high school boys' bathroom, it seemed impossible that Bezos was not in on the joke—until you remembered that he was Jeff Bezos. Nine days earlier, British magnate Richard Branson had nipped Bezos in the space race, successfully completing his own suborbital flight in Virgin Galactic's VSS *Unity*, a supersonic plane. Then there was Elon Musk, the Tesla mogul, undeterred by the fact that his own prototype "Starships" spacecraft had crashed and burned in multiple test flights, and now busy working on two fronts:

planning a program of Martian colonization with his "space transportation" concern SpaceX, while, in his capacity as founder of the
Boring Company—either brilliantly or idiotically named, you
pick—he was pioneering a new system of subterranean transit in
which driverless Teslas would ferry passengers between cities via a
network of "Hyperloop" tunnels.

You couldn't really blame the billionaires for wanting to jet into
space or head underground. Earth was experiencing a bad run of
weather. The same morning that Bezos took off on the New Shepherd, I stepped out of my apartment building, unchained my bike,
and started riding. Soon, I noticed that my eyes were stinging, my
throat itched, and the sky was tinged a hazy hue of reddish orange.
For weeks, dozens of wildfires had been ravaging the West Coast,
burning millions of acres. The extreme heat generated by one of
those infernos, the Bootleg Fire in Oregon, created ash-filled pyro-
cumulus clouds, which rode high-level winds three thousand miles
east to drop a dusty veil on Brooklyn. There is no such thing any-
more as local weather.

Several weeks later, another sign of the times descended from
the skies. On September 1, a Wednesday evening, torrential rains
fell on New York, causing flash flooding that swamped the town.
The storm was the remnant of Hurricane Ida, which had struck
Louisiana forty-eight hours earlier. Cars floated in the streets, bobbing in water that carried raw sewage. The Brooklyn-Queens Expressway filled up like a Venetian canal. The flood burst through the
ceilings of subway stations, cascading onto trains and platforms.
Thirteen people died in New York City, nearly all of them immigrants in Queens who were trapped in basement apartments as the
water rose. A viral Twitter post showed video of a Grubhub worker
on a Brooklyn street that had become a river, pushing his bicycle
through driving rain in waist-high water. On the handlebars of his
bike you can see a plastic bag dangling: he is making a food delivery.
Later, it emerged that some apps incentivized *deliveristas* to keep

working in the life-threatening conditions by offering "severe weather incentives": a few extra dollars per job.

The next morning, September 2, was bright, breezy, and dry, one of those preposterously crystalline days that seem to follow the once-in-a-century climatic events that now take place every month or so. Overnight, the MTA had shut down the inundated subway, so New Yorkers woke up and got on bicycles. Citi Bike recorded 126,360 trips that day: the largest single-day ridership in the service's eight-year existence to that date. Ice is melting at the top and bottom of the planet, forests are aflame, political systems are fracturing, a pandemic has shaken daily life at its foundations, and amid the tumult, a new global bicycle culture is emerging. Today's bike boom is, without question, the largest in history, taking in untold millions of cyclists, just about everywhere on earth. It is a mass movement, of epic proportions. But is it too little, too late?

———

Over the past two decades, Ai Weiwei, the dissident Chinese artist, has created a series of sculptures that bear the evocative title *Forever Bicycles*. The first of these, from 2003, featured a couple dozen bikes, with handlebars, pedals, and chains removed, rigged up in circular pattern to form a single structure—a kind of a bicycle ouroboros, a Dada freak bike. Ai continued to evolve the work on an increasingly massive scale, producing site-specific *Forever Bicycles* installations in which hundreds, or occasionally thousands, of bikes are arranged in vast symmetrical configurations that tower and arc overhead. The effect is strobic: gazing upward, the viewer takes in a psychedelic infinitude of frames and wheels.

There are art historical allusions here: a nod to Duchamp, certainly, and perhaps to M. C. Escher's optical echo chambers. There are other resonances, too. The title, *Forever Bicycles*, contains a pun, a reference to the famous Shanghai bicycle brand Forever, which, along with Flying Pigeon, ruled the roads of Ai's youth in the 1960s and '70s. (In many versions of the sculptures, Ai has used Forever bikes.)

No one familiar with Ai will doubt that there are politics in this monumental assemblage of bikes without riders: an evocation of the vanished cycling multitudes of yesteryear, including those who pedaled together to Tiananmen Square. But Ai also speaks to the deeps of bike lore and bike love. *Forever Bicycles* is a poetic, symphonic tribute to the pure and timeless beauty of the bicycle's form: all those bikes—or, rather, a single bike, the Bike Eternal, refracted endlessly—hovering on high, as if floating in the heavenly vault.

Of course, the bike probably isn't eternal. In our age of collapse, what is? But the bicycle is resilient; it has a way of staging comebacks. In recent years, China has evinced second thoughts about the demise of its bicycle kingdom. The nation's conversion to car culture has had a predictable series of environmental and social effects: increased pollution and greenhouse gas emissions, rising rates of lung disease and other respiratory maladies, an obesity crisis, and an epidemic of auto accidents. Today, China's roads are the world's most dangerous, and traffic accidents are the leading cause of death for Chinese people age forty-five and younger.

Bicycles remain a fixture of the nation's economy. China is, by far, the world's leading producer and exporter of bikes and bike components. And recently, the government has embarked on ambitious efforts to revive cycling at home. After years of building roads for cars on a gargantuan scale, the CCP has undertaken cutting-edge cycling infrastructure projects, including the construction of bicycle expressways in Beijing and the coastal city of Xiamen.

Bike-share systems are another key to China's bicycle revival. The nation's experiment with share bikes started badly: the boom-and-bust debacle of the latter 2010s, which left those mountain ranges of discarded Mobikes and Ofos piled on urban outskirts. But in the last half decade, especially since the onset of the pandemic, the industry has regained ground, with new bike-share brands, funded by corporate giants, operating in a moderately more regulated market. Dockless Hellobikes (backed by tech goliath Alibaba) and Meituan Bike (which acquired Mobike in 2018) are increasingly fixtures of Chinese cities, popular among a new generation of urban professionals who are, perhaps, less invested in the cult of the car and harbor fewer stigmatized associations with bikes. A growing number of the share cycles are electric bikes, which have emerged as the focal point of China's cycling renaissance. Today, there are an astounding three hundred million e-bikes, both share bikes and privately owned, on China's roads.

In historical terms, this is a pretty big deal. The rise of e-bikes—whose global market will grow to $70 billion by 2027, according to industry forecasters—may well be the most significant development in bicycle culture since the invention of the safety. A bike that requires minimal use of human muscle and pedal power represents a huge ontological shift, a great big reconceptualization of *what a bike is*. But what matters on the ground is that lots of people really, really like electric bikes, and are reconfiguring their lives around them. In China, the e-bike is clearly the new "national bike," the successor to the iconic black roadsters of yore.

Those roadsters are still around, though. There are millions of them in China, quite possibly hundreds of millions, in various states of working order. I rode one when I visited Beijing, long before Covid hit. I was staying at a big corporate hotel in the center of town, not too far from the Forbidden City and Tiananmen Square, and the hotel had a half dozen or so Forever bikes, of 1990s vintage, available for the use of guests. I pedaled the bike all over town, and kept my eyes peeled for others of its ilk. I spied a lot of battered old roadsters—Forevers and Flying Pigeons and Golden Lions and the like—in Beijing's extant residential *hutongs*, set against walls and leaning on crates. For a while I entertained the fantasy that these were well-loved bikes, treasured by old-timers who had ridden them for decades and couldn't bear to part with them. Later, I learned that many people drag roadsters out of cold storage and use them in *hutongs* to hold parking spots for their cars.

Yet you do see Beijingers pedaling the classic bikes. Usually they are middle-aged or elderly, and not particularly well-to-do. Many Chinese people never graduated to a car, and will never ride an e-bike. In the city's wholesale marketplaces and hardscrabble proletarian districts, cargo bicycles and tricycles are ubiquitous. Old-fashioned bicycle trades endure as well. You can still spot sidewalk bicycle repairmen, operating out of "shops" defined by a couple of concrete blocks laid out on a street corner, performing speedy surgery on snarled chains and punctured tires and bent forks. There are places where the Kingdom of the Bicycle never fell, where pedal power still has primacy, where the bicycle culture of yesteryear is intact and, by all appearances, unchanged.

In fact, it's inaccurate to speak of "China's bicycle culture," as if it's monolithic, or even comprehensible. There are only bicycle cultures, plural—too many of them to inventory or to wrestle into a grand unified theory. For some young people in Beijing, the appeal of the bicycle is that it is subcultural: something they're into that's a little bit weird and niche.

Certain Beijing cycling scenes that, in the Chinese context, are exotic may strike non-Chinese as rather mainstream. In recent years, the city has seen a proliferation of clubs focused on road biking. The members of these collectives own high-end racing and touring bikes; they take group rides en masse to the mountains north and west of Beijing. The membership of these clubs is almost entirely male, and they have, it seems fair to say, a recognizably male fixation on athletic achievements that can be quantified and compared—miles ridden, hills surmounted, speeds reached. They're also really into stuff: top of the line gear and components, titanium bike frames, "technical" cycling clothing. Two generations ago, it was unimaginable in China that riding a bicycle could distinguish an individual from his fellow citizens. Today, Beijing's sport cyclists know better. Pedaling the streets of the ancient capital wearing lycra uniforms and shiny helmets and pricey sunglasses with photochromatic lenses, they represent a novelty: bicycling as style and lifestyle, available to the discerning at a hefty price point.

There are other new Beijing bicycle subcultures. I discovered one, by accident, when I was tooling around one afternoon in a fashionable corner of the Dongcheng district, in east-central Beijing. There, in a *hutong* lined with slick stores, I stumbled on Natooke, a custom bicycle shop, run by a German expat named Ines Brunn, which exclusively sells single-speed fixed-gear bikes. Brunn is a character: a professional trick cyclist with a master's degree in physics who has lived, and performed, all over the world. She had opened Natooke to spread the fixed-gear gospel to Beijingers, and evidently she had succeeded. Attractive young people with difficult haircuts were milling around, looking more or less like the kind of patrons you'd see at a boutique fixie emporium in Brooklyn.

But there is no analogous store, in Brooklyn or, as far as I know, anywhere else. Without question, it was the most beautiful bicycle shop I'd ever seen. Everywhere I turned my gaze, stacked in rows and hanging from hooks and wall racks, were bicycle bits and parts in an explosion of rainbow colors: frames, forks, rims, tires, hubs, spokes, chainrings, chains, handlebars, handlebar grips, in reds and blues and yellows and purples and pinks. The gimmick of the shop was that you could customize every component of your bike, in hues of your choosing.

I was struck by the difference, semiotically speaking, between the heavy-duty Forever that I had locked up on the street outside— a blunt and anonymous big black boat of a bike, built to ferry China's proletariat masses—and Natooke's lightweight, almost cartoonishly fun fixies, available in whatever candy-colored set-up a shopper desires. I was also struck by how badly I wanted one of these things for myself. For a good while I stood there, with a wildish look in my eyes, I'm sure, contemplating the color combinations I'd select, and how exactly I might manage to get a Natooke bike, or two, back to New York.

Instead, I decided to rent one for a few hours, an option the shop offered. I was given a bicycle with a white frame and white tires, and various other components in a shade best described as Kermit the Frog green. I left the Forever locked in the *hutong* and strolled north, rolling the fixie alongside me. I was heading to Ditan Park, about ten minutes away, an oasis of stretching trees and paved paths where I had spent a pleasant couple of hours reading the day before. Ditan Park is home to the Temple of the Earth, a sixteenth-century Ming dynasty edifice. It's a serene park, a little bit sleepy, and was therefore good for my purposes. I'd have some room to experiment. I'd only ridden a fixed-gear bike once, briefly and not very successfully, back in high school. And a fixie takes some getting used to.

Most bicycles have a hub that is equipped with a freewheel, the mechanism that allows the pedals to remain stationary as the bike rolls along. It's the freewheel that permits cyclists to ride without pedaling forward—to coast, one of the dreamiest and most pleasurable of all cycling sensations. (Iain Boal, the historian, has called "freewheeling" the bicycle's greatest contribution to the English language.)

But on a fixed-gear bike, the drivetrain is attached directly to the rear wheel's hub, a coupling arrangement that makes coasting impossible. When you pedal forward, the rear wheel is thrown into motion, and the bike moves forward. As long as the rear wheel continues to rotate—whether you're actively pedaling or not—the pedals will continue to rotate. The relationship is reciprocal and unequivocal. The pedals spin the wheel; the wheel spins the pedals.

Devotees maintain that this makes a fixie the truest bike, the bikiest bike, the purist's choice. It is the bicycle that most directly and efficiently deploys its human motor, without any extraneous hardware to interfere with the energy transfer. The feeling of merging with the machine is experienced more profoundly on a fixie than on any other species of bike.

There are other advantages touted by fixie fans. Fixies offer riders a greater degree of control. Trick cyclists often use fixies because they allow you to "ride fakie," to pedal the bike backward. Fixies are fast. Because they operate so efficiently, fixie riders can maintain higher pedaling cadences than riders of geared bicycles in the same ratio. Some people refer to fixies by their traditional name, "track bikes," because they were originally designed for races staged in velodromes and on outdoor tracks. Speed is also the reason that fixies were favored by New York's hell-for-leather bike messengers back in the '80s and '90s.

Then there is the matter of aesthetics. Fixies are beautiful, in the Loosian, less-is-more sense, since they're uncluttered by the extra parts necessary for a fully geared drivetrain. The fixie is the elemental bike—the bicycle reduced to its essence.

Brakes are one of the components not found on a classic fixed-gear bike. (Natooke sells fixies both with and without brakes; the bike I rented was a brakeless model.) The challenge, for a novice on a fixie, is not how to ride, but how to stop riding. To bring the bike safely to a halt, you have to apply reverse pressure, using your legs and body weight to push back against the rotation of the cranks. It's an action I was used to performing: my own bike, at home, was a cruiser with a coaster brake, or foot brake, which is activated by that same backward-kicking motion. But a coaster brake is a separate mechanism, integrated into a bicycle's internal hub; when you back-pedal, the brake engages and does the hard work for you.

To arrest the movement of a brakeless fixie is a task of a different order. It calls for greater strength and more finesse. There are various techniques that can be employed. There is the basic method of applying steady back-pressure to the pedals to slow the bike's roll. You can "skip stop," rising out of the saddle and lifting the rear wheel off the ground a few times in rapid succession. Or if you're moving fast, you can do a skid—a flashier move, where you jam the pedals back so forcefully that the rear wheel locks up and you slide to a halt. It all sounds simple enough, but braking a fixie is a feel thing, the kind of maneuver that you need to commit to muscle memory. It's a skill.

If don't have a skill, you have to acquire it. I reached Ditan Park, which at that hour, about two P.M., was busyish but not buzzing. A postprandial languor hung over the place. There were young mothers pushing strollers, and old men sitting at tables playing *xiangqi*, the Chinese version of chess. There were a few people in a little fitness area outfitted with monkey bars, parallel bars, and a stationary bicycle. I walked around the park a bit, until I found a nice, long, mostly unpeopled pathway. It was September, but the weather was summery. A balmy breeze was blowing. It was a more or less perfect day for a bike ride.

I swung my right leg over the fixie, hoisted myself onto the saddle, and set the thing in motion, pedaling slowly and deliberately. I built up a bit of momentum, allowing the bike to roll forward maybe forty feet. And then I pushed the pedals backward, coaster brake–style.

But the bicycle pushed back. The pedals didn't yield, they kept spinning forward, and I lurched forward in turn, rising up out of the saddle and dropping down to a standing position. I was straddling the top tube—a physically unpleasant position to be in, to be totally frank—while dragging my feet across the ground, trying to slow the bike down, a bit like Fred Flintstone in his Stone Age car. Eventually, the fixie came to rest.

All things considered, this wasn't a great way to brake a bike. What I needed to do, I realized, was perform the maneuver more fluidly. The action required wasn't the single violent jerk that I used when coaster-braking my cruiser. What I needed to do was to truly *pedal* backward, exerting steady pressure until the wheel reversed course. So I remounted, turned the bike around, launched it forward, and tried again—and again, the pedals disobeyed. My feet flew up, I was off the saddle, yanking the handlebars right and then left, teetering and swerving. My legs were spread akimbo over the top tube, and my feet were pawing the pavement in an ugly effort to slow the bike and keep it upright.

I managed to wrestle the fixie to a standstill. I glanced around. *Is anyone watching this?* A passerby might conclude that they were witnessing a maiden voyage: a man trying to ride a bike for the first time in his life. But there were just a handful of people strolling in this corner of the park. Off to my right, a dozen or so older women were doing *tai chi*. Everyone appeared to be perfectly indifferent to the struggles, to the existence, of the foreigner with the bicycle.

It occurred to me that I might have put myself at a disadvantage, riding a fixie that wasn't equipped with toe straps. These little devices, which hitch a rider's feet to the pedals, are helpful, some would say essential, for bringing a fixie to a stop. They prevent the problem I was experiencing—your feet zooming up and off the pedals—while affording a greater degree of power and control, allowing a rider to push down with his back foot while pulling up with his front one. Still, I'd seen many fixie riders over the years, biking around without toe straps. The issue, I decided, wasn't the equipment I lacked, or even my poor technique. It was a question of conviction. This apprehensive attitude wouldn't do. I had to go for it.

So I turned the bike around once more. I pointed the wheels down the long flagstone causeway, centered my weight on the seat, and shoved off, pedaling smoothly and steadily.

Two wheels hummed over the ground. The bike sliced the air. Overhead, ginkgo trees waved. There was no doubt about it: the Natooke was legit. It rode just about as good as it looked.

I'd traveled maybe twenty-five yards, building up a fair bit of speed. The time was nigh. I shifted my weight toward the rear of the bike, braced my thighs against the top tube, and gave a mighty backward shove. But again I felt the force of the pedals pushing back, again my feet flew up, again the bike wobbled and weaved, and I had to jerk the handlebars several times to steady the ship.

My feet sought the pedals. The only course of action now, it seemed, was to make peace with the bike, not fight against it. If you're a person familiar with bicycle history, this is the kind of scenario that puts you in mind of the past: the testimonies of all those nineteenth-century cyclists who regarded their velocipedes and boneshakers as unruly beasts, machines with minds of their own. My feet were back on the pedals now. Was I pedaling the bike or was it pedaling me? It wasn't quite clear. In any case, the fixie was barreling along and picking up speed. The situation presented a stark choice: I could either bail out—choose the softest-looking patch of pavement I could find and pour myself onto it—or tighten my white-knuckle grip and go along for the ride. With or without me, the bicycle was headed up the road.

ACKNOWLEDGMENTS

I racked up many debts of gratitude while working on this book. Some people are aware—all too aware, possibly—of the ways they helped me out. Others may be surprised to find their names listed here. Every one of them was crucial to the completion of this project. Words on a page can't convey how grateful I am, but it's a start.

My first thanks go to those who endured my questions, shared their stories, and allowed me to write about their lives. Thank you, Mohammed Abul Badshah, Syed Manzoorul Islam, Sonam Tshering, Barb Samsoe, Bill Samsoe, Greg Siple, June Siple, Danny MacAskill, Rev. Harry Latham, Ted White, and George Bliss.

My agent, Elyse Cheney, guided the book from inception to conclusion. I'm grateful for her advocacy, advice, and good humor. Thanks also to the entire team at the Cheney Agency, including Alex Jacobs, Claire Gillespie, Allison Devereux, Isabel Mendia, and Danny Hertz.

I am exceedingly fortunate to have landed at Crown, and am grateful to everyone there who has had a hand in publishing *Two Wheels Good*. Thank you to my wonderful editor, Libby Burton, for her sharp mind, shrewd judgment, patience, and kindness. Thank you, Aubrey Martinson, who did so much to ensure a smooth editorial, production, and publication process. Thank you, Gillian Blake, a great publisher and editor, whose support means the world to me. Thank you, David Drake and Annsley Rosner. Thanks to Evan Camfield, Bonnie Thompson, Stacey Stein, and Melissa Esner. Thanks also to Rachel Klayman and Molly Stern, who believed in this book way back when.

I owe special thanks to those who helped me during my travels. In Dhaka, I was assisted by Rifat Islam Esha, who served as a translator, facilitated my reporting, and shared many insights about her home city. Thanks also to K. Ahmed Anis and Imran Khan in Dhaka.

Ina Zhou was my translator and fixer in China, and was hugely helpful in the months that followed my reporting there. I am grateful to others whose generosity and knowledge I relied on in China: Andrew Jacobs, Xu Tao, Li Tao, and Shannon Bufton.

Without the assistance of Dhamey Norgay, I never would have traveled to Bhutan, or accomplished anything while I was there. Thank you, Dhamey.

Jake Rusby welcomed me into his studio in South London, showed me his beautiful hand-built bikes, and taught me valuable lessons about bicycle design and engineering.

I owe thanks to everyone at Rasoulution in Munich for all they did to coordinate my time in Scotland with Danny MacAskill.

I'm grateful to the intrepid cyclists of Longyearbyen, 78 degrees north latitude, who opened my eyes in new ways to the beauty, and insanity, of winter cycling.

Thanks to Franchesca Alejandra Ocasio and the Ovarian Psycos for allowing me to tag along with them in Los Angeles. This experience changed the way I think about bicycles and politics.

Thank you to the staffs at the New York Public Library, the Brooklyn Public Library, the Elmer Holmes Bobst Library at NYU, the Library of Congress, the British Library, the Royal Geographical Society, and the Bibliothèque Nationale de France.

Thank you, Omar Ali and everyone at Cobble Hill Variety. Thanks also to the staffs of a hundred coffee shops, or maybe it's a thousand, in Brooklyn and elsewhere.

I am especially indebted to the bicycle scholars, activists, and aficionados whose ideas and expertise informed this book. Some of these people I have had the pleasure of communicating with directly; others I know only through the words they've written. I'm grateful to all of them, and to many others whose work is cited in the Notes. Thank you: Iain Boal, Zack Furness, Melody Hoffmann, Adonia Lugo, Aaron Golub, Gerardo Sandoval, Evan Friss, James Longhorst, Paul Smethurst, Peter Cox, Randy Rzewnicki, Hans-Erhard Lessing, Tony Hadland, Tiina Männistö-Funk, Timo Myllyntaus, Glen Norcliffe, Margaret Guroff, Robert Turpin, Steven Alford, Suzanne Ferriss, Nicholas Oddy, and Carlton Reid. Thank you, Gary Sanderson, Jennifer Candipan, and Evan P. Schneider. Thanks to the International Cycling History Conference.

Thank you to cherished colleagues at *The New York Times Magazine*, who have supported my career, such as it is, and in various ways aided my reaching the finish line on this book: Nitsuh Abebe, Jake Silverstein, Jessica Lustig, Bill Wasik, Sasha Weiss, Erika Sommer.

I'm grateful to the many family members, friends, colleagues, treasured acquaintances, et al., who offered camaraderie, advice, encouragement, ideas, and recommendations on sources, among other mitzvot. Thanks also to many of you for providing the inspiration of your own great writing and thinking. Gillian Kane, Ann Powers, Carl Wilson, Whitney Chandler, Dan Adams, Craig Marks, Eric Weisbard, Julia Turner, Michael Agger, John Swansburg, Adam Gopnik, Dana Stevens, Josh Kun, Stephen Metcalf, Ali Colleen Neff, Karl Hagstrom Miller, Sean Howe, Jennifer Lena, Karen Tongson, Garnette Cadogan, Nathan Heller, Daphne Brooks, Forrest Wickman, Emily Stokes, Eddy Portnoy, Eric Harvey, Mark Lamster, Erin MacLeod, Joe Schloss, Frankie Thomas, Miles Grier, Steve Waksman, Ari Kelman, Ken Wissoker, Jason King, John Shaw, Ari Y. Kelman, Christopher Bononos, David Greenberg, Joey Thompson, Steacy Easton, Stuart Henderson, George Rosen, Seth Redniss.

Thank you to my parents, biological and otherwise, whose support and love was essential to the writing of this book: Marc Rosen, Susan Rosen, Roberta Stone, Amy Hoffman. Many thanks also to my wonderful in-laws, Rick and Robin Redniss.

This book is dedicated, with all my love, to Lauren Redniss, Sasha Rosen, and Theo Rosen.

NOTES

PROLOGUE VOYAGE TO THE MOON

x   **"been brought to such perfection"**: "A Revolution in Locomotion," *New York Times*, August 22, 1867.

x   **A cartoon from the same period**: Artist unknown, *Voyage à la lune*, publisher unknown (France, c. 1865–1870). Hand-colored lithograph. A copy of the print is in the collection of the Library of Congress's Prints and Photographs Division, Washington, D.C. It can be viewed online at loc.gov/item/2002722394/.

xi   **"a beautiful golden road"**: John Kendrick Bangs, *Bikey the Skicycle and Other Tales of Jimmieboy* (New York: Riggs, 1902), 35–37.

xi   **"A miner's bike would have looked odd in the streets of Stockholm"**: Robert A. Heinlein, *The Rolling Stones* (New York: Ballantine, 1952), 68–69.

xi   ***Trans-Galactic Bike Ride*, published in 2020**: Lydia Rogue, ed., *Trans-Galactic Bike Ride* (Portland, Ore.: Elly Blue, 2020).

xii   **"The art of flight will be the practical outcome"**: Benjamin Ward Richardson, "Cycling as an Intellectual Pursuit," *Longman's Magazine* 2, no. 12 (May–October 1883): 593–607.

xii   **A NASA photograph documents a test run**: For more on NASA's flirtation with "lunar cycling," see, e.g., Amy Teitel, "How NASA Didn't Drive on the Moon," April 6, 2012, AmericaSpace, americaspace.com /2012/04/06/how-nasa-didnt-drive-on-the-moon/.

xiii   **The bicycles Wilson proposed . . . were semi-recumbent**: For a comprehensive description of Wilson's proposed moon vehicles and other details of his vision for transport in space, see "Human-Powered Space Transportation," *Galileo* no. 11–12 (June 1979): 21–26.

xiii   **"the freedom conferred with having no wind resistance"**: Ibid., 24.

xiii   **"The 'cruising' speed for an astronaut"**: Ibid., 22.

xiii   **"a space colony established on an artificial satellite"**: Ibid., 25.

xiii   **"The picture I have tried to portray of human-powered transportation"**: Ibid., 26.

xiv   **John Boyd Dunlop was a forty-seven-year-old Belfast-based veterinarian**: For Dunlop's account of his invention of the pneumatic tire, see

John Boyd Dunlop, *The Invention of the Pneumatic Tyre* (Dublin: A. Thom & Company, 1925). Also see Jim Cooke, *John Boyd Dunlop* (Tankardstown, Garristown, County Meath, Ireland: Dreolín Specialist Publications, 2000).

xiv   **"an abiding interest in the problems of road, rail and sea transport":** Jim Cooke, "John Boyd Dunlop 1840–1921, Inventor," *Dublin Historical Record* 49, no. 1 (Dublin: Old Dublin Society, 1996), 16–31.

xv   **"It occurred to me," he wrote years later:** Dunlop, *Invention of the Pneumatic Tyre,* 9.

xv   **"eager to have a speed trial of his new machine":** Ibid., 15.

xvi   **Robert William Thomson, had made the same imaginative leap:** See Charles Barlow, Esq., ed., *The Patent Journal and Inventors' Magazine,* vol. 1 (London: Patent Journal Office, 1846): 61. Thomson, incidentally, was also the inventor of the fountain pen.

xvi   **"intercepted vibration from the road":** Cooke, *John Boyd Dunlop,* 16.

xvi   **The name Thomson gave to his creation had a poetic ring:** T. R. Nicholson, *The Birth of the British Motor Car, 1769–1897,* vol. 2, *Revival and Defeat, 1842–93* (London: Macmillan, 1982), 241.

INTRODUCTION BICYCLE PLANET

3   **"Cycle tracks will abound in Utopia":** H. G. Wells, *A Modern Utopia* (New York: Charles Scribner's Sons, 1905), 47.

3   **"Mankind has invested more than four million years":** This vivid passage appears in P. J. O'Rourke's "A Cool and Logical Analysis of the Bicycle Menace," originally published in *Car and Driver Magazine* in 1984. Like most of O'Rourke's stuff, it was satirical but also not—an exaggerated expression of earnestly held views. (O'Rourke published another anti-bicycle broadside, "Dear Urban Cyclists: Go Play in Traffic," on *The Wall Street Journal's* op-ed page, April 2, 2011.) "A Cool and Logical Analysis of the Bicycle Menace" is anthologized in P. J. O'Rourke, *Republican Party Reptile: The Confessions, Adventures, Essays and (Other) Outrages of P. J. O'Rourke* (New York: Atlantic Monthly Press, 1987), 122–27.

4   **"You are traveling":** "The Winged Wheel," *New York Times,* December 28, 1878.

5   **"Bicycling . . . has done more to emancipate women":** "Champion of Her Sex," *World* (New York), February 2, 1896.

5   **"It would not be at all strange":** See "Mark of the Century," *Detroit Tribune,* May 10, 1896.

5   **"Perhaps an interface between East and West is the bicycle":** James C. McCullagh, ed., *Pedal Power in Work, Leisure, and Transportation* (Emmaus, Penn.: Rodale, 1977), x.

5   **"the noblest invention":** Lance Armstrong, ed., *The Noblest Invention: An Illustrated History of the Bicycle* (Emmaus, Penn.: Rodale, 2003).

5   **"the most benevolent machine":** Sharon A. Babaian, *The Most Benevolent Machine: A Historical Assessment of Cycles in Canada* (Ottawa, Ont.: National Museum of Science and Technology, 1998).

5   **"rideable art that can just about save the world":** This aphorism,

attributed to the American bicycle designer and author Grant Peterson, is widely quoted in "inspirational" bicycle literature and internet memes. See, e.g., Chris Naylor, *Bike Porn* (Chichester, West Sussex, Eng.: Summersdale, 2013).

5   **There are twice as many bikes:** See, e.g., Michael Kolomatsky, "The Best Cities for Cyclists," *New York Times*, June 24, 2021, nytimes .com/2021/06/24/realestate/the-best-cities-for-cyclists.html; Leszek J. Sibiliski, "Why We Need to Encourage Cycling Everywhere," *World Economic Forum*, February 5, 2015, weforum.org/agenda/2015/02 /why-we-need-to-encourage-cycling-everywhere/.

6   **the linear course of technological advancement:** See David Edgerton, *The Shock of the Old: Technology and Global History Since 1900* (New York: Oxford University Press, 2007).

6   **"Get a bicycle," wrote Mark Twain:** From Mark Twain, "Taming the Bicycle" (1886). Anthologized in Mark Twain, *Collected Tales, Sketches, Speeches & Essays: 1852–1890* (New York: Library of America, 1992), 892–99.

6   **"The cyclist is a suicide apprentice":** Julio Torri, "La bicicleta," in *Julio Torri: Textos* (Saltillo, Coahuila, Mex.: Universidad Autónoma de Coahuila, 2002), 109. Translation from the Spanish by Jody Rosen.

7   **by migrants navigating the no-man's-land:** For an account of the role played by bicycles in migration at the U.S.-Mexican border and in border policing, see Kimball Taylor, *The Coyote's Bicycle: The Untold Story of Seven Thousand Bicycles and the Rise of a Borderland Empire* (Portland, Ore.: Tin House Books, 2016).

8   **"A curious two-wheeled vehicle called the Velocipede":** *Evening Post* (New York), June 11, 1819.

8   **An American newspaper editorial urged citizens to "destroy" veloci-pedes:** *Columbian Register* (New Haven), July 10, 1819.

8   **"kyphosis bicyclistarum":** "A Terrible Disease," *Neenah Daily Times* (Neenah, Wisc.), July 17, 1893.

8   **"[The] bicycle runs for Satan":** "Reformers in a New Field," *San Francisco Chronicle*, July 2, 1896.

9   **A 2019 Australian study explored the negative view of cyclists:** Alexa Delbosc, Farhana Naznin, Nick Haslam, and Narelle Haworth, "Dehumanization of Cyclists Predicts Self-Reported Aggressive Behaviour Toward Them: A Pilot Study," *Transportation Research, Part F: Traffic Psychology and Behaviour* 62 (April 2019): 681–89.

9   **analysts predict that the market will hit $80 billion by 2027:** "Bicycles— Global Market Trajectory & Analytics," Research and Markets, January 2021, researchandmarkets.com/reports/338773/bicycles_global_market _trajectory_and_analytics.

10   **A manifesto issued by the Provo:** Joseph Lelyveld, "Dadaists in Politics," *New York Times*, October 2, 1966. Cf. Alan Smart, "Provos in New Babylon," *Urbânia 4*, August 31, 2011, urbania4.org/2011/08/31 /provos-in-new-babylon/.

11   **One of Adolf Hitler's first acts upon assuming power:** See Iain Boal's 2010 lecture at the Museum of Copenhagen, accessible online in five videos posted on Vimeo, especially "The Green Machine—Lecture by

Iain Boal, Bicycle Historian. Part 3 of 5," Vimeo, 2010, vimeo.com /11264396.

11 German soldiers . . . confiscated bicycles: See, e.g., Mikkel Andreas Beck, "How Hitler Decided to Launch the Largest Bike Theft in Denmark's History," *ScienceNordic*, October 23, 2016, sciencenordic .com/denmark-history-second-world-war/how-hitler-decided-to-launch -the-largest-bike-theft-in-denmarks-history/1438738.

11 "Women are riding to suffrage on a bicycle": "Riding to Suffrage on a Bicycle," *Fall River Daily Herald* (Fall River, Mass.), June 8, 1895.

11 Authoritarian governments in Asia and the Middle East have periodically imposed bans: See, e.g., Daniel Defraia, "North Korea Bans Women from Riding Bicycles . . . Again," CNBC, Jan 17, 2013, cnbc .com/id/100386298; "Saudi Arabia Eases Ban on Women Riding Bikes," Al Jazeera, April 2, 2013, aljazeera.com/news/2013/4/2/saudi-arabia -eases-ban-on-women-riding-bikes.

11 In 2016, Iran's supreme leader, Ali Khamenei, proclaimed a fatwa: Andree Massiah, "Women in Iran Defy Fatwa by Riding Bikes in Public," BBC, September 21, 2016, bbc.com/news/world-middle -east-37430493.

11 "attracts the attention of male strangers and exposes society to corruption": Hannah Ross, *Revolutions: How Women Changed the World on Two Wheels* (New York: Plume, 2020), 99. See also: "Khamenei Says Use of Bicycles for Women Should Be Limited," Radio Farda, November 27, 2017, en.radiofarda.com/a/iran-women-bicycles-rstricted -khamenei-fatwa/28882216.html.

11 "Do not be sexually tempted": "Women Banned from Riding Bikes in Iran Province Run by Ultra-Conservative Cleric," Radio Farda, August 5, 2020, en.radiofarda.com/a/women-banned-from-riding-bikes-in -iran-province-run-by-ultra-conservative-cleric/30767110.html.

12 "Islamic punishment": Ross, *Revolutions*, 99. Also: "Iran's Regime Bans Women from Riding Bicycles in Isfahan," *National Council of Resistance of Iran*, May 15, 2019, ncr-iran.org/en/news/women/iran-s-regime -bans-women-from-riding-bicycles-in-isfahan/.

12 reported physical attacks and sexual assaults: "Iranian Cyclists Endure Physical, Sexual Abuse and Bans," *Kodoom*, July 30, 2020, features. kodoom.com/en/iran-sports/iranian-cyclists-endure-physical-sexual -abuse-and-bans/v/7164/.

12 scholars have begun unearthing a less hagiographic history: Of particular note is the groundbreaking work of Zack Furness, *One Less Car: Bicycling and the Politics of Automobility* (Philadelphia: Temple University Press, 2010); Paul Smethurst, *The Bicycle: Towards a Global History* (New York: Palgrave Macmillan, 2015); Steven A. Alford and Suzanne Ferriss, *An Alternative History of Bicycles and Motorcycles: Two-Wheeled Transportation and Material Culture* (Lanham, Md.: Lexington Books, 2016); and Iain Boal, "The World of the Bicycle," in *Critical Mass: Bicycling's Defiant Celebration*, ed. Chris Carlsson (Oakland, Calif.: AK Press, 2002), 167–74.

13 the Quadricycle: See Paul Ingrassia, *Engines of Change: A History of the American Dream in Fifteen Cars* (New York: Simon & Schuster,

2012), 5–6; "1896 Ford Quadricycle Runabout, First Car Built by Henry Ford," *The Henry Ford*, thehenryford.org/collections-and-research /digital-collections/artifact/252049/#slide=gs-212191.

13 **"macadamization":** See Peter J. Hugill, "Good Roads and the Automobile in the United States 1880–1929," *Geographical Review* 72, no. 3 (July 1982): 327–49; Charles Freeman Johnson, "The Good Roads Movement and the California Bureau of Highways," *Overland Monthly* 28, no. 2 (July–December 1896): 442–55.

13 **"bicycle bloc":** Michael Taylor, "The Bicycle Boom and the Bicycle Bloc: Cycling and Politics in the 1890s," *Indiana Magazine of History* 104 (September 2008): 213–40.

13 **"It is the task of critical historians of the bicycle":** Iain A. Boal, "The World of the Bicycle," in *Critical Mass: Bicycling's Defiant Celebration,* ed. Chris Carlsson (Oakland, Calif.: AK Press, 2002), 171.

14 **"maps of gentrification":** Elizabeth Flanagan, Ugo Lachapelle, and Ahmed El-Geneidy, "Riding Tandem: Does Cycling Infrastructure Investment Mirror Gentrification and Privilege in Portland, OR and Chicago, IL?," *Research in Transportation Economics* 60 (December 2017): 14–24.

14 **The term "invisible riders" has gained currency:** See, e.g., Melody L. Hoffmann, *Bike Lanes and White Lanes: Bicycle Advocacy and Urban Planning* (Lincoln: University of Nebraska Press, 2016); Adonia E. Lugo, *Bicycle/Race: Transportation, Culture, & Resistance* (Portland, Ore.: Microcosm, 2018); Aaron Golub, Melody L. Hoffmann, Adonia E. Lugo, and Gerardo F. Sandoval, eds., *Bicycle Justice and Urban Transformation: Biking for All?* (New York: Routledge, 2016); Tiina Männistö-Funk and Timo Myllyntaus, *Invisible Bicycle: Parallel Histories and Different Timelines* (Leiden, Neth.: Brill, 2019); and Glen Norcliffe, *Critical Geographies of Cycling* (New York: Routledge, 2015).

15 **Mikael Colville-Andersen has popularized "Copenhagenize":** See Mikael Colville-Andersen, *Copenhagenize: The Definitive Guide to Global Bicycle Urbanism* (Washington, D.C.: Island Press, 2018). Colville-Andersen's book, spun off from his popular website, bills itself as *The Definitive Guide to Global Bicycle Urbanism,* yet Asian, African, and Latin American cities barely warrant a mention.

15 **"cycle chic":** Mikael Colville-Andersen, *Cycle Chic* (London: Thames & Hudson, 2012).

15 **Researchers say that motor vehicles are the largest net contributor:** Emily Atkin, "The Modern Automobile Must Die," *New Republic,* August 20, 2018, newrepublic.com/article/150689/modern-automobile -must-die.

16 **tire wear and other non-tailpipe pollutants account for a large percentage:** "Tyres Not Tailpipe," *Emissions Analytics,* January 29, 2020, emissionsanalytics.com/news/2020/1/28/tyres-not-tailpipe.

16 **Globally, some 1.25 million people die in car crashes each year:** World Bank, "The High Toll of Traffic Injuries: Unacceptable and Preventable," Open Knowledge Repository, 2017, openknowledge .worldbank.org/handle/10986/29129.

16 "The bicycle is the most civilized transport known to man": Iris Murdoch, *The Red and the Green* (New York: Viking, 1965), 29.

16 "Two wheels good, four wheels bad": The phrase riffs on the maxim "Four legs good, two legs bad," from Orwell's *Animal Farm*.

17 "The bicycle is the perfect transducer": Ivan Illich, *Energy and Equity* (New York: Harper & Row, 1974), 60.

17 "a bicycle for our minds": This was one of Steve Jobs's favorite riffs. See, e.g., the excerpt of Jobs talking about bicycles and computers in the 1990 film *Memory and Imagination: New Pathways to the Library of Congress.* Available online at "Steve Jobs, 'Computers Are Like a Bicycle for Our Minds'—Michael Lawrence Films," YouTube, youtube .com/watch?v=ob_GX50Za6c.

I THE BICYCLE WINDOW

19 "Elegy Written in a Country Churchyard": See Thomas Gray, "Elegy Written in a Country Churchyard," poets.org/poem/elegy-written -country-churchyard.

21 "The Passion Considered as an Uphill Bicycle Race": Alfred Jarry, *La passion considérée comme course de côte—et autres speculations* (1903; repr., Montélimar, France: Voix d'Encre, 2008). An English translation is available online at *Bike Reader: A Rider's Digest,* notanothercycling forum.net/bikereader/contributors/misc/passion.html.

22 "Bicycles appear in the bas reliefs": Walter Sullivan, "Leonardo Legend Grows as Long-Lost Notes Are Published," *New York Times,* September 30, 1974.

23 A raft of evidence has since confirmed: For a comprehensive (and entertaining) debunking of "Leonardo's bicycle," see Hans-Erhard Lessing's "The Evidence Against 'Leonardo's Bicycle,'" presented at the Eighth International Conference on Cycling History, Glasgow School of Art, August 1997. Available online from Cycle Publishing, cycle publishing.com/history/leonardo%20da%20vinci%20bicycle.html.

23 "The Italian cultural bureaucracy . . . still upholds: Tony Hadland and Hans-Erhard Lessing, *Bicycle Design: An Illustrated History* (Cambridge, Mass.: MIT Press, 2014), 501.

23 "In Italy, the bicycle belongs to the national art heritage": Curzio Malaparte, "Les deux visages de l'Italie: Coppi et Bartali," *Sport-Digest* (Paris) no. 6 (1949): 105–09. The translation appears in Lessing, "The Evidence Against 'Leonardo's Bicycle.'"

23 "As soon as individuals—and by extension nations—are credited": Paul Smethurst, *The Bicycle: Towards a Global History* (New York: Palgrave Macmillan, 2015), 53.

24 Efim Artamonov, a Russian serf who invented a high-wheeled bicycle: The Artamonov hoax is detailed in Derek Roberts, *Cycling History: Myths and Queries* (Birmingham: John Pinkerton, 1991), 27–28; Slava Gerovitch, "Perestroika of the History of Technology and Science in the USSR: Changes in the Discourse," *Technology and Culture* 37, no. 1 (January 1996): 102–34; "Artamonov's Bike," *Clever Geek Handbook,* clever-geek.imtqy.com/articles/1619221/index.html;

"The Story of a Hoax," *historyntagil.ru/*, historyntagil.ru/people/6_82
.htm; "Artamonov's Bike: Legends and Documents," *historyntagil.ru/*,
historyntagil.ru/history/2_19_28.htm. See also a 1989 scholarly article,
transcribed and posted on the website of the State Public Scientific and
Technical Library of Russia: B. C. Virginsky, S. A. Klat, T. V. Komshi-
lova, and G. N. Liszt, "How Myths Are Created in the History of
Technology: On the History of the Question of 'Artamonov's Bicycle,'"
State Public Scientific and Technical Library of Russia, gpntb.ru/win
/mentsin/mentsin2b5c1.html.

24   "Artamonov, who with his invention anticipated the modern bicycle":
Roberts, *Cycling History*, 28.

25   *Histoire générale de la vélocipédie:* L. Baudry de Saunier, *Histoire
générale de la vélocipédie* (Paris: Paul Ollendorff, 1891).

25   "M. de Sivrac's invention was but a poor little naked seed!": Ibid, 7.
Translation from the French by Jody Rosen.

26   "Could a brain from the other side of the Rhine": Hadland and
Lessing, *Bicycle Design*, 494.

26   "The Badenian was merely a thief of ideas": Ibid., 494.

26   The basic facts of the story: For my account of Drais's life and his
invention of the *Laufmaschine*, I have relied in particular on the
indispensable work of Hans-Erhard Lessing. See Hadland and Lessing,
Bicycle Design, 8–21; Hans-Erhard Lessing, *Automobilität—Karl Drais
und die unglaublichen Anfänge* (Leipzig: Maxime-Verlag, 2003);
Hans-Erhard Lessing, "Les deux-roues de Karl von Drais: Ce qu'on en
sait," *Proceedings of the International Cycling History Conference* 1
(1990): 4–22; Hans-Erhard Lessing, "The Bicycle and Science—from
Drais Until Today," *Proceedings of the International Cycling History
Conference* 3 (1992): 70–86; Hans-Erhard Lessing, "What Led to the
Invention of the Early Bicycle?," *Proceedings of the International
Cycling History Conference* 11 (2000): 28–36; Hans-Erhard Lessing,
"The Two-Wheeled Velocipede: A Solution to the Tambora Freeze of
1816," *Proceedings of the International Cycling History Conference* 22
(2011): 180–88. Other helpful sources include David V. Herlihy, *Bicycle:
The History* (New Haven, Conn.: Yale University Press, 2004), and the
website Karl Drais: All About the Beginnings of Individual Mobility,
karldrais.de/. I also drew on the short Drais biography available online
at mannheim.de/sites/default/files/page/490/en_biography.pdf.

27   "The instrument and the traveller are kept in equilibrio": For an
English translation of Drais's "account . . . of [the *Laufmaschine's*]
nature and properties," see "The Velocipede or Draisena," *Analectic
Magazine* (Philadelphia) 13 (1819).

27   "turned a man into a horse": Herlihy, *Bicycle: The History*, 24.

28   "When roads are dry and firm": Ibid.

29   "the year without a summer": William K. Klingaman and Nichols P.
Klingaman, *The Year Without Summer: 1816 and the Volcano That
Darkened the World and Changed History* (New York: St. Martin's, 2013).

31   "environmentalist revisionism": Smethurst, *The Bicycle*, 56.

32   medieval land-surveying tool known as a waywiser: Hadland and
Lessing, *Bicycle Design*, 495–96.

33   "The church window cyclist of 1642": Harry Hewitt Griffin, *Cycles and Cycling* (New York: Frederick A. Stokes, 1890), 3.

33   "clue to the student who is desirous of tracing manual locomotion": Ibid., 2.

33   "Every visitor to Stoke Poges visits Gray's tomb": Charles G. Harper, *Cycle Rides Round London* (London: Chapman & Hall Ltd., 1902), 208.

2 DANDY CHARGERS

39   **The story is recorded in a pamphlet:** See Roger Street, *The Pedestrian Hobby-Horse at the Dawn of Cycling* (Christchurch, Dorset, Eng.: Artesius, 1998), 102–03.

39   **Then there is the kicker to the story:** The final sentence of Fairburn's account of the "Dandy-Race," in which he reports that it was impossible to determine the winner of the contest, contains a final punning joke. Fairburn writes: "It is hard to tell which of these two nobles merited first to arrive at <u>Tyburn</u> and win <u>by the neck</u>, but as both did their best, their claims <u>to be exalted</u> might be considered as equal." (The underlinings are present in Fairburn's original text.) As Roger Street points out, the sentence appears to make satirical reference to "the use of the old gallows at Tyburn which apparently stood near the North East corner of Hyde Park." See ibid., 103.

39   **a patent for "a Pedestrian Curricle or Velocipede":** *The Modern Velocipede: Its History and Construction* (London: George Maddick, 1869), 3.

39   **Johnson's machine incorporated modifications:** For an excellent technical and historical discussion of Denis Johnson's velocipedes, see Tony Hadland and Hans-Erhard Lessing, *Bicycle Design: An Illustrated History* (Cambridge, Mass.: MIT Press, 2014), 22–25.

40   **a woman was killed when her horse, startled by a passing velocipede:** *Star* (London), June 8, 1819.

40   **Denis Johnson, hoping to drum up sales, went on tour:** Street, *The Pedestrian Hobby-Horse at the Dawn of Cycling*, 53–55.

40   **There were velocipede races:** For example, on May 8, 1819, *The Suffolk Chronicle* (Ipswich, Suffolk, England) reported on a "grand velocipede match between four amateurs," covering a course of fifty miles, for a "sweepstakes of 25 guineas." In another race in Ipswich that same year, velocipede riders clad in "jockey dresses" competed for a subscription purse. A race in York "pitted a dandy charger against an opponent mounted on a jackass." In Londonderry, in the north of Ireland, velocipede races were run at the city's horse track.

40   **"In the New Road [velocipedes] might be seen in great numbers":** Hadland and Lessing, *Bicycle Design*, 505. One of the "rooms for practice" was a velocipede riding school operated by Denis Johnson, not far from his workshop in Long Acre, where he filled orders for new machines.

40   **"To-day, nothing is spoken of but the Persian Ambassador":** *Morning Advertiser* (London), May 6, 1819.

40   **On the variety stage, skits:** In March 1819, a velocipede-themed

comedy, *The Accelerators; or, The Modern Hobby-Horses*, debuted at the Strand Theatre. See advertisement, "Miss E. BROADHURST's Night; STRAND THEATRE, the *Sans Pareil*," in *The Times* (London), March 27, 1819. The popular songs that cast a skeptical eye on the new invention included: "London Fashions, Follies, Dandies, and Hobby Horses" and "Riding on a Real Jackass, the Velocipedes, Alias Hobby Horses."

40   "The nothing of the day is a machine called the velocipede": John Gilmer Speed, ed., *The Letters of John Keats* (New York: Dodd, Mead, 1883), 67.

42   the regent's birthday celebration at Windsor Castle: *Morning Post* (London), August 16, 1819.

42   "It is now become quite common": "Miscellaneous Articles," *The Westmorland Gazette and Kendal Advertiser* (Kendal, Cumbria, Eng.), June 26, 1819.

42   "all the wagon-train pomp of a peaceful military parade": Street, *The Pedestrian Hobby-Horse at the Dawn of Cycling*, 103–4.

42   "In Hyde Park, all fashionable men cross its saddle": *Morning Advertiser* (London), March 25, 1819.

42   "If we are *literally* to shoot the folly as it flies": Quoted in Street, *The Pedestrian Hobby-Horse at the Dawn of Cycling*, 67.

43   Pray have you not seen: "Ode on the Dandy-Horses," *Monthly Magazine; or, British Register* (London), 48, part 2 (December 1, 1819): 433.

43   "disgrace and odium of Dandyism": "Lewes," *Sussex Advertiser* (Lewes, Sussex, Eng.), May 31, 1819.

43   "What are these lay-lords": *Gorgon: A Weekly Political Publication* (London), March 27, 1819.

44   "the bloodiest political event of the nineteenth century on English soil": Robert Poole, *Peterloo: The English Uprising* (New York: Oxford, 2019), 1.

44   "all those with the slightest pretension to fashion or taste": Venetia Murray, *An Elegant Madness: High Society in Regency England* (New York: Viking, 1999), 9.

44   "hanker[ing] after Paris as their spiritual home": Ibid., 9.

44   a comedian appeared onstage at London's Covent Garden Theatre: "Lines Spoken by Mr. Liston, Riding on a Velocipede on Tuesday Night, *Star* (London), June 17, 1819.

44   The most vivid satire was the work of caricaturists: Roger Street, *Before the Bicycle: The Regency Hobby-Horse Prints* (Christchurch, Dorset, Eng.: Artesius, 2014), includes eighty full-color reproductions of velocipede-themed prints from the period.

44   "contributes to the amusement of passengers in the streets": *Public Ledger and Daily Advertiser* (London), May 19, 1819.

45   One print, thought to be the work of the famous illustrator George Cruikshank: Artist possibly George Cruikshank, *R°°°l Hobby's!!!*, published by J. L. Marks, London, c. April 1819. Hand-colored etching, 9 x 13½". A copy of the print is in the collection of the British Museum and can be viewed online at britishmuseum.org/collection/object/P_1868-0808-8435.

45   "The crowded state of the metropolis does not admit": *Public Ledger and Daily Advertiser* (London), March 19, 1819.

46   "indulged themselves in the Sunday use of this vehicle": "Important Caution," *Windsor and Eton Express* (Windsor, Berkshire, Eng.), August 1, 1819. The article reported that "the fatal efficacy of the Velocipede, in producing ruptures, [had] been formally announced by the London Surgeons."

46   When quietly disposed people saw a velocipede: Hadland and Lessing, *Bicycle Design: An Illustrated History*, 508–09.

46   In Hyde Park, gangs of youths swarmed riders: David V. Herlihy, *Bicycle: The History* (New Haven, Conn.: Yale University Press, 2004), 34.

46   "the hobbies ultimately became objects of attack and were demolished": *Morning Advertiser* (London), April 13, 1819.

46   In 1819, a ban on velocipede riding was decreed in London: "[The velocipede] has been put down by the Magistrates," *Public Ledger and Daily Advertiser* (London), March 19, 1819.

47   "seize, break, destroy, or convert to their own use": *Columbian Register* (New Haven, Conn.), July 10, 1819.

47   "It would seem that the Dandies of Calcutta": *The Sun* (London), May 17, 1820.

47   "Great expectations were at one time formed of those things called Velocipedes": "Land Conveyance by Machinery," *Morning Post* (London), July 22, 1820.

47   "All the catalogue of dandy chargers hitherto invented": "Steam-Boats," *Caledonian Mercury* (Edinburgh, Scotland), June 26, 1819.

47   "A more contemptible, cowardly, selfish, unfeeling dog": Charles C. F. Greville, *The Greville Memoirs: A Journal of the Reigns of King George IV and King William IV*, ed. Henry Reeve, vol. 1 (New York: D. Appleton, 1886), 131.

47   "as ephemeral as a Brummel or a Velocipede": "Extracts," *Perthsire Courier* (Perth, Perthshire, Scotland), April 16, 1822.

48   an 1829 letter: *The Mechanics' Magazine* (London) 12 (1830), 237.

48   Thomas Stephens Davies delivered a speech: Thomas Stephens Davies's speech is included in an appendix to Hadland and Lessing, *Bicycle Design: An Illustrated History*, 503–17.

3   ART VÉLO

51   "so lissome, so slender": Quoted in Jeremy Withers and Daniel P. Shea, eds., *Culture on Two Wheels: The Bicycle in Literature and Film* (Lincoln: University of Nebraska Press, 2016), 143.

52   "To see that wheel turning was very soothing, very comforting": Excerpt from *MoMA Highlights: 375 Works from the Museum of Modern Art, New York* (New York: Museum of Modern Art, 2019) for Marcel Duchamp's *Bicycle Wheel*, Museum of Modern Art website, moma.org/collection/works/81631.

52   "as beautiful as a bicycle": Joseph Masheck, *Adolf Loos: The Art of Architecture* (New York, I. B. Tauris, 2013), 26.

52   "petro-fetishism": See Sheena Wilson, Adam Carlson, and Imre Szeman, eds., *Petrocultures: Oil, Politics, Culture* (Montreal: McGill–Queen's University Press, 2017).

53   "comes to us . . . naked": Roderick Watson and Martin Gray, *The Penguin Book of the Bicycle* (London: Penguin Books, 1978), 97.

53   "In every art there are forms so implicit in the process": Lewis Mumford, *The Culture of Cities* (New York: Harcourt, Brace, Jovanovich, 1970), 444.

53   The writer Robert Penn has made the amusing observation: Robert Penn, *It's All About the Bike: The Pursuit of Happiness on Two Wheels* (New York: Bloomsbury, 2010), 112.

54   The bike wheel has a combination of strength and lightness: The canonical study of the bicycle wheel, which I draw on extensively in this chapter, is Jobst Brandt, *The Bicycle Wheel,* 3rd ed. (Palo Alto, Calif.: Avocet, 1993).

54   capable of supporting approximately four hundred times its own weight: Max Glaskin, *Cycling Science* (London: Ivy, 2019), 112.

55   A young Frank Zappa appeared on *The Steve Allen Show* in 1963: Zappa's performance can be viewed on YouTube: "Frank Zappa Teaches Steve Allen to play the Bicycle (1963)," youtube.com/watch?v=QF0PYQ8IOL4.

57   "Cycling with regular pedals and cranks": Penn, *It's All About the Bike,* 89.

58   "It is unlikely that the diamond frame will ever be surpassed": Sheldon Brown, "Sheldon Brown's Bicycle Glossary," sheldonbrown.com/gloss_da-o.html.

58   The raw materials in . . . a road bike: See, e.g., "Bicycle Life Cycle: Dissecting the Raw Materials, Embodied Energy, and Waste of Road-bikes," *Design Life-Cycle,* designlife-cycle.com/bicycle; Margarida Coelho, "Cycling Mobility—A Life Cycle Assessment Based Approach," *Transportation Research Procedia* 10 (December 2015), 443–51; Papon Roy, Md. Danesh Miah, Md. Tasneem Zafar, "Environmental Impacts of Bicycle Production in Bangladesh: a Cradle-to-Grave Life Cycle Assessment Approach," *SN Applied Sciences* 1, link.springer.com/content/pdf/10.1007/s42452-019-0721-z.pdf; Kat Austen, "Examining the Lifecycle of a Bike—and Its Green Credentials," *Guardian* (London), March 15, 2012, theguardian.com/environment/bike-blog/2012/mar/15/lifecycle-carbon-footprint-bike-blog.

59   the exploitation of child bike factory workers: See Zacharias Zacharakis, "Under the Wheels," *Zeit Online,* December 4, 2019, zeit.de/wirtschaft/2019-12/cambodia-bicycles-worker-exploited-production-working-conditions-english?utm_referrer=https%3A%2F%2Fwww.google.com%2F; "Global Bike Manufacturers Guilty of Using Child Labour, Claims Green Mag," *bikebiz,* October 3, 2003, bikebiz.com/global-bike-manufacturers-guilty-of-using-child-labour-claims-green-mag/.

60   In Brazil, one person perished . . . in Congo: "The Past Is Now: Birmingham and the British Empire," *Birmingham Museum and Art Gallery,* birminghammuseums.org.uk/system/resources/W1siZiIsIjIwMTgvMTIvMDcvMXVocndzcjBkcV9UaGVVfUGFzdF9pc19Ob3bdf

TGFyZ2VfUHJpbnRfTGFiZWxzLnBkZiJdXQ/The%20Past%20is%20
Now%20Labels.

60   "If you were one of the millions": Maya Jasanoff, *The Dawn Watch: Joseph Conrad in a Global World* (New York: Penguin Books, 2017), 208.

60   asphalt: See, e.g., Kenneth O'Reilly, *Asphalt: A History* (Lincoln: University of Nebraska Press, 2021), 60–62, 206–7.

60   "atom of the Machine Age": Lance Armstrong, ed., *The Noblest Invention: An Illustrated History of the Bicycle* (Emmaus, Penn.: Rodale, 2003), 142.

60   The record is muddled by the usual disputes about provenance: For a thorough and even-handed hashing through of the bicycle's technical development and the competing narratives thereof, see Tony Hadland and Hans-Erhard Lessing, *Bicycle Design: An Illustrated History* (Cambridge, Mass.: MIT Press, 2014).

61   "There are two ways you can get exercise out of a bicycle": Jerome K. Jerome, *"Three Men on a Boat" and "Three Men on the Bummel"* (New York: Penguin, 1999), 205.

62   "When we finally get a full-rigged bicycle": *Norfolk Journal* (Norfolk, Neb.), February 18, 1886.

62   The bicycle first arrived in Vietnam: David Arnold and Erich DeWald, "Cycles of Empowerment? The Bicycle and Everyday Technology in Colonial India and Vietnam," *Comparative Studies in Society and History* 53, no. 4, (October 2011), 971–96.

62   "Sometimes the bicycle itself is the instrument of death": "A Study: Viet Cong Use of Terror," *United States Mission in Vietnam* (May 1966), pdf.usaid.gov/pdf_docs/Pnadx570.pdf. It has been suggested that the earliest waves of bicycle bombing in Saigon, in the 1950s, were perpetrated by the U.S.-backed Vietnamese nationalist Trinh Minh Thé, with the knowledge and support of American intelligence operatives. According to the theory, the goal was to sew opposition to the Communist cause by perpetrating terrorist atrocities and blaming them on Ho Chi Minh. This is the scenario depicted in Graham Greene's famous Vietnam roman à clef, *The Quiet American*. See, e.g., Sergei Blagov, *Honest Mistakes: The Life and Death of Trinh Minh Thé* (Hauppauge, New York: Nova Science Publishers, 2001), and Mike Davis, *Buda's Wagon: A Brief History of the Car Bomb* (New York: Verso, 2007).

62   The origins of the modern mountain bicycle: For the history of the mountain bike's origins in the 1970s, see Charles Kelly, *Fat Tire Flyer: Repack and the Birth of Mountain Biking* (Boulder, Colo.: VeloPress, 2014), and Frank J. Berto, *The Birth of Dirt: Origins of Mountain Biking*, 3rd ed. (San Francisco: Van der Plas / Cycle Publishing, 2014). See also John Howard, *Dirt! The Philosophy, Technique, and Practice of Mountain Biking* (New York: Lyons, 1997); Hadland and Lessing, *Bicycle Design*, 433–45 and 139–55; Margaret Guroff, *The Mechanical Horse: How the Bicycle Reshaped American Life* (Austin: University of Texas Press, 2016), 139–55; and Paul Smethurst, *The Bicycle: Towards a Global History* (New York: Palgrave Macmillan, 2015), 61–65.

63   The "freak bike" or "mutant bike" movement: See Zack Furness's

superb analysis of "DIY bike culture": Zack Furness, *One Less Car: Bicycling and the Politics of Automobility* (Philadelphia: Temple University Press, 2010), 153–58.

64   "To consider the endless perfection of the chain": Hugh Kenner, *Samuel Beckett: A Critical Study* (New York: Grove, 1961), 123.

64   "a new animal / . . . Half wheel and half brain": Théodore Faullain de Banville, *Nouvelles odes funambulesques* (Paris: Alphonse Lemerre, 1869), 130.

64   "people in these parts who nearly are half people and half bicycles": Flann O'Brien, *The Third Policeman* (Funks Grove, Ill.: Dalkey Archive, 1999), 85.

4 SILENT STEED

66   "The hoofs of the horses!": Will H. Ogilvie, "The Hoofs of the Horses," *Baily's Magazine of Sports and Pastimes* 87 (1907): 465.

67   "All who dwell in the land will wail": Jeremiah 47:3, New International Version (2011 translation), accessed at biblia.com/books/niv2011/Je47.3.

67   "There is something weird, almost uncanny": Charles B. Warring, "What Keeps the Bicycler Upright?," *Popular Science Monthly* (New York) 38 (April 1891): 766.

67   eliminate the "harsh rattle and clatter": Sylvester Baxter, "Economic and Social Influences of the Bicycle," *Arena* (Boston) 6 (1892): 581.

67   in Flanders, the bicycle was a *vlosse-peerd:* David Perry, *Bike Cult: The Ultimate Guide to Human-Powered Vehicles* (New York: Four Walls Eight Windows, 1995), 98.

67   the Schwetzinger Relaishaus: Robert Penn, *It's All About the Bike: The Pursuit of Happiness on Two Wheels* (New York: Bloomsbury, 2010), 49.

68   the arrival of the steam locomotive: For a revelatory cultural history of the railroad, see Wolfgang Schivelbusch's classic study. Wolfgang Schivelbusch, *The Railway Journey: The Industrialization of Time and Space in the Nineteenth Century* (Berkeley: University of California Press, 1977).

68   "a single horse that obeyed only one master": David V. Herlihy, *Bicycle: The History* (New Haven, Conn.: Yale University Press, 2004), 24.

68   "The shadow of my silent steed": Paul Pastnor, "The Wheelman's Joy," *Wheelman* (Boston) 3, no. 2 (November 1883): 143.

68   "[The velocipede] is light, and little, and leans lovingly against you for support": J. T. Goddard, *The Velocipede: Its History, Varieties, and Practice* (New York: Hurd and Houghton, 1869), 20.

69   "It quivers like an animal under its thick skin of nickel and enamel": The quotation is taken from L. Baudry de Saunier, the French historian and fabulist behind the *célérifère* myth. Quoted in Christopher S. Thompson, *The Tour de France: A Cultural History* (Berkeley: University of California Press, 2006), 144.

69   "It runs, it leaps, it rears and writhes, and shies and kicks": Charles E. Pratt, *The American Bicycler: A Manual for the Observer, the Learner, and the Expert* (Boston: Houghton, Osgood, 1879), 30.

69   "will try all the lowest dodges to get rid of their riders": Jerome K. Jerome, "A Lesson in Bicycling," *To-Day: A Weekly Magazine Journal* (London), December 16, 1893, 28.

69   **Mark Twain recounted his struggle:** Mark Twain, "Taming the Bicycle" (1886). Anthologized in Mark Twain, *Collected Tales, Sketches, Speeches & Essays: 1852–1890* (New York: Library of America, 1992), 892–99.

69   **A satirical etching from 1819:** Charles Williams, *Anti-Dandy Infantry Triumphant or the Velocipede Cavalry Unhobby'd,* published by Thomas Tegg, London, 1819. Hand-colored etching. 9½ x 13½". A copy of the print is in the collection of the British Museum and can be viewed online at britishmuseum.org/collection/object/P_1895-0408-22.

70   **"What an expense would be saved in feeding, littering, farriering, and doctoring!":** *Inverness Journal and Northern Advertiser* (Inverness, Inverness-Shire, Scotland), May 28, 1819.

70   **"We think the bicycle an animal, which will, in a great measure, supersede the horse":** Goddard, *The Velocipede,* 20.

70   **"We may imagine the race courses devoted to contests of this description":** "The Velocipede Mania," *New York Clipper,* September 26, 1868.

70   **A French cartoonist went further:** The caricature, published in *Le journal amusant* (Paris), October 29, 1868, is reproduced in Herlihy, *Bicycle: The History,* 99.

70   **In 1869, a tournament hosted by the Liverpool Velocipede Club:** "Liverpool Velocipede Club: Bicycle Tournament and Assault at Arms, in the Gymnasium, Saturday Afternoon Next" (advertisement), *Albion* (Liverpool), April 19, 1869. Cf. "A Bicycle Tournament," *Illustrated London News,* May 1, 1869.

70   **"A new race of servants has come into being—the bicycle groom":** Arsène Alexandre, "All Paris A-Wheel," *Scribner's Magazine* (New York), August 1895.

71   **"no steed but trusty Wheel":** Basil Webb, "A Ballade of This Age," *Wheelman* (Boston) 3, no. 2 (November 1883): 100.

71   **"five hundred mailed and belted knights on bicycles":** Mark Twain, *A Connecticut Yankee in King Arthur's Court* (New York: Harper & Brothers, 1889), 365.

71   **"When the horse is badly injured he becomes an encumbrance":** Charles H. Muir, "Notes on the Preparation of the Infantry Soldier," *Journal of the Military Service Institution of the United States* 19 (1896): 237.

71   **"Trust the English to invent a way of traveling while sitting down":** Martin Caidin and Jay Barbree, *Bicycles in War* (New York: Hawthorn, 1974), 66.

72   **"crack horseman":** Frederik Rompel, *Heroes of the Boer War* (London: Review of Reviews Office, 1903), 155.

72   **"the hardest thorn in the flesh of the British advance":** Siegfried Mortkowitz, "Bicycles at War," *We Love Cycling,* October 14, 2019, welovecycling.com/wide/2019/10/14/bicycles-at-war/.

72   **"an inferno of lyddite and shrapnel":** Pieter Gerhardus Cloete, *The Anglo-Boer War: A Chronology* (Pretoria: J. P. van der Walt, 2000), 186.

73   **"I think Jesus might ride a wheel if He were in our place":** "The Man

on the Wheel," *The Sketch: A Journal of Art and Actuality* (London), August 30, 1899.

73   **"One of the most interesting things in life":** *North-Eastern Daily Gazette* (Middlesbrough, North Yorkshire, Eng.), July 1, 1895.

73   **"What is the one symbol that used to mark the rich man":** "Safety in the Safety," *Morning Journal-Courier* (New Haven, Conn.), June 5, 1899.

74   **In American cities, ordinances banning bicycles:** For a superb account of the bicycle battles in late-nineteenth-century American cities, see Evan Friss, *The Cycling City: Bicycles and Urban America in the 1890s* (Chicago: University of Chicago Press, 2015). Cf. Friss's *On Bicycles: A 200-Year History of Cycling in New York City* (New York: Columbia University Press, 2019).

74   **"a teamster's horse [had] knocked it over":** "Wheel Gossip," *Wheel and Cycling Trade Review* (New York), October 30, 1891.

74   **"who appear to take delight in annoying those who ride the wheel":** "Cyclers' Street Rights," *New York Times,* July 24, 1895.

75   **"Delight in the dangerous pastime of driving skittish":** Karl Kron, *Ten Thousand Miles on a Bicycle* (New York: Karl Kron, 1887), 3.

75   **"Her mighty limbs sent the bicycle spinning round the track":** "Horse Against Bicycle," *Daily Alta California* (San Francisco), April 15, 1884.

76   **Samuel Franklin Cody, a Buffalo Bill imitator from Iowa:** See Garry Jenkins, *Colonel Cody and the Flying Cathedral: The Adventures of the Cowboy Who Conquered the Sky* (New York: Picador USA, 1999).

76   *Le tombeur de vélocipédistes:* Jenkins, *Colonel Cody and the Flying Cathedral,* 59.

76   **the League of American Wheelmen:** For primers on the LAW and the Good Roads Movement, see Michael Taylor, "The Bicycle Boom and the Bicycle Bloc: Cycling and Politics in the 1890s," *Indiana Magazine of History* 104, no. 3 (September 2008): 213–40; Carlton Reid, *Roads Were Not Built for Cars: How Cyclists Were the First to Push for Good Roads and Became the Pioneers of Motoring* (Washington, D.C.: Island Press, 2015); James Longhurst, *Bike Battles: A History of Sharing the American Road* (Seattle: University of Washington Press, 2015); Martin T. Olliff, *Getting Out of the Mud: The Alabama Good Roads Movement and Highway Administration, 1898–1928* (Tuscaloosa: University of Alabama Press, 2017); Friss, *The Cycling City;* and Lorenz J. Finison, *Boston's Cycling Craze, 1880–1900: A Story of Race, Sport, and Society* (Amherst: University of Massachusetts Press, 2014).

77   **"great bicycle parade":** "Novelties of a Great Bicycle Parade," *The Postal Record Monthly* 10, nos. 10–11 (October–December 1897): 233.

77   **minstrel show performances were staples:** The depth and breadth of this phenomenon is revealed by even a cursory survey of newspaper coverage of LAW events and turn-of-the-century bicycle club gatherings. It's a subject that merits further study. Start by searching under "blackface," "minstrel show," and "wheelmen" in a decent newspaper archive, e.g., newspapers.com or the Library of Congress's Chronicling America: Historic American Newspaper (chroniclingamerica.loc.gov)

site. See also, e.g., Jesse J. Gant and Nicholas J. Hoffman, *Wheel Fever: How Wisconsin Became a Great Bicycling State* (Madison: Wisconsin State Historical Society Press, 2013), 86.

77   "sand, gravel, mud, stones and muck holes": Quoted in Sister Caitriona Quinn, *The League of American Wheelmen and the Good Roads Movement, 1880–1912* (academic thesis), August 1968. Available online at john-s-allen.com/LAW_1939-1955/history/quinn-good-roads.pdf.

77   "No nation can advance in civilization": Albert A. Pope, *A Memorial to Congress on the Subject of a Road Department* (Boston: Samuel A. Green, 1893), 4.

78   "the bicycle, which has to a great extent superseded the use of horses": "Hay and Oats," *Sun* (New York), January 22, 1897.

78   "The saddle- and harness-makers are . . . turning their attention": J. B. Bishop, "The Social and Economic Influence of the Bicycle," *Forum* (New York), August 1896.

78   "The bicycle has come to stay and the reign of the horse is over": "The Steel Horse—the Wonder of the Nineteenth Century," *Menorah Magazine* 19 (1895): 382–83.

78   In this period, the horse assumed a new character: See Ann Norton Greene, *Horses at Work: Harnessing Power in Industrial America* (Cambridge, Mass.: Harvard University Press, 2008), 259–65. Cf. Clay McShane and Joel A. Tarr, *The Horse in the City: Living Machines in the Nineteenth Century* (Baltimore: Johns Hopkins University Press, 2008).

79   The following year, just 160,000 bikes were sold: Hank Chapot, "The Great Bicycle Protest of 1896," in *Critical Mass: Bicycling's Defiant Celebration,* ed. Chris Carlsson (Oakland, Calif.: AK Press, 2002), 182.

79   "infernal noise": Mikael Colville-Andersen, *Copenhagenize: The Definitive Guide to Global Bicycle Urbanism* (Washington, D.C.: Island Press, 2018), 231.

79   "stress-related illnesses": "Driving Kills—Health Warnings," *Copenhagenize,* July 27, 2009, copenhagenize.com/2009/07/driving-kills-health-warnings.html.

79   the horse reemerged as a marketing angle: Robert J. Turpin, *First Taste of Freedom: A Cultural History of Bicycle Manufacturing in the United States* (Syracuse, N.Y.: University of Syracuse Press, 2018), 169–70.

79   "Stallion Black" and "Palomino Tan": The digital scan of a 1951 print advertisement for the Gene Autry Western Bike can be viewed online: onlinebicyclemuseum.co.uk/wp-content/uploads/2015/04/1951-Monark-Gene-Autry-14.jpg.

79   Gene Autry Western Bike: Ibid.

80   "the leading bike-horse hybridiser in the world": You can see—and hear—the Trotify on YouTube: "Trotify in the Wild" (2012), youtube.com/watch?v=cfyC6NJqt2o.

5 BICYCLE MANIA: 1890s

82   Chris Heller has filed a petition: "Bicycle Craze," *Akron Daily Democrat* (Akron, Ohio), August 29, 1899.

82   The bicycle has appeared in a new role: "Bicycle Disrupts a Home:

Suit for Divorce the Outgrowth of a Woman's Passion for Wheeling," *Wichita Daily Eagle* (Wichita, Kansas), October 31, 1896.

82   Henry Cleating and his wife once lived happily: "No New Woman for Him: Mr. Cleating Got Tired of Washing Dishes and Chopped Up His Wife's Bicycle," *The World* (New York, New York), July 21, 1896.

83   Philip Pearce, alias *Spurgeon:* "A Youth Ruined by a Bicycle Mania," *The Essex Standard* (Colchester, Essex, Eng.), August 29, 1891.

83   They arrived at Glen Island [N.Y.] on Thursday, July 11: "Gay Girls in Bloomers: Father Objects to New Woman Tendencies and Takes Them Home," *The Journal and Tribune* (Knoxville, Tennessee), July 21, 1895.

84   Sunday the police developed a case of extreme cruelty: *The Des Moines Register* (Des Moines, Iowa), September 2, 1896.

84   A dispatch from Unadilla, N.Y.: "Wedded as They Scorched: A Pair of Amorous Bicyclists Married While They Flew Along on Wheels," *The Allentown Leader* (Allentown, Pennsylvania), September 9, 1895.

85   As a revolutionary force in the social world: "Bicycle Problems and Benefits," *The Century Illustrated Monthly Magazine* (New York, New York), July 1895.

86   In every civilized land, the bicycle has become a familiar object: "The World Awheel: The Wheel Abroad: Royalty on Wheels," *Munsey's Magazine* (New York, New York), May 1896.

86   American bicycles have made their appearance in Arabia: *The Muncie Evening Press* (Muncie, Indiana), February 17, 1897.

87   In all the wonder story of commerce and money dealings: "The Almighty Bicycle," *The Journal* (New York, New York), June 7, 1896.

88   The economic effects of this new force in human affairs: "Social and Economic Influence of the Bicycle," *The Forum* (New York, New York), August 1896.

89   The Rev. Thomas B. Gregory of Chicago: *The Anaconda Standard* (Anaconda, Montana), July 5, 1897.

89   Whenever a healthful amusement becomes a mania: "Abuse of the Wheel," *The Oshkosh Northwestern* (Oshkosh, Wisconsin), August 23, 1895.

89   Doctors seem to agree: "A Bicycle Malady," *Buffalo Courier* (Buffalo, New York), September 3, 1893.

90   The wheel is often the primary or exciting cause: "Bicycle-riding," *The Medical Age* (Detroit, Michigan), March 25, 1896.

90   Of all the deformities produced by biking: "Bike Deformities: Some of the Effects of Too Close Devotion to the Wheel," *The Daily Sentinel* (Grand Junction, Colorado), May 7, 1896.

91   The wry-faced, hunchbacked, human monkey: "Want the Scorcher Suppressed," *Chattanooga Daily Times* (Chattanooga, Tennessee), July 25, 1898.

91   The bicycle maniac should be shot on sight: *Toronto Saturday Night* (Toronto, Canada), October 17, 1896.

92   Doctors of France are puzzled by a new mania: "Bicycle Makes Women Cruel," *The Saint Paul Globe* (Saint Paul, Minnesota), June 14, 1897.

93   The question, it seems to me: "Is It the New Woman?," *The Chicago Tribune* (Chicago, Illinois), October 7, 1894.

93 **Miss Charlotte Smith:** "Miss Smith's Smithereen," *The Nebraska State Journal* (Lincoln, Nebraska), July 12, 1896.

93 **A very grave objection:** "Sexual Excitement," *The American Journal of Obstetrics and Diseases of Women and Children* (New York, New York), January 1895.

94 **To my brethren I feel I must speak plainly:** "As to the Bicycle," *The Medical World* (Philadelphia, Pennsylvania), November 1895.

94 **A word in regard to the tandem:** "The Bicycle and Its Riders," *The Cincinnati Lancet-Clinic* (Cincinnati, Ohio), September 1897.

95 **Among the bicyclists of the Boulevard:** "Woman Scorcher Nabbed," *The Sun* (New York, New York), May 2, 1896.

95 **An extraordinary incident:** "Her First Bloomers Created a Scene," *Cheltenham Chronicle* (Cheltenham, Gloucestershire, U.K.), April 18, 1896.

96 **Cambridge University today:** "Press Dispatch, Cambridge, England, May 21," *Public Opinion* (New York, New York), May 27, 1897.

96 **The bicycle fever will not have spent its fury:** "The Horseless Vehicle the Next Craze," *The Glencoe Transcript* (Glencoe, Ontario, Canada), June 18, 1896.

96 **Are the days of the bicycle numbered:** "To Take the Place of the Bicycle," *The Philadelphia Times* (Philadelphia, Pennsylvania), November 22, 1896.

97 **There are some who claim the automobile:** *Comfort* (Augusta, Maine), September 1899.

97 **Those people who affect to believe:** *Fort Scott Daily Monitor* (Fort Scott, Kansas), July 8, 1896.

6 BALANCING ACT

98 **Angus MacAskill was one of the biggest men:** For a brisk account of Angus MacAskill's life, see James Donald Gillis, *The Cape Breton Giant: A Truthful Memoir* (Montreal: John Lovell & Son, 1899). Despite its subtitle, Gillis's book inclines toward legend and overstatement throughout—which, given its Barnumian subject matter, feels appropriate.

99 **"were always literally great features in my establishment":** P. T. Barnum, *Struggles and Triumphs; or, Forty Years' Recollections of P. T. Barnum* (Buffalo, N.Y.: Courier Company, 1882), 161.

100 **The following year, MacAskill's youngest child, four-year-old Danny:** Unless otherwise noted, all the biographical information about, and quotations from, Danny MacAskill come from interviews with him conducted by the author. See also his autobiography: Danny MacAskill, *At the Edge: Riding for My Life* (London: Penguin, 2017).

101 **a Norse word meaning "isle of cloud":** David R. Ross, *On the Trail of Scotland's History* (Edinburgh: Luath, 2007), 10.

101 **can be viewed as a mighty bird:** Terry Marsh, *Walking the Isle of Skye: Walks and Scrambles Throughout Skye, Including the Cuillin*, Fourth Edition (Cicerone: Kendal, Cumbria, Eng.), 15.

102   Skye is the setting for many legends: Otta Swire, *Skye: The Island and Its Legends* (Edinburgh: Berlinn, 2017).

104   a 1997 film called *Chainspotting*: *Chainspotting—Full Movie—1997—UK Mountain Bike Movie*, youtube.com/watch?v=L_A2exFmvn0.

106   they called the video *Inspired Bicycles*: *Inspired Bicycles—Danny MacAskill April 2009*, youtube.com/watch?v=Z19zFlPah-o.

106   *Bicycle Trick Riding No. 2* (1899) and *The Trick Cyclist* (1901): Both videos can be viewed, back to back, at: *First Bike Trick EVER. Edison All*, youtube.com/watch?v=aZjd9pBmLoU.

107   the Cycling Elliotts: See Viona Elliott Lane, Randall Merris, and Chris Algar, "Tommy Elliott and the Musical Elliotts," *Papers of the International Concertina Association* 5 (2008): 16–49. See also Margaret Guroff, *The Mechanical Horse: How the Bicycle Reshaped American Life* (Austin: University of Texas Press, 2016), 111–14.

108   a cycling version of a Parisian quadrille: "The Elliotts: A Family of Trick Cyclists," *Travalanche*, December 7, 2012, travsd.wordpress.com/2012/12/17/the-elliotts-a-family-of-trick-cyclists/.

108   a poem published in *The Sporting and Theatrical Journal:* The poem is titled "To the Elliotts," and is credited to a "Mrs. Anne E. Capron." A subtitle adds: "Written by a lady who was infatuated with the Elliott children bicycle act at Barnum's Circus." I have an electronic version of the newspaper clipping in my possession; unfortunately, I have no information regarding its provenance or publication. If you are a researcher—or just a fancier of odes to youth trick cycling troupes—and wish to see the clipping, feel free to email me, and I will send it along. You can reach me at jody@jody-rosen.com.

108   the Elliotts came to the attention of the New York Society for the Prevention: See, e.g., "The Child-Performers," *New-York Tribune*, March 29, 1883; "Why P. T. Barnum Was Arrested," *New York Times*, April 3, 1883; and *Brooklyn Daily Eagle*, April 3, 1883.

108   the Cycling Elliotts gave a special demonstration: "Barnum's Arrest," *Daily Evening Sentinel* (Carlisle, Penn.), April 3, 1883.

108   "a dozen or more leading doctors": "Mr. Barnum Not Cruel to the Little Bicycle Riders," *Brooklyn Daily Eagle*, April 5, 1883.

108   the regimen of a trick cyclist was "very beautiful and beneficial": "Barnum Not Guilty," *New York Times*, April 5, 1883.

108   "if all children took similar exercise, it would be better than doctors or drugs": "The Elliott Children," *New York Herald*, April 5, 1883. Quoted in Guroff, *The Mechanical Horse*, 113.

108   "The Revolving Wheel of Fire": Lane, Merris, and Algar, "Tommy Elliott and the Musical Elliotts," 42–43.

109   "He was [a] . . . small, but beautifully built fellow, supple as a cat": Berta Ruck, *Miss Million's Maid: A Romance of Love and Fortune* (New York: A. L. Burt, 1915), 377.

109   Kaufmann's Cycling Beauties: See David Goldblatt, "Sporting Life: Cycling Is Among the Most Flexible of All Sports," *Prospect Magazine*, October 19, 2011, prospectmagazine.co.uk/magazine/sporting-life-9. For a photograph of the troupe in their form-fitting attire, see commons.wikimedia.org/wiki/File:Kaufmann%27s_Cycling_Beauties.jpg.

110   **Annie Oakley did a bicycle turn**: Sarah Russell, "Annie Oakley, Gender, and Guns: The 'Champion Rifle Shot' and Gender Performance, 1860–1926" (Chancellor's Honors Program Projects, University of Tennessee, Knoxville, 2013), 28; trace.tennessee.edu/utk_chanhonoproj /1646.

110   **"Hatsley the Boy Wonder"**: Wade Gordon James Nelson, "Reading Cycles: The Culture of BMX Freestyle" (PhD thesis, McGill University, August 2006), 63; core.ac.uk/download/pdf/41887323.pdf.

110   **The British cyclist Sid Black did a thrilling variation**: "The King of the Wheel," *Sketch: A Journal of Art and Actuality* (London), September 7, 1898.

111   **At a performance in Bremen, Germany**: "Secrets of Trick Cycling," *Lake Wakatip Mail* (Queenstown, Otago, N.Z.), July 24, 1906.

111   **The Villions, a family troupe**: William G. Fitzgerald, "Side-Shows," *Strand Magazine* (London) 14, no. 80 (August 1897): 156–57.

112   **The signature stunt of vaudevillian Joe Jackson**: Frank Cullen with Florence Hackman and Donald McNeilly, *Vaudeville Old & New: An Encyclopedia of Variety Performers in America*, vol. 1 (New York: Routledge, 2004), 558–59.

112   **"A Bear and a Monkey Race on Bicycles"**: The video can be viewed on YouTube: "A Bear and a Monkey Race on Bicycles, Then Bear Eats Monkey," youtube.com/watch?v=cteBe4gCUKo.

112   **One lavishly illustrated instructional manual**: Isabel Marks, *Fancy Cycling: Trick Riding for Amateurs* (London: Sands & Company, 1901), 5–6.

112   **The chief instructor at a popular New York cycling school**: "Fancy Bicycle Riding," *Indianapolis News*, April 10, 1896.

113   **Sixty years ago the belles and beaux**: I have in my possession an electronic version of this newspaper clipping, a fifty-five-word report on the vogue for "gymkhana tricks" and "swagger cycle schools" among London's swanky set. The newspaper clipping makes clear that the item is an excerpt of a piece that appeared first in *Hearth and Home*, a London-based women's magazine. Unfortunately, I cannot determine what newspaper the clipping is taken from, or when exactly it was published, nor can I locate the issue of *Hearth and Home* in which the item originally appeared. The electronic footprint for this intriguing tidbit appears to have been covered up by the sands of time, or the digital equivalent thereof. If you are a researcher or other interested party, I would be happy to email you the clipping. I can be reached via email: jody@jody-rosen.com.

113   **The teenage Prince Albert**: "Prince Albert as Trick Cyclist," *Yorkshire Evening Post*, June 18, 1912.

113   **the Code of Ordinances for Memphis, Tennessee**: See "Code of Ordinances, City of Memphis, Tennessee," specifically "Sec. 12-84-19.— Instruction in operating automobiles, and other vehicles and trick riding prohibited"; available online at library.municode.com/tn/memphis /codes/code_of_ordinances?nodeId=TIT11VETR_CH11-24BI.

114   *Broadway Weekly* **complained that trick cyclists**: "The Way to Make a Hit in Vaudeville," *Broadway Weekly* (New York), September 21, 1904.

114 **In 1907, an audience at the Belfast Hippodrome:** "Fatal Accident to a
Lady Trick Cyclist," *Stonehaven Journal* (Stonehaven, Kincardineshire,
Scotland), June 20, 1907.

114 **"He fell into a dry moat":** "Trick Cyclist Killed in Paris," *Nottingham
Evening Post* (Nottingham, Nottinghamshire, Eng.), March 19, 1903.

114 **Charles Kabrich, a self-styled "bike-chute-aeronaut":** "Chas. H.
Kabrich, the Only Bike-Chute Aeronaut: Novel and Thrilling Bicycle
Parachute Act in Mid-air" (publicity poster), Library of Congress, loc
.gov/resource/var.0525/.

114 **"The Terrible Trip to the Moon" . . . "An Awful Holding of Life as
a Pawn":** See the publicity poster, available online at Alamy, alamy
.com/stock-photo-the-great-adam-forepaugh-and-sells-bros-americas
-enormous-shows-united-83150063.html.

114 **"It is a terrible leap, such as pinches the heart":** "Most Daring Performance," *Morning Press* (Santa Barbara, Calif.), September 13, 1906.

115 **Ray Sinatra:** See "Ray Sinatra and His Cycling Orchestra—Picture #1,"
Dave's Vintage Bicycles: A Classic Bicycle Photo Archive, nostalgic.net
/bicycle287/picture1093.

115 **the most prominent forms of stunt riding:** Stunt riding is not just sport
or showbiz, of course. It's also a folk art that serves surprising social
functions. In a 1977 study of the role played by bicycles in the life of
Umuaro, a "village cluster" in southeastern Nigeria, the social psycholo-
gists Rex Uzo Ugorji and Nnennaya Achinivu reported on the tradition
of "magic cyclists . . . men who ride bicycles with juju": troupes of trick
cyclists who traveled to the rural region from the city of Aba to stage
performances on festive occasions. See Rex Uzo Ugorji and Nnennaya
Achinivu, "The Significance of Bicycles in a Nigerian Village," *The
Journal of Social Psychology* 102, no. 2 (1977), 241–46.

116 ***The Ridge*** **(2014):** *Danny Macaskill: The Ridge,* youtube.com/watch
?v=xQ_IQS3VKjA.

116 ***Imaginate*:** *Danny MacAskill's Imaginate,* youtube.com/watch?v=Sv3x
VOs7_No.

116 ***Danny Daycare*:** *Danny MacAskill: Danny Daycare,* youtube.com
/watch?v=jj0CmnxuTaQ.

118 ***Back on Track*:** *Martyn Ashton—Back on Track,* youtube.com/watch
?v=kX_hn3Xf90g.

119 **"The management of our aeroplane, like that of the bicycle":** "Have
Long Sought Mastery of Air," *Clinton Republican* (Wilmington, Ohio),
June 6, 1908.

119 **"The aviator of the present day":** Reprinted in Waldemar Kaempffert,
The New Art of Flying (New York: Dodd, Mead, 1911), 233.

7 PUT SOME FUN BETWEEN YOUR LEGS

122 **"I want to fuck a bicycle":** Vi Khi Nao, *Fish in Exile* (Minneapolis:
Coffee House, 2016), 131.

123 **"moving his hips back and forth as if to simulate sex":** "Man Admits to
Sex with Bike," UPI, October 27, 2007, upi.com/Odd_News/2007/10/27
/Man-admits-to-sex-with-bike/10221193507754/; "Bike Sex Case Sparks

Legal Debate," BBC News, November 16, 2007, news.bbc.co.uk/2/hi
/uk_news/scotland/glasgow_and_west/7098116.stm; "'Cycle-Sexualist'
Gets Probation," UPI, November 15, 2007, upi.com/Odd_News/2007
/11/15/Cycle-sexualist-gets-probation/26451195142086/.

124   "a coalition of the horny": Bike Smut, bikesmut.com.

125   *Fuck Bike #001:* Andrew H. Shirley, *Fuck Bike #001* (2011), vimeo
.com/20439817.

125   project Bikesexual aims to "challenge body norms": *Bikesexual,*
bikesexual.blogsport.eu/beispiel-seite/.

125   "combines principles of DIY, vegan, ecological, and bicycle culture":
Ibid.

126   "bring about constant friction over the clitoris and labia": "Bicycling
for Women from the Standpoint of the Gynecologist," *Transactions of
the New York Obstetrical Society from October 20, 1894 to October 1,
1895,* published by *The American Journal of Obstetrics* (New York:
William Wood, 1895), 86–87.

126   "Daisy Bell (Bicycle Built for Two)": Harry Dacre, "Daisy Bell (Bicycle
Built for Two)" (New York: T. B. Harms, 1892).

126   James Joyce writes of a young *"prostituta in herba"*: James Joyce,
Finnegans Wake (Ware, Hertfordshire, Eng.: Wordsworth Editions,
2012), 115.

126   "We had abandoned the real world": Georges Bataille, *Story of the Eye
by Lord Auch,* trans. Joachim Neugroschel (San Francisco: City Lights,
1978), 32–34.

127   "a long 'spin' in the country": C. C. Mapes, "A Review of the Dangers
and Evils of Bicycling," *The Medical Age* (Detroit), November 10, 1897.

128   "The road rose and fell over gentle slopes": Maurice Leblanc, *Voici
des ailes!* (Paris: Ink Book, 2019), 49–51, e-book. Translation from the
French by Jody Rosen.

128   "The concept of riding a bike naked": Steve Hunt, "Naked Protest
and Radical Cycling: A History of the Journey to the World Naked Bike
Ride," Academia.edu, academia.edu/35589138/Naked_Protest_and
_Radical_Cycling_A_History_of_the_Journey_to_the_World_Naked
_Bike_Ride, 4.

129   Philip Carr-Gomm has written: Philip Carr-Gomm, *A Brief History of
Nakedness* (London: Reaktion, 2010), 12.

129   "By cycling naked we declare our confidence in the beauty": World
Naked Bike Ride, Portland, Oregon, "Why," pdxwnbr.org/why/.

129   "It's impossible to feel like a grown-up when you're on a bicycle":
P. J. O'Rourke, "Dear Urban Cyclists: Go Play in Traffic," *Wall Street
Journal,* April 2, 2011.

130   Social scientists have reported: Cf. Dag Balkmar, "Violent Mobilities:
Men, Masculinities and Road Conflicts in Sweden," *Mobilities* 13, no. 5
(2018): 717–32.

130   "double-tall bike adorned with a giant papier-mâché vulva": Adriane
"Lil' Mama Bone Crusher" Ackerman, "The Cuntraption," in *Our
Bodies, Our Bikes,* ed. Elly Blue and April Streeter (Portland, Ore.: Elly
Blue Publishing / Microcosm, 2015), 75–76.

131   "phallic powers of penetration and thrust": Zoë Sofoulis, "Slime in the

Matrix: Post-phallic Formations in Women's Art in New Media," in *Jane Gallop Seminar Papers*, ed. Jill Julius Matthews (Canberra: Australian National University, Humanities Research Centre, 1993), 97.

131   **"In northern Europe we save our private bodies for the indoors"**: Jet McDonald, "Girls on Bikes," *Jet McDonald*, jetmcdonald.com/2016/12 /08/girls-on-bikes/.

131   **the memoir *My Bike and Other Friends:*** See Henry Miller, *Henry Miller's Book of Friends: A Trilogy* (Santa Barbara, Calif.: Capra Press, 1978), 223.

8 WINTER

133   **Now, on April 27, 1827, she was setting out:** For an account of the journey by the *Hecla*'s captain, see William Edward Parry, *Narrative of an Attempt to Reach the North Pole, in Boats Fitted for the Purpose, and Attached to His Majesty's Ship Hecla, in the Year MDCCCXXVII* (London: John Murray, 1828).

134   **"When Peruvians first saw a Spaniard on horseback":** *Morning Advertiser* (London), February 1, 1827.

135   **"dilettante who sends his bicycle to winter quarters directly":** R. T. Lang, "Winter Bicycling," *Badminton Magazine of Sports & Pastimes* 14 (January–June 1902): 180.

135   **"When . . . the snow [is] whirling and twisting and twirling":** Ibid., 189.

135   **wintertime biking:** For a peppy overview of winter cycling, see Tom Babin, *Frostbike: The Joy, Pain and Numbness of Winter Cycling* (Toronto: Rocky Mountain Books, 2014).

136   **There is a 1948 photograph of Joe Steinlauf:** The photograph can be viewed online at "Early Ice Bike," *Cyclelicious*, cyclelicio.us/2010/early -ice-bike/. Check it out, it's worth the clicks.

137   **"Ice velocipedes are the latest novelty on the Hudson":** *Brooklyn Daily Eagle*, January 12, 1869.

137   **a new wave of winterized bicycle designs:** See, e.g., "The Cyclist in a Winter Paradise," *Sunday Morning Call* (Lincoln, Neb.), January 24, 1897. Cf. *Bicycle: The Definitive Visual History* (London: DK, 2016), 62–63.

137   **"any style or make of modern safety bicycle":** "Ice-Bicycle Attachments," *Hardware: Devoted to the American Hardware Trade*, November 25, 1895.

137   **"swifter than summer speed":** "Chicago Ice Bicycle Apparatus . . ." (advertisement), *Gazette* (Montreal), November 23, 1895, 6.

137   **The company boasted:** "Ice-Bicycle Attachments," *Hardware: Devoted to the American Hardware Trade*, November 25, 1895.

137   **"Klondike Bicycle":** "Klondike Bicycle Freight Line," *Boston Globe*, August 2, 1897.

138   **the Klondike Bicycle could serve as both a passenger and a cargo vehicle:** "To Klondyke by Bicycle," *Democrat and Chronicle* (Rochester, N.Y.), July 30, 1897.

138   **"tenderfoot prospectors who have taken bicycles"** to the Yukon:

A. C. Harris, *Alaska and the Klondike Gold Fields: Practical Instructions for Fortune Seekers* (Cincinnati: W. H. Ferguson, 1897), 77.

138 **Proponents of bicycles . . . "had overlooked the one thing necessary":** Ibid., pp. 442–43. In 1897, a Newark, New Jersey, entrepreneur, Charles H. Brinkerhoff, announced a plan to alleviate the problem of poor road conditions by building "a bicycle track to the Klondike . . . lightly constructed of steel, clamped to the sides of the mountains." The roadway, Brinkerhoff said, would be engineered such that "the mountain climbing will be done almost without the bicyclist being aware of any uphill work." Brinkerhoff's plan called for cozy pit stops: "Every twenty-five miles of the journey there will be a station, lighted and heated by electricity and provided with seats and tables and a restaurant so that pilgrims to the gold district can rest and refresh themselves." Needless to say, the track was never built. See "A Bicycle Route to the Klondike," *Buffalo Courier-Record*, November 28, 1897.

139 **"The heartbreak and suffering which so many have undergone":** Jennifer Marx, *The Magic of Gold* (New York: Doubleday, 1978), 410.

139 **the *Skagway Daily Alaskan* estimated that 250 cyclists were heading:** Terrence Cole, ed., *Wheels on Ice: Bicycling in Alaska, 1898–1908* (Anchorage: Alaska Northwest Publishing, 1985), 6.

140 **"A red short haired dog frozen hard as stone":** Ibid., 14.

140 **"took about 25 headers into the snow":** Ibid., 10.

141 **"I split a nice straight grained piece of spruce":** Ibid., 14–15.

141 **Max Hirschberg:** Hirschberg's vivid first-person account of his Klondike journey, written at the request of his wife in the 1950s, is anthologized in Cole, ed., *Wheels on Ice*, 21–23.

143 **"A thrill shot through me as I caught sight of Old Glory waving":** Ibid., 22.

143 **Robert McDonald, an Anglican priest and missionary:** Patrick Moore, "Archdeacon Robert McDonald and Gwich'in Literacy," *Anthropological Linguistics* 49, no. 1 (Spring 2007): 27–53.

145 **"Without my chain I could not control the speed of my bicycle":** Cole, ed., *Wheels on Ice*, 23.

145 **There is a video of the historic ride on the internet:** "(OFFICIAL) Eric Barone—227,720 km/h (141.499 mph)—Mountain Bike World Speed Record—2017," youtube.com/watch?v=7gBqbNUtr3c.

146 **"hold his body together in a crash.":** Patty Hodapp, "How a Mountain Biker Clocked 138 MPH Riding Downhill," *Vice*, April 16, 2015, vice .com/en/article/yp77jj/how-a-mountain-biker-clocked-138-mph-riding -downhill.

9 UPHILL

153 **"guiding directive for development":** See Michael S. Givel, "Gross National Happiness in Bhutan: Political Institutions and Implementation," *Asian Affairs* 46, no. 1 (2015), 108.

153 **According to one story, it was a Raleigh racing bike:** "Cycling in Bhutan," *Inside Himalayas*, April 11, 2015, insidehimalayas.com /cycling-in-bhutan/.

153   "along mud trails at perilous speed": Karma Ura, *Leadership of the Wise: Kings of Bhutan* (Thimphu, Bhutan: Centre for Bhutan Studies, 2010), 108.

153   **The average elevation in Bhutan is 10,760 feet:** "Countries with the Highest Average Elevations," *World Atlas,* worldatlas.com/articles /countries-with-the-highest-average-elevations.html.

153   **According to one study:** Devi Maya Adhikari, Karma Wangchuk, and A. Jabeena, "Preliminary Study on Automatic Dependent Surveillance-Broadcast Coverage Design in the Mountainous Terrain of Bhutan," in *Advances in Automation, Signal Processing, Instrumentation, and Control,* ed. Venkata Lakshmi Narayana Komanapalli, N. Sivakumaran, and Santoshkumar Hampannavar (Singapore: Springer, 2021), 873.

154   **"to make Bhutan a bicycling culture":** Madhu Suri Prakash, "Why the Kings of Bhutan Ride Bicycles," *Yes! Magazine* (Bainbridge Island, Wash.), January 15, 2011, yesmagazine.org/issue/happy-families-know /2011/01/15/why-the-kings-of-bhutan-ride-bicycles.

154   **"There is a reason we in Bhutan like to cycle":** Author interview with Tshering Tobgay. Unless otherwise noted, all direct quotations in this chapter come from interviews conducted by the author in Bhutan.

155   **The national anthem, "The Thunder Dragon Kingdom":** The translation of the anthem's lyrics can be found in Dorji Penjore and Sonam Kinga, *The Origin and Description of the National Flag and National Anthem of the Kingdom of Bhutan* (Thimphu, Bhutan: Centre for Bhutan Studies, 2002), 16.

158   **Bhutan's success in combating the Covid-19 pandemic:** See, e.g., "Bhutan, the Vaccination Nation: A UN Resident Coordinator Blog," *UN News,* May 23, 2021, news.un.org/en/story/2021/05/109242; Madeline Drexler, "The Unlikeliest Pandemic Success Story," *The Atlantic,* February 10, 2021, theatlantic.com/international/archive/2021/02 /coronavirus-pandemic-bhutan/617976/.

159   **Bhutan's constitution mandates:** See the .pdf posted on the website of the National Assembly of Bhutan: *The Constitution of the Kingdom of Bhutan,* National Assembly of Bhutan website, nab.gov.bt/assets /templates/images/constitution-of-bhutan-2008.pdf.

159   **a carbon sink:** Mark Tutton and Katy Scott, "What Tiny Bhutan Can Teach the World About Being Carbon Negative," CNN, October 11, 2018, cnn.com/2018/10/11/asia/bhutan-carbon-negative/index.html; "Bhutan Is the World's Only Carbon Negative Country, So How Did They Do It?," *Climate Council,* April 2, 2017, climatecouncil.org.au /bhutan-is-the-world-s-only-carbon-negative-country-so-how-did-they -do-it/.

159   **"the real Shangri-La":** Jeffrey Gettleman, "A New, Flourishing Literary Scene in the Real Shangri-La," *New York Times,* August 19, 2018.

160   **the scholar Lauchlan T. Munro has argued:** Lauchlan T. Munro, "Where Did Bhutan's Gross National Happiness Come From? The Origins of an Invented Tradition," *Asian Affairs* 47, no. 1 (2016): 71–92.

160   **"One Nation, One People":** See, e.g., Rajesh S. Karat, "The Ethnic Crisis in Bhutan: Its Implications," *India Quarterly* 57, no. 1 (2001),

39–50; Vidhyapati Mishra, "Bhutan Is No Shangri-La," *New York Times,* June 28, 2013, nytimes.com/2013/06/29/opinion/bhutan-is-no-shangri-la .html; Kai Bird, "The Enigma of Bhutan," *The Nation,* March 7, 2012, thenation.com/article/archive/enigma-bhutan/.

161   "ethnic cleansing": Bill Frelick, "Bhutan's Ethnic Cleansing," *Human Rights Watch,* February 1, 2008, hrw.org/news/2008/02/01/bhutans -ethnic-cleansing.

161   "world's biggest creator of refugees by per capita": Maximillian Mørch, "Bhutan's Dark Secret: The Lhotshampa Expulsion," *The Diplomat,* September 21, 2016, thediplomat.com/2016/09/bhutans-dark -secret-the-lhotshampa-expulsion/.

161   "the image of a small, landlocked, plucky country": Munro, "Where Did Bhutan's Gross National Happiness Come From?," 86.

166   "I was scorched by the sun, stifled by the dust, drenched by the rain": Elizabeth Robins Pennell, *Over the Alps on a Bicycle* (London: T. Fisher Unwin, 1898), 105.

166   "I wanted to see if I could cross the Alps on a bicycle": Ibid.

166   "I did not think I was very original": Ibid., 11.

10 NOWHERE FAST

168   "electric camel": Seán O'Driscoll, "Electric Camels and Cigars: Life on the Titanic," *Times* (London), April 21, 2017, thetimes.co.uk/article /electric-camels-and-cigars-life-on-the-titanic-8kznbpcnw.

169   a large dial whose red and blue arrows marked the rider's progress: Walter Lord, *A Night to Remember* (New York: Henry Holt and Company, 1955), 40.

169   There is a famous photograph: See Lawrence Beesley, *The Loss of the S.S. Titanic: Its Story and Its Lessons* (Boston: Houghton Mifflin Company, 1912), 12–13.

170   the Gymnasticon, a machine patented in 1796: See "Specification of the Patent Granted to Mr. Francis Lowndes, of St. Paul's Churchyard, Medical Electrician; for a new-invented Machine for exercising the Joints and Muscles of the Human Body," in *The Repertory of Arts, Manufactures, and Agriculture,* vol. 6 (London: printed for the proprietors, 1797), 88–92.

170   roller-bike contests in vaudeville theaters: See Marlene Targ Brill, *Marshall "Major" Taylor: World Champion Bicyclist, 1899-1901* (Minneapolis: Twenty-First Century Books, 2008), 70.

170   "The use of a home trainer gives the best sort of indoor exercise": Luther Henry Porter, *Cycling for Health and Pleasure: An Indispensable Guide to the Successful Use of the Wheel* (New York: Dodd, Mead, 1895), 138.

171   "We may expect to find some idiot advertising": The piece, originally published, apparently, in the London magazine *Pall Mall,* is quoted in an item in an American hardware trade journal: "Trade Chat from Gotham," *Stoves and Hardware Reporter* (St. Louis and Chicago), August 1, 1895, 22.

171   **an ambitious home cyclist:** The story of this enterprising stationary cyclist was published in an 1897 issue of the London-based periodical *The Rambler* (Tagline: "A Penny Magazine Devoted to Out-door Life") under the title "The Cycle in the House: Curious Domestic Uses of the Bicycle." A clipping of the piece can be viewed online at upload .wikimedia.org/wikipedia/commons/thumb/0/09/Home_cycling _trainer_1897.jpg/640px-Home_cycling_trainer_1897.jpg.

172   **Aaron Puzey:** "Meet the Man Cycling the UK Using Virtual Reality," BBC News, August 16, 2016, bbc.com/news/av/uk-37099807.

173   **in 1899, a research team led by Professor W. O. Atwater:** "The Human Machine at the Head," *Mind and Body: A Monthly Journal Devoted to Physical Education* (Milwaukee, Wisc.) 12 (March 1905–February 1906), 54–55; "Experiments on a Man in a Cage," *New York Journal,* June 18, 1899; and Jane A. Stewart, "Prof. Atwater's Alcohol Experiment," *School Journal* (New York) 59 (July 1, 1899–December 31, 1899), 589–90. Also: W. O. Atwater and F. G. Benedict, "The Respiration Calorimeter," *Yearbook of the United States Department of Agriculture: 1904* (Washington, D.C.: Government Printing Office, 1905), 205–20. Available online at naldc.nal.usda.gov /download/IND43645383/PDF.

174   **These ideas were elaborated in one of the more fascinating artifacts:** James C. McCullagh, ed., *Pedal Power in Work, Leisure, and Transportation* (Emmaus, Penn.: Rodale, 1977).

174   **"this age of lasers and deep space probes":** Ibid., ix.

175   **"climate of bikology":** Ibid., 58.

175   **"full human potential inherent in the use of bicycles for work":** Ibid., x.

175   **"Researchers report that when working with cherries":** Ibid., 62–64.

175   **"As the bicycle in a sense 'liberated' people at the turn of the century":** Ibid., 144.

176   **the global stationary cycle market is valued at nearly $600 million:** "Exercise Bike Market: Global Industry Trends, Share, Size, Growth, Opportunity and Forecast 2021–2026," Imarc Group, available online at imarcgroup.com/exercise-bike-market.

177   **"The stationary bike, potentially the most boring piece of equipment":** For this quotation and all the other quotations from Goldberg's book, see Andrea Cagan and Johnny G, *Romancing the Bicycle: The Five Spokes of Balance* (Los Angeles: Johnny G Publishing, 2000), 77.

178   **a "cardio party":** "Who We Are," SoulCycle, soul-cycle.com/our-story/.

179   **SoulCycle has endured financial setbacks:** Abby Ellin, "SoulCycle and the Wild Ride," *Town and Country,* April 21, 2021, townandcountry mag.com/leisure/sporting/a36175871/soul-cycle-spin-class-scandals/.

179   **a record twenty-three thousand Peloton members:** Eric Newcomer, "Peloton Attracts a Record 23,000 People to Single Workout Class," *Bloomberg,* April 24, 2020, bloomberg.com/news/articles/2020-04-24 /peloton-attracts-a-record-23-000-people-to-single-workout-class.

180   **Cycle Ergometer with Vibration Isolation and Stabilization System, or CEVIS:** "Cycling on the International Space Station with Astronaut Doug Wheelock," youtube.com/watch?v=bG3hG3iB5S4.

181 "Lance Armstrong, eat your heart out!": "Ed Lu's Journal: Entry #7: Working Out," SpaceRef, July 29, 2003, spaceref.com/news/viewsr .html?pid=9881.

II CROSS COUNTRY

182 "Daisy Bell (Bicycle Built for Two)": Harry Dacre, "Daisy Bell (Bicycle Built for Two)," (New York: T. B. Harms, 1892).

183 The Old Pali Highway: Kristen Pedersen, "The Pali Highway: From Rough Trail to Daily Commute," Historic Hawai'i Foundation, August 22, 2016, historichawaii.org/2016/08/22/thepalihighway/.

183 When Barb Brushe was a young woman: Unless otherwise noted, the stories told in this chapter about Barb Samsoe (née Brushe) and Bill Samsoe come from the author's interviews with the Samsoes.

183 "It's called Bikecentennial": See Michael McCoy and Greg Siple, *America's Bicycle Route: The Story of the TransAmerica Bicycle Trail* (Virginia Beach, Va.: Donning , 2016); and Dan D'Ambrosio, "Bikecentennial: Summer of 1976," Adventure Cycling Association, February 15, 2019, adventurecycling.org/blog/bikecentennial-summer-of-1976/.

185 John Denver's "Sweet Surrender": John Denver, "Sweet Surrender," from the album *Back Home Again* (RCA Records, 1974).

191 grasshopper swarm: See John L. Capinera, ed., *Encyclopedia of Entomology*, 2nd edition (Springer: Dordrecht, Netherlands, 2008), 141–44.

192 "great grasshopper plagues" of the 1870s: See Thomas C. Cox, *Everything but the Fenceposts: The Great Plains Grasshopper Plague of 1874–1877* (Los Angeles: Figueroa Press, 2010); and Jeffrey A. Lockwood, *Locust: The Devastating Rise and Mysterious Disappearance of the Insect that Shaped the American Frontier* (New York: Basic Books, 2015).

192 a man named Greg Siple: Unless otherwise noted, the accounts of Greg Siple's life, travels, and planning of the Bikecentennial with his wife, June Siple, and friends Dan and Lys Burden come from the author's interviews and correspondence with Greg and June Siple.

193 "My original thought was to send out ads": D'Ambrosio, "Bikecentennial: Summer of 1976."

194 "combine the best features of the TOSRV and Hemistour": McCoy and Siple, *America's Bicycle Route*, 25.

195 "BONETINGLING, Kaleidoscopic, Multitudinous": June J. Siple, "The Chocolate Connection: Remembering Bikecentennial's Beginnings," *Adventure Cyclist*, June 2016, 27.

196 *Around the World on a Bicycle* (1887): Thomas Stevens, *Around the World on a Bicycle* (1887; repr. Mechanicsburg, Penn.: Stackpole, 2000).

197 "In summery locales like Florida and Southern California": Margaret Guroff, *The Mechanical Horse: How the Bicycle Reshaped American Life* (Austin: University of Texas Press, 2016), 128.

197 An ad for the AMF Roadmaster: Ibid., 128.

197   **A 1972 federal government report:** Ibid., 135.

198   **bicycles outsold cars:** Ibid., 135.

198   **"Survival Faire":** "Remembering the Survival Faire, Earth Day's Predecessor," *Bay Nature*, March 24, 2020, baynature.org/article /remembering-the-survival-faire-earth-days-predecesor/.

198   **"As the local citizenry looked on":** Sam Whiting, "San Jose Car Burial Put Ecological Era in Gear," *San Francisco Chronicle*, April 20, 2010, sfgate.com/green/article/San-Jose-car-burial-put-ecological-era-in-gear -3266993.php.

199   **"Pollution Solution":** Guroff, *The Mechanical Horse*, 133.

199   **"poetic velo-rutionary tendency":** Peter Walker, "People Power: the Secret to Montreal's Success as a Bike-Friendly City," *Guardian*, June 17, 2015, theguardian.com/cities/2015/jun/17/people-power -montreal-north-america-cycle-city.

199   **"the biggest bicycle touring event in world history":** McCoy and Siple, *America's Bicycle Route*, 26.

199   **"Let 1976 be the year":** Ibid., 26.

200   **Four-thousand-sixty-five cyclists:** Bikecentennial statistics and demographic information was gleaned from Greg Siple, "Bikecentennial 76: America's Biggest Bicycling Event," in *Cycle History 27: Proceedings of the 27th International Cycling History Conference* (Verona, New Jersey: ICHC Publications Committee, 2017), 110–15; and McCoy and Siple, *America's Bicycle Route*, 48.

200   **"seeing rural America close-up":** McCoy and Siple, *America's Bicycle Route*, 48.

200   **Bridget O'Connell:** "Flute-Toting Cyclist Bridget O'Connell Gilchrist Shares Bikecentennial Memories," Adventure Cycling Association, June 29, 2015, adventurecycling.org/resources/blog/bridget-gilchrist -my-favorite-places-to-sleep-outdoors-were-pine-forests-corn-fields-and -near-a-babbling-brook/.

201   **The audience would boo:** "Bikecentennial 76 Shuttle Truck Driver Remembers Cyclists' Appreciation," Adventure Cycling Association, September 21, 2015, adventurecycling.org/resources/blog/bike centennial-76-shuttle-truck-driver-remembers-cyclists-appreciation/.

201   **Wilma Ramsay:** "Theresa Whalen Leland: Remembering Bikecentennial 1976," Adventure Cycling Association, June 1, 2015, adventure cycling.org/resources/blog/theresa-whalen-leland-remembering -bikecentennial-1976/. Theresa Whalen Leland's lovely Bikecentennial reminiscence was my source for the stories of Wilma Ramsay and her brother Albert Schultz.

201   **a freak blizzard:** Siple, "Bikecentennial 76," 115.

202   **slept among grunting hogs:** McCoy and Siple, *America's Bicycle Route*, 45.

202   **Lloyd Sumner:** Ibid., 46.

202   **slalomed between turtles:** "Theresa Whalen Leland: Remembering Bikecentennial 1976."

206   **They wrote many letters:** I am grateful to the Samsoes for sharing copies of their letters with me.

12 BEAST OF BURDEN

217 **Global Liveability Index:** See, e.g., "The Global Liveability Index 2021," *Economist Intelligence,* eiu.com/n/campaigns/global-liveability-index-2021/.

218 **Each year, four hundred thousand migrants arrive in Dhaka:** Md Masud Parves Rana and Irina N. Ilina, "Climate Change and Migration Impacts on Cities: Lessons from Bangladesh," *Environmental Challenges* 5 (December 2021), available online at sciencedirect.com/science/article/pii/S2667010021002213?via%3Dihub; and Poppy McPherson, "Dhaka: The City Where Climate Refugees Are Already a Reality," *Guardian* (London), December 1, 2015, theguardian.com/cities/2015/dec/01/dhaka-city-climate-refugees-reality.

218 **authoritarianism and extremism:** See K. Anis Ahmed, "Bangladesh's Choice: Authoritarianism or Extremism," *New York Times,* December 27, 2018, nytimes.com/2018/12/27/opinion/bangladesh-election-awami-bnp-authoritarian-extreme.html.

218 **A 2021 study:** Cascade Tuholske, Kelly Caylor, Chris Funk, Andrew Verdin, Stuart Sweeney, Kathryn Grace, Pete Peterson, and Tom Evans, "Global Urban Population Exposure to Extreme Heat," *PNAS* 118, no. 41 (2021), pnas.org/content/pnas/118/41/e2024792118.full.pdf.

218 **"5 Things to Do While Stuck in Traffic":** Naziba Basher, "5 Things to Do While Stuck in Traffic," *Daily Star* (Dhaka), August 28, 2015.

220 **"Juts and jags to fill up any bubble of navigable space":** K. Anis Ahmed, *Good Night, Mr. Kissinger: And Other Stories* (Los Angeles: Unnamed Press, 2014), 27.

221 **Studies have determined:** See, for example, "Dhaka's Noise Pollution Three Times More Than Tolerable Level: Environment Minister," *Daily Star* (Dhaka), April 28, 2021, thedailystar.net/environment/news/dhakas-noise-pollution-three-times-more-tolerable-level-environment-minister-2085309; "Noise Pollution Exceeds Permissible Limit in Dhaka," *New Age* (Dhaka), January 11, 2020, newagebd.net/print/article/96222.

221 **There are about eighty thousand licensed rickshaws in Dhaka:** Rezaul Karim and Khandoker Abdus Salam, "Organising the Informal Economy Workers: A Study of Rickshaw Pullers in Dhaka City," *Bangladesh Institute of Labour Studies-BILS,* March 2019, bilsbd.org/wp-content/uploads/2019/06/A-Study-of-Rickshaw-Pullers-in-Dhaka-City.pdf, 21.

221 **an estimate of 1.1 million:** Ibid., 12.

221 *The Rickshaws of Bangladesh:* Rob Gallagher, *The Rickshaws of Bangladesh* (Dhaka: University Press, 1992), 1–2.

222 **three million citizens of Dhaka:** Karim and Salam, "Organising the Informal Economy Workers," 25.

222 **"nearly double the output of London's underground railway":** Gallagher, *The Rickshaws of Bangladesh,* 6.

223 **a rear-mounted "luggage board" and fittings for panniers:** Tony Hadland and Hans-Erhard Lessing, *Bicycle Design: An Illustrated History* (Cambridge, Mass.: MIT Press, 2014), 14.

224 **The same is true of nearly every bicycle:** For a historical survey of bicycle racks, carriers, and other "luggage," see ibid., 351–84.

224 **Salisbury's testimony startled the committee:** *Harrison E. Salisbury's Trip to North Vietnam: Hearing Before the Committee on Foreign Relations, United States Senate, Ninetieth Congress, First Session with Harrison E. Salisbury, Assistant Managing Editor of the New York Times* (Washington, D.C.: U.S. Government Printing Office, 1967). Available online at govinfo.gov/content/pkg/CHRG-90shrg74687/pdf /CHRG-90shrg74687.pdf.

225 **"I literally believe that without bikes":** Ibid., 11.

225 **"Why don't we concentrate on bicycles?":** Ibid., 16.

225 **"The corps of bicycle newspaper carriers in London":** "The Trick Cyclist on the Road," *Yorkshire Post and Leeds Intelligencer* (Leeds, Yorkshire, Eng.), August 4, 1905.

226 **"riders raced cargo tricycles loaded with up to 40 kg of ballast":** Peter Cox and Randy Rzewnicki, "Cargo Bikes: Distributing Consumer Goods," in *Cycling Cultures,* ed. Peter Cox (Chester, Cheshire, Eng.: University of Chester Press, 2015), 137.

226 **The cult of Dutch and Danish-style "cargo cruisers":** See, e.g., filmmaker Liz Canning's 2019 film *MOTHERLOAD,* "an award-winning documentary that uses the cargo bike as the vehicle for exploring parenthood in this digital age of climate change," motherloadmovie .com/welcome.

227 **It is also an indelible image of human toil:** A remarkable document of this phenomenon is French photographer Alain Delorme's *Totems* (2010), a series of photos, shot in Shanghai, of cargo tricyclists carting gargantuan loads. See alaindelorme.com/serie/totems.

227 **"between 40–60 million working tricycles":** Glen Norcliffe, *Critical Geographies of Cycling* (New York: Routledge, 2015), 221.

227 **"The passenger-carrying cycle—in its various passenger rickshaw forms:** Cox and Rzewnicki, "Cargo Bikes: Distributing Consumer Goods," 133.

228 **The rickshaw was invented in Japan:** For the historical background on the rickshaw, especially in the East Asian and Chinese contexts, see David Strand, *Rickshaw Beijing: City People and Politics in the 1920s* (Berkeley: University of California Press, 1989). For an overview of the rickshaw in South Asia, see M. William Steele, "Rickshaws in South Asia," *Transfers* 3, no. 3 (2013), 56–61. See also: Tony Wheeler and Richard l'Anson, *Chasing Rickshaws* (Hawthorn, Victoria, Australia: Lonely Planet Publications, 1998).

229 **In Dhaka, the rickshaw's history:** For background on the rickshaw's history in Dhaka see Gallagher, *The Rickshaws of Bangladesh;* and *Of Rickshaws and Rickshawallahs,* ed. Niaz Zaman (Dhaka: University Press, 2008).

229 **proposals to ban rickshaws in Dhaka:** See Musleh Uddin Hasan and Julio D. Davila, "The Politics of (Im)Mobility: Rickshaw Bans in Dhaka, Bangladesh," *Journal of Transport Geography* 70 (2018), 246–55; Mahabubul Bari and Debra Efroymson, "Rickshaw Bans in Dhaka City: An Overview of the Arguments For and Against," published by *Work for a Better Bangladesh Trust and Roads for People,* 2005, wbbtrust.org /view/research_publication/33; Mohammad Al-Masum Molla, "Ban on Rickshaw: How Logical Is It?," *Daily Star* (Dhaka), July 7, 2019,

thedailystar.net/opinion/politics/news/ban-rickshaw-how-logical-it
-1767535.

229 **Shahnaz Huq-Hussain and Umme Habiba make a populist and feminist case:** Shahnaz Huq-Hussain and Umme Habiba, "Gendered Experiences of Mobility: Travel Behavior of Middle-Class Women in Dhaka City," *Transfers: Interdisciplinary Journal of Mobility Studies* 3, no. 3 (2013).

230 **The workforce is exclusively male:** For sociological and economic analysis of the lives and working conditions of Dhaka's *rickshawallahs,* see, e.g., M. Maksudur Rahman and Md. Assadekjaman, "Rickshaw Pullers and the Cycle of Unsustainability in Dhaka City," 99–118; Syed Naimul Wadood and Mostofa Tehsum, "Examining Vulnerabilities: The Cycle Rickshaw Pullers of Dhaka City," Munich Personal RePEc Archive, 2018, core.ac.uk/download/pdf/214004362.pdf; Meheri Tamanna, "Rickshaw Cycle Drivers in Dhaka: Assessing Working Conditions and Livelihoods"(Master's Thesis, International Institute of Social Studies, Erasmus University, The Hague, Netherlands), 2012, semantic scholar.org/paper/Rickshaw-Cycle-Drivers-in-Dhaka%3A-Assessing -Working-Poor/4708d8065f3ee07c02dd39e6e939a4e57e10e050; Sharifa Begum and Binayak Sen, "Pulling Rickshaws in the City of Dhaka: A Way Out of Poverty?," *Environment & Urbanization* 17, no. 2 (2005), journals.sagepub.com/doi/pdf/10.1177/095624780501700202.

230 **Their health is often poor:** Hafiz Ehsanul Hoque, Masako Ono-Kihara, Saman Zamani, Shahrzad Mortazavi Ravari, Masahiro Kihara, "HIV-Related Risk Behaviours and the Correlates Among Rickshaw Pullers of Kamrangirchar, Dhaka, Bangladesh: a Cross-Sectional Study Using Probability Sampling," *BMC Public Health* 9, no. 80 (2009), pubmed .ncbi.nlm.nih.gov/19284569/.

230 **The Covid pandemic:** Joynal Abedin Shishir, "Income Lost to Covid, Many Take to Pulling Rickshaws in Dhaka," *The Business Standard,* August 31, 2021, tbsnews.net/economy/income-lost-covid-many-take -pulling-rickshaws-dhaka-295444.

230 **"Hafiz and Abdul Hafiz":** Mahbub Talukdar, "Hafiz and Abdul Hafiz," trans. Israt Jahan Baki, in Zaman, ed., *Of Rickshaws and Rickshawal- lahs,* 57.

231 **Mohammed Abul Badshah:** Unless otherwise noted, all the biographi- cal information about and quotations from Mohammed Abul Badshah come from interviews with him conducted by the author. These conver- sations were translated by Rifat Islam Esha.

234 **85 percent of Dhaka's roads:** Khaled Mahmud, Khonika Gope, Syed Mustafizur, Syed Chowdhury, "Possible Causes & Solutions of Traffic Jam and Their Impact on the Economy of Dhaka City," *Journal of Management and Sustainability* 2, no. 2 (2012), 112–35.

235 **battery-powered "easy bikes":** See "Government to Ban Battery-Run Rickshaws, Vans," *Dhaka Tribune,* June 20, 2021, dhakatribune.com /bangladesh/2021/06/20/govt-to-ban-battery-run-rickshaws-vans; Rafiul Islam, "Battery-Run Rickshaws on DSCC Roads: Defying Ban, They Keep on Running," *Daily Star* (Dhaka), January 30, 2021, thedailystar .net/city/news/defying-ban-they-keep-running-2036221.

238 "We eke out our living in this country": Dilip Sarkar, "The Rickshawal-lah's Song," trans. M. Mizannur Rahman, in Zaman, ed., *Of Rickshaws and Rickshawallahs,* 31.

238 Badshah lives in Kamrangirchar: Md. Abul Hasam, Shahida Arafin, Saima Naznin, Md. Mushahid, Mosharraf Hossain, "Informality, Poverty and Politics in Urban Bangladesh: An Empirical Study of Dhaka City," *Journal of Economics and Sustainable Development* 8, no.14 (2017), 158–82; "Slum Conditions in Bangladesh Pose Health Hazards, and Malnutrition Is a Sign of Other Illnesses," *Médecins Sans Frontières,* October 13, 2010, msf.org/slum-conditions-bangladesh-pose-health -hazards-and-malnutrition-sign-other-illnesses.

239 "one of the most polluted places on the planet": Hal Hodson, "Slum-dog Mapmakers Fill in the Urban Blanks," *New Scientist,* October 23, 2014, newscientist.com/article/mg22429924-100-slumdog-mapmakers -fill-in-the-urban-blanks/.

239 dozens of leather tanneries: "Toxic Tanneries: The Health Repercus-sions of Bangladesh's Hazaribagh Leather," *Human Rights Watch,* October 8, 2012, hrw.org/report/2012/10/08/toxic-tanneries/health -repercussions-bangladeshs-hazaribagh-leather; Sarah Boseley, "Child Labourers Exposed to Toxic Chemicals Dying Before 50, WHO Says," *Guardian,* March 21, 2017, theguardian.com/world/2017/mar/21 /plight-of-child-workers-facing-cocktail-of-toxic-chemicals-exposed-by -report-bangladesh-tanneries.

239 hundreds of small-scale factories: See "Poor Bangladesh Kids Work to Eat, Help Families," *Jakarta Post,* June 14, 2016, thejakartapost.com /multimedia/2016/06/14/poor-bangladesh-kids-work-to-eat-help -families.html; Jason Beaubien, "Study: Child Laborers In Bangladesh Are Working 64 Hours a Week," NPR, December 7, 2016, npr.org /sections/goatsandsoda/2016/12/07/504681046/study-child-laborers-in -bangladesh-are-working-64-hours-a-week; Terragraphics International Foundation, "Hazaribagh & Kamrangirchar, Bangladesh," terragraphics international.org/bangladesh.

240 toxic e-waste: Mahbub Alam and Khalid Md. Bahauddin, "Electronic Waste in Bangladesh: Evaluating the Situation, Legislation and Policy and Way Forward with Strategy and Approach," *PESD* 9, no. 1 (2015), 81–101; Mohammad Nazrul Islam, "E-waste Management of Bangla-desh," *International Journal of Innovative Human Ecology & Nature Studies* 4, no. 2 (April–June, 2016), 1–12.

245 "moving museums": Sonya Soheli, "Canvas of Rickshaw Art," *Daily Star* (Dhaka), Mar. 31, 2015, thedailystar.net/lifestyle/ls-pick/canvas -rickshaw-art-74449.

247 Avijit Roy: "Bangladesh Court Sentences Five to Death for Killing American Blogger," *New York Times,* February 16, 2021, nytimes.com /2021/02/16/world/asia/bangladesh-sentence-avijit-roy.html.

248 "Nowhere else do people talk as much": Unless otherwise noted, all quotations from Syed Manzoorul Islam come from the author's inter-views with Islam.

249 "form of life threatened by the chaos and alienation": *Of Rickshaws and Rickshawallahs,* 91.

249   Islam has published studies of rickshaw painting: See, e.g., "Rickshaw Art of Bangladesh," in *Of Rickshaws and Rickshawallahs*, 83–92.

13 PERSONAL HISTORY

252   a greater understanding of the processes that guide our mastery of bike riding: Boris Suchan, "Why Don't We Forget How to Ride a Bike?," *Scientific American*, November 15, 2018, scientificamerican.com/article/why-dont-we-forget-how-to-ride-a-bike/.

252   "One morning I no longer heard the sound of someone running": Paul Fournel, *Need for the Bike*, trans. Allan Stoekl (Lincoln: University of Nebraska Press, 2003), 26.

252   "so pervasive was the idea that bicycles and children belonged": Robert J. Turpin, *First Taste of Freedom: A Cultural History of Bicycle Manufacturing in the United States* (Syracuse, N.Y.: University of Syracuse Press, 2018), 1.

253   "Nothing equals the bicycle as a developer of sturdy bodies": Quoted in ibid., 85.

253   *Bike Riding Lesson* (1954): The image can be viewed online here: saturdayeveningpost.com/wp-content/uploads/satevepost/bike_riding_lesson_george_hughes.jpg.

266   Ghost bikes are painted entirely white: Ghost bike memorials are a familiar New York sight, but they are a global phenomenon, found in cities across the world. As art objects, ghost bikes have a stark power. They resonate with history, too, calling to mind the white bicycles of the Dutch Provo's guerrilla bike sharing effort. The Provo chose to paint their bikes white to evoke the "simplicity and cleanliness" of the bicycle in contrast to the "vanity and foulness of the authoritarian car." See Robert Graham, *Anarchism: A Documentary History of Libertarian Ideas. Volume Two: The Emergence of the New Anarchism (1939–1977)* (Montreal: Black Rose Books, 2009), 287.

266   "Is It O.K. to Kill Cyclists?": Daniel Duane, "Is It O.K. to Kill Cyclists?," *New York Times*, November 9, 2013, nytimes.com/2013/11/10/opinion/sunday/is-it-ok-to-kill-cyclists.html.

268   "Cars make you stupid": Eula Biss, *Having and Being Had* (New York: Riverhead Books, 2020), 248.

268   "Dogs become dogs again and snap at your raincoat": Bill Emerson, "On Bicycling," *Saturday Evening Post*, July 29, 1967.

272   "It is by riding a bicycle that you learn the contours of a country": Ernest Hemingway, *By-Line Ernest Hemingway: Selected Articles and Dispatches of Four Decades* (New York: Touchstone, 1998), 364.

273   "[The cycleur] has discovered cycling to be an occupation": Valeria Luiselli, "Manifesto à Velo," in *Sidewalks*, trans. Christina MacSweeney (Minneapolis: Coffee House, 2014), 36.

273   "slow cycling": See e.g., Ian Cleverly, "The Slow Cycling Movement," *Rouleur*, June 15, 2021, rouleur.cc/blogs/the-rouleur-journal/the-slow-cycling-movement.

273   "as if through the lens of a movie camera": Luiselli, *Sidewalks*, 37.

275   "allows the rider to sail past pedestrian eyes:" Ibid., 34.

276   "A memory of motion lingers in the muscles of your legs": H. G. Wells, *The Wheels of Chance: A Bicycling Idyll* (New York: Grosset & Dunlap, 1896), 79.

278   a woman in rural Chile named Elena Galvez: "Cerrillos' 90-Year-Old Cyclist Shows No Signs of Slowing Down," Reuters, September 9, 2016, reuters.com/article/us-chile-elderly-idCAKCN11F2HK.

14 GRAVEYARDS

281   When the canal was emptied in 2016: Marine Benoit, "Les improbables trouvailles au fond du canal Saint-Martin," *L'Express,* January 5, 2016, lexpress.fr/actualite/societe/environnement/en-images-les -improbables-du-trouvailles-au-fond-du-canal-saint-martin_1750737 .html; Mélanie Faure, "Vidé, le canal Saint-Martin révèle ses surprises," *Le Figaro,* January 20, 2016, lefigaro.fr/actualite-france/2016/01/20 /01016-20160120ARTFIG00416-vide-le-canal-saint-martin-revele-ses -surprises.php; and Henry Samuel, "Pistol Found in Paris' Canal St-Martin as 'Big Cleanup' Commences," *Telegraph,* January 5, 2016, telegraph.co.uk/news/worldnews/europe/france/12082794/Pistol-found -in-Paris-Canal-St-Martin-as-big-clean-up-commences.html.

282   Her body, still manacled to the bike, was found a week later: Douglass Dowty, "DA: DeWitt Woman Handcuffed Herself to Bike, Rode into Green Lake in Suicide," Syracuse.com, March 22, 2019; originally published on October 17, 2016, syracuse.com/crime/2016/10 /fitzpatrick_woman_committed_suicide_at_green_lakes.html.

282   stirs deep urges in certain vandals: Something along these lines was suggested by the author of an unsigned article in the London *Times* in 1940. The writer diagnosed a "demon of destructiveness" lurking "within each one of us" and described the "fierce joy" to be found in "hurling away saucepans and bedsteads, in uprooting railings, in dismembering bicycles." *The Times* (London), July 20, 1940. Quoted in Peter Thorsheim, "Salvage and Destruction: The Recycling of Books and Manuscripts in Great Britain During the Second World War," *Contemporary European History* 22, no. 3, *"Special Issue: Recycling and Reuse in the Twentieth Century"* (2013), 431–52.

283   In one clip, a teenage boy faces the camera: "Throwing My Friends [*sic*] Bike into a Lake," youtube.com/watch?v=OcysvVwDFK8.

283   "a boat snagged on . . . an underwater mountain of bicycles": Mike Buchanan, *Two Men in a Car (a Businessman, a Chauffeur, and Their Holidays in France)* (Bedford, Bedfordshire, Eng.: LPS), 2017, 34.

284   devotes several pages to bicycle drowning: Pete Jordan, *In the City of Bikes: The Story of the Amsterdam Cyclist* (New York: Harper Perennial, 2013). See chapter 18, "A Typical Amsterdam Characteristic: The Bike Fisherman," 327–42.

285   "those traditional garbage cans where we take our visitors": Ibid., 332.

285   "Dockless Bikes Keep Ending Up Underwater": Steve Annear, "Dockless Bikes Keep Ending Up Underwater," *Boston Globe,* July 13, 2018.

285   In Britain: See, e.g., "What Lurks Beneath the Waterline?," Canal & River Trust, March 24, 2016, canalrivertrust.org.uk/news-and-views

/news/what-lurks-beneath-the-waterline; "Bikes, Baths and Bullets Among Items Found in Country's Waterways," *Guardian* (London), March 24, 2016; and Isobel Frodsham, "Fly-tippers Dump Hundreds of Bikes, a Blow Up Doll and a GUN in Britain's Canals and Rivers to Avoid a Crackdown on the Streets," *Daily Mail* (London), April 16, 2017, dailymail.co.uk/news/article-4415872/Fly-tippers-dump-GUN-Britain-s-canals.html.

286   **The Canal & River Trust:** "What Lurks Beneath?," Canal & River Trust video, youtube.com/watch?v=NkTuGmigJZM.

286   **"Based on the oysters on the handlebar":** Jen Chung, "Barnacle Bike Was Likely in the Hudson River Since Last Summer," *Gothamist,* February 26, 2019, gothamist.com/news/barnacle-bike-was-likely-in-the-hudson-river-since-last-summer.

286   **One widely circulated video:** "Footage Shows Man Throwing Shared Bikes into River, Claim They Disclose Privacy Information," youtube.com/watch?v=EsidHmfEpKg.

286   **"It is common to hear people describe bike-sharing":** Javier C. Hernández, "As Bike-Sharing Brings Out Bad Manners, China Asks, What's Wrong with Us?," *New York Times,* September 2, 2017, nytimes.com/2017/09/02/world/asia/china-beijing-dockless-bike-share.html.

286   **"The chips in Mobikes are unsafe":** See YouTube video caption for "Footage Shows Man Throwing Shared Bikes into River."

287   **more than seventy dockless bike-share start-ups:** Hernández, "As Bike-Sharing Brings Out Bad Manners."

287   **but in overhead photos and videos captured by drone:** "Drone Footage Shows Thousands of Bicycles Abandoned in China as Bike Sharing Reaches Saturation," *South China Morning Post* YouTube channel, youtube.com/watch?v=Xlms-8zEcCg. See also Alan Taylor, "The Bike-Share Oversupply in China: Huge Piles of Abandoned and Broken Bicycles," *Atlantic,* March 22, 2018.

288   **the scrapyard was fined $85,000:** Reuven Blau, "Two Scrap Metal Recyclers Busted for Dumping Waste into Gowanus Canal; One Slapped with $85K Fine," *Daily News* (New York), December 4, 2012.

289   **"Broken Bicycles":** Tom Waits, "Broken Bicycles," from the album *One from the Heart* (CBS Records, 1982).

15 MASS MOVEMENT

292   **dozens of bicycles . . . left behind in a heap:** Fred Strebeigh, "The Wheels of Freedom: Bicycles in China" originally published in *Bicycling,* April 1991, available at strebeigh.com/china-bikes.html.

292   **"took a bicycle and a loudspeaker to organize the chaotic crowd":** "Voices from Tiananmen," *South China Morning Post* (Hong Kong), June 3, 2014.

293   **"needed to propose something to the government":** Louisa Lim, "Student Leaders Reflect, 20 Years After Tiananmen," NPR, June 3, 2009, npr.org/templates/story/story.php?storyId=104821771.

293   **"I wrote down seven requests":** Ibid.

293   **"a well-planned plot":** Liang Zhang (Andrew J. Nathan and Perry Link,

eds.), *The Tiananmen Papers: The Chinese Leadership's Decision to Use Force Against Their Own People—In Their Own Words* (New York: Public Affairs, 2001), 76.

293   One observer compared the procession to a fleet of tall ships: Strebeigh, "The Wheels of Freedom."

294   "The mad dash across Tiananmen Square": Philip J. Cunningham, *Tiananmen Moon: Inside the Chinese Student Uprising of 1989* (Lanham, Md.: Rowman & Littlefield, Inc., 2009), 50.

295   One evening in October 1992, a few dozen people: The accounts of that evening at Fixed Gear in San Francisco and of Ted White and George Bliss's 1991 trip to China are based on the author's interviews with Ted White. See also Ted White, "Reels on Wheels," in *Critical Mass: Bicycling's Defiant Celebration*, ed. Chris Carlsson (Oakland, Calif.: AK Press, 2002), 145–52.

295   *Return of the Scorcher:* Ted White, *Return of the Scorcher* (1992, USA, 28 minutes). The film can be viewed online, with a director's commentary: "*Return of the Scorcher* 1992 Bicycle Documentary: A Cycling Renaissance," youtube.com/watch?v=K1DUaWJ6KGc.

296   "Kingdom of the Bicycle": For the history of the bicycle in China see, e.g., Qiuning Wang, *A Shrinking Path for Bicycles: A Historical Review of Bicycle Use in Beijing,* Master's Thesis, University of British Columbia, May 2012; Xu Tao, "Making a Living: Bicycle-related Professions in Shanghai, 1897–1949," *Transfers* 3, no. 3 (2013), 6–26; Xu Tao, "The popularization of bicycles and modern Shanghai," *Shilin* 史林 (Historical Review) 1 (2007): 103–13; Neil Thomas, "The Rise, Fall, and Restoration of the Kingdom of Bicycles," *Macro Polo,* October 24, 2018, macropolo.org/analysis/the-rise-fall-and-restoration-of-the-kingdom-of-bicycles/; Hua Zhang, Susan A. Shaheen, and Xingpeng Chen, "Bicycle Evolution in China: From the 1900s to the Present," *International Journal of Sustainable Transportation* 8, no. 5 (2014): 317–35; and Anne Lusk, "A History of Bicycle Environments in China: Comparisons with the U.S. and the Netherlands," *Harvard Asia Quarterly* 14, no. 4 (2012): 16–27. Paul Smethurst, *The Bicycle: Towards a Global History* (New York: Palgrave Macmillan, 2015), 105–20.

296   "On the avenues people ride on a vehicle with only two wheels": Tony Hadland and Hans-Erhard Lessing, *Bicycle Design: An Illustrated History* (Cambridge, Mass.: MIT Press, 2014), 38.

296   ordered the removal of the doorway thresholds: Henry Pu Yi (Paul Kramer, ed.), *The Last Manchu: The Autobiography of Henry Pu Yi, Last Emperor of China* (New York: Skyhorse Publishing, 2010), 16.

296   500,000 bicycles in use across the country: Wang, *A Shrinking Path for Bicycles,* 1.

297   230,000 in the city of Shanghai: Gijs Mom, *Globalizing Automobilism: Exuberance and the Emergence of Layered Mobility, 1900–1980* (New York: Berghahn, 2020), 81.

297   "an egalitarian social system that promised little comfort: Kevin Desmond, *Electric Motorcycles and Bicycles: A History Including Scooters, Tricycles, Segways, and Monocycles* (Jefferson, N.C.: McFarland, 2019), 142.

297   "three rounds and a sound": Evan Osnos, *Age of Ambition: Chasing Fortune, Truth, and Faith in the New China* (New York: Farrar, Straus and Giroux, 2014), 56.

297   "Ford and GM of China": Stephen L. Koss, *China, Heart and Soul: Four Years of Living, Learning, Teaching, and Becoming Half-Chinese in Suzhou, China* (Bloomington, Ind.: iUniverse, 2009), 167.

298   "a Flying Pigeon in every household": Hilda Rømer Christensen, "Is the Kingdom of Bicycles Rising Again?: Cycling, Gender, and Class in Postsocialist China," *Transfers* 7, no. 2 (2017): 2.

298   Flying Pigeon produced four million bicycles per year: Thomas, "The Rise, Fall, and Restoration of the Kingdom of Bicycles."

298   By the end of the decade: Ibid.

298   The bicycle, writes Paul Smethurst, "was so absorbed into the state-sponsored culture": Smethurst, *The Bicycle*, 107.

300   "Aren't you sick & tired of having to fight for your life on city streets?": A scan of the flyer is online here: FoundSF ("Shaping San Francisco's digital archive"), foundsf.org/index.php?title=File:First-ever -flyer.jpg.

301   *Critical Comments on the Critical Mass*: A scan of Carlsson's pamphlet is online here: FoundSF ("Shaping San Francisco's digital archive"), foundsf.org/index.php?title=File:Critical-Comments-on-the-Critical -Mass-nov-92.jpg.

303   around 2028, experts estimate: Larry Elliott, "China to Overtake US as World's Biggest Economy by 2028, Report Predicts," *Guardian* (London), December 25, 2020, theguardian.com/world/2020/dec/26/china -to-overtake-us-as-worlds-biggest-economy-by-2028-report-predicts.

304   China's GDP per capita was $310: See "GDP per Capita (Current US$)—China," The World Bank, data.worldbank.org/indicator/NY.GDP .PCAP.CD?locations=CN.

304   the per capita GDP had reached $10,216: Ibid.

304   1.6 billion cellphone subscriptions: "Number of Mobile Cell Phone Subscriptions in China from August 2020 to August 2021," Statista, statista.com/statistics/278204/china-mobile-users-by-month/.

304   a reported 1 billion Chinese have internet access: Evelyn Cheng, "China Says It Now Has Nearly 1 Billion Internet Users," CNBC, February 4, 2021, cnbc.com/2021/02/04/china-says-it-now-has-nearly-1 -billion-internet-users.html.

304   more than 200 million: "China has over 200 million private cars," *Xinhua*, January 7, 2020, xinhuanet.com/english/2020-01/07/c_138685873.htm.

304   only 1 in 74,000: Marcia D. Lowe, "The Bicycle: Vehicle for a Small Planet," *Worldwatch Paper 90* (Washington, D.C.: Worldwatch Institute, 1989), 8.

304   In 2009, the year China surpassed the United States: "China Car Sales 'Overtook the US' in 2009," BBC News, January 11, 2010, bbc.co.uk/2 /hi/8451887.stm.

305   the most passenger cars sold: Hilde Hartmann Holsten, "How Cars Have Transformed China," University of Oslo, September 28, 2016, partner.sciencenorway.no/cars-and-traffic-forskningno-norway/how-cars -have-transformed-china/1437901.

305   "So many past events and recollections that were once clearly
        inscribed": Li Zhang, "Contesting Spatial Modernity in Late-Socialist
        China," *Current Anthropology* 47, no. 3 (June 2006): 469. Available
        online at jstor.org/stable/10.1086/503063.

305   "most of the old neighborhoods of Boston, New York": Beth E. Notar,
        "Car Crazy: The Rise of Car Culture in China," in *Cars, Automobility
        and Development in Asia,* ed. Arve Hansen and Kenneth Nielsen
        (London: Routledge, 2017), 158.

306   an all-time high of 523 million: Thomas, "The Rise, Fall, and Restora-
        tion of the Kingdom of Bicycles."

306   a 40 percent reduction in bicycle commuting by the year 2013:
        Zhang, Shaheen, and Chen, "Bicycle Evolution in China," 318.

307   by 2003, bicycle usage in the city had decreased: Wang, *A Shrinking
        Path for Bicycles,* 3.

307   "non-bicycle city": Zhang, Shaheen, and Chen, "Bicycle Evolution in
        China," 318.

307   an estimated nine million bicycles in the capital: Wang, *A Shrinking
        Path for Bicycles,* 10.

307   2.5 bikes per household: Ibid., 3.

307   nearly two-thirds of all trips: Ibid., 3.

307   Within fifteen years: Ibid., 3.

307   "abandoned by the thousands": Glen Norcliffe and Boyang Gao,
        "Hurry-Slow: Automobility in Beijing, or a Resurrection of the Kingdom
        of Bicycles?," in *Architectures of Hurry:—Mobilities, Cities and
        Modernity,* ed. Phillip Gordon Mackintosh, Richard Dennis, and
        Deryck W. Holdsworth (Oxon: Routledge, 2018), 88.

308   "for losers": Debra Bruno, "The De-Bikification of Beijing," April 9,
        2012, *Bloomberg CityLab,* bloomberg.com/news/articles/2012-04-09
        /the-de-bikification-of-beijing.

308   "for the poor": Anne Renzenbrink and Laura Zhou, "Coming Full
        Cycle in China: Beijing Pedallers Try to Restore 'Kingdom of Bicycles'
        amid Traffic, Pollution Woes," *South China Morning Post,* July 26, 2015,
        scmp.com/news/china/money-wealth/article/1843877/coming-full-cycle
        -china-beijing-pedallers-try-restore.

308   "choosing skirts instead of pants": Philip P. Pan, "Bicycle No Longer
        King of the Road in China," *Washington Post,* March 12, 2001,
        washingtonpost.com/archive/politics/2001/03/12/bicycle-no-longer-king
        -of-the-road-in-china/f9c66880-fcab-40ff-b86d-f3db13aa1859/.

308   "I'd rather cry in a BMW": Osnos, *Age of Ambition,* 56.

309   Each year, millions of cars: Norihiko Shirouzu, Yilei Sun, "As One
        of China's 'Detroits' Reopens, World's Automakers Worry About
        Disruptions," Reuters, March 8, 2020, reuters.com/article/us-health
        -coronavirus-autos-parts/as-one-of-chinas-detroits-reopens-worlds
        -automakers-worry-about-disruptions-idUSKBN20V14J.

310   "What do bikes and toilet paper have in common?": Emily Davies,
        "What Do Bikes and Toilet Paper Have in Common? Both Are Flying
        Out of Stores amid the Coronavirus Pandemic," *Washington Post,*
        June 15, 2020, washingtonpost.com/local/what-do-bikes-and-toilet
        -paper-have-in-common-both-are-flying-out-of-stores-amid-the-corona

virus-pandemic/2020/05/14/c58d44f6-9554-11ea-82b4-c8db161ff6e5
_story.html.

310 **year-over-year bicycle sales rose nearly 60 percent nationally:** Felix Richter, "Pandemic-Fueled Bicycle Boom Coasts Into 2021," Statista, June 16, 2021, statista.com/chart/25088/us-consumer-spending-on -bicycles/.

310 **"sleep with it next to you":** Kimiko de Freytas-Tamura, "Bike Thefts Are Up 27% in Pandemic N.Y.C.: 'Sleep with It Next to You,'" *New York Times,* October 14, 2020.

311 **one in ten American adults:** Adrienne Bernhard, "The Great Bicycle Boom of 2020," BBC, December 10, 2020, bbc.com/future/bespoke /made-on-earth/the-great-bicycle-boom-of-2020.html.

311 **"transit upheaval":** Natalie Zhang, "Covid Has Spurred a Bike Boom, but Most U.S. Cities Aren't Ready for It," CNBC, December 8, 2020, cnbc.com/2020/12/08/covid-bike-boom-us-cities-cycling.html.

311 **"Great Covid-19 Bicycle Boom":** John Mazerolle, "Great COVID-19 Bicycle Boom Expected to Keep Bike Industry on Its Toes for Years to Come," CBC News, March 21, 2021, cbc.ca/news/business/bicycle -boom-industry-turmoil-covid-19-1.5956400.

311 **"Corona cycleways":** Liz Alderman, "'Corona Cycleways' Become the New Post-Confinement Commute," *New York Times,* June 12, 2020, nytimes.com/2020/06/12/business/paris-bicycles-commute-coronavirus .html.

311 **In the Philippines:** Regine Cabato and Martin San Diego, "Filipinos Are Cycling Their Way Through the Pandemic," *Washington Post,* March 31, 2021, washingtonpost.com/climate-solutions/interactive/2021 /climate-manila-biking/.

311 **"cycling revolution":** "'India Cycles4Change' Challenge Gains Momentum," Press Release, Indian Ministry of Housing & Urban Affairs, June 2, 2021, pib.gov.in/PressReleaseIframePage.aspx?PRID=1723860.

311 **"havens for cycling":** Nivedha Selvam, "Can City Become More Bikeable? Corporation Wants to Know," *Times of India,* August 15, 2020, timesofindia.indiatimes.com/city/coimbatore/can-city-become -more-bikeable-corporation-wants-to-know/articleshow/77554660.cms.

311 **A study published in the spring of 2021:** Sebastian Kraus and Nicolas Koch, "Provisional COVID-19 Infrastructure Induces Large, Rapid Increases in Cycling," *PNAS* 118, no. 15 (2021), https://www.pnas.org /content/pnas/118/15/e2024399118.full.pdf.

312 **"the joy of . . . cities as they could be":** Quoted in Bernhard, "The Great Bicycle Boom of 2020."

313 **New York was the global epicenter of the pandemic:** For New York City COVID statistics, see "New York City Coronavirus Map and Case Count," *New York Times,* nytimes.com/interactive/2020/nyregion/new -york-city-coronavirus-cases.html.

313 **"the equivalent of an ongoing 9/11":** Alistair Bunkall, "Coronavirus: New York Could Temporarily Bury Bodies in Park Because Morgues Nearly Full," April 6, 2020, *Sky News,* news.sky.com/story/coronavirus -new-york-could-temporarily-bury-bodies-in-park-because-morgues -nearly-full-11969522.

316   "focus on the bicyclists": Tweet, Catherina Gioino (@CatGioino), posted to Twitter, June 5, 2020, 1:35 A.M.: twitter.com/catgioino/status /1268778355169669122?lang=en.

316   **Mayor Bill de Blasio's executive order:** "Emergency Executive Order No. 119," City of New York, Office of the Mayor, June 2, 2020. Available online at www1.nyc.gov/assets/home/downloads/pdf/executive-orders /2020/eeo-119.pdf.

316   **an NYPD officer body-slammed a Critical Mass rider:** Jen Chung, "10 Years Ago, a Cop Bodyslammed a Cyclist During Critical Mass Ride," *Gothamist,* July 27, 2018, gothamist.com/news/10-years-ago-a -cop-bodyslammed-a-cyclist-during-critical-mass-ride.

316   **"ticket blitzes":** Jillian Jorgensen, "De Blasio Defends Ticket Blitz of Bicyclists Following Deadly Crashes," *New York Daily News,* February 19, 2019, nydailynews.com/news/politics/ny-pol-deblasio-nypd -bicycle-tickets-20190219-story.html.

317   **"war on e-bikes":** Christopher Robbins, "De Blasio's 2018 War On E-Bikes Targeted Riders, Not Businesses," *Gothamist,* January 18, 2019, gothamist.com/news/de-blasios-2018-war-on-e-bikes-targeted-riders -not-businesses.

317   **"that we did not intend or design them to be used":** Jonny Long, "Fuji Bikes Suspend Sale of American Police Bikes Used in 'Violent Tactics' During Protests as Trek Faces Criticism," *Cycling Weekly,* June 6, 2020, cyclingweekly.com/news/latest-news/fuji-bikes-suspend -sale-of-american-police-bikes-used-in-violent-tactics-as-trek-faces -criticism-457378.

317   **the NYPD's own "elite" unit:** Larry Celona and Natalie O'Neill, "NYPD Bike Cops Break Out 'Turtle Uniforms' Amid George Floyd Protests," *New York Post,* June 4, 2020, nypost.com/2020/06/04/nypd -bike-cops-break-out-turtle-uniforms-amid-riots/.

317   **"planned assault" and "police brutality":** "'Kettling' Protesters in the Bronx: Systemic Police Brutality and Its Costs in the United States," *Human Rights Watch,* September 30, 2020, hrw.org/report/2020/09/30 /kettling-protesters-bronx/systemic-police-brutality-and-its-costs-united -states.

317   **The SRG Bike Squad's "Instructor Guide":** "SRG Bicycle Management Instructor's Guide," documentcloud.org/documents/20584525 -srg_bike_squad_modules.

318   **30 percent and 23 percent:** League of American Bicyclists and The Sierra Club, *The New Majority: Pedaling Towards Equity,* 2013, bikeleague.org/sites/default/files/equity_report.pdf.

318   **Studies also confirm:** Dan Roe, "Black Cyclists Are Stopped More Often than Whites, Police Data Shows," *Bicycling,* July 27, 2020, bicycling.com/culture/a33383540/cycling-while-black-police/.

318   **A survey in Oakland:** "Biking While Black: Racial Bias in Oakland Policing," Bike Lab, May 20, 2019, bike-lab.org/2019/05/20/biking -while-black-racial-bias-in-oakland-policing/.

318   **in Chicago:** Adam Mahoney, "In Chicago, Cyclists in Black Neighborhoods Are Over-Policed and Under-Protected," *Grist,* October 21, 2021, grist.org/cities/black-chicago-biking-disparities-infrastructure/.

318 **and Tampa:** Kameel Stanley, "How Riding Your Bike Can Land You in Trouble With the Cops—If You're Black," *Tampa Bay Times,* April 18, 2015, tampabay.com/news/publicsafety/how-riding-your-bike-can-land -you-in-trouble-with-the-cops---if-youre-black/2225966/.

318 **In New York, 86 percent:** Julianne Cuba, "NYPD Targets Black and Brown Cyclists for Biking on the Sidewalk," June 22, 2020, nyc.streets blog.org/2020/06/22/nypd-targets-black-and-brown-cyclists-for-biking -on-the-sidewalk/.

319 **A *Los Angeles Times* investigation:** Alene Tchekmedyian, Ben Poston, and Julia Barajas, "L.A. Sheriff's Deputies Use Minor Stops to Search Bicyclists, with Latinos Hit Hardest," *Los Angeles Times,* November 4, 2021, latimes.com/projects/la-county-sheriff-bike-stops-analysis/.

319 **"riding a bicycle on the wrong side of the road":** Jessica Myers, "Family of Dijon Kizzee, a Black Man Killed by LA Sheriff's Deputies, Files $35 Million Claim," CNN, February 12, 2021, cnn.com/2021/02 /11/us/dijon-kizzee-los-angeles-claim/index.html. See also: Leila Miller, "Dijon Kizzee Was 'Trying to Find His Way' Before Being Killed by L.A. Deputies, Relatives Say," *Los Angeles Times*, September 4, 2020, latimes.com/california/story/2020-09-04/dijon-kizzee-was-trying -to-find-his-way-relatives-say.

319 *Deliveristas* **staged demonstrations:** Claudia Irizarry Aponte and Josefa Velasquez, "NYC Food Delivery Workers Band to Demand Better Treatment. Will New York Listen to Los Deliveristas Unidos?," *The City*, December 6, 2020, thecity.nyc/work/2020/12/6/22157730/nyc -food-delivery-workers-demand-better-treatment. For a brilliant and moving chronicle of the plight of New York's *deliveristas* see Josh Dzieza, "Revolt of the Delivery Workers," *Curbed*, September 13, 2021, curbed.com/article/nyc-delivery-workers.html. See also Jody Rosen, "Edvin Quic, Food Deliveryman, 31, Brooklyn" in "Exposed. Afraid. Determined.," *New York Times Magazine*, April 1, 2020, nytimes.com /interactive/2020/04/01/magazine/coronavirus-workers.html#quic, and Jody Rosen, "Will We Keep Ordering Takeout?" in "Workers on the Edge," *New York Times Magazine*, February 17, 2021, nytimes.com /interactive/2021/02/17/magazine/remote-work-return-to-office.html.

320 **Darnell Meyers:** See Rachel Bachman, "The BMX Bikes Getting Teens Back on Two Wheels—or One," *Wall Street Journal,* May 3, 2017, wsj .com/articles/the-bike-getting-teens-back-on-two-wheelsor-one-1493 817829.

320 **posting online videos:** DBlocks's Instagram feed can be viewed at instagram.com/rrdblocks/.

321 **the policing of "Bicycle Ride Outs":** "SRG Bicycle Management Instructor's Guide," 8.

322 **In a concurring opinion, Justice Neil Gorsuch:** Heather Kerrigan, ed., *Historic Documents of 2020* (Thousand Oaks, Calif.: CQ Press, 2021), 694–95.

322 **Buttigieg made sensible statements:** See Carlton Reid, "Design for Human Beings Not Cars, New U.S. Transport Secretary Says," *Forbes,* March 22, 2021, forbes.com/sites/carltonreid/2021/03/22/design-for

-human-beings-not-cars-new-us-transport-secretary-says/?sh=156033
907d86.

323 **bills that grant immunity to drivers who strike protesters with their cars:**
Reid J. Epstein and Patricia Mazzei, "G.O.P. Bills Target Protesters (and
Absolve Motorists Who Hit Them)," *New York Times,* April 21, 2021,
nytimes.com/2021/04/21/us/politics/republican-anti-protest-laws.html.

324 **A viral Twitter post showed video of a Grubhub worker:** Tweet,
Unequal Scenes (@UnequalScenes), posted to Twitter, September 1, 2021,
10:16 P.M.: twitter.com/UnequalScenes/status/1433252530713243648.

325 **"severe weather incentives":** Lauren Kaori Gurley and Joseph Cox,
"Gig Workers Were Incentivized to Deliver Food During NYC's Deadly
Flood," *Vice,* September 2, 2021, vice.com/en/article/5db8zx/gig
-workers-were-incentivized-to-deliver-food-during-nycs-deadly-flood;
Ashley Wong, "After Delivery Workers Braved the Storm, Advocates
Call for Better Conditions," *New York Times,* September 3, 2021,
nytimes.com/2021/09/03/nyregion/ida-delivery-workers-safety.html; and
Alex Woodward, "'We Deserve Better': New York's 'Deliveristas'
Working Through Deadly Floods Demand Workplace Protections,"
Independent, September 3, 2020, independent.co.uk/climate-change
/news/new-york-flood-delivery-bike-b1914084.html.

325 *Forever Bicycles:* See "Ai Weiwei's Bicycles Come to London,"
Phaidon, August 25, 2015, phaidon.com/agenda/art/articles/2015
/august/25/ai-weiwei-s-bicycles-come-to-london/.

326 **bicycle expressways in Beijing and the coastal city of Xiamen:** Don
Giolzetti, "It's Complicated: China's Relationship With the Bicycle,
Then and Now," *SupChina,* January 8, 2020, supchina.com/2020/01/08
/its-complicated-chinas-relationship-with-the-bicycle/; Leanna Garfield,
"China's Dizzying 'Bicycle Skyway' Can Handle over 2,000 Bikes at a
Time—Take a Look," *Business Insider,* July 21, 2017, businessinsider
.com/china-elevated-cycleway-xiamen-2017-7; Du Juan, "Xiamen
Residents Love Cycling the Most in China," *China Daily,* July 17, 2017,
chinadaily.com.cn/china/2017-07/17/content_30140705.htm.

327 **a global market share of $70 billion by 2027:** "The Global E-Bike
Market Size Is Projected to Grow to USD 70.0 Billion by 2027 from
USD 41.1 Billion in 2020, at a CAGR of 7.9%," *Globe Newswire,*
December 8, 2020, globenewswire.com/news-release/2020/12/08/2141352
/0/en/The-global-e-bike-market-size-is-projected-to-grow-to-USD-70-0
-billion-by-2027-from-USD-41-1-billion-in-2020-at-a-CAGR-of-7-9
.html.

330 **"freewheeling":** See "The Green Machine—Lecture by Iain Boal,
Bicycle Historian. Part 3 of 5" (2010), vimeo.com/11264396.

PHOTO CREDITS

Page 182: Barb Brushe and Bill Samsoe's Bikecentennial I.D. cards, 1976. Courtesy of Barb and Bill Samsoe. Used by permission.

Page 216: "Traffic jam in the suburbs of the city of Dhaka, the capital of Bangladesh in August 20, 2007." Photo by Frédéric Soltan /Corbis via Getty Images. Used by permission.

Page 251: Photograph by Lauren Redniss. Used by permission.

Page 280: "Drainage and Cleaning Operation at Canal Saint-Martin, bicycle in the water, in Paris on May 10, 2017." Photo by Frédéric Soltan/Corbis via Getty Images. Used by permission.

Page 291: "Brooklyn Drag Queens March to Celebrate Pride," June 26, 2020. Photo by Stephanie Keith/Getty Images. Used by permission.

INDEX

Page numbers in *italics* indicate illustrations.

The Rolling Stones (Heinlein), xi
*Romancing the Bicycle: The Five
    Spokes of Balance* (Goldberg),
    176–77
Rothpetz, Emil, 74
Rover bicycle (1885), 7, 21
Roy, Avijit, 247
rubber, xv–xvi, 59–60
Rzewnicki, Randy, 227

safety, chain drives and, 57
Salai (student of Leonardo), 22–23
Salisbury, Harrison, 224–25
Salvo, 114–15
Samsoe, Barb (Brushe), *182*, 183–92,
    199–200, 202–15
Samsoe, Bill, 186–88, 204–11, 213–15
    Bikecentennial, *182*, 188–91, 192,
        199–200, 202–4, 211, 212–13
    "Southern Tier" trek, 211–12
Samsoe, Erik, 207, 208, 213
Samsoe, Kelly, 208, 210, 213
Samsoe, Marge, 209
San Francisco Chronicle, 198–99
Sarkar, Dilip, 238
Saturday Evening Post, 253
Sayre, Louis A., 108
Schmidt, Conrad, 128–29
Schultz, Albert, 201
Schwinn Sting-Ray, 52
sculpture, *Bicycle Wheel*, 52
Second Boer War (1899–1902), 71–72
sexual purity, bicycles as threat to, 8,
    45, 93–94
Sheldon, Charles, 72–73
"the Shock Twat," 130
"the Silent Steed," 67
Sinatra, Ray, 115
Siple, Charles, 193
Siple, Greg, 192–94, 211
Siple, June, 192–94, 211
Skagway Daily Alaskan, 139
Smethurst, Paul
    on Drais's invention of bicycle, 31
    importance of bicycles in China,
        298, 299
    political battles over lineage of
        bicycles, 23–24
Smith, Charlotte, 93

Snow, Jerome, 85
socialism, bicycles as egalitarian mode
    of transportation, 10, 57
SoulCycle, 178–79
"Southern Tier" trek, 211–12
Soviet Union, 24–25
Sowerby, Dave, 105–6
spinning, 172, 176–78
Spitsbergen, Norway, 134, 147–48,
    149–50
The Sporting and Theatrical Journal,
    108, 357n108
St. Giles' Church, Buckinghamshire,
    England, *18*, 18–20, 32–36
Starley, John Kemp, 7
stationary bicycles
    as alternative energy sources,
        173–76
    diagnostic uses of, 172–73
    early, 170
    home trainers, 170–71
    Peloton, 179–80
    physical therapy and, 172
    SoulCycle, 178–79
    in space, 180–81
    spinning, 172, 176–78
    on *Titanic*, *168*, 168–69
    value of global market, 176
    virtual-reality journeys with,
        171–72
Steinlauf, Joe, 136–37
The Steve Allen Show, 55
Stevens, Thomas, 196
Stewart, Robert, 123–24
Story of the Eye (Bataille), 126–27
Stranger Things (television program),
    253
Street Riders NYC, 319
stunt riding. *See* trick cycling
Sumner, Lloyd, 202
Sun (London), 47
The Sun (New York City), 95
Suriray, Jules-Pierre, 60

Talukdar, Mahbub, 230–31
"Taming the Bicycle" (Twain), 69
tandem bicycles, 94
Taylor, Marshall "Major," 170
The Tennessean, 92–93

ABOUT THE AUTHOR

JODY ROSEN is a contributing writer for *The New York Times Magazine*. His writing has appeared in *Slate, New York, The New Yorker,* and many other publications. He lives in Brooklyn with his family.